KT-442-501

THE SOVIET UNION
AN ECONOMIC GEOGRAPHY

R. S. MATHIESON
Senior Lecturer in Geography
University of Sydney

NEWMAN COLLEGE
BARTLEY GREEN
BIRMINGHAM, 32.

CLASS	330.947
ACCESSION	52758
AUTHOR	MAT

HEINEMANN EDUCATIONAL BOOKS · LONDON
BARNES & NOBLE BOOKS · NEW YORK
(A division of Harper & Row Publishers Inc.)

Published by Heinemann Educational Books Ltd.
48 Charles Street, London W1X 8AH
ISBN 0 435 35601 1
© R. S. Mathieson 1975
First published 1975

Published in the U.S.A. 1975 by
Harper & Row Publishers Inc.
Barnes & Noble Import Division
ISBN 0–06–494647–9
LC No. 75–10018

**To
My Wife,
Sylvia and Stuart**

Filmset in Photon Times 11 on 12 pt. by
Richard Clay (The Chaucer Press), Ltd., Bungay, Suffolk
and printed in Great Britain by
Fletcher & Son Ltd., Norwich

CONTENTS

PREFACE

The initial decision to write this book was made in 1968, following the visit of some Russian fellow geographers to Australia. In my courses at the University of Sydney, I had long contemplated the need for a specifically *economic geography* of the Soviet Union in English, and consequently, I finally seized the opportunity to put together the basic material from many scattered sources.

Sabbatical leave in 1969 permitted me to return to the London School of Economics, and I was thus able to use the resources of both the British Library of Economic and Political Science and those of the Royal Geographical Society's Library in Kensington. During an earlier period of leave, I had assembled material in the Institut für Weltwirtschaftsforschung in Kiel, Germany.

During visits to Europe, I had been able to travel quite extensively throughout European Russia, meeting and talking with numerous Russian geographers and gaining many insights that have since proved invaluable in matters of geographical interpretation.

The central purpose of this book is to introduce university and senior school students and the general reader to the economic geography of the Soviet Union. In writing the book I have striven to retain the advantages of hindsight, but I have deliberately focused most attention on the 1950–73 period. This has been an epoch of great change in Soviet economic geography, and one that I feel deserves careful study as a guide to future developments.

I should be most appreciative if readers would draw to my attention any errors or obscurities found in the text, diagrams, or maps, in care of my publishers, Heinemann Educational Books Limited. It will then be possible to ensure improvements to any subsequent edition.

R.S.M.
Sydney

ACKNOWLEDGEMENTS

In writing this book I have received the most friendly and courteous help from many individuals and institutions. I want to express thanks to all who in any way contributed to the material or formation of this book.

First, my thanks must go to my former London School of Economics teachers for their assistance and encouragement; the late Professor Sir Dudley Stamp, Professor Emeritus R. O. Buchanan, and Professor Michael Wise.

I am also indebted to many Russian geographers who have expressed interest and in many instances provided published statistical material and monographs to assist me in my research. I acknowledge too the work of Russian and other geographers not known to me personally, whose writings have formed the background for this book.

To the University of Sydney, I express my deepest appreciation for its financial support, the granting of sabbatical and special leave, and the purchase of specialized books. In this regard too, I am indebted to successive Heads of Department, Professors George Dury, David Simonett, and Trevor Langford-Smith, who have supported my project with the best provision of all: short periods of unfettered research time.

The stimulation provided by my University students, past and present, some of whom have now done postgraduate research on the Soviet Union themselves, I gratefully acknowledge. They above all have helped to focus attention, motivate enquiry, and suggest new insights. They have also helped to ferret out the obscure and the novel, and generally created that teacher–student amalgam in which the teacher disappears and we are all learners together.

I greatly appreciate the assistance of the Embassy of the U.S.S.R., Canberra, which, through their Counsellor, Dr. Boris Galat, saw that I received a great volume of up-to-date source material, and kindly provided most of the photographs used in the book.

I acknowledge the help and unerring efficiency of my typist, Miss Peggy Holmes. She converted my often obtuse and illegible manuscript into a clear record for my Publishers. I am grateful to my friend, Alan Bartlett, for rendering my rough maps and diagrams into their final cartographic form.

Finally, I thank my wife who has assisted in many ways during the preparation of this book, not least in her encouragement and the stoicism with which she accepted disturbances in the family's domestic arrangements. Coupled to this I want to thank my two children, Sylvia and Stuart, who have accepted the non-availability of a parent over weekends and many evenings with a forbearance beyond their years.

As is customary, I add that none of these individuals is to be held responsible for any of the book's shortcomings, but to the contrary, I gladly honour them for any features worthy of merit it may possess.

For me, the preparation of the book has not been without its fascination. It is my earnest hope that my readers too will experience something of the interest and awakening curiosity latent in a study of the economic geography of one of the world's largest and most powerful countries.

LIST OF TABLES

PART FOUR: SOVIET ECONOMIC REGIONS

LIST OF PLATES

PART ONE: ENVIRONMENTAL RESOURCES

PART TWO: HUMAN RESOURCES AND SPATIAL ORGANIZATION

PART THREE: APPRAISAL OF SOVIET SYSTEMATIC ECONOMIC GEOGRAPHY

PART FOUR: SOVIET ECONOMIC REGIONS

LIST OF FIGURES

NOTE ON THE SYSTEM OF TRANSLITERATION FROM RUSSIAN

In general the system of transliteration from the Cyrillic alphabet for place-names and proper names is that recommended by the British Permanent Committee on Geographical Names. Where words in Russian have an anglicized version, e.g. Archangel, the normal Russian form has been retained nevertheless, i.e. Arkhangel'sk. Exceptions occur only where the Russian name may be so unfamiliar to readers that confusion might arise; the English Georgia is preferred to its Russian equivalent, Gruziya. The use of Moscow has been preferred to Moskva as being more familiar to English-speaking readers.

Throughout the text the apostrophe ' has been used to represent the Russian 'soft sign', denoting that the preceding consonant is palatalized, as in the names, Arkhangel'sk, Perm', Stavropol', and Tyumen'.

Place-names with the prefix Novo- (= New) have been rendered as one word, e.g. Novokuybyshev (= New Kuybyshev) where this is customary in the Russian literature, but as two separate words, e.g. Novo Ufa, where it is not usually so contracted. The index makes clear the most common usage in this regard, especially as the Russians themselves do not always apply such contractions consistently.

Exceptions to the foregoing transliteration rules occur in minor instances. Also where transliteration is provided in an already translated reference, the original transliteration has been retained.

Russian words that are commonly known to English readers: kolkhoz, sovkhoz, oblast, kombinat, etc., have been used in their English forms, especially in their plurals. Thus sovkhozes rather than the Russian *sovkhozi*. Words of Russian origin otherwise found in the text are shown in italics.

NOTE ON UNITS

Where possible, S.I. units have been used. References to *tons* are to *metric tons* throughout.

LIST OF ABBREVIATIONS USED IN THE BIBLIOGRAPHIES

AAAG	Annals of the Association of American Geographers, Chicago
GJ	Geographical Journal, London
GR	Geographical Review, New York
G and K	Geografiya i Khozyaystvo (Geography and Economics), Moscow
Iz.A.N.	Izvestiya Akademii Nauk SSSR, Geographical Series, Moscow
PM	Petermanns Mitteilungen, Gotha
QJE	Quarterly Journal of Economics, Cambridge, USA
SG	Soviet Geography: Review and Translation, American Geographical Society, New York
VP	Voprosy Geografii (Problems in Geography), Moscow

PART ONE

ENVIRONMENTAL RESOURCES

CHAPTER ONE

INTRODUCTION

There are two vital reasons for the writing of this book: first, the growing economic significance of the Soviet Union in world affairs. It is a country that ranks third in terms of size of population (241·7 million in 1970) after Mainland China and India, but well ahead of the aggregate population of Western European countries or North America (U.S.A. and Canada). Moreover, the Soviet Union covers one-sixth of the world's land surface, and divides unevenly at the Urals into Soviet Europe and Soviet Asia. Astride two continents, the Soviet Union is a vital economic link between two cultural realms; the 'Western' and the 'Oriental'.

Secondly, over the past fifteen years or so, the Soviet Union has undertaken vigorous and manifold economic developments of great moment. It has harnessed an energy resource system and established a heavy industrial base approaching those of the United States. Its methods of utilizing its vast resource potential have also felt the impact of great technological transformations: in industries; in agricultural pursuits; in transport means; and above all in the material well-being of its population.

These facts make an in-depth study of the Soviet Union's economic geography a fascinating and, it would seem, timely event.

Since the early 1960s, several new Russian books on the country's economic geography have appeared, but only one has been translated into English. This is A. N. Lavrishchev's *Economic Geography of the USSR*, published in Moscow in 1969. As a matter of interest, the authors and titles of these Russian works are cited in the end-of-chapter bibliography. Also included are particulars of the several books by specialists writing in English relevant to economic geography that have been published in the West. These include, for example, L. Symon's *Russian Agriculture*; T. Shabad's *Basic Industrial Resources of the Soviet Union*; E. W. Williams' *Freight Transportation in the Soviet Union*, and F. L. Pryor's *The Communist Foreign Trade System*.

Many other specialist studies and the geographical and economic periodical literature have been combed for the basic data that make-up the ground work for the current study. These sources are all cited in the bibliographies to assist readers in their further studies.

This book attempts to provide a definitive assessment of the *economic geography* of the Soviet Union with special emphasis on the 1960–73 period. To this writer such an objective appraisal of recent Soviet economic geography would seem long overdue. The aim throughout has been to provide as much up-to-date information and practical insights as are currently feasible. Some effort has been made to present a value-free assessment with a treatment that is neither pro-Soviet nor pro-Western in its perspectives.

It is thus apparent that the general aims and purpose of the book are comparatively simple. This has called for a considered framework to give the book some value as a textbook and a reference work. To this end, the treatment has been to break the subject matter down into four parts, each given the amount of space considered appropriate to its importance, consistent with the overall objectives. These parts are:

Part I (three chapters), **Environmental Resources**, pinpoints the essential elements of land, mineral resources, climate, soils, and natural plant cover.

Part II (three chapters), **Human Resources and Spatial Organization**, gives some insights into Soviet demographic, ethnic, and occupational trends; into urbanization and the urban structure, and into the regional framework. These two parts set down the essential parameters for the systematic and regional parts that follow; providing the stage as it were for the economic characteristics discussed within the systematic and regional contexts.

Part III (ten chapters), **An Appraisal of Soviet**

Systematic Economic Geography, covers a consideration of *Soviet Agriculture, Soviet Industry* and *Soviet Transportation and Foreign Trade and Overseas Aid* in some detail in three sub-sections. The first sub-section deals with Soviet agricultural policies, agricultural structure, and agricultural landscapes; the second, with Soviet industrial policies, the power and energy industries, metal mining operations, heavy industries, and finally, the light industries and consumer markets; and the third sub-section discusses transportation, trade and overseas aid.

Part IV (twelve chapters), **Soviet Economic Regions**, provides a regional treatment of Soviet economic geography, and closes with a concluding chapter on Soviet perspectives and the future.

The method adopted for the regional chapters is to group together some of the Soviet Union's nineteen major economic regions – the essential statistical-administrative regions of the country – to facilitate study. This technique is essentially due to limitations of space. Nevertheless, in many respects, this grouping has been advantageous since the book's regions demonstrate the common features and deep economic affinities possessed by some of the official, Soviet-devised economic regions with their neighbours (Fig. 7.1). The regional treatment thus seeks to highlight each region's personality: its fundamental position, environmental characteristics, its economic resources, and its technological status in the Soviet economy as a whole.

No satisfactory yardstick exists to measure the economic geography of the Soviet Union with that of other areas of comparable size and population, although numerous attempts have been made in the past to do just this.

Superficially, the North American continental land mass and the Soviet Eurasian land mass have strong geographical resemblances (Table 1.1). None-

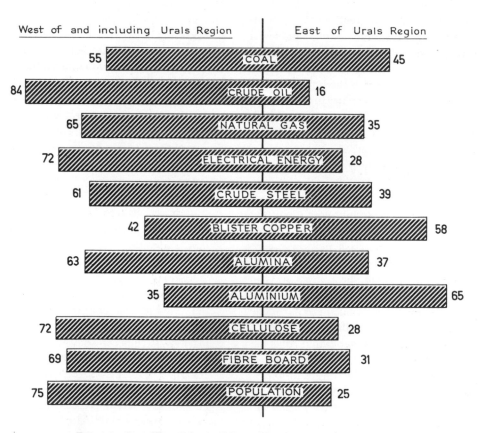

FIG. 1.1 East–West Balance of Population and Economic Indicators.

TABLE 1.1

Basic Statistical Comparison: The Soviet Union and North America (U.S.A. and Canada) 1970

Quantum (and units)	Soviet Union	North America (U.S.A. and Canada)
Total Population (millions)	241·7	224·6
Urban Population (millions)	136·0	165·0
Rural Population (millions)	105·7	59·6
Area (million square kilometres)	22·4	19·3
Population Density (persons per sq. km)	10·8	11·6
Crude Birth Rate (live births/1000)	17·0	17·7
Crude Death Rate (deaths/1000)	8·1	9·4
Land-Uses (percentage of total area)	100·0	100·0
Arable lands and orchards	10·6	11·7
Meadows and permanent pasture	16·6	14·3
Forests and woodlands	36·9	34·6
Wastelands and Urban Area	35·9	39·4

Sources: *Statesman's Year Book*, 1972–73, *passim*; *U.N. Statistical Year Book*, 1970, *passim*; and E. L. Shubalov, *Ekonomicheskaya Geografiya SSSR*, Geografizdaz, Moscow, 1965. (All figures adapted to conform to a 1970 date-line by the author.)

theless, environmental and human homologues should not be pressed too far.

If there exist in the Soviet Union the same basic empathy between Man and Nature, there are important and deep-seated differences arising from the voluntarist approach to environmental and human resources in that country. In other words, the Russians have great faith in Man's ability to transform and mould Nature, ostensibly following the course of the Marxist–Leninist dialectic. This is brought out clearly in Matley's paper, cited in the bibliographies.

Moreover, the vast differences in the incidence of government planning and control, and in attitudes to resource management, mark off the two continental areas quite sharply one from the other. Peaceful coexistence has never implied conformity in the ways in which nations grow.

As examples of the immediate continental differences one can cite the case of the Soviet penchant for exploiting marginal resources. This is clearly shown in the Virgin Lands Scheme; in desert irrigation projects; in the exploitation of remote mineral resources; and in excessively long and probably uneconomic railway freight hauls. It is doubtful whether North American entrepreneurs would find that many such decisions made by

Soviet authorities are economically viable. But it is equally clear that the Russians do. Failure to distinguish between these two approaches to Nature can only lead to the gravest errors of interpretation.

The Russian attitude has led to virtual national self-sufficiency in the production of energy and metals, and in the basic support-structure for its huge population.

For these reasons, unless a great deal of attention is given to detailed considerations, any intercontinental comparisons tend to break down, or worse, are accepted equivocally at their apparent face value. Such an approach is naïve. If agriculture is taken as an example, then it is clear that the natural environments of the two continents impinge quite differently on their agricultural productivity. But in essence there are no strictly scientific homologues between North American and Russian climates, soils, and other environmental traits. Precipitation provenance is different in character, intensity, and seasonal incidence in both continents. On the human and technological side there are immense structural differences between North American and Soviet agricultural systems, not to mention the acutely different political and social climates in which they have grown in the past.

Nevertheless, if it is clearly recognized that deep-seated geographical differences may exist between superficially analogous regions, then, with caution, the comparison of inter-continental data becomes instructive. The following table gives some insight into the position of the Soviet Union *vis-à-vis* the United States in a selection of industries (Table 1.2). It is evident that the Soviet Union's position ranks below that of the United States, but it is equally clear that many key material indices in Soviet production are improving in relation to those of the United States (Table 1.3).

It seems clear, however, that the Soviet Union with its vast area, varied natural environments — embracing all climatic and landscape zones with the exception of the tropics — its rich mineral and agricultural resources, and its disciplined man-power, stands on the threshold of great advances in levels of production for many raw materials, producer goods, and indeed consumer industries. The following pages will spell out some of the transformations accomplished during the seventh Seven-Year Plan (1959–65), the eighth Five-Year Plan (1966–70), and those currently under way in

TABLE 1.2

Industrial Production: The Soviet Union and the United States, 1969

Production and Units	Soviet Union	United States
Manufacturing Production Workers (millions)	26·7	21·5
Bituminous Coal (million tons)	425·8	513·4
Brown Coal (million tons)	137·7	4·5
Crude Oil (million tons)	328·3	455·6
Natural Gas (thousand million cubic metres)	181·1	586·1
Electrical Energy (thousand million kwh)	689·0	1,552·3
Coke-oven Coke (million tons)	73·5	58·7
Iron Ore (Fe. Content) (million tons)	101·0	52·5
Crude Steel (million tons)	110·3	128·1
Cement (million tons)	89·7	66·6
Sulphuric Acid (million tons)	10·66	26·06
Caustic Soda (million tons)	1·66	8·73
Copper: Refined Primary (million tons)	1·02	2·03
Aluminium: Primary (million tons)	1·10	3·44
Magnesium: Primary (thousand tons)	45·00	90·61
Lead: Primary (thousand tons)	440·0	594·1
Zinc: Primary (thousand tons)	610·0	944·0
Wood Pulp: Mechanical (thousand tons)	1,546·0	5,284·0
Wood Pulp: Chemical (thousand tons)	4,252·0	31,964·0
Newsprint (thousand tons)	1,051·0	2,878·0
Rayon–Acetate Fibres (thousand tons)	441·0	715·0
Synthetic Fibres (thousand tons)	142·5	1,581·0
Plastics and Resins (thousand tons)	1,452·6	7,278·7
Cotton Yarn inc. mixtures (thousand tons)	1,421·0	1,637·1
Wool Yarn inc. mixtures (thousand tons)	322·0	175·9
Tyres, Rubber (millions)	20·88	207·83
Motor Vehicles (thousands)	293·6	8,223·7
Radio Receivers (thousands)	7,266·0	17,646·0
Television Receivers (thousands)	6,595·0	8,914·0

Source: *United Nations Statistical Yearbook*, 1970, *passim*.

Notes: Manufacturing production workers in the U.S. do not include salaried grades; the Soviet figure however includes all manufacturing workers (wage earners and salaried).

'Primary' means metals extracted from ores. The U.S. produces considerable amounts of secondary metals derived from scrap metals.

Rayon–Acetate and Synthetic Fibres include both continuous filament and staple types.

TABLE 1.3
Soviet Union – United States: Industrial Index Numbers 1950–70 (1950 Base = 100)

Type of Production	1950		1960		1965		1970	
	U.S.S.R.	U.S.A.	U.S.S.R.	U.S.A.	U.S.S.R.	U.S.A.	U.S.S.R.	U.S.A.
All Industrial Production	100	100	304	145	458	191	689	224
Electricity Output	100	100	320	218	555	299	812	424
Iron and Steel Industry	100	100	269	98	396	129	522	127
Chemicals and Petrochemicals	100	100	392	198	766	296	1366	411
Machine Production and Metal Working	100	100	422	165	757	229	1321	260
Forest Industries	100	100	216	133	276	171	363	194
Building Materials	100	100	543	136	831	166	1244	182
Glass and Porcelain	100	100	335	129	522	165	839	201
Light Industries	100	100	250	121	283	152	427	155
Food Industries	100	100	234	128	334	148	442	169

Source: *Narodnoe Khozyaistvo, 1970*, Moscow, 1971, p. 91.

response to the ninth Five-Year Plan (1971–75) approved by the 24th Communist Party of the Soviet Union Congress in 1970.

One of the measures which suggest the attainment of specific production goals has been the rate of growth in various production indices over the last twenty years (Table 1.3). The speed with which the manifest gap between Soviet and United States production for specific products is being closed is little short of phenomenal. It is a measure of the Soviet penchant for setting their production goals realistically, particularly in the post-Khrushchev period. The speed with which the Soviet Union has approached, and, in some cases, overtaken production levels in the foremost capitalist countries is viewed by some with considerable misgiving, if not foreboding. But the economic geographer (if he values his scholarly objectivity and impartiality at all) cannot comment on the relative merits of different political systems. He must nevertheless present the cogent facts – and industrial growth rates are just one such set of facts – without fear or favour.

The comparisons afforded by Table 1.3 illustrate the growth of various industrial sectors in the Soviet Union against those in the United States over the period, 1950–70. One should hasten to add that this shows the relative rate of growth over that time period, and not the absolute positions in these industrial sectors. Therefore as a cautionary note, the author draws attention to the absolute production levels in 1969 for a number of important industrial products (Table 1.2).

What is frequently not apparent, however, is that for all the vigorous growth elements to be found in Soviet industrial sectors, the performance is often very uneven. To take just one instance, the chemical and petrochemical industries have advanced nearly fourteen-fold in the Soviet Union since 1950, but there are wide discrepancies in growth rates within the class (Table 1.4).

This underlines the need in writing this economic geography of the Soviet Union, to look closely at the facts and figures behind the unfolding story of current changes.

It is particularly desirable to assess correctly the relative rates of change not only in the means of production – the Russian term for the producer goods industries – but also in the light industries, consumer goods sectors, and also in agriculture, external trade, and transport. Such analyses have been undertaken in the chapters that follow. The spatial distribution aspects of these changes are also covered in the regional part of this book.

Without prejudging the issues involved, it is clear that in the fifty years since its formation the Soviet Union has, on the whole, achieved a remarkable and sustained economic growth, notwithstanding World War II which destroyed much of the country's productive capacity, and the many internal upheavals that unbalanced the economy for short periods.

ENVIRONMENTAL RESOURCES

TABLE 1.4

Soviet Union: Chemical Production (thousand tons)

	1950	1960	1970	Growth % 1950–70
Mineral Fertilizers	5,497	13,867	55,400	907·8
Sulphuric Acid (monohydrate)	2,125	5,398	12,059	467·5
Caustic Soda	325	765	1,938	496·3
Plastics and Resins	67·1	311·6	1,672·0	2,391·8
Chemical Fibres	24.2	211·2	623·0	2,474·4
Synthetic Dyes	46·2	84·1	98·0	112·1
Tyres (millions)	7·4	17·2	34·6	367·6

Source: R. Belousov, *USSR Heavy Industry*, Novosti Press Agency, Moscow, 1972, p. 72.

CHAPTER TWO

SOVIET EURASIA: STRUCTURE AND LAND FORMS

The Soviet Union is an Eurasian sub-continent with a total area of about 22·4 million square kilometres (8·65 million square miles); it covers a considerable part of the European continent and a substantial portion of mainland Asia. The European part of the Soviet Union comprises 5·6 million square kilometres and that of the Asian Territories, 16·8 million. Thus, as far as territory is concerned, the country is more closely bonded to Asia than Europe.

With its great size – almost three times the size of the U.S.A. or Australia and 90 times the size of Britain – the Soviet Union encompasses manifold geological structures and a diversity of land forms. It is a country in which rocks of all geological ages are represented and one in which a whole gamut of geomorphological land forms abound.

Geological history has given the Soviet Union vast mineral resources; fossil fuels, ferrous and non-ferrous metals, rare earths, and precious gemstones in abundance, while its geomorphological build, with glacial, fluvio-glacial, fluvial, and arid land forms in conspicuous array, has set the stage for many aspects of the country's economy.

The east–west extent of the country is more than 9000 kilometres (5580 miles). It runs from the centre of the Bering Strait, where a line between the Diomede Islands separates Soviet and U.S. territory, to the Baltic Republics and beyond. The Big Diomede Island (called Ratmanov Island by the Russians) is the easternmost extent of the Soviet Union. The western limit is near Kaliningrad (formerly Königsberg) on the Soviet–Polish border.

The north–south territorial span is more than 4500 kilometres (2790 miles). Cape Fligely on Rudolf Island in the Arctic Ocean is the Soviet Union's most northerly point, while the southernmost point is near the town of Kushka in Turkmenistan. Thus from the blizzard-swept *sastrugi* of the polar north to the *inselbergs* and other arid land forms of the extreme south of the Soviet Union a great variety of economic land-uses exist.

The external borders of the Soviet Union are somewhat longer than 60,000 kilometres (37,200 miles). Two-thirds of this length is maritime border, mainly along the margins of the Barents, Kara, Laptev, and East Siberian Seas of the Arctic north. On the 'sector principle' Soviet territory extends northward to the North Pole and embraces such island territories as Novaya Zemlya, Franz Josef Land, and Severnaya Zemlya. Around 20,000 kilometres (12,400 miles) however, are land borders with Korea, China, Mongolia, Afghanistan, Iran, and Turkey in the south; with Rumania, Hungary, Czechoslovakia, and Poland in the COMECON west, and Finland and Norway in the northwest.

The Pacific Ocean approaches to the Soviet Union are controlled by Komandorskye Islands, the terminal islands of the Aleutian chain, and the Kuriles and southern Sakhalin, both of which were ceded by Japan following World War II.

The geological structure of the Soviet Union can be described as two large platforms, the Russian and the Siberian. These form the elemental structure on which the manifold detail of Soviet geology is based.

The Russian platform spreads out between the mountain ranges of the Carpathians, the Caucasus, and the Crimea and the Ural Mountains covering the whole of European Russia (Figure 2.1). The crystalline rocks of this platform are exposed in two places forming the Baltic and Ukrainian Shields. The former is exposed in the Kola Peninsula and in Karelia as low-lying crystalline rocks contiguous with the Fenno-Scandinavian Shield. Major water surfaces occur in this Shield including the White Sea, Lakes Ladoga and Onega and Chudskoe (Peipus).

The southwestern Ukranian or Azov–Podolsk Shield forms the basement of ancient crystalline rocks which have been overlaid by successive layers of young rocks throughout geological history. Paleozoic deposits cover the intervening area from the Shields to the Ural Mountains and, in turn, are overlaid by Mesozoic and Tertiary rocks like a huge layer cake. In places, the sedimentary rocks reach thickness of up to 2000 metres (6560 feet) depending on the undulations in the underlying platform. Everywhere either glacial or fluvial action has stripped away the upper layers to expose the deeper rocks of the earth's crust. In the case of the Baltic and Azov–Podolian Shields the upper geological series have been completely eroded. Differential erosive action on different parts of the Russian platform have thus brought metallic minerals and other useful resources to light. Discussion of these resources is deferred until the appropriate following chapters.

The Siberian platform coincides with the Central Siberian Plateaux extending from the Yenisey heights in the west to the Aldan and Lena mountain complexes, and to the Sayan Mountains, Yablonovyy, and Stanovoy Mountains in the south. Two ancient crystalline shield areas are exposed in the Siberian platform, the Aldan Shield and the Anabar Massif. Again mineral and fuel resources of great significance are associated with the Siberian platform.

The structural build of the Soviet Union has been greatly affected by the relative movement of the two platforms deep within the earth's mantle at various geological times. In Paleozoic times the broad geosyncline between the Russian and Siberian platforms in-filled with thick sediments. Subsequent movement of the platforms towards each other raised up the Ural fold mountain during the Hercynian orogen. Similar orogenic action between the Siberian and Laurentian (American) platforms raised up the fold mountains of Soviet Far East –

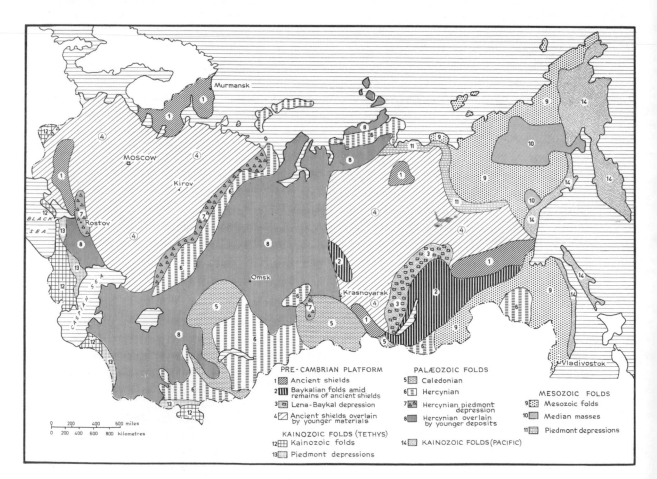

FIG. 2.1   Geological Structure and Build of the Soviet Union.

the Sikhote-Alin, Verkhoyansk, Cherskiy, and Anadyr Mountains. These were all raised up during the Mesozoic geological era. This action also moulded the tethys or basin of the North Pacific.

The most recent movement of the platforms southward folded deep sediments in a great east–west geosyncline and thus created the high Alpine mountain systems which flank the Soviet Union's southern border areas–the Crimean and Caucasus Mountains, the Pamirs and associated chains of the Hindu Kush and Himalayas, while in the east, the mountain ranges of Sakhalin and Kamchatka, and also the drowned mountain archipelago of the Kuril Islands were formed contemporaneously with the Alpine folding of Tertiary times. As in the case of North American Sierras and the Himalayas, the high Tertiary fold mountains of the Soviet Union have been a serious impediment to economic development, lying athwart the most direct routes to the interior and impeding the inflow of moist, growth-promoting summer monsoon. On the other hand these mountain bastions have been of great benefit throughout Russian history because of the protection afforded against i̶ from more numerous peoples of the so̶ the Indian and Chinese sub-

Associated with the flank̶ tains are some of the S̶ petroleum resources. I̶ geologists have prospecte̶ the far northeast where̶ suitable for the oc̶ Excitement has grown ̶ up of the Barrow̶ geological conditions a̶

The geomorpholog̶ Union rests primaril̶ fundamental geologi̶ processes of gla̶ insolation. In detail,̶ is too complex for ̶ only the broad outlines are given.

In the west, the European Plain, rarely more than 200 metres above sea-level, stretches to the Urals. Here and there low ranges of hills protrude above the general elevation; up to 400 metres in some parts. Typical are the Valdai Hills, the Russian Uplands south of Moscow, and the Volga Heights. During the Pleistocene glaciation these higher areas

had a significant effect in impeding continental glaciations. Further they played a part in the fluvial and aeolian sorting of sedimentary materials contributing significantly to the more fertile agricultural areas of the southern European Plain.

Within the general bounds of the European Plain of Russia are numerous lowland basins. In particular, the following can be noted: the Poles'ye, Dnieper, Oka-Don, Meshchera, and Sukhona, as well as the Black Sea and Sea of Azov coastal plains and the huge Caspian Depression. In parts, the latter is 25 metres below sea level. With the exception of the Caspian Depression these lowlands form by far the most intensively exploited agricultural areas of the Soviet Union based on geomorphology and pre-eminent soil groups, especially the black-earths (chernozems) and chestnut soils. Throughout Russian history these lowland areas of European Russia have supported dense agrarian populations and this land-use pattern has been but slightly modified during the Soviet period.

East of the Urals and advancing to the Yenisey Heights lies an extensive lowland plain of the Ob' Basin. Considerable areas of this great West Siberian lowland, drained by the Ob' and its trib-̶ extensive marshes, particularly in the ̶ of ice in the north as the ̶ inundation of ̶nd. At the ̶erian Basin ̶ularly where ̶bsoil, com-̶nage.

̶he low folded ̶gay Uplands. ̶ are the low ̶azakhstan and ̶rt Plateau and ̶ and Kyzyl Kum ̶ands, marked by ̶ave been brought ̶Soviet period. The ̶olved are discussed in Chapters ̶.

East of the Yenisey, ̶ iet Union's landmass is dominated by extensive high plateaux and mountain ranges already discussed above. In the southern border areas great lake basins are found within mountain fastnesses. Lake Balkhash (18,000 square kilometres) and Lake Baykal (31,500 square kilometres) are the most prominent. These lakes together with their associated deeply entrenched river valleys provide some of the Soviet Union's best hydroelectric power potential. Numerous sites on the upper Yenisey and Angara are being developed currently and are scheduled to generate sufficient power for local electrical energy-intense industries and still allow a surplus for long-distance transmission to the industrial areas of the west.

Although there are few exceptions to the general highland character of Siberia and the Far East, some lowlands of conspicuous value nevertheless exist. In the Maritime Kray of the Far East extensive lowlands occur within the lower courses and interfluves of the Amur, Sungari, and Ussuri rivers. Similar basins occur in the Zeya–Bureya lowlands and in northern Sakhalin Island. Historically, these fertile basins have been a bone of contention between Russian and Ukrainian farmers on the one hand, and Chinese, Korean, and Japanese settlers on the other. Currently China and Russia share riparian rights on parts of the Amur, Sungari, and Ussuri systems.

The importance of the geological structure and geomorphological development of the Soviet Union can be seen in their effects on economic activities. Resources of fuel, energy, metallic minerals, and similar 'geological' raw materials clearly depend on the antecedent earth history. Similarly the richness and diversity of agriculture and forestry depend on what Nature has accomplished in bygone ages. The fact that Russian scientists have identified some forty-two different primary land-use systems in the Soviet Union indicates the diversity of land resources that actually exists.

1. Shelter belt of birch trees in the eastern Ukraine. (Photograph by the author.)

CHAPTER THREE

CLIMATES OF THE SOVIET UNION: THEIR ECONOMIC ASPECTS

In essence the climatic diversity of the Soviet Union arises from its great size, one-seventh of the world's land surface. It is bounded by a broad latitudinal range (36° N to 82° N) and an even greater longitudinal range (20° E to 192° E). Considerable variations in surface roughness and morphological build exist, including a variety of mountain ranges, plateaux, and extensive plains, and on the west, north, and east, proximity to large ocean masses, gives the Soviet Union great macro-climatic diversity. The westerly winds too, characteristic of the northern hemisphere, play their part in regional differentiation of climate. Taken together, these genetic factors divide the Soviet Union into a ragged chequerboard of regional climates, unsurpassed in number by any other continental mass.

Since the primary purpose of this chapter is to examine closely some of the applied aspects of climate, particularly as they affect economic activity, we shall not spend time on the Soviet Union's fundamental climatology. Several comprehensive books mentioned in the bibliography deal quite adequately with these more general matters, especially Borisov and Berg.

It is nevertheless expedient to enumerate the major climatic zones and their regional divisions according to one Soviet climatologist, Alisov (1956) (Figure 3.1). This provides the broad framework for our discussion of the economic impact of climate within each zone (Table 3.1).

Throughout the Soviet Union, climatic limitations impose severe restrictions on agricultural land-use and many other economic activities. Inadequate warmth or excessive cold; relative drought or excessive moisture give rise to a series of landscapes, marshlands, steppes, permafrost zones, and taiga, that man has only won over with great difficulty.

The Soviet Union suffers greatly from inclement winds at particular seasons of the year. The hot, dry desiccating *sukhovey* wind of late summer blows in from the deserts of the southeast causing drought conditions as plants suffer from excessive transpiration and soil moisture stress. While a technical definition of the *sukhovey* has been devised — temperatures in excess of 25° C, wind velocity in excess of 5 metres per second and relative humidity of less than 30 per cent — this is not entirely satisfactory because *sukhovey*-type droughts can occur well outside these limits.

The bora wind brings a surge of very cold air streaming from the Siberian high pressure zone in winter far to the south, reaching as far as the Great Caucasus Range. Temperatures plunge to minus 8° C overnight and very cold conditions persist until the situation is relieved by an in-flow of maritime air causing a temporary thaw (*ottepel'*).

A similar but more severe condition to the bora occurs in the northern parts of the Soviet Union. This is the *purga* wind (*buran*) of the tundra and taiga causing snow blizzards driven by bitterly cold winds outblowing from the Siberian high pressure zone in winter. This makes all activities in these latitudes hazardous.

Only those areas sheltered from continental winds from the north and east enjoy really subtropical conditions with long and humid summers. Fortunately, much of the Soviet Union enjoys a summer incidence of rainfall thus promoting vegetative growth. However, despite adequate rainfall, high evaporation rates cause moisture stress in many areas of the Southeast as well as in Kazakhstan and Central Asia.

Typical growing seasons are less than 100 days and are almost everywhere unsuited to the best development of cereal crops from the physiological point of view. Frost-free seasons are short, and this greatly restricts the northern and eastern limits of cultivation for cotton, maize, and similar crops for which longer warm growing seasons are essential.

The European parts of the Soviet Union experience considerable snow accumulation over the winter months which provides snow-melt moisture in

TABLE 3.1

Climatic Regions of the Soviet Union (by absolute zonal area and percentage of total)

Zones and Regions	%	Zones and Regions	%
I Eastern Temperate		*IV Arctic*	
1. Monsoonal Forest Type	2·7	13. Sub-polar Type	2·7
2. East Coast Forest Type	5·4	14. Atlantic Type	1·3
II Central Temperate		15. E. Siberian Type	1·8
3. W. Siberian Continental Forest Type	9·5	16. Pacific Type	2·3
4. E. Siberian Continental Forest Type	11·5	*V Sub-Arctic*	
5. W. Siberian Continental Steppe Type	4·5	17. Atlantic Type	8·6
6. Altai-Sayan Montane Type	0·8	18. Siberian Type	12·2
7. Central Asian Continental Desert Type	3·6	19. Pacific Type	13·4
8. Tien Shan Montane Type	0·8	*VI Sub-Tropical*	
III Western Temperate		20. W. Trans-Caucasian Type	0·5
9. Arctic-Atlantic Type	2·2	21. E. Trans-Caucasian Type	0·7
10. Atlantic Continental Forest Type	9·7	22. Trans-Caucasian Montane Type	0·3
11. Atlantic Continental Steppe Type	2·7	23. S. Turanian Desert Type	1·5
12. N. Caucasian Montane Type	0·8	24. Pamir-Altai Montane Type	0·5

Summary of Macro-climatic Regions

		(in Millions of Hectares)	%
I	Eastern Temperate	180	8·1
II	Central Temperate	678	30·7
III	Western Temperate	340	15·4
IV	Arctic	180	8·1
V	Sub-Arctic	755	34·2
VI	Sub-Tropical	78	3·5
	Total Soviet Union	2211·0	100·0

Sources: Estimated by the author from planimeter surveys of Soviet references, particularly, Grigor'yev and Budyko, *op. cit.*, Alisov, *op. cit.*, and Borisov, *op. cit.*

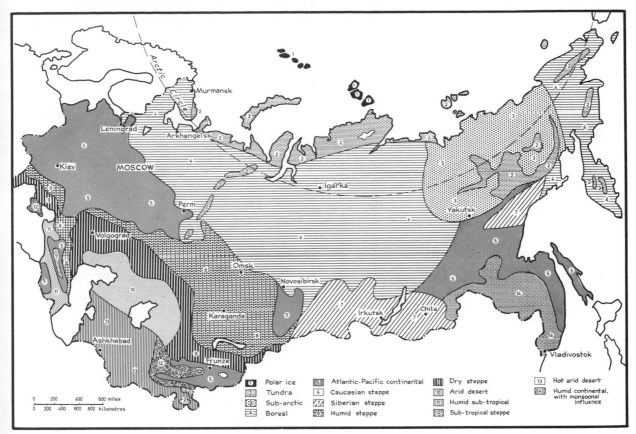

FIG. 3.1 Climatic Zones of the Soviet Union.

spring and has the effect of protecting soils and crops from severe winter temperatures and the cold *purga*, outblowing winds from Siberia. Winter wheat can be successfully grown only in the western parts of Central Region (Orel–Voronezh) and the Ukraine, and consequently most Russian wheat is spring-sown.

Where oceanic air masses do not penetrate, winters are especially severe; the sub-soil becomes permanently frozen. Throughout the Siberias and much of Northern Russia, frozen soil and sub-soil make it impossible for crops to over-winter, and since the hard-frozen ground thaws only slowly during the spring, ploughing and planting is very much delayed. Even in the temperate forest-steppe and steppe, cold outblowing winds from the Siberian 'High' may reduce the winter snow-cover to a thin layer. Here again, the freezing of the surface soil delays the onset of spring agricultural activities. One side effect of this annual freeze-thaw

action is the continual breakdown of soil particles. These become free-flowing and easily erodable surface horizons. In many instances, seasonal wind action on such soils has removed the upper layers so that only degraded profiles now remain; in fact, fossil B-horizons of low fertility.

The southern areas of the Soviet Union are bordered by high mountain ranges. These act as barriers to tropical and especially monsoonal influences for most of the Soviet Union's territory. Continentality is thus strengthened. In the Far East however, monsoonal influences prevail and usefully stimulate land-use in favoured areas.

Over most areas of the Soviet Union the balance between moisture-gain by precipitation, and moisture-loss by evaporation and transpiration, is acute. With the perversity of Nature, only the north has a seasonal moisture surplus which, however, is of little value since temperatures become the limiting factor for most types of land-use. Only in the higher rainfall areas of the West is there an adequate moisture regime to support multi-seasonal agriculture. In the pastoral areas, the scarcity of stock-water in autumn and winter as well as the lack of green herbage until well into summer, impose severe limitation on the stock-carrying capacity of the grasslands. More importantly, this limits the number of stock that can be accommodated on the land from one summer production peak to the next.

The northern and eastern rivers and sea-ports of the Soviet Union are greatly affected by climatic severity (Fig. 3.2). Frozen and impassable for the most part in winter, they become surcharged with flows in the warm season. Since the head-waters thaw some months earlier than the downstream reaches, the Northern Dvina, Ob', Yenisey, and Lena overflow their banks in tremendous seasonal floods. Again, this restricts any extensive agricul-

tural activities on the better soils of the super flood-plains until well into summer.

Even the southern rivers, like those of the Volga system, suffer from a fluctuating water regime; dominantly low-water stages in summer and autumn when water-stress on crop-land is at its worst.

In the extreme north and west of the Soviet Union, where precipitation exceeds evapotranspiration, extensive areas of bog and marshland occur. Mostly these are developed in areas of impeded drainage on glacial or fluvio-glacial soils of which the Poles'ye is typical.

The moisture-surplus areas have acid, low-fertility soils, most frequently leached podzols. The natural vegetation here is coniferous forest, but clearings of quick-growing coarse-grains, especially barley, and fodder crops, are found in more favoured areas.

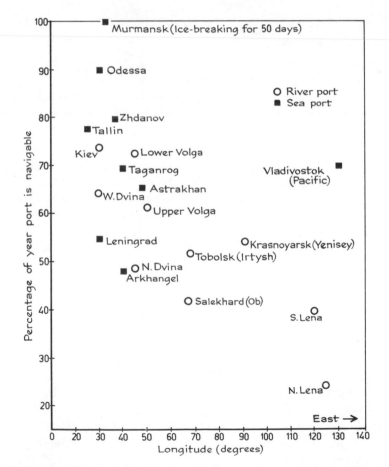

FIG. 3.2   The Effects of Climatic Severity (Indicated by Longitude) on Navigability of River and Sea Ports.

Cool summers and heavy cloud-cover render the Baltic Republics, Belorussia, and the Northwest marginal for much agriculture, quite apart from the poor, low-fertility soils and waterlogged condition of much of the surface. More activity results in the cultivation of hygrophytes; flax, hemp and meadow-hays associated with cattle-raising.

Responses to Climate

Only the western temperate climatic zone has provided really adequate conditions for the full economic development of climatic potential. The other five zones are either limited in area (sub-tropical zone) or have climates that greatly inhibit full economic growth (Fig. 3.3).

Soviet agronomists have developed quick-maturing cereal grains and crops so that these may be grown in areas that would be otherwise climatically unsuitable, particularly the eastern and central temperate zones and the sub-arctic zone. The vernalization of crops – or subjecting seed to artificial heat to cause premature germination – has permitted reduction of the natural growing season requirements in marginal climates.

Everywhere special care is needed to combat the ever-present risk of failure through normal climatic deficiencies, and more particularly with the unseasonal development of a particular stringency. Climatic risk is a very special hazard in Russian agriculture.

The more elements of climate that are hazardous, the less likely is a sound land-system to be developed. For example, where permafrost and shortfalls in annual warmth coincide, any land-use based on agriculture or pastoral activity becomes a highly risky venture.

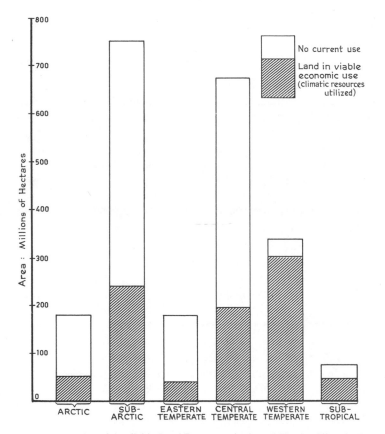

FIG. 3.3   Quantity of Available Land Resources in Actual Use by Climatic Zones.

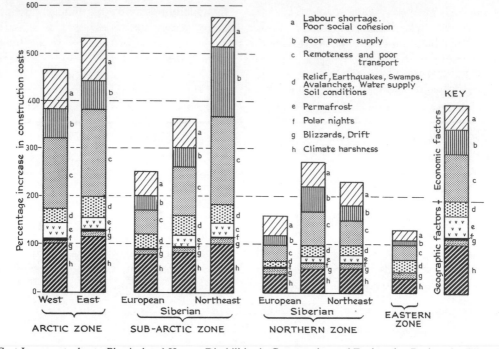

Fig. 3.4   Cost Increments due to Physical and Human Disabilities in Construction and Engineering Projects by Climatic Zone.

Also it should be recognized that very severe cost disabilities may arise from attempts to open up marginal regions where climatic inhibitions are severe. By way of example, the cost increments arising from natural hazards and economic problems in various climatic zones are shown (Figure 3.4).

In the marshlands of the European parts of the Soviet Union, drainage work and mole ploughing have assisted reclamation and promoted the up-grading of bog-soils. Removal of boulders from the fields and also the application of lime and fertilizers have all promoted greater agricultural efficiency, especially in recent years.

The southern steppe and desert climatic zones are marked by high temperatures, long periods of sunshine, dry winds, and consequently high evaporation. At the turn of the season, a small moisture surplus is converted to a marked deficiency by late summer. In the worst affected areas of Central Asia, wind erosion and moving sand dunes render agriculture all but impossible. The careful conservation of a few favoured oases of older times as well as modern irrigation canals of great length have,

however, brought higher levels of agricultural and pastoral production. These irrigated lands are especially valuable, as warmth-loving and generally specialized crops of many kinds may be grown.

It is perhaps doubtful whether the Soviet Union's many costly irrigation works are entirely justified by simple economic criteria. Nevertheless, year-to-year variability in moisture supply makes vast engineering works essential if production is to be sustained at all. Such activity has permitted drought-resistant, but low-yielding crops, like millet and barley to be grown in association with the more sought-after grains, particularly spring wheat. Even in the non-irrigated lands, dry-farming methods in which soil moisture is conserved by ploughing followed by fallow, and the planting of shelter belts, have extended the useful areas of agriculture.

The wooded steppe, extending as a thin wedge from the Ukraine to the Middle Volga and Urals and a few small pockets deep into the Siberias, has for centuries been the most reliable zone for spring-sown grain production. Chernozems and similar pedocal soils have developed from a favourable moisture regime, especially on the underlying high-potential loess soils. However, generations of bonanza-use have left much of this country's soils degraded and not infrequently heavily gullied, resulting from solifluction due to successive summer downpours working on over-cultivated land. There have been some half-hearted attempts by Soviet authorities to repair these erosional ravages of time, but achievements to date are not particularly propitious. However, larger applications of mineral fertilizers and the use of cover-crops is substantially rehabilitating former degraded soils.

Disabilities of Soviet Climates

1. Great areas of the country do not basically support climatic regimes favouring agriculture. Thus much production is at hazard involving marginal or low yields in a majority of years. To combat this difficulty expensive works are needed. Inevitably, this makes for high-cost agriculture.
2. The growth season for crops is unduly restricted by cold in the northlands on the one hand, and by general aridity, or at least seasonal drought, in the southlands on the other. This involves a farm-year cycle that must be premised on higher than normal manpower requirements – a feature of collective and state farming – and an altogether inordinate need for expensive and specialized farm machinery. The Soviet system has not so far been able to afford adequate investments in this regard, although current policies stress these needs. Much of the manpower and machinery is inevitably under-utilized for much of the year, since all Soviet farming activities are telescoped into a period of not more than 120 days or so.
3. The Soviet Union's areas of land suited for the growth of sub-tropical and Mediterranean crops is very small. This means that marginal climatic zones must be pressed into service if the country's growing needs for cotton, rice, oilseeds, tobacco, vine-fruit, tea and other specialized crops are to be met. Again, this

2. Aircraft spraying for pest and weed control in the Trans-Ilian Ala-Tau. This region grows choice apples and other fruit, and as in many parts of the Soviet Union agricultural aircraft play an important role.

premises lower than optimum yields and relatively high-cost agriculture, or alternatively more intensive agriculture based on increasingly more costly irrigation.

Planning of Soviet agricultural production depends to a considerable degree on a correct assessment of the impact of weather and climate on cropping and animal husbandry. In earlier times the selection of particular land-use patterns was a process of trial and error evolved over centuries. Thus emerged the grain regions of the Ukraine, the Centre, and North Caucasus; the cotton areas of Central Asia, and viticulture and tea-growing in the Trans-Caucasus.

Nevertheless, these long-term agricultural systems are not always as well suited to present-day needs as might be supposed. First, new crops have to be accommodated (e.g. maize), or new strains and varieties of crops and animals create new land-type requirements. Again, the pattern of demand causes shifts of emphasis in the need for particular kinds of agricultural output. All of these factors impinge on the redistribution of agricultural activity. Soviet scientists attempt more and more to attain the best use of pedo-climatic resources and thus secure more rational regionalization of agricultural production. Emphasis has been given to early and late-maturing varieties of crops: the first pushing production into areas formerly too cold to secure economic production, and the second

3. Erecting pre-cast irrigation troughs in the Golodnaya Steppe, Uzbekistan.

promoting higher yields by establishing longer growing periods. In some cases, the use of early-maturing varieties has permitted the double-cropping of favourable areas, significantly increasing unit-area production.

The measures Soviet scientists commonly used to work out the agro-climatic potential of given regions are primarily heat and moisture indicators (Table 3.2). Temperature standards are established by summing the mean daily temperatures for the growing period, that is, when these temperatures are higher than 10° C. This indicator permits the Soviet Union to be divided into four temperature accumulation zones: the arctic, sub-arctic, temperate, and sub-tropical. Each of these zones is then sub-divided into sub-zones or regions (Table 3.2).

The temperature accumulation parameter is only one of those needed to define a region's suitability for a given crop. The moisture regime is also vital, particularly in regard to productivity. The measures Soviet scientists use here are both the annual precipitation and the amount falling during the vegetative period. Since, however, evaporation plays a part in the effectiveness of this precipitation, the indicator preferred is the moisture supply (annual or seasonal). This is the amount of annual or seasonal precipitation minus the potential evapotranspiration which in turn depends on insolation, wind conditions, and plant cover. The major zones for moisture availability are the humid, semi-arid, and arid, and these again are broken down into smaller regions. In this way, the Soviet Union is divided into agro-climatic regions.

The regionalization of climatic indices in this way has great significance in the Soviet Union not only for the selection of the land-use system, but also for practical questions, such as setting differential norms for kolkhoz revenue; planning of optimum investment in crop or animal land-use systems, the need for supplementary irrigation, the establishment of 'insurance' food stocks and similar questions.

In order to ensure the most rational use of climatic resources, attention is given to the stability factor in each agro-climatic region. For the arid regions where instability of crop yields is greatest, an 80 per cent certainty factor is required to establish suitability of the land for a given crop. This means that greater than normal deviations from the

TABLE 3.2

Agro-Climatic Resources of the Soviet Union

Accumulated Temperature* °C	Precipitation†					
	Very Humid	Humid	Sub-Humid Subject to some drought	Semi-Arid Subject to drought	Semi-Arid Frequent drought	Arid
	Vo	V	Zs	Z	Zo	S
1500–2000	Northwest Latvia Estonia	West Siberia Volga–Vyatka Urals Far East Krasnoyarsk Kray		East Siberia		
2000–2500	Lithuania Belorussia	The Centre Kaliningrad Oblast	Central Black Earth Altay Kray	Virgin Lands Kray		East Kazakhstan
2500–3000		Maritime Kray Trans-Carpathian Oblast Poles'ye / Forest Steppe		Volga	Aktyubinsk Oblast	Semipalatinsk Oblast
3000–3500				North Caucasus Moldavia Steppe		Astrakhan Oblast Western, Central and Southeastern Kazakhstan
3500–4000			Krasnodar Kray			
4000–4500						Uzbekistan South Kazakhstan
4500–5000						Turkmenistan

Source: Davitaya and Sapozhnikova, *op. cit.*, Table 1, pp. 58–61. Adapted by the author.

* Sum of the Mean Daily Temperatures for the period when they *exceed* 10 °C.

† Precipitation levels are not given in the source, but the following classification is appropriate.

Precipitation (Mean Annual) mm		
>840	(Vo)	Very humid
700–840	(V)	Humid
560–700	(Zs)	Sub-Humid
420–560	(Z)	Semi-Arid with drought
280–420	(Zo)	Semi-Arid with frequent drought
0–280	(S)	Arid

average yield will occur in less than 20 per cent of the years. In other words, the land-use system 'budgets' for a climatic shortfall in output once in every five years.

The effects of ground cover on climatic conditions have been discussed by Feldman (1971). Disturbance of the ground cover by man, most frequently by the substitution of crops or pastures for the natural vegetation, has an effect on the local climate of an area. The change may be beneficial or harmful, promoting or constraining economic use of the land.

Once the major problems found in specific climatic regions have been identified, Russian scientists have sought to ameliorate them. Indeed, it is not too much to claim that the Russian climate in its severity and capriciousness has greatly favoured research into physical constraints and land-use systems.

Briefly, each zone has particular problems: in the Arctic and Sub-Arctic regions the problems are the low accumulation of useful temperatures (above 10° C daily mean) and the need to extend the growing period by averting late spring and early autumn frosts. These conditions are assisted by proper logging operations that allow standing timber of various ages to co-exist and by the restriction of animal husbandry and cropping to small, sheltered clearings. Such an organization of the landscape on the micro-level favourably alters the rainfall pattern (without changing its annual amount) and raises temperatures somewhat.

In the temperate zones, the task perceived is on the one hand to ameliorate drought or excess moisture in specific seasons, and to combat frost hazards on the other. The planting of tree shelter belts traps and distributes snow and holds a potential moisture supply on higher ground. Without shelter belts, some 60 per cent of the snow accumulation would be blown into ravines and depressions with consequent rapid loss to the agricultural system in the spring thaw. Also a blanket of snow, even if only 30–50 centimetres thick, insulates the soil from frost conditions and holds soil and soil moisture at temperatures 10–15° C higher than they would be otherwise. However, snow cover decreases air temperatures by some 5–10° C, and shelter belts may therefore be quite inimical in fruit-growing areas where spring-thaw temperatures are often critical. Similarly, in areas of excessive spring soil moisture, or where the crops grown are sensitive to waterlogging, shelter belts are not good cultural practice, since they provide even more thaw moisture in spring than would be the case from cleared land.

4. The Kazalin dam on the Syr-Darya river. One of the hundreds of irrigation control works that dot the arid areas of Kazakhstan and Soviet Central Asia. These provide irrigation water for cotton, rice, curbis, and other oasis crops as well as thousands of hectares of improved grazing land.

5. Tomato-growing hothouses in Vikhorevka, Irkutsk oblast. Soviet horticultural technology helps overcome the disabilities of a severe continental climate.

In areas of drought, afforestation and shelter belts ameliorate considerably the deleterious effects of the hot *sukhovey* winds of summer, or the bleak *purga* winds of winter.

The moderating influence of reservoirs and man-made lakes on local climate is considerable, extending some 20 kilometres (12·4 miles) from the water margins. These areas can be of very considerable size. Soviet authorities have utilized the micro-climates created by these warmer conditions and moisture provenance of reservoirs to good effect. For example, the creation of the Kuybyshev reservoir caused hot season temperature to decrease by 0·4–0·6° C, but increased the late summer–early autumn temperatures by 1·7–2·2° C. Moreover, warmer conditions were prolonged and the relative humidity of the air increased in spring and early summer when moisture is most beneficial to crops, and the surrounding areas would be most drought-prone without the reservoirs' moderating influence.

According to Vernander *et al.* (1964), effective control measures against drought, the *sukhovey*, and dust storms are irrigation, windbreak-tree plantings and rows of tall-stalk crops. In an average year, the steppe areas under agricultural use require additional ground moisture equivalent to 150 mm of precipitation to ensure high crop yields. This is needed, for example, to secure either 55 centners per hectare of winter wheat, 70 centners per hectare of maize or 540 centners per hectare of sugar beet. Successful furrow irrigation systems provide this moisture in four applications: an autumn charging of 60–70 mm, followed by two anti-desiccation charges of 30–40 mm in the early part of the growing season, and a final summer watering of 30–40 mm when the ears or tubers fill.

In semi-arid areas tall-stalk plants, such as maize or sunflower, are planted in bands 6–9 metres wide and separated by the 'nursed' crop for distances of 70–80 metres with very beneficial effect on the moisture regime of steppe areas. Both 'protector' and 'nurse' crops are harvested at the normal time but the high stubble is left to trap snow until the next ploughing.

Another form of land-use amelioration is the drainage of water-logged land. Considerable areas of the Pripyat marshlands (Belorussia) have been drained quite successfully. These now yield up to 800 centners of potatoes or 25 centners of grain per

hectare, once nitrogen potash fertilizers and copper-trace applications have been made to correct deficiences in the soils. Such treatments give humus-rich soils of good tilth, free from the hard, waxy surfaces common in drained, but otherwise untreated peat-lands.

It is clear that economic land-use in the Soviet Union has benefited by Soviet science. The past two decades have revealed a closer understanding of how climatic potential can be best translated into effective land-use both in order to obtain the greatest possible physical output from land-use, and equally importantly, in order to secure this output in the most economical way.

6. The taiga yields vast quantities of oil, natural gas, and metallic ores. Here one of the thirty-five wells drilled to depths of 3000 metres in the Vuktyl' area yields condensate oil and dry gas which is treated at nearby Ukhta, Komi A.S.S.R. In 1972 about 13,000 million cubic metres of condensate gas were drawn from the Vuktyl' fields.

CHAPTER FOUR

SOILS AND NATURAL VEGETATION: ECONOMIC ASPECTS

Planning higher agricultural and forestry production in the Soviet Union is founded on scientific evaluation of land resources, particularly of the soil characteristics and the potentially commercial vegetation cover, such as natural pastures and forests. Such an evaluation can be used in conjunction with data on climatic characteristics, and also with current production statistics from those regions already exploited. In this way, an accurate resource and land-use potential map can be extrapolated for the whole of the Soviet Union. At present, precise large-scale and detailed soil maps are available for less than half of the agricultural area, so that correct estimation of the potential of unmapped and new areas rests heavily on indirect data at the present time.

The best nation-wide soil map on a scale of 1 : 4 million prepared by this method was published by the Dokuchayev Soil Institute under the supervision of N. N. Rozov (Fig. 4.1). This map divides the Soviet Union's vast area into 42 genetic soil types. These are then combined into 17 sub-zonal types, and again into 5 macro-zonal groups (Table 4.1).

The Soviet Union's soil zones, the result of climatic conditions for the most part, present a pattern for land-use potential which is far from favourable. Of the country's total area of 2211 million hectares of land surface, only 10·7 per cent is currently used for arable cultivation, horticulture, orchards, or long-term fallow (*zalezh'*); a further 2·6 per cent for hay production; and 14·2 per cent for pasturage or grazing, making a total of only

7. A desert solar desalination plant at the Bakharden sovkhoz in Turkmenistan. Brackish water drawn from artesian sources passes through the desalination unit before being fed into sheep troughs. A single unit can economically supply enough drinking water to support 2000 sheep.

27·5 per cent in any form of intensive or extensive land-use. There are only very limited soil resources available which have not been utilized so far. Consequently future increases in land productivity must come from intensification of land-use rather than from an augmentation of area. The best soils for future extension of area are some of the desert grey-brown soils and sierozems which are currently being brought into production by irrigation (Table 4.2) and at the other extreme, some of the water-logged peaty and bog soils which are being reclaimed by drainage (Table 4.3). The provision of drinking water for the farm population is a critical factor in the further development of the desert soils no less than the availability of canal or ground water irrigation. To this end the Soviet Union is in

TABLE 4.1
Soviet Soil Zones and Sub-Zones

Zones and Sub-Zones	Total Area (million hectares)	Percentage by Texture			Main Inter-Zonal Types
		Alluvials	Clays and Loams	All other †	
POLAR TUNDRA					
1. Arctic Soil	60	—	85·0	15·0	Clay-loams
2. Tundra Soils	120	1·7	83·3	15·0	Clay-loams
TAIGA					
3. Gleyey Podzolic	240	3·3	16·7	80·0	Permafrost
4. Podzolic Soils	255	3·9	17·3	78·8	Permafrost
5. Peaty Podzolic *	260	5·8	59·2	35·0	Clay-loams
FOREST STEPPE AND STEPPE					
6. Grey Forest Soils	64	3·0	89·5	7·5	Clay-loams
7. Podzolized, Leached and Typical Chernozems	89	4·5	74·2	21·3	Clay-loams
8. Ordinary and Southern Chernozems	100	3·0	76·0	21·0	Clay-loams
9. Dark and Chestnut Soils	68	4·3	44·2	51·5	Solonized clay-loams
SEMI-DESERT AND DESERT					
10. Light Chestnut and Brown Desert Steppe Soils	130	3·0	19·3	77·7	Solonetz
11. Grey-Brown Desert Soils	140	4·3	30·7	65·0	Sands and clay-loams
12. Grey Soils	33	—	69·7	30·3	Clay-loams
MOUNTAIN					
13. Mountain Tundra	165	—	—	100·0	⎫
14. Mountain Meadow	27	—	—	100·0	⎪
15. Mountain Podzolic	400	—	1·8	98·2	Stony Mountain
16. Mountain Brown Forest	18	—	—	100·0	Regoliths
17. Mountain Steppe and Desert Soils	42	—	16·6	83·4	⎭
Total Soviet Union	2211	2·6	37·2	60·2	

Source: N. N. Rozov *in* Gerasimov *et al., op. cit.,* 1971, p. 110.

 * This Taiga soil is described in the original translation as 'turfy' podzolic, but the term 'peaty' is considered more correct.

 † 'All other' includes one or more of the following types: sandy soils, stony soils, bogs, meadow steppe, solonized soils, solonetz, solonchaks and takyr soils, and taiga permafrost soils.

the forefront of electrodialysis desalination of brackish water. Many such plants have been set-up in Central Asia and Kazakhstan.

Two things should be noted, however, about such winning of new land in the Soviet Union; first, reclamation can contribute only marginally to the total stock of usable soils, and secondly, each successive stage of development brings in less economically viable areas for intensive forms of production. As in the United States, the Soviet Union's new irrigation and drainage projects are being increasingly challenged on grounds of capital costs in relation to their prospective returns in the farming system.

In addition to the land-uses already mentioned, the Soviet Union has vast areas of forests and taiga scrubland (37·2 per cent of the country's total area), much of them too remote or low in commercial return to justify exploitation. Furthermore, the tundra and taiga possess immense areas of so-called reindeer pastures (14·8 per cent of total area), but only a minute area of this is actually used for reindeer herding. In 1969 the reindeer population was officially quoted at 2·5 million head, an increase of over 500,000 since 1961. During this period there has been a consolidation of reindeer grazing into sovkhoz management – from 20 to 60 per cent of all reindeer. The remaining animals were either on kolkhozes (27 per cent) or under personal ownership of national minority groups (13 per cent). In recent years transhumance of reindeer herds has been greatly reduced. Control has

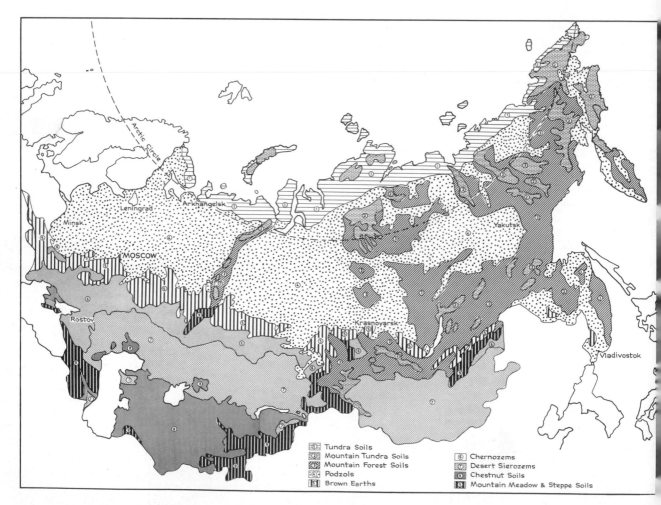

FIG. 4.1   Soil Zones of the Soviet Union.

TABLE 4.2

Development and Utilization of Irrigation in the Soviet Union, 1945, 1960

Republic	Agricultural Land with an Irrigation Network		Lands Actually Irrigated		Percentage Growth of Lands Irrigated	Irrigated Lands as Percentage of Agricultural Land	
	(in thousands of hectares)						
	1945	1960	1945	1960	1945–60	1945	1960
R.S.F.S.R.	649	1537	450	966	121·3	69·3	64·8
Kazakhstan	1027	1479	938	1134	20·9	91·3	76·7
Turkmenia	397	480	370	434	17·3	93·2	90·4
Uzbekistan	1972	2675	1918	2389	24·5	97·3	89·3
Tadzhikistan	289	425	283	394	39·2	97·9	92·7
Kirghizia	887	1146	756	889	17·6	85·2	77·6
Azerbaydzhan	722	1272	712	1036	45·5	98·6	81·4
Georgia	228	333	170	233	37·0	74·6	70·0
Armenia	190	225	182	198	8·8	95·8	88·0
Ukraine	62	287	26	237	811·5	41·9	82·6
Moldavia	0·2	34	0·2	26	...	100·0	76·5
Total	6424	9893	5806	7936	36·7	90·4	80·2

Source: For basic figures S. L. Mirkin (1960) quoted by S. F. Averyanov *in* Gerasimov *et. al.*, *op. cit.*, p. 140. Growth and utilization calculated by author.

8. Land drainage machinery has transformed the reclamation of new farming areas from waterlogged marshlands. Here ditch-diggers prepare trenches for tile-drains on a Lithuanian farm.

TABLE 4.3

Drainage Developments in the Soviet Union

Republic	1945	1960	Percentage Growth 1945–1960
	(in thousands of hectares)		
R.S.F.S.R.	1129	2440	116·1
Belorussia	665	971	46·0
Latvia	1619	1598	1·3
Lithuania	498	922	85·1
Estonia	265	660	149·0
Ukraine	707	1056	49·4
Moldavia	—	31	...
Georgia	20	103	415·0
Total	4903	7781	58·7

Source: S. L. Mirkin (1960) quoted by S. F. Averyanov *et. al.*, *op. cit.*, p. 151. Adapted by the author.

become more and more a sedentary occupation, based in permanent villages. This has resulted in increasing domestication of the semi-wild herds, harvesting of natural fodder for winter feeding, and veterinary oversight to ensure healthy herds. While the reindeer sovkhozes tend to be specialized, collective farmers and other herders tend to have secondary occupations of hunting, sealing, and fishing.

Forest Resources of the Soviet Union

The Soviet Union has the largest forest resources in the world: 37 per cent of the world's forested area (Fig. 4.2). Much of this vast extent of forest cannot be worked economically, given the remoteness from lines of communication and the present technological status of forestry. Nevertheless, the Soviet Union leads the world in the volume of its annual timber cut; 378 million cubic metres in 1965.

Forest lands in the Soviet Union have an area of 747 million hectares (515 million hectares in the Asian part) mostly administered and worked by the central government. About 39 million hectares have been granted for the use of collective farmers free of all charges; a hangover from the old hereditary rights of peasant usage since Czarist times.

Of the Asian forests (515 million hectares) 51·4 million hectares of exploited forest were along the northern margin, 25·4 million in the Urals and 17·9 million in the northeast. The European forests,

currently exploited, amount to 232 million hectares, and are dominantly in the northwest.

Crop-protecting forest belts in the steppe and forest-steppe are located especially in the European R.S.F.S.R. including the Volga region. By mid-1952 some 2·6 million hectares of shelter-belt with associated ponds and reservoirs had been planted. In 1970 afforestation other than shelter-belts covered 2·3 million hectares.

Eighty per cent of timber production comes from the Soviet Union's northern coniferous forest. Here the dominant species logged are pine, spruce, larch, cedar, and fir. Pine is cut from the forests from Karelia to the northern Urals. Spruce stands are interdigitated with pine in the Ural piedmontain zones. It is cut principally to manufacture high quality paper. Larch is the predominant tree in the forests of Siberia and the Far East, and it is therefore still little used. It is, however, very suitable for the manufacture of kraft papers and paperboards, and it therefore forms a useful reserve at the present time. In 1973 agreements were signed with Japanese interests to develop wood pulp industries in the Far East for export to Japanese paper-mills.

The southern taiga is forested by mixed species, the conifers are found in mixed stands of birch, aspen, alder, and other deciduous trees. Oak, beech, and ash are among the trees essentially over-exploited in the past in the mixed forest zone of the wooded steppe. Great encouragement to the preservation and rational exploitation of second-growth deciduous forest is now official policy. In recent years exploitation of these has grown considerably, although conifers still yield more than three-quarters of Soviet timber production.

In the 1960s much readily exploitable forest land was lost through the construction of hydroelectric power schemes which created immense inundation of forest valleys (Table 4.4).

Soviet forest management practice has established a norm for prudent forest exploitation. For coniferous forest, 40 per cent of the stand should be young trees (under 40 years old), and 20 per cent are permitted as mature and over-ripe trees (over 80 years old), while the remaining 40 per cent are the developing trees (40–80 years old). Definite signs of past over-exploitation therefore show up where there exist a paucity of mature trees or alternatively a surfeit of under-age trees.

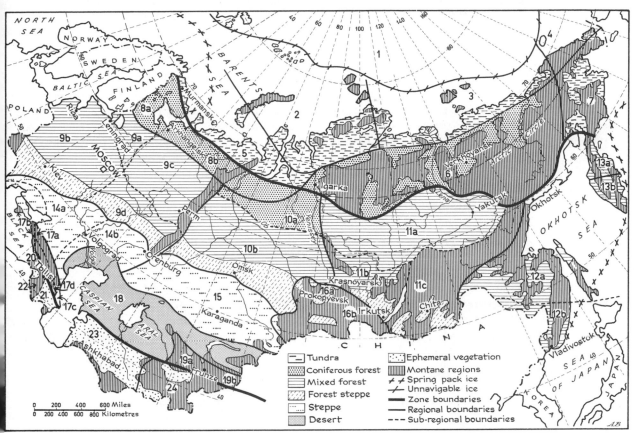

FIG. 4.2   Natural Vegetation Zones of the Soviet Union.

TABLE 4.4

Inundated Area and Timber Loss Due to Hydroelectric Power Schemes, c. 1960

Region or River Basin	Inundated Area (millions of hectares)		Timber Loss (millions of cubic metres)	
	Total	Forested	Total	Exploitable
Western Siberia	15·0	8·6	770	460
Eastern Siberia	4·0	3·7	370	260
Volga	4·2	1·7	160	80
Dnieper–Dniester–Don	2·1	0·5	60	30
Pechora–Vychegda–Kama	1·6	1·4	110	80
Other Regions	3·7	1·7	170	100
Total Area	30·6	17·6	1640	1010

Source: P. V. Vasilyev, *in* Gerasimov, *op. cit.*, p. 192, quoting Vyzgo; and Fogel and Shiglovskiy.

Vladimir oblast, Voronezh oblast, the Ukraine S.S.R. and Belorussian S.S.R. provide examples of imbalanced forest age-structure. In these areas the percentages indicate ruthless past exploitation with some 50 to 80 per cent of the present forest trees less than 40 years old. Clearly, these forests need time to recover, and hence timber production has shifted progressively away from the old centres of production to the Northwest, the Urals, Western and Eastern Siberia, and the Far East. These regions now account for more than 60 per cent of the country's logging and timber-milling. At the moment, they provide only 35 per cent of the paper production (1959), but a further shift eastward of this industry is *en train*. Concomitantly, however, heavy rail shipments and long hauls are now required because of the imbalance between timber production areas and market areas. For instance, although the eastern regions produce 58 per cent of the milled timber, they generate only 22 per cent of the total demand for timber. This is because

they have only 21 per cent of the country's population.

Several new timber projects were set into operation in recent years. These are the Verkhne–Kondinskiy, Tavda, and Bratsk lumber centres. The giant Bratsk mill will produce 1 million cubic metres of lumber annually. Others are located at Asino, Yeniseysk, and Chuna. These new milling centres exploiting virgin forests will permit the older centres, like those at Kirov, Gor'kiy, Kalinin, Kostroma, and Arkhangel'sk in the Northwest to cut back their output to levels commensurate with tree-growth and forest regeneration in their respective supply areas. This will also apply to the Volga milling centres, such as Kazan' and Kuybyshev. In this way the Soviet authorities have placed forestry husbandry on secure foundations, matching lumber cut with the biological yield of timber in the best 'tree-farming' tradition.

Existing eastern mills are located at Krasnoyarsk, Irkutsk, Barnaul, Novosibirsk, and numerous

9. The broad chernozem plain near Poltava shows vast expanses of standing grain and occasional hillocks of glacial sands used for building material. (Photograph by the author.)

TABLE 4.5

Annual Timber Cut From Soviet Forests and Degree of Logging Mechanization

	1940	1950	1960	1970
Total Forest Cut (in millions cubic metres)	246·1	266·0	369·5	385·1
Sawn Timber Production (in millions cubic metres)	117·9	161·0	261·5	298·6
Forest Efficiency (per cent)	47·9	60·5	70·8	77·5
Mechanization (percentage of work performance)				
Felling (power saws)	—	38·0	97·0	99·2
Extraction (snagging, high lines, etc.)	2·8	56·7	94·4	99·6
Haulage (jinkers, etc.)	5·6	29·0	91·2	97·8

Source: R. Belousov, *USSR Heavy Industry*, Novosti Press Agency Publishing, Moscow, 1972, pp. 76–77.

other centres in the Siberias. Recently the Far East has come into greater prominence in the lumber industry by the expansion of mills at Blagoveshchensk, Iman, Khabarovsk, and Lesozavodsk.

In post-war years, the Soviet timber industry has undertaken massive re-organization. This has not only involved shifts in regions of exploitation, but also in uses of the output and in the degree of mechanization of the industry. Around 1940 some 14·3 per cent of the forest timber output was required as a fuel supply, but the rise of oil, natural gas and electricity output since then has greatly reduced the place of timber as fuel. In 1970 only 2·2 per cent of the cut was needed for this purpose, and then only in the remotest areas of marginal development

Logging operations involving felling, extraction, and haulage to timber mills were almost completely mechanized by 1970 (Table 4.5).

Plywood and particle-board production has also shifted to the East, although considerable segments of the industry still remain in the initial centres of the European zone. Smolensk, Vladimir (Murom), Gomel, and Vitebsk remain important plywood centres. To some degree, spruce and pine forests are being replaced by quick-growing deciduous species, such as birch and alder, to sustain these plywood plants. New plywood and particle-board plants have been set up in the Urals and Siberia.

Despite the utter dependence of the wood pulp and paper industry on cheap and easily accessible supplies of pulpwood, electrical energy, heat energy, and process water, this industry is still marked by a high degree of geographical inertia. Under present circumstances, former large investments in plant and machinery in the European areas – at Gor'kiy, Kondopoga in Karelia, in Leningrad, and various centres of Belorussia – have served to retain pulpwood and paper industries long after their wood supply areas and the needed electrical energy generating capacity became inadequate. However, recent attempts have been made to shift the industries to the Urals and beyond, where more than adequate supplies of pulpwood, oil for heat energy, hydroelectric power to drive wood-grinding machines, and process water are readily available. In the early 1970s about one-third of Soviet paper and paperboard production took place east of the Urals. Large new facilities were built in Bratsk (Eastern Siberia), at Komsomol'sk-on-Amur (Far East) and on Sakhalin Island.

Recent increases in the Soviet pulp and paper industries have been very great indeed. Not only is pulp required for the manufacture of paper, newsprint, and cardboard, but a portion of the stock is now sent to mills for conversion to rayon and other man-made fibres. At the same time there has been a relative switch away from mechanical pulp to chemical or semi-chemical (mechanical-chemical) pulps, quite an innovation for the Soviet Union.

Present production of Soviet pulp and paper is shown below (Table 4.6).

TABLE 4.6
Soviet Pulp and Paper Production (Million Tons)

	1940	1950	1960	1970	1972	Plan 1975
Pulp	0·5	1·1	2·3	5·1	5·7	8·5
Paper	0·8	1·2	2·3	4·2	4·6	5·5

Source: R. Belousov, *USSR Heavy Industry*, Novosti Press Agency Publishing, Moscow, 1972, p. 78. 1972 production figures only, *Moscow News Supplement*, 1153, 1973.

It is evident from the foregoing discussion that great emphasis is given to the rational development and exploitation of soils and natural vegetation in the Soviet Union. Despite the vastness of Soviet territory, economically viable resources are strictly limited in extent and accessibility. It cannot be said that the country has yet reached that ill-defined threshold where the further exploitation of soils, irrigation supplies, drainage projects, and forests becomes uneconomic, but assuredly Soviet scientists are as wary of growing man-made pressures on the environment as those of the Western World.

10. The biological purification of heavily polluted effluents from industrial plants has made great progress in the Soviet Union. Here in Perm, as in similar installations elsewhere, micro-organisms introduced into the treatment tanks are capable of reducing noxious chemicals like phenols and thiocyanates to release harmless carbon dioxide and purified, oxygenated water.

PART TWO

HUMAN RESOURCES AND
SPATIAL ORGANIZATION

CHAPTER FIVE

HUMAN RESOURCES IN THE SOVIET UNION

More important than the physical environment and natural resources of the Soviet Union are its human resources. The Soviet Socialist system of resource development and planning of the country's socio-economic structure are based on the proper utilization of its human resources. From the Leninist precept of 'from each according to his ability and to each according to his work' flows the marrying of the country's physical endowment with Soviet man-power.

The human resources of the country are examined under three distinct headings in this chapter: (1) population trends and shifts, (2) ethnic structure and nationalities, and (3) the Soviet work-force and employment structure.

Population Trends and Shifts

The 1970 census of the Soviet Union enumerated a total population of 241·7 million persons. Distribution of this population is shown in Fig. 5.1. Population has increased by 32·9 million or 13·6 per cent since the last census taken in 1959. The urban population by 1970 had increased by 36 million to reach a total of 136 million in all urban centres and cities. At the same time the urban percentage of the total population rose from 48 per cent to 56 per cent. Rural population declined slightly from 108·8 million to 105·7 between 1959 and 1970. The Soviet Union ranks third after the People's Republic of China and India as the world's most populous country. It should also be noted that this population is almost totally literate (99·6 per cent for men, 99·4 for women) and endowed with high levels of education, technical competence and skills. Further, it is highly organized in both the political and social senses. These characteristics of size and attributes give the Soviet Union very considerable advantages in its fund of human resources. Population growth in the Soviet Republics is shown in Table 5.1.

The demographic pattern of the Soviet population is set by past trends in both birth and death rates. In 1970 the Soviet birth rate was 17·4 per thousand and the death rate 8·2 per thousand. Thus increasing urbanization and the trend to a sophisticated industrial society have had exactly the same effects in the Soviet Union as those previously experienced in other technically advanced countries: falling birth rates and falling death rates. Within the Soviet period birth rates have dropped from 45 to near 18 per thousand; death rates from around 25 to near 8 per thousand (Fig. 5.2). As Soviet population has become more urbanized, fertility rates have fallen so that fewer children are born to families. Also improved hygiene and medical science advances have cut the death rate. No longer are the decimating epidemics of the past encountered.

Nonetheless since a wide margin exists between birth and death rates, the rate of natural increase in the Soviet population is considerable; 17·8 per thousand in 1959. This should have meant that total population would double in some 40 years. However, by 1970 the rate of natural increase had fallen dramatically to 9·2 per thousand due to a heavy decline in birth rate.

The distribution of population by age group has changed since 1959 (Table 5.2). With a current expectation of life of 70 years, a higher proportion of the total population are now approaching this threshold than in the 1959 Census. Over 11·8 per cent of the population are now over 60 years of age against only 9·4 per cent in 1959. At the other end of the age pyramid by 1970 about the same percentage of the population (30·9 per cent) are under 16 years as in 1959 (30·4 per cent) (Table 5.2). The net result, however, was an increased number of dependents in the population; retired workers on the one hand and dependent youngsters on the other (Fig. 5.3). In aggregate, the Soviet economy had to support more than 111 million persons who were not gainfully employed. This represents 46 per cent of the total population; 3·4 per cent more than in 1959. Another segment of the population not available in the labour-force are the university and polytechnic students as well as other adolescents under training.

The high incidence of women in the labour-force has some surprising side effects. For instance, the number of children born to women in the most fertile age group, 20–29, is far lower in the Soviet Union than in most Western countries. This is a result of employment and career orientation *within* marriage. There are, however, marked differences in family-size characteristics, depending on whether this relates to rural or urban population and also the ethnic cultural parameters of these population segments.

Thomas (1967) gives some values that are significant in this context. Kazakhstan and the Ukraine are given as examples indicative of these trends for the 'Oriental' Soviet Union and the 'western' Soviet Union respectively.

For the European parts of the Soviet Union

families of more than parents and two children are comparatively rare, especially in urban environments. In the Moslem communities however, especially of Kazakhstan and the Central Asian republics, families of more than three children are common; about a 12–15 per cent greater incidence than in the 'western' Soviet Union. For these reasons, population growth in the Soviet realm is very unequally distributed. There has been differential growth in various major regions not only in terms of absolute population change, but also with respect to growth of urban population and the gain or loss of rural population (Table 5.3).

Some major regions, such as Kazakhstan, Central Asia, the Trans-Caucasus, Eastern and Northwestern Siberia, and the Northwest of European Russia, have population growth rates above the median rate of 7·14 per cent (1959–64); most frequently considerably above this rate (Table

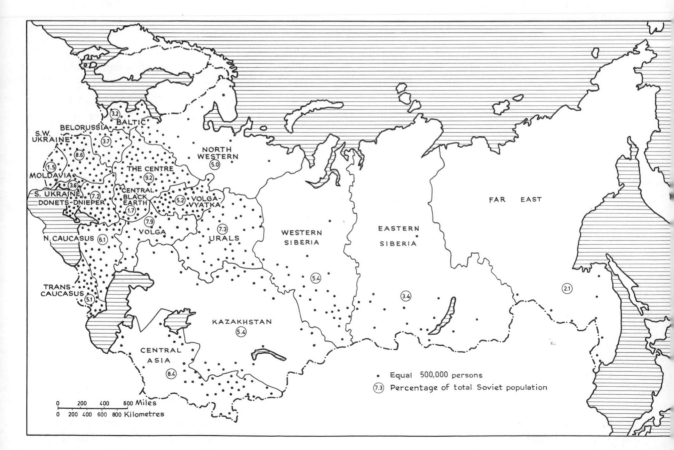

Fig. 5.1 Population Distribution in the Soviet Union.

TABLE 5.1

Population Growth in the Soviet Republics and Principal Ethnic Groups in Republics

Republic	Population (in thousands) 1959	Population (in thousands) 1970	Percentage Growth 1959–70	Three most important ethnic-linguistic groups with percentage of republic's population in 1970 1		Three most important ethnic-linguistic groups with percentage of republic's population in 1970 2		Three most important ethnic-linguistic groups with percentage of republic's population in 1970 3	
S.F.S.R.	117,534	130,079	10·7	Russians	82·8	Tatars	3·7	Ukrainian	2·6
kraine	41,869	47,126	12·5	Ukrainian	74·9	Russians	19·4	Jews	1·6
elorussia	8,056	9,002	11·7	Belorussians	81·0	Russians	10·4	Poles	4·3
zbekistan	8,261	11,960	44·8	Uzbeks	64·7	Russians	12·5	Tatars	4·8
azakhstan	9,153	12,849	40·4	Russians	42·8	Kazakhs	32·4	Ukrainians	7·2
eorgia	4,044	4,686	15·9	Georgians	66·8	Armenians	9·7	Russians	8·5
zerbaydzhan	3,698	5,117	38·4	Azerbaydzhani	73·8	Russians	10·0	Armenians	9·4
thuania	2,711	3,128	15·4	Lithuanians	80·1	Russians	8·6	Poles	7·7
oldavia	2,885	3,569	23·7	Moldavians	64·6	Ukranians	14·2	Russians	11·6
atvia	2,093	2,364	12·9	Latvians	56·8	Russians	29·8	Belorussians	4·0
rghizia	2,066	2,933	42·0	Kirghiz	43·8	Russians	29·2	Uzbeks	11·3
dzhikistan	1,981	2,900	46·4	Tadzhiks	56·2	Uzbeks	23·0	Russians	11·9
rmenia	1,763	2,492	41·3	Armenians	88·6	Azerbaydzhani	5·9	Russians	2·7
rkmenistan	1,516	2,159	42·4	Turkmen	65·6	Russians	14·5	Uzbeks	8·3
tonia	1,197	1,356	13·3	Estonians	68·2	Russians	24·7	Ukrainians	2·1
S.S.R.	208,827	241,720	13·6	Russians	129,015	Ukrainians	40,753	Uzbeks	9,195

rce: *Narodnoe Khozyaistvo SSSR, 1970*, Moscow, 1971, pp. 18–21. Adapted by the author.

TABLE 5.2

Changes in the Soviet Population Pyramid, 1939– 70
(Percentage of Total)

Age Group	1939	1959	1970
Over 70	2·3	3·8	4·5
55–69	7·6	9·8	12·3
40–54	12·6	15·9	16·7
25–39	24·7	23·4	21·4
16–24	15·1	16·7	14·2
5–15	25·3	18·7	22·4
0–14	12·4	11·7	8·5
	100·0	100·0	100·0
Total (in thousands)	190,678	208,827	241,720
Percentage in Working Age Groups *	53·6	57·4	54·0

Source: *Narodnoe Khozyaistvo SSSR, 1970*, p. 13.

* 16–59 years for men
16 54 years for women.

5.4). Kazakhstan and Central Asia for instance had absolute population increases of 2·36 million and 2·63 million persons respectively, giving population gain rates of 25·75 and 19·06 per cent. At the other extreme, the Centre, Central Black Earth and Volga–Vyatka regions experienced comparatively minor growth, gaining 2·69, 2·69, and 0·48 per cent in absolute population respectively between 1959 and 1964.

In some cases inordinate growth rates are attributable to the incidence of high rates of natural increase in the region concerned; that is, in the internal demographic trend *within* the region. In other cases, in-migration from neighbouring or distant regions undergoing depopulation is the primary reason for a given region's absolute increase in population. In those regions where absolute regional population gains exceeded 10 per cent between 1959 and 1964 and urban growth involved rates of 20 per cent or more, both influences, natural increase and in-migration, played dominant roles in bringing about the change. Notable regions exhibiting the dual effects are

Kazakhstan, Central Asia, the Trans-Caucasus, and Eastern Siberia.

In general, the bi-polar effect of either massive urban concentration of population as shown in the 'Northwest' segment of the matrix (Table 5.4) or an equally dramatic rural depopulation as indicated in the 'Southwest' segment group of republics in the same table. It is evident that a belt of high urban growth runs across the country from the Northern Caucasus to Eastern Siberia. North of this belt and extending from the Centre through Povolzhe and the Urals to the Far East is a zone of absolute rural population decline.

Pokshishevskiy (1963) has noted that 'an average

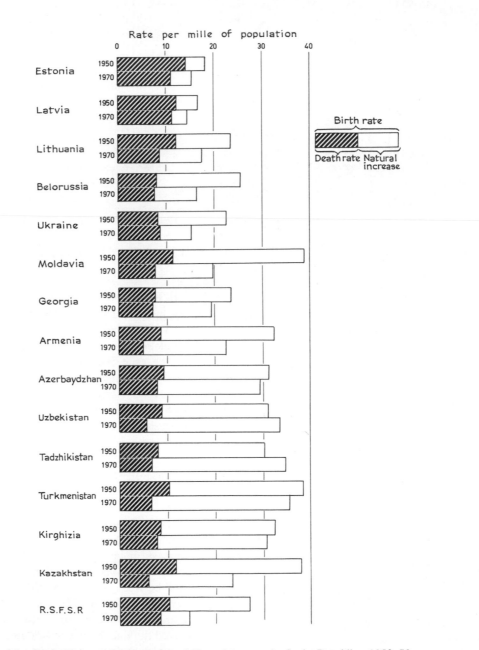

FIG. 5.2   Crude Birth and Death Rates, and Natural Increase by Soviet Republics, 1950–70.

annual natural increase of 1 per cent accounts for a population growth of 28 per cent in 25 years, and a natural increase of 2·5 per cent for a growth of 85 per cent [in the same period]'. Thus, it is certain that the differential rates of natural increase indicated (Fig. 5.1) must bring about markedly different population growth rates in various regions of the Soviet Union. On the whole the European parts of the Russian Federation and its neighbours are experiencing a slow rate of population growth, while in the areas east of the Urals and within the Kazakhstan and Central Asian republics growth is extremely rapid. Over the next two decades the existing ascendancy of the Soviet Union's western population concentration will begin to wither away. In 1959 the respective percentages of 'western' and 'eastern' population were 71·4 per cent for the west and 28·6 per cent east of the Urals. By 1970 the distribution had changed to 69·6 per cent 'west' and 30·4 per cent 'east', and this trend will continue at an accelerating rate.

Shifts in the Soviet population have been from rural to urban environments. Between 1965 and 1970 urban settlements gained 15·3 million persons principally by natural increase but also by net in-migration from rural to urban areas and the reclassification of formerly rural terrain on the margins of cities as incorporated urban area. On the other hand the rural areas lost 3·2 million persons for these reasons.

But in addition to the progressive urbanization of the Soviet Union – 49 per cent of the population

TABLE 5.3

Number of Persons in Family (Percentage of All Families)

Size of Family	Kazakhstan		Ukraine	
	Urban	Rural	Urban	Rural
2–4	68·4	59·9	83·0	74·0
5–8	30·3	37·9	16·4	25·5
more than 9	1·3	2·2	0·6	0·5
	100·0	100·0	100·0	100·0
Average No. in Families	3·9	4·3	3·4	3·7

Source: C. Thomas, 'Population Trends in the Soviet Union: 1959–64', *Geography*, **52**, 1967: 193–97.

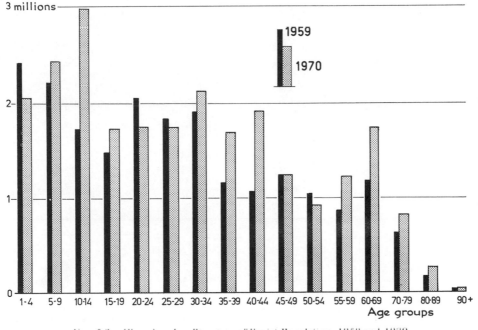

FIG. 5.3 Changing Age Structure of Soviet Population, 1959 and 1970.

TABLE 5.4

Population Change Characteristics of Major Regions 1959–64. In Percentage Gain (+) or Loss (−)

	Urban Change: Above Median		Urban Change: Median (19·50%) or Below Median	
	Rural Gain (+) or Loss (−)	Urban Gain	Rural Loss (−)	Urban Gain
Rural Change: Above Median	+21·13 Kazakhstan 31·61			
	+14·74 Central Asia 27·18		−1·60 Ukraine 17·81	
	no change Northwestern Siberia 26·96		−2·35 Baltic 15·68	
	+4·54 Northern Caucasus 23·00			
	+7·68 Trans-Caucasus 22·15			
	−0·48 Eastern Siberia 20·18			
Rural Change: Median (−2·72%) or Below Median			−11·65 Volga–Vyatka 19·50	
	−5·05 Black Earth 23·75		−2·72 Povolzhe 19·16	
	−4·75 Belorussia 26·80		−4·33 Southwestern Siberia 16·16	
			−11·98 Northwest 15·84	
			−4·06 Ural 14·75	
			−7·27 Far East 14·21	
			−11·40 Centre 13·48	

Source: Thomas, *op. cit.*, for figures. Re-ordered about medians by author.

TABLE 5.5

Nationality Groups in the Soviet Union, 1959–70 (in millions)

Nationality	1959 Census	1970 Census	Nationality	1959 Census	1970 Census
Great Russians	114·11	129·01	Tadzhiks	1·40	2·14
Ukrainians	37·25	40·75	Germans †	1·62	1·85
Uzbeks	6·01	9·19	Chuvash	1·47	1·69
Belorussians	7·91	9·05	Turkomen	1·00	1·52
Tatars	4·97	5·93	Kirghiz	0·97	1·45
Kazakhs	3·62	5·30	Latvians	1·40	1·43
Azerbaydzhanis	2·94	4·38	Mordovians	1·28	1·26
Armenians	2·79	3·56	Poles †	1·38	1·17
Georgians	2·69	3·24	Bashkirs	0·99	1·24
Moldavians	2·21	2·70	Estonians	0·99	1·01
Lithuanians	2·33	2·66	All Other Groups	7·23	9·04
Jews *	2·27	2·15			
			Soviet Citizens	208·83	241·72

Source: *Narodnoe Khozyaistvo SSSR, 1970*, Moscow, 1971, pp. 15–16.

  * In the Soviet Union Jews are classed as a national group, and consequently there is no necessary religious connotation associated with persons returning themselves as Jews in the Census.

  † Germans and Poles are permanent residents *and* Soviet citizens. Long-term visitors and 'guest-workers' are excluded.

was urban in 1960, 53 per cent in 1965, 56 per cent in 1970, and 58 per cent in 1972 – there have been regional shifts in population too. By 1970 the Soviet Union's population centre of gravity had shifted considerably to the east, partly as a result of higher natural increase in the eastern population, and partly due to government-sponsored internal migration.

Excluding for the moment the Russian Federation (R.S.F.S.R.), whose population straddles both the European and Asiatic parts of the Soviet Union, an analysis of population growth shows 9·7 million additional population in the five 'oriental' republics in 1970 compared to the 1959 situation. This is a 42 per cent increase in population over the 1959–70 period. On the assumption that the mean natural increase for these two reference years in these five republics (Table 5.5) represents fairly well the natural growth of population, then somewhat over 5·7 million was added to the total population through this cause alone. This leaves 4·0 million as the net in-migration into Kazakhstan and the Central Asian Republics from outside regions.

A similar analysis for the Russian Federation reveals an additional population in eastern areas (including the Urals) of 3·9 million in 1970 compared with the 1959 situation; a 10·3 per cent increase. Since however the eastern R.S.F.S.R. had a mean natural increase of about 10·9 per thousand between 1959 and 1970 then virtually the whole of the addition to population was due to this cause. Indeed, there is some evidence that the earlier massive in-migration from the European parts of the Soviet Union has now been reversed, with out-migration exceeding new arrivals. Should the eastern Russian Federation be forced in future to rely only on natural increase for its population growth, then its human resources must be greatly restricted for many years to come.

Ethnic Structure and Nationalities

The Soviet Union is a multi-national state comprising over 100 distinct national groups, some very large and some small. The largest ethnic group is the Great Russians, or simply Russians, who number 129 million people, or 53·4 per cent of the country's total population. Next in size come the Ukrainians with 40·7 million people (17 per cent of

the Soviet population) (Table 5.5). These two ethnic groups dominate the overall pattern of the country's structure and indeed in most Republics they account for substantial minority populations within the national groups present (Table 5.1).

Other ethnic groups each of which number more than four million people are: Uzbeks (9·2 million), Belorussians or White Russians (9·1 million), Tatars (5·9 million), Kazakhs (5·3 million), and Azerbaydzhanis (4·4 million). At the other end of the scale are very small national groups with only about a thousand or fewer people; the Orochi, Nganasani, and the Yukagirs. National identity in the Soviet Union is based on major and minor linguistic divisions of the respective national groups. There are some fifteen major ethnic–linguistic groups including six Indo-European language types (Slavonic, Letto-Lithuanian, Romance, Iranic, Armenian, and Caucasian types) and six Uralic–Altaic language types (Finnish base, Ugrian, Samodian, Turkic, Mongolian and Tungus–Manchurian types). In addition there are interesting survivals of the Palaeo-Asiatic, Eskimo-Aleutian, and Ket language types.

11. Academician Nikolay Tsytsyn, a Michurin geneticist, who successfully developed perennial wheat by cross-breeding wheat with the wild cereal grain 'witch grass'. He also achieved hybrids of rye and witch grass and of wheat and wild rye, and he has six new varieties of wheat to his name including the high-yielding winter 'branchy' wheat he is seen holding.

It is a creditworthy achievement of the Soviet regime that over a period of little more than fifty years such diverse ethnic, linguistic, and cultural groupings should be welded into a monolithic identity, namely the Soviet citizen. To a marked degree this unity in diversity has been achieved by the official promotion of cultural attributes of each ethnic group; the side-by-side development of native consciousness along with the national affinities of the whole Soviet people. The native consciousness is encouraged by the teaching of local languages in schools, the promotion of cultural activities and identification with national hero-images of the past and present, particularly writers, scientists, and sportsmen. The national Soviet identity is achieved by the common language (Russian) and the 50-year heritage of the Soviet people as a whole.

TABLE 5.6

Employment Structure of the Soviet Union
(*In Percentages of Total Working Population*)

	1939	1959	1971
Factory Workers	32·5	48·2	58·0
Office Employees	17·7	20·1	22·0
Collective Farmers (including craftsmen)	47·2	31·4	20·0
Individual Farmers and Artisans not organized in collectives	2·6	0·3	—
Total	100·0	100·0	100·0

Source: *Novosti Press Agency Yearbook*, Moscow, 1972, pp. 39–40.

12. The Frunze Plant Breeding and Agricultural Research Institute has developed high-yielding varieties of club wheat suitable for the high mountain irrigation farms of Kirghizia.

It should not be thought that these objectives have always been pursued smoothly. Indeed, at times, the imprint of the Russian has proved stultifying to national identity. Most recently some Ukrainian and Jewish national groups have felt themselves oppressed by the Russian majority. However, this is not the place to scrutinize such political issues, and it should be readily admitted that by and large the ethnic diversity of the country's human resources is more of an asset than a liability.

The Soviet Work-force and Employment Structure
The Soviet work-force has changed remarkably over the last thirty-year period. Greater numbers are now employed in industry and tertiary activities and many fewer in agriculture. Broadly, the working population is made up of state and collective farmers, the working classes in industry, transport, and trade, and the working intelligentsia as writers, scientists, university staffs, and party functionaries are called.

Employment structure of the entire Soviet population is shown in Table 5.6.

In regard to a further breakdown of the employment structure the following figures for 1940 and 1970 may be noted (Table 5.7). This shows quite dramatically the swing away from primary employment in agriculture and forestry towards other classes of employment, particularly industrial employment. In 1970 about 115·5 million people were gainfully occupied in the Soviet economy, or 47·8 per cent of the country's population.

The two most noteworthy facts to emerge from this table are the heavy relative and absolute decline

13. Handling experimental rats in the radio-isotope laboratory of the Skryabin Helminthological Institute, Vilnius, Lithuania.

14. Soviet scientific and industrial growth is increasingly based on sophisticated technology. Shown here is the control console of the Minsk-32 electronic computer at the Ukrainian Institute of Scientific and Technical Information.

TABLE 5.7

Employment by Major Branches of the Soviet Economy. Percent of Total Employment (excluding students)

	1940	1970	Change in Percentage 1940–70
Industry and Building Trades	23	37	+14
Agriculture and Forestry	54	27	−27
Transport and Communications	5	8	+3
Trade, Public Catering, Purchase, and Sale	5	7	+2
Education, Health Services, Science, and Arts	6	15	+9
State and Public Organization	3	2	−1
Housing Administration, Municipal and Auxiliary Services, Other Services	4	4	no change
	100	100	

Source: *Novosti Press Agency Yearbook*, Moscow, 1972, p. 37.

in employment in agriculture and a somewhat lesser fall in the numbers engaged in forestry (the two together down 27 per cent). On the other hand there has been a steep rise in employment in construction and industry (up 14 per cent) and in the tertiary service industries (up 10 per cent). Considering the marked overall growth of the Soviet economy the one per cent decline in public service employment is notable. This has been achieved by the greater application of computers and office machines in the business of government as well as by some worthwhile gains in labour productivity in these fields.

According to the Soviet census of 1970 there were 130·5 million able-bodied persons within the working age-groups of 16–59 years for men and 16–54 years for women. Of this number 120·6 million, or 92·4 per cent, were either employed in some sector of the Soviet economy or were full-time students at secondary schools or tertiary-level institutions, such as universities. However, with older age levels of the Soviet population pyramid and an increasing expectancy of life, there are now more than 42 million pensioners in the Soviet Union. Of these, seven million contribute as workers to the Soviet economy through part-time or full-time cmployment.

Another aspect of Soviet employment is the rising number of specialists employed in various branches of the economy. A specialist is a worker with higher education. In 1972 there were 17·9 million such specialists, thus making up about one-sixth of all those gainfully employed. The continued fostering of higher technical education in the Soviet Union has done much to support recent technological advances and scientific achievements. At the other end of the scale, illiteracy, which as recently as 1939 involved 16 per cent of the population in the 9–49 age group, has now been all

15. Automatic control equipment at the North Lutuginskaya mine (Voroshilovgrad oblast) oversees coal-mining operations at all locations. A UM-1 computer automatically registers work performed, output by heads and levels, and movement of the coal to the surface. The system quickly pin-points areas of hazard or production breakdown.

16. The space and hydro-meteorological research ship 'Cosmonaut Yuri Gagarin' in its home port of Odessa. This vessel carries out space research programmes in Arctic and Antarctic seas and contributes data to the World Meteorological Organization and International Council of Scientific Associations.

but eliminated with beneficial results on working expertise and attitude. In 1970 illiteracy in the age group mentioned was 0·5 per cent, comparable to the norms of western industrial countries. There was also no distinguishable differences between male and female literacy; a very marked change from the earlier situation when illiteracy of women was considerably higher than for men.

The distribution of the Soviet population is very uneven. The European parts of the Russian Federation, the Ukraine and Moldavia, are very densely settled, approaching the high densities of Western Europe. Within a 500-kilometre radius of Moscow about 20 per cent of the entire Soviet population lives, and authorities have tried to inhibit further growth in the immediate vicinity of Moscow by regulation. Average density within this circle exceeds 280 persons per square kilometre. On the other hand, remoter areas of the Russian Federation and many of the mountainous and desert-strewn Republics have fewer than one person per square kilometre, while remote Far Eastern areas like Kamchatka and the Evenki national

okrug have only 0·2 and 0·02 inhabitants per square kilometre respectively.

In recent years Soviet policy has endeavoured to spread population more in accordance with known or newly discovered resources. In this the authorities have been assisted greatly by fortuitous differences in the rates of natural increases in republics (Table 5.5). In general, resource-rich, but previously sparsely settled republics have high rates of natural increase and moreover they are very attractive to the Soviet Union's highly mobile labour-force. Incentive wage-levels in these areas have the effect of building up population quickly. This is again reflected in high natural growth and heavy annual in-migration from de-populating and densely settled areas of the European parts of the country (Table 5.4).

All in all, Soviet human resources are important parameters in the continued expansion of the Soviet economy. It is for this reason that the government and planning agencies are doing more research on the geographical spread and characteristics of the Soviet population.

CHAPTER SIX

URBAN DEVELOPMENT AND URBANIZATION: ECONOMIC CHANGES

Soviet economic growth has generated vast and powerful changes in the urban structure of the country. Since the 1945 war, the number of the Union's largest cities (>500,000 inhabitants) has increased nearly threefold. The aggregate population of these largest cities (*krupneyshie goroda*) has also grown quite remarkably, indeed at a significantly greater rate than the growth recorded in the total urban population of the country (Table 6.1). Over the same period from 1939 to 1970 the urbanization rate of the Soviet Union – the proportion of the total population living in an urban environment – rose from 32 per cent to over 56 per cent and continues to rise.

It is thus certain that more and more of the country's population is living within the total urban environment and contributes to urban-based economic activities, particularly secondary industries, service functions, and commerce. Between 1940 and 1966 the urban population increased by 61·6 million, almost a two-fold growth rate, while rural population decreased from 130·9 to 107·1 million. It is also evident that the 34 largest cities exceeding 500,000 inhabitants make a disproportionate contribution to the Soviet gross domestic product; perhaps far in excess of the 15 per cent of the total population living in these cities in 1972.

This economic intensification of large cities within territorial production complexes has been a major phenomenon since pre-war days. In 1939 there were only 11 large cities of more than 500,000 population, about one-third of the 1972 figure, and these contained only 6·7 per cent of the country's population then. A similar pattern is discernible in the general rate of urbanization, 32 per cent in 1939, and around 58 per cent in 1972. In consequence the economically dominant landscape in the Soviet Union is urban and it far transcends the rural areas in its contribution to total output by value and perhaps, more importantly, yields greater production efficiency through economies of scale and harnessing technology, and better promotes the division of socialist labour.

The high growth rates in urban development have been sustained by two forces; (*a*) the long-range impact of demographic structure in which the Union's relatively 'young' population pyramid has, until recently, given a high rate of natural increase to the population, and (*b*) the continued and indeed accelerated growth of urban centres due to rural–urban migration (Table 6.2).

While birth rates are somewhat lower in urban areas than in rural areas (in 1968, 15·5 per 1000 population, as against 19·6 – a difference of 4·1 per 1000), more than 50 per cent of the natural increase in population (9·6 per thousand in 1968) occurred in towns and cities and, moreover, the rural increase indirectly spawned more rural–urban migration. These forces, as shown above, accounted for quite a dramatic upsurge in urban growth, particularly in the higher order towns and cities of the Soviet Union. There is some suggestion that the huge exodus from countryside to city in the Soviet Union, combined at the same time with the emergence of new city growth poles in the Urals, Siberia, and Kazakhstan, was the Russian counterpart of the European overseas migration to the Americas, Africa and other colonial countries during the 19th and early 20th centuries. The Russian migrations involved an estimated 43 million persons over a period of some 32 years before 1959. This compares with Lorimer's estimate of a net overseas migration of some 40–45 million Europeans during a 140-year period up to 1940.[1] It is obvious that such structural changes in the distribution of Soviet population, occurring over such a short period of time, have involved enormous pressures on the country's infrastructure of cities as

---

[1] Lorimer (1965), 'Population' in *Encyclopedia Britannica*, 1965 ed., Vol. 18, p. 234.

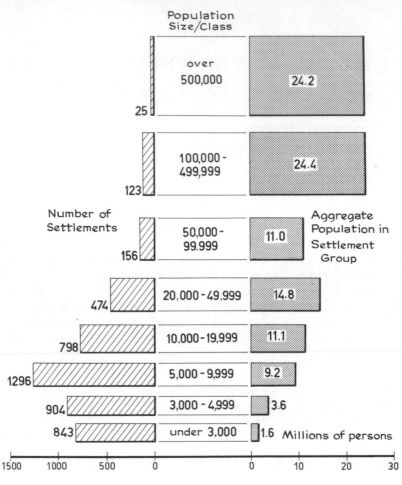

FIG. 6.1   Numbers of Settlement (Cities) by Size-Class and Aggregate Populations, 1970.

TABLE 6.1

Urban Development

	1939	1955	1959	1962	1965	1972
Number of cities exceeding 500,000 inhabitants	11	21	25	27	31	34
Aggregate population in these cities (in millions)	12·8	20·0	24·1	29·0	34·3	38·6
Total urban population	60·4	84·6	99·8	111·8	120·7	142·6
Total population of Soviet Union	190·7	200·1	208·8	219·7	229·6	246·3
Urban population as % of total population (= urbanization rate)	32·0	43·4	48·0	51·0	52·9	57·8
Population in cities >500,000 as % of total population	6·7	10·0	11·5	13·2	15·0	15·1

Sources: Meckelein, p. 262, and for 1965, Harris, *op. cit.*, pp. 15ff., 1972. Yaroslavl', Karaganda, and Novokuznetsk
   are assumed to have attained 500,000 class by 1972 as they were near this threshold in 1967.
(There were 209 cities greater than 100,000 persons in 1969; 222 cities in 1971.)

17. The simple log-cabin remains the standard home of the Russian countryside – sometimes with thatched roof and earthen floors (background) or with a weatherproofed burlap roof and board floor (middle). A scene near Rovno, Southwest Ukraine. (Photograph by the author.)

well as on the capacity of industries to absorb manpower. Without comprehensive planning and a command-type economy the Soviet Union might well have found that such achievements were quite impossible, at least during the 50 years of Soviet rule.

Urban settlements in the Soviet Union are classified under two heads, cities proper (*goroda*) and other settlements of urban type (*poselki gorodskogo tipa*).[1] In 1967 there were 1888 cities and 3460 urban settlements, compared with 1679 and 2940

respectively at the 1959 census. By 1971 there were 1943 large cities and no less than 3576 other urban settlements. The cities, although smaller in number, comprise about 85 per cent of the total urban population and contrast strongly with urban-type settlements which range down from 20,000 persons to units as small as urbanized villages of under 3000 inhabitants. Fig. 6.1 gives the frequency distribution of each settlement group by number and aggregate population in each size-class.

It is evident that the European parts of the Soviet Union possess two-thirds or more of all major cities in the country (Table 6.3). Further, there is a marked concentration of these cities in the Ukraine and Southern region as well as in the Centre and Volga, accounting for 102 of the 143 cities greater than 100,000 inhabitants in the European part of the Soviet Union in 1970. This concentration of

[1] Soviet statistics are not uniform in regard to the definition of urban areas. For the R.S.F.S.R. all centres with populations greater than 12,000 are classified as towns with the additional proviso that not more than 15 per cent of this population is agriculturally based. In the Ukraine, the figure is 10,000 with a 'preponderance of industrial and office workers'; while in the other Union Republics, a lower level is accepted; 5000 persons constitute a town community.

urban development is associated with the chief centres of mining, heavy industry, and the light consumer goods industries of the European core. It is further supported by the immense scale of the close-knit and intensive agriculture of the Ukraine, the Centre, Central Chernozem, and Volga regions.

TABLE 6.2

Soviet Urban–Rural Population, 1959 and 1970 (in millions)

	Total	Urban	Rural
1959 Census	208·8	100·0	108·8
Natural Increase (1959–70)	+32·9	+14·6	+18·3
Reclassification (1959–70)	—	+5·0	−5·0
Rural–urban Migration (1959–70)	—	+16·4	−16·4
1970 Census	241·7	136·0	105·7

Between 1959 and 1971 the number of cities in the greater than 100,000 class increased from 148 to 222; an increase of 74 in twelve years. By 1971 the aggregate population of these cities reached 77·5 million, compared to only 48·6 million at the 1959 census.

Metropolitan and some of the largest cities in this European core zone include the following (Fig. 6.1): Moscow, the U.S.S.R. capital (1967 and 1970 populations in thousands: 6507 and 6942), Gor'kiy (1120 and 1170), Kuybyshev (992 and 1047), Kazan' (821 and 869), Voronezh (611 and 660), Ufa (704 and 773), Saratov (720 and 757), Volgograd (743 and 818), and Yaroslavl' (498 and 517). These cities give a very heavy population density in the Central–Volga region. A second node

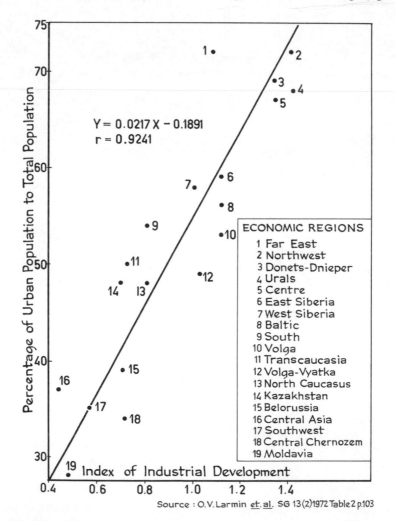

Source : O.V. Larmin *et. al.* SG 13(2)1972 Table 2 p.103

Fig. 6.2   Urbanization Ratio Plotted Against Index of Industrial Development.

TABLE 6.3

Regional Distribution of Larger Cities (Exceeding 100,000 Population) in the Soviet Union, 1970

Region*	100,000 to 199,000	200,000 to 299,000	300,000 to 399,000	400,000 to 499,000	500,000 to 749,000	Greater than 750,000	Total
Western	18	5	4	0	2	2	31
Southern	28	9	5	2	2	8	54
Central and Volga	20	12	5	3	2	6	48
Northwestern and Northern	6	1	2	0	0	1	10
Total European Regions (excluding Urals)	72	27	16	5	6	17	143
Urals	8	2	4	1	0	4	19
Kazakhstan and Central Asia	18	5	1	1	2	1	28
Western Siberia	5	2	2	2	0	2	13
Eastern Siberia	2	3	0	1	1	0	7
Far East	6	1	0	2	0	0	9
Total Asian Regions	39	13	7	7	3	7	76
Total Soviet Union	111	40	23	12	9	24	219

Source: *Narodnoe Khozyaistvo, 1970*, Moscow, 1971, pp. 37 ff. Abstracted by the author.

* Regions adopted by this book. See Chapters 18–28 following.

It should be noted that the total number of cities in excess of 500,000 population in 1970 was 33. Novokuznetsk in Western Siberia passed this threshold by 1972, hence the number at that date is 34 cities as per Table 6.1 above.

is apparent in the Ukraine–Southern region including such important cities as Khar'kov (1125 and 1223), Donetsk (840 and 879), Dnepropetrovsk (816 and 863), Odessa (776 and 892), Krivoy Rog (510 and 573), and Zaporozh'ye (595 and 658). In a very real sense, the peripheral areas of the Soviet Union have suffered in the past because of this inordinate concentration of city-building in the European core. However, recent Five-Year Plans devised by the Soviet authorities have taken corrective measures to promote better balanced urban growth by the prohibition of new industrial construction in Moscow oblast and in other large cities. Further, the government has promoted a shift in city growth through decentralization policies, particularly eastward, stimulating the growth of smaller and medium-sized cities by the injection of industry or other economic stimuli. Had not the core-zone cities been de-emphasized in this way, the headlong agglomeration of population in the European parts of the Soviet Union would have led to massive problems. Nevertheless, despite government

proscriptions, the larger cities are gaining population at far higher rates than small cities (Table 6.4).

The 'million' cities in 1959 were Kiev, Moscow, and Leningrad; six new 'million' cities had been added by 1971: Kiev, Khar'kov, Moscow, Gor'kiy, Kuybyshev, Leningrad, Sverdlovsk, Tashkent, and Novosibirsk. This table clearly shows the tendency for the largest cities to grow more rapidly than the other classes. However, the marked increase in the 100–500,000 class was supported by Gosplan's insistence on the growth of smaller centres.

Work by the Soviet geographers Listengurt, Khorev, and others sets out the economic planning procedures for the development of smaller cities. Particular emphasis is given to locating many complementary industrial complexes at the same time and planning the necessary infrastructure, residential areas and service functions generated, as a single planning operation. This method contrasts strongly with the more piecemeal growth and self-generation of facilities favoured by Western planners.

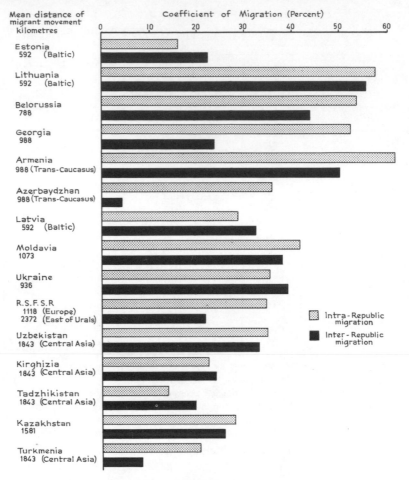

FIG. 6.3   Mean Distances of Migration Movements.

The central importance of urbanization and city growth in the non-core areas of the Soviet Union is their contribution to a rather more balanced distribution of economic activity and so too of population. In a sense these forces iron out vast differences in the economic revenue-earning capacity of the various regions, moving towards an optimal status in which each region maximizes its contribution to the Soviet gross domestic product, while incurring minimum costs of doing so.

At the time of the 1959 census, urban-type employment involved 46·8 million workers against 52·3 million workers in rural activities. By 1970 employment had increased by 21·5 million making a total of 120·6 million. Of these about 88 million were urban workers and 32·6 million rural workers engaged in farming or forestry or ancillary rural activities.

Because city-type employment adds considerably more value per unit of output than the rural processes, the recent moves towards greater urban development can be viewed as a rational contribution to Soviet economic efficiency. It now appears that more than three-quarters of the Soviet Union's gross domestic product originates within the urban environment. There is evidently a very close correlation between urbanization and degree of industrialisation (Fig. 6.2.).

Of the total urban employment of 88 million in the Soviet Union, industry, building and construction, transport and communications account for the lion's share: industry and construction for 50·7 per cent of total employment and transport and communications for 11·0 per cent. Trade and distributive services account for 9·6 per cent, and cultural and social services such as housing adminstration,

18. Log-houses and shiplap timber houses of Estonian style dot the Russian plain south of Leningrad. (Photograph by the author.)

19. A modern kolkhoz settlement in Turkmenistan. Houses are well-designed and functional, constructed of rendered brick and corrugated iron, and set in extensive garden-estate surroundings.

TABLE 6.4

Population Classes of Cities by Numbers and Aggregate Population

Population Class	No. of Cities 1959	Total Population (in millions) 1959	%	No. of Cities 1971	Total Population (in millions) 1971	%	Population Increase 1959–71 Absolute (millions)	Per cent
Under 50,000	4315	40·4	40·4	5095	47·5	34·2	7·1	17·5
50,000–100,000	156	11·0	11·0	202	14·0	10·1	3·0	27·3
100,000–500,000	123	24·4	24·4	188	38·9	27·9	14·5	59·5
500,000–1 million	22	14·1	14·1	25	19·5	14·0	5·4	38·3
Over 1 million	3	10·1	10·1	9	19·1	13·8	9·0	89·1
Total	4619	100·0	100·0	5519	139·0	100·0	39·0	39·0

Sources: *S.G.*, Sept., 1970, p. 582; and *Narodnoe Khozyaistvo, 1970*, Moscow, 1971, p. 46.

municipal, educational, and public health services absorb a total of 28·7 per cent of the total urban employment. It is estimated that the agricultural sector of urban employment – agricultural specialists, veterinary services, and public service personnel in Agricultural Departments, resident in cities – accounts for 4·7 per cent of the total urban employment. Strictly therefore about 4·1 million workers are ancillary to the support of rural activities although they are classified as urban residents. Thus in terms of economic structure the breakdown between rural and non-rural activities is about 36·7 million persons against 83·9 million in industry and other types of urban employment.

Outside the core areas, industry and transport group employment is well below the national average of about 60 per cent as a general rule, although this varies from city to city. Khorev (1966) has used the ratio of employment in industry alone to

TABLE 6.5

A. Cities with Populations greater than 100,000 (N = 148)
B. Cities with Populations less than 100,000 (Sample N = 173)

Percentage Employment in Industry and Transport	Percentage Employment in Industry Alone																
	Above National Average								Below National Average								
	Greater than 60%		50% to 60%		40% to 50%		Total Above National Average		40% to 30%		Less than 30%		Total Below National Average		Aggregate Number of Cities	
	A	B	A	B	A	B	A	B	A	B	A	B	A	B	A	B
Greater than 70%	10	20	27	30	10	8	47	58	1	4	—	3	1	7	48	65
60%–70%	—	—	10	6	33	21	43	27	18	16	1	5	19	21	62	48
50%–60%	—	—	—	—	3	2	3	2	25	22	7	14	32	36	35	38
Less than 50%	—	—	—	—	1	—	1	—	2	2	—	20	2	22	3	22
Total	10	20	37	36	47	31	94	87	46	44	8	42	54	86	148	173

Source: Adapted from Khorev, *op. cit.*, pp. 36–37.
N.B. to total of 321 (148 + 173) urban settlements.

20. A housing estate at Belgorod, Central Chernozem Region. Such stereotyped flat dwellings have been built in many areas devastated during World War II. (Photograph by the author.)

that in industry and transport to devise a typology of city-types in the greater than 100,000 class and less than 100,000 class at the 1959 census (Table 6.5).

It is quite evident from this table that a high percentage of employment in industry and a high percentage of employment in transport are associated. Of the 321 cities Khorev studied, no less than 105 had in excess of 40 per cent of their workers engaged in industry alone or aggregating more than 70 per cent in industry and transport. Thus nearly a third of these cities could be classified as super-industrial cities. Another 70 cities were above average in industrial employment and above average in industrial plus transport employment. At the other end of the scale, 92 cities were below the national average in industrial and industrial plus transport employment, but over one half of these were in the under 100,000 class sample. This suggests that from 1959 onwards the 100,000 plus class cities were undergoing rapid industrialization, shown by an upward swing in the percentage of all workers engaged in industrial and/or transport activities.

Functional Classification of Soviet Cities
A general functional classification of Soviet cities indicates a preponderance of diversified administrative centres; capitals of republics or subordinate capitals of oblasts (Table 6.6). These cities are marked by a wide range of economic activities including industry, but have also well-formed services

and socio-cultural functions such as theatres, 'palaces of culture', pioneer centres, etc. Next in order of importance are the principal manufacturing centres, dominantly located within the Southern, Central and Volga, and Urals regions. Then follow the manufacturing centres in which the element 'mining' is also present, again following the previous pattern. The broad geographical distribution of these 304 cities is shown. This also distinguishes between the functional types indicated by Khorev (1966) and Harris (1970).

As can be seen from Table 6.6, Soviet cities with more than 50,000 population can be divided into two roughly equal groups: those which are primarily industrial centres, and those that are administrative centres of the Union Republics, oblasts, or krays, but which as major central places are highly diversified in their functional structure. The larger cities in particular, such as Moscow, Leningrad, Kiev, and Tashkent, derive their livelihood from many different economic activities, administration, industry, transport, trade, and building activity.

Regional Occurrence of City Growth Due to Migration

As indicated earlier in this chapter rural–urban migration as well as migration within and between republics of the Soviet Union have had a marked effect on city growth. Between 1959 and 1970 some 16·4 million people transferred from rural to urban environments in the Soviet Union and a further 5 million lived in rural areas around cities which were subsequently taken within their municipal boundaries (Table 6.2). Again, natural increase added 14·6 million to the urban populations between 1959 and 1970.

Although these increases in urban population were very significant in themselves – they added 36 per cent to that population in eleven years – the geographical distribution and impact of these urban growth attributes are even more fundamental.

Tatevosyan (1972) produced a seminal paper that discusses an analytical technique to assess inter-regional migration and its impact on urbanization in the Soviet Union. Intra-republic migration has been very high within many republics, notably Lithuania, Belorussia, Georgia, Armenia, and Moldavia, involving migration within the republic, both rural to city and city to city movements. But in some instances inter-republic migration involving migration between republics has been almost as great. Here again Lithuania, Belorussia, and Armenia, and to a somewhat lesser extent, the Ukraine and Moldavia, figured

TABLE 6.6
Functional Classification of Soviet Cities (>50,000) 1967

Region	Diversified Administrative Centres		Local Centres	Industrial Centres			Transport Centres	All Other Types and Moscow Suburbs	Total
	Union Capitals	Oblast and Similar Centres		Manufacturing	Manufacturing and Mining	Mining, Primary Processing and Energy			
Western	6	16	5	8	—	—	—	1	36
Southern	3	22	1	16	15	2	2	6	67
Central and Volga	1	29	3	33	7	—	1	6	80
Northwestern and Northern	1	8	1	3	1	—	—	—	14
Urals	—	6	1	13	10	2	—	—	32
Kazakhstan and Central Asia	5	19	2	3	3	2	—	—	34
Siberias and Far East	—	18	2	6	8	4	2	1	41
Total U.S.S.R.	16	118	15	82	44	10	5	14	304

Source: Adapted from data in C. D. Harris, *op. cit.*, pp. 69–78.

21. One of Moscow's many radial roads (Prospects), broad and lined with high-rise apartment buildings, shows well the forward planning of major traffic arteries in the country's major cities. Note the disciplined pedestrian traffic on crossings, despite the absence of vehicular flows. (Photograph by the author.)

22. Moscow at night during the celebrations of the 50th anniversary of the October Revolution. Absence of advertising illuminations makes Russian cities rather austere after night-fall.

TABLE 6.7
Major Cities of the Soviet Union by Region (All Cities exceeding 290,000 persons in 1970)

	Population (in Thousands) 1959	1970	Growth % 1959–70		Population (in Thousands) 1959	1970	Growth % 1959–70
Western Region				*Central and Volga*—contd.			
Tallin	282	363	29	Volgograd	591	818	38
Riga	580	733	26	Kuybyshev	806	1047	30
Vilnius	236	372	57	Penza	255	374	31
Kaunas	219	306	40	Saratov	579	757	43
Kaliningrad	204	297	46	Kazan	667	869	30
Minsk	509	907	78	*Northwest and*			
Kiev	1110	1632	47	*Northern*			
L'vov	411	553	35	Arkhangel'sk	258	343	33
Kishinev	216	357	65	Leningrad	2985	3513	18
Southern Region				Murmansk	222	309	39
Dnepropetrovsk	661	863	31	*Urals Region*			
Krivoy Rog	401	573	43	Ul'yanovsk	206	351	70
Donetsk	708	879	24	Ufa	547	773	41
Makeyevka	371	393	6	Orenburg	267	345	29
Zhdanov	284	417	47	Perm	629	850	35
Gorlovka	308	335	9	Sverdlovsk	779	1026	32
Zaporozh'ye	449	658	46	Nizhniy Tagil	338	378	12
Voroshilovgrad	275	382	39	Chelyabinsk	689	874	27
Khar'kov	953	1223	28	Magnitogorsk	311	364	17
Nikolayev	235	331	40	Izhevsk	285	422	48
Odessa	664	892	34	*Kazakhstan and*			
Tbilisi	703	889	27	*Central Asia*			
Yerevan	493	767	55	Alma-Ata	456	730	60
Baku	643	847	32	Karaganda	383	522	36
Krasnodar	313	465	48	Tashkent	927	1385	49
Rostov	660	789	32	Frunze	220	431	96
Groznyy	250	341	37	Dushanbe	227	374	65
Central and Volga				*Western Siberia*			
Bryansk	207	318	53	Barnaul	303	439	45
Ivanovo	335	419	25	Kemerovo	289	385	33
Kalinin	261	345	32	Novokuznetsk	382	499	31
Moscow	6009	6942	16	Novosibirsk	885	1161	31
Ryazan'	214	351	64	Omsk	581	821	41
Tula	351	462	32	Tomsk	249	339	36
Yaroslavl'	407	517	27	*Eastern Siberia*			
Gor'kiy	941	1170	24	Krasnoyarsk	412	648	57
Kirov	252	332	32	Irkutsk	366	451	23
Voronezh	447	660	48	*Far East Region*			
Lipetsk	157	290	85	Vladivostok	291	442	52
Astrakhan'	305	411	35	Khabarovsk	323	437	35

Source: *Narodnoe Khozyaistvo, 1970*, Moscow, 1971, pp. 37–45 for population.

prominently. The overall pattern of movement is shown (Fig. 6.3). In terms of the average distance travelled by migrants to their new city the Soviet Union mean is 1317 kilometres. Not unnaturally the European areas show the shortest migration distances – Baltic mean, 592 kilometres, Belorussia, 788 kilometres, the Southwest, 832 kilometres, and Donets-Dnieper, 902 kilometres.

As the Urals and the Siberias and Far East migrations are measured so the mean distance travelled increases, according to Tatevosyan. These mean distances are: Urals, 988 kilometres, Western Siberia, 1310 kilometres (approximately the nation-wide mean), and for Eastern Siberia, 1941 kilometres, and the Far East, 3865 kilometres. The last two values indicate that across-the-country migration is the common norm for the new populations of these remote economic regions.

Rural–urban, intra- and inter-republic migration streams have been responsible for the very significant growth of cities in the various economic regions of the Soviet Union. The largest cities – those in excess of 290,000 persons – are listed by region in Table 6.7.

From this table it is evident that some cities of this size group are growing at an extraordinary rate; many increasing their population by 50, 60, 70, or even 90 per cent in the eleven years, 1959–70. However, as can be seen from the frequence tabulation (Table 6.8), the highest percentage of all cities in the 290,000-plus class were growing at a rate between 30–39 per cent for the 1959–70 period. Another group of 14 cities was growing at 40–49 per cent and yet another group of 11 cities at between 20–29 per cent. It is clear that the growth norm for this group of 70 cities is within the 30–39 per cent growth class.

For the 1959–69 period all types of migration – rural–urban, intra- and inter-regional migration – accounted for a 16·4 million increase in the Soviet Union's urban population. A further 14·6 million growth was due to natural increase in population within the urban environment and another 5·0 million to engrossment of cities by the inclusion of outlying areas into the *de jure* city boundaries. Thus urban growth for the period was 36 millions, of which internal migration accounted for 45·5 per cent.

23. The Bolshoy Theatre in Moscow. The Soviet people take great pride in their cultural achievements. Even small towns no less than the big cities will have their repertory theatres, choirs, and orchestras.

TABLE 6.8

Frequency of Growth Percentages for 290,000-Plus Class Cities

Growth Rate (Per cent)	No. of Cities	Percentage of Cities
Less than 19	6	8·6
20–29	11	15·7
30–39	26	37·2
40–49	14	20·0
50–59	5	7·1
60–69	4	5·7
Greater than 70	4	5·7
	70	100·0

Source: Derived from Table 6.7.

CHAPTER SEVEN

ECONOMIC REGIONALIZATION

Economic regionalization in the Soviet Union has reflected two things: the demands of a rapidly changing economy for a rational division of productive facilities between various regions, and the changing attitude of the Soviet government towards economic criteria in determination of optimum locations. The post-war emergence of many new territorial complexes caused industry and other intensive forms of economic activity to agglomerate in regions hitherto lightly developed. There was thus a need to define new economic regions at all levels. At the same time successive Soviet governments experimented with numerous economic organizations to achieve a sensitive and rational territorial division of the vast economic realm, recognizing the changing patterns of production and consumption.

In discussing regionalization, Melezin (1968) delineates the main trends in Soviet regionalization based on areas of in- and out-migration; areas of deficit and surplus manpower; freight flows generated in, and destined for, particular regions, giving an active or negative balance for each macro-region (i.e. active equal to excess of out-flow over in-flow, and negative equal to excess of in-flow over out-flow). In this highly generalized model of Soviet regionalization, Melezin concludes that there are at present three supra-regional entities in the Soviet Union; the Soviet West, the Soviet Mid-east, and the Soviet South (Fig. 7.1). These three integrated regions embrace less than half of the Soviet landmass, but contain rather more than 90 per cent of its population. They also contain most of the country's industrial and agricultural activity. Each of these integrated supra-regions contains substantial cores of industrial agglomeration, some old-established, but others dating their major growth only from the post-war years.

A sub-division of these three supra-regions breaks down into various alternative regionalization patterns; in essence sub-divisions of Melezin's classification.

Soviet geographers have sub-divided their country variously into 15, 19, and 47 economic regions for purposes of studying their composition and inter-relationships. In the Khrushchev era, these regions were even further broken down for both administrative and statistical purposes into Sovnarkhozes (regional economic councils), which numbered 104 in all. For practical reasons such a fine-mesh pattern of economic regionalization is unmanageable in the present economic context of the Soviet Union. The author has therefore endeavoured to devise a regionalization pattern that interprets the thinking of Soviet geographers, while at the same time remaining a useful framework for systematic discussion and for the regional chapters that follow.

In the Soviet Union changes in administrative and economic divisions of the country are frequent and often far-reaching. Territorial divisions, based on ethnic structure and national autonomy, seemingly change according to political caprice or governmental convenience. For example, the former Finno-Karelian Republic was reduced to the status of an autonomous republic in 1956, leaving just 15 constituent republics of the Union.

The largest territorial unit is the Russian Soviet Federative Socialist Republic (R.S.F.S.R.), embracing four-fifths of the country's area and nearly 60 per cent of its population. Other republics, such as the Ukraine, Belorussia, Uzbekistan, and Kazakhstan, for example, also cover vast territories and each contains substantial populations of distinct ethnic composition. Essentially these republics make a patchwork quilt of nations within the federation of the U.S.S.R.

For the purpose of economic planning, the Soviet Union is at present divided into nineteen macro-economic regions (*krupnyy ekonomicheskiy raion*). Over the years however this number has not been constant. Indeed, it has fluctuated according to the groupings at particular times of the smaller territorial divisions, whether these are the smaller union republics, autonomous republics, or national okrugs. In effect, these macro-regions are statistical divisions related to national planning and data collections required by various levels of Gosplan, the Soviet Union's chief planning agency.

From 1939 onwards there were 13 macro-economic regions. In 1960, the number was increased by Gosplan to 16, and the next year the number changed to 17 first by amalgamating two regions (Arkhangel'sk oblast joined the North-West), and then sub-dividing the formerly single Ukraine into three separate regions, named respectively after their chief nodal cities, Kiev, Khar'kov, and Odessa. Since 1961 two union republics, Belorussia and Moldavia, were subsequently added, so that there are currently nineteen such macro-economic regions in the Soviet Union. As can be seen, changes in the economic regionalization of the Soviet Union have occurred frequently in the past.

The present economic regionalization embraces 10 economic macro-regions in the R.S.F.S.R. (6 in Europe; 4 in Asia, including the Urals); Ukraine, 3; Baltic Republics together, 1; the Trans-Caucasian republics together, 1; the Central Asian republics together, 1; and Kazakhstan, 1; Belorussia, 1, and Moldavia, 1 (Table 7.1).

Since these economic macro-regional divisions have been established there have been several experiments to achieve even greater devolution of planning and control of the nation's economic activities. Under Khrushchev's influence the major reorganization occurred from mid-1957 onwards. Economic administrative regions, already mentioned and known as sovnarkhozes and numbering a maximum of 104, were then set up. The word sovnarkhoz is abbreviated from Soviet Narodnogo Khozyaistva (National Economy Soviet). Most sovnarkhozes in densely settled areas embraced one single *oblast*

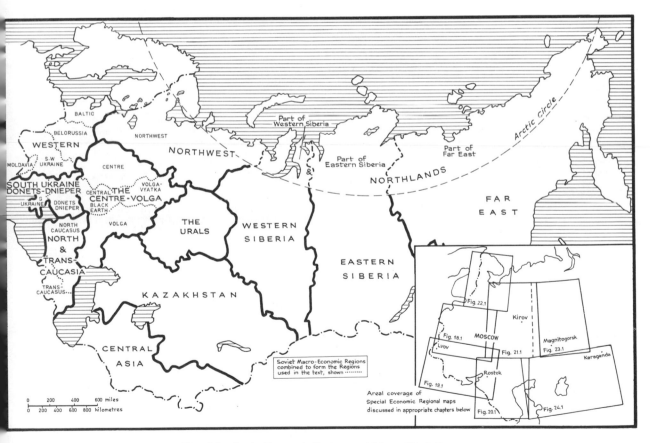

FIG. 7.1   Soviet Economic Regions and Macro-Regions.

TABLE 7.1

Administrative and Economic Divisions of the Soviet Union

Union Republics	Administrative Divisions				Economic Divisions		
	Oblasts and Krays	A.S.S.R.s	Autonomous Oblasts or (National Territories)	Total Subordinate Administrative Territorial Divisions	Sovnarkhozes	Enlarged Sovnarkhozes = Industrial Management Regions (1963–65)	Major Economic Regions* 1970
R.S.F.S.R.	55	16	15	86	68	24	10
Estonia				—	11	1 ⎫	
Latvia				—	9	1 ⎬	1
Lithuania				—	5	1 ⎭	
Belorussia	6	—	—	6	1	1	1
Ukraine	25	—	—	25	1	7	3
Moldavia	—	—	—	—	1	1	1
Georgia	—	2	1	3	1	1 ⎫	
Armenia	—	1		—	1	1 ⎬	1
Azerbaydzhan		1	1	2	1	1 ⎭	
Kazakhstan	17	—	—	17	1	7	1
Uzbekistan	10	1		11	1	1 ⎫	
Turkmenistan	3			3	1	1 ⎬	
Tadzhikistan	1		1	2	1	1 ⎬	1
Kirghizia	3			3	1	1 ⎭	
	120	20	18	158	104	50	19

Sources: Adapted from Bernard, *op. cit.*, p. 32; Lavrishchev, *op. cit.*, Map p. 16; and Harris, *op. cit.*, Table 20, pp. 150–4.

  * The Major Economic Regions are: For R.S.F.S.R.: Northwest, Central, Volga–Vyatka, Central Chernozem, Volga, North Caucasus, Urals, West Siberia, East Siberia, and Far East. For Ukraine, Donets-Dnieper, Southwest, and Southern. For Estonia, Latvia, and Lithuania together; Western Region. For Georgia, Armenia, and Azerbaydzhan together; Trans-Caucasian Region. For Uzbekistan, Turkmenistan, Tadzhikistan, and Kirghizia; Central Asia. Belorussia and Moldavia are known by their Republic's name.

(administrative province) or *kray* (territory) or Autonomous Soviet Socialist Republic or *okrug* (national territory). In other cases, where 'economic density' of the landscape was less intensively developed, several administrative territorial units, such as oblasts, were frequently combined to make up a single sovnarkhoz. For example, both Belorussia with 10 oblasts and Kirgizia with 4 oblasts each formed a single sovnarkhoz. In this way, some 165 politico-administrative units, whether oblasts, krays, A.S.S.R's, or national territories, formed the 104 sovnarkhozes. Of this number of sovnarkhozes, the R.S.F.S.R. had 68, the Ukraine 11 (14 in 1962), Kazakhstan and Uzbekistan 9 then 5 (1 only in 1960) respectively, and the 11 remaining Union republics had one each. Thus, as of 1960, there were 102 sovnarkhozes: 67 in the R.S.F.S.R., 14 in the Ukraine, 9 in Kazakhstan, and 1 each in the other republics. By the end of 1962, the number of sovnarkhozes had been reduced by amalgamation to 47, each being on

average twice the size in terms of population and economic 'quantum' than the earlier sovnarkhoz territorial organization. Not only was amalgamation of statistical entities involved in these reforms, but real political thresholds were crossed to secure more viable economic units. For instance, the four Central Asian republics, each different in ethnic structure and cultural attributes, were combined to form a single macro-sovnarkhoz, or industrial management unit as they were called.

In all essentials, the nineteen economic macro-regions now form the exclusive basis for the subdivision of the Soviet Union into statistical collection zones, used also for all purposes of economic regionalization.

Before the 1960s there had been very little specific *regional* planning in the Soviet Union. Decisions were then made by either the central ministries, by sovnarkhozes or oblasts and similar local authorities without very much apparent coordination. But by 1962 new co-ordination councils were at work. They were responsible for over-seeing the regional planning and co-ordinating decisions taken at all levels of government pertaining to each of the ten major economic regions of the R.S.F.S.R. and 7 other major regions existing at that time. These co-ordinating councils, one for each major region, were very large. They consisted of some 50–100 members drawn from communist party secretaries for each of the territorial divisions, chairmen of sovnarkhozes (before these were abandoned), directors of large industrial plants, specialists (e.g. Gosplan officials), and certain elected members.

The role of the co-ordinating councils and the permanent commissions which formed their executive branches was to maximize regional resource utilization, direct the expansion of agriculture, industry, construction, transport, and services. Actual implementation of the plans was the responsibility of individual enterprises with government assistance, where the scope of the project warranted this. These co-ordinating councils were short-lived, however, and their planning functions in the regional context have been added to the responsibilities of the All-Union Gosplan. Since its inception in the 1920s, Gosplan has mainly emphasized sectoral planning, planning by particular branches of the economy. With the urgent tasks of building the productive systems at large, questions of regional balance and the regional allocation of production were pushed into the background quite severely.

Since the 1960s, however, a greater awareness has developed concerning the importance of correct regional distribution of economic activities based pre-eminently on the natural condition, raw material endowment, the availability of transport, and population distribution. A major impact on the regionalization of production problems resulted from the work of a Gosplan department; The Council for the Study of Productive Forces (S.O.P.S.). This organization examines the underlying conditions and forces contributing to the dynamic economic growth of each particular region (Nekrasov, 1964, p. 14). Emphasis is given to 'the productive specialization of the region, and the development of the complex of service sectors'. It is generally envisaged that correct specialization and the proper development of the region as a 'territor-

ial productive complex' – i.e. one in which key industries or economic activities are linked with each other and with an appropriate service infra-structure – will lead to an optimum pattern of regionalization. The goal is to maximize Soviet output of all types of product at minimum costs, costs being measured in terms of minimum labour inputs. In this way, the quality of life of the major economic regions is improved, while assisting the over-all growth of the Soviet Union.

Soviet geographers define two major types of spatial productive organization:

1. the highly concentrated industrial complex, and
2. the disseminated territorial complex, in which two further sub-types are recognized:
   (i) the energy-industrial complex which marries industrial activities with a particular energy base; hydroelectric power, oil, natural gas, coal, or nuclear power, and
   (ii) the industrial–agrarian complex that seeks to disseminate agriculturally based processing industries and rural service industries throughout regions of intensive agriculture.

In substance, the first type of territorial complex, the highly concentrated industrial complex, has been the most natural outgrowth over 50 years of Soviet endeavour. But under Leninist principles which demand the merging of town and country, the second type of spatial productive organization, that merging energy and industry with agriculture, have been favoured in recent years. Here the Soviet Union is following the Commune model of Communist China. There is, however, no apparent consensus among Soviet geographers as to whether the concentration principle or the dissemination principle is the correct route to optimum regionalization, and indeed this parallels similar doubts expressed by Western geographers concerning their own countries.

Belousov (1964) injects a further point in the discussion of Soviet regionalization when he stresses the importance of transport in the formation of economic regions. 'The criterion of effectiveness', he says, 'of various models of regional complexes would be the minimum total cost of production and transportation'. Regionalization according to Belousov depends on correctly relating production factors and circulation factors, i.e., transportation *flows*; the balances of production and consumption for each commodity in various regions, and the influence of technology and economics on these elements.

Kistanov (1965) works out a measure for the regional specialization of given industries or other economic activities, using the following formula:

$$Su_1 = \frac{\dfrac{\text{Output of Given Industry in Region}}{\text{Total Output of Region}}}{\dfrac{\text{Output of Given Industry in U.S.S.R.}}{\text{Total Output of U.S.S.R.}}}$$

where Su_1 means specialization level. Where Su_1 is equal to or greater than 1, the given industry is in the specialized category. For the purposes of these calculations regional statistics of industries were derived from the series collected by the Central Statistical Administration as 131 individual production categories, which are combined into 14 industrial groups.

The industrial specialization of seven of the major economic regions using Kistanov's method are shown by way of example (Table 7.2). In this case, the specialization levels are grouped I, II, and III on the basis of the magnitude of Su_1; the level of specialization.

That Soviet regionalization is moving towards a rational distribution of major industries, is clear from much of recent research. There are substantial overtones of the adoption of comparative cost theory in Soviet regionalization. 'An economic requisite for an inter-regional division of labour', says Probst (1964), 'is a difference in the level of regional labour costs for the production of a given product. Some regions specialize in a given product because its production there is more efficient than elsewhere, and, having satisfied local requirements, these specialized regions can export their surplus to other regions'. Such specialization, however, can only be justified if the sum of the production costs in

TABLE 7.2

Regional Specialization of Industries in Typical Major Regions

Major Region	$Su_1 > 2\cdot0$ Group I (Very High)	$Su_1\ 1\cdot5–2\cdot0$ Group II (Moderately High)	$Su_1\ 1\cdot0–1\cdot5$ Group III (High)
Centre	—	light industries	chemicals, machinery
Volga	fuel-energy	—	machinery, building materials, chemicals
North Caucasus	—	fuel-energy, light industries	building materials
Western Siberia	fuel-energy	—	chemicals, iron and steel, machinery
Far East	timber and wood processing, non-ferrous metals	food processing, building materials	non-ferrous metals
Donets-Dnieper	iron and steel, fuel-energy	—	building materials, machinery
Kazakhstan	non-ferrous metals	—	fuel-energy, food processing

Source: Kistanov (1965) *op. cit.*, p. 22.

the specialized region plus the transport costs to the final market do not exceed production costs for the same product in the consuming area. The limiting transport radius (x) for a product made in the specialized region can be calculated from:

$$x = \frac{P_2 + LT - P_1}{2T}$$

where P_1 and P_2 are the price of the product in the specialized production zone and the market respectively, L is the distance separation, and T is the unit cost of transport per kilometre. Further, the optimum regionalization of consumption of a given product obtained from a specialized region is:

$$P_1 + xT = P_2 + (L - x)\,T$$

When this is applied to all directions and to all markets, the optimum regionalization of consumption is derived. Probst, to whom these methods of calculation are due, also shows that 'national savings' accrue all the time. Costs of producing and transporting goods from specialized regions do not exceed those costs in non-specialized production regions.

A great deal of the current industrialization in the eastern and southern parts of the Soviet Union arises from the application of the new concepts of economic regionalization. The manifest need for balanced growth in all regions of the country and a continuing commitment to regional specialization on a basis of comparative production and transport costs has meant that sophisticated analytical techniques have become even more important to the Soviet economy.

PART THREE

APPRAISAL OF SOVIET SYSTEMATIC ECONOMIC GEOGRAPHY

CHAPTER EIGHT

SOVIET AGRICULTURAL POLICIES

Soviet agriculture is faced with two fundamental problems:

(1) the need to grow greater quantities and a greater variety of crops, particularly grain crops, in a country that seeks self-sufficiency in all agricultural produce;

(2) the comparative backwardness of the Russian countryside.

Agriculture has not kept pace with the rest of the the Soviet economy. In consequence, both economic and ideological problems loom large in Soviet agriculture. The government's hope is to create an agricultural system that will meet the demands of agricultural product markets and at the same time be a model of Communist efficiency. Since World War II, neither of these objectives have been spectacularly successful. In particular, grain harvests have fluctuated in a series of climatic disasters and vacillating administrative policies, and especially during the Sovnarkhoz interlude. These have greatly inhibited the efficiency of crop production.

Nevertheless, with the attainment of some technological progress, especially in the greater provision of farm machinery, Soviet agriculture is now becoming far more co-ordinated than in the recent past. Large state farms (sovkhozes) as well as certain of the more efficient collective farms (kolkhozes) are approaching factory-like organization. Many advanced state farms have introduced cost-accounting systems. In these circumstances, rural labour can be thought of as a type of specialized industrial manpower. Skill for skill the income gap between industrial workers and farmers is being narrowed. The location of Soviet agricultural zones is shown in Fig. 8.1.

Soviet Agricultural Policies

Since the stultifying effects created by the policies of Stalin and Malenkov, Soviet agricultural policies have taken a turn for the better. The abandonment of the Machine Tractor Station (MTS) has meant that more intensive use of mechanical equipment under the direct control of each farm has induced

24. Newly planted vineyards in the Carpathian foothills near L'vov, Southwest Ukraine. (Photograph by the author.)

25. The self-propelled 'Niva' grain harvester is capable of rapidly harvesting crops — essential in the Soviet Union's inclement climatic conditions. The machine features a dust-tight driver's cab with an air-conditioning unit. It is seen operating in Rostov oblast. Note the shelter belt in background.

greater productivity. Formerly the Machine Tractor Stations promoted inefficiency since their limited equipment was necessarily spread over a great number of individual collective farms; up to 30 in some regions. The extension of rural electrification has also had a beneficial effect, and the marked improvement in the application of agricultural chemistry has rendered gains in yields and quality of produce feasible. Thus the improvements in the technological foundations of agriculture that began under Khrushchev have been some of the reasons for quite marked increases in production, especially in years of favourable climate.

Other reasons that are perhaps equally cogent, are the enormous extension of farming area that has augmented cropped area in post-war years. Another factor, perhaps even more important, was the material and monetary incentives given that have improved the lot of collective farmers and state farm workers immeasurably after decades of de-

privation and neglect. At long last, agriculture has been given adequate priorities in the Communist scheme of things.

Under Khrushchev, Soviet agriculture underwent a plethora of changes; administrative, organizational, and technical. Most changes have had some far-reaching consequences. Perhaps the most significant administrative change was the devolution of the power of the Ministry of Agriculture so that decision-making in agriculture could be carried out at much lower levels in the hierarchy. This gave a substantial degree of initiative to collective farm managers and local committees and also to regional agricultural authorities.

Swearer (1963) in his study of these changes puts forward the view that such devolution of the decision-process '... is incompatible with a centralized political structure', and it is clear that agriculture has now returned to central control.

During the period of the Sovnarkhozes (Regional

Economic Councils) the creation of territorial production administrations (T.P.A.) managed agricultural policies along with those of other economic activities. In effect, these T.P.A.s determined regional specialization and diversification in particular crops, and thus also the amount of agricultural produce as well as the product-mix coming from each T.P.A. area.

Nevertheless, the allocation of State procurement quotas remains hard and inflexible, although contracts are now freely negotiated. Often, demands on agriculture are made without adequate regard for local differences in climate, soils, and micro-environment. This often renders the attainment of specific goals difficult. Nonetheless, outside the State's responsibility to secure agricultural production as best it may, there remains a substantial initiative for collectives to assess their produce market prospects for themselves, providing that their State procurement goals have been achieved. Such a system represents a very great relaxation over former rigid policies.

In these incentives, differences in agricultural productivity, remoteness or harshness of environment and such other 'land rent' factors give rise to price zones for particular crops. Also differential taxation is applied by the State, according to the natural productivity of particular regions. This is intended to compensate for the physical hazards faced by some collective farmers and to provide monetary incentives for undertaking risks.

One marked policy of post-war years has been the extension of agriculture into less favourable environments. W. A. Douglas Jackson (in Laird, *op. cit.*) has stated that the concept 'of a fabulous reserve of cultivable land is a Soviet myth ... the best lands in Russia ... had been occupied and utilized by the outbreak of World War I'. While this is essentially a true assessment, it does ignore the Soviet penchant for pushing cultivation, not neces-

26. Gathering in the grain quickly by the two-stage group operating technique (cutting and wind-rowing followed by pick-up and threshing) is customary in most Soviet grain-growing areas. The scene is on the Lenin kolkhoz, Gorodokskiy area, Ukraine, where each machine can handle 12–15 hectares daily.

sarily cultivation on the 'best' land, into marginal environments. In recent times agriculture has moved into short- and long-term fallow lands, the forest-steppe margins, the virgin steppe, and, with the help of massive irrigation programmes, into semi-arid desert lands of Central Asia and Kazakhstan. Also production has increased after costly drainage of the marshlands and coastal lagoons. Changes over time are summarized in Table 8.1.

TABLE 8.1

Indices of Agricultural Change in the Soviet Union

Agricultural Land Use (in millions hectares)	1940	1950	1960	1970
Grain crops	110·7	103·7	115·6	119·3
Industrial crops	11·8	12·9	13·1	14·5
Vegetables and potatoes	10·0	10·7	11·2	10·1
Fodder crops	18·1	20·9	63·1	62·8
Total (under all crop types)	150·6	148·2	203·0	206·7
of which:				
Irrigated land	8·0	8·6	9·4	11·1
Drained land	5·5	6·5	9·4	10·2
*Gross Crop Production** (in million tons, unless otherwise stated)				
Grains	95·6	81·2	125·5	186·8
of which: wheat	31·8	31·1	64·3	99·7
Maize for grain	5·2	6·6	9·8	9·4
Raw cotton	2·24	3·54	4·29	6·89
Sugar-beet	18·0	20·8	57·7	78·3
Flax fibre (thousand tons)	349·0	255·0	425·0	456·0
Sunflower	2·64	1·80	3·97	6·14
Potatoes	76·1	88·6	84·4	96·8
Vegetables	13·7	9·3	16·6	20·3
Productivity (Yields) (Centners per Hectare)				
Grains	8·6	7·9	10·9	15·6
Winter wheat	10·1	9·1	15·1	22·8
Spring wheat	6·6	7·6	9·5	12·3
Maize for grain	13·8	13·8	19·3	28·0
Rice	17·3	14·6	19·7	36·5
Raw cotton	13·8	19·6	19·6	25·1
Sugar-beet	146·0	159·0	191·0	237·0
Flax fibre	1·7	1·3	2·6	3·6
Sunflower	7·4	5·0	9·4	12·8
Potatoes	99·0	104·0	92·0	120·0
Vegetables	91·0	72·0	110·0	138·0

Sources: V. Matskevich, *Agriculture*, Novosti Press Agency, Moscow, 1971, p. 84 and *Narodnoe Khozyaistvo, 1970*, Moscow, 1971, p. 278.

* Includes production of state farms, collectives, and personal plots.

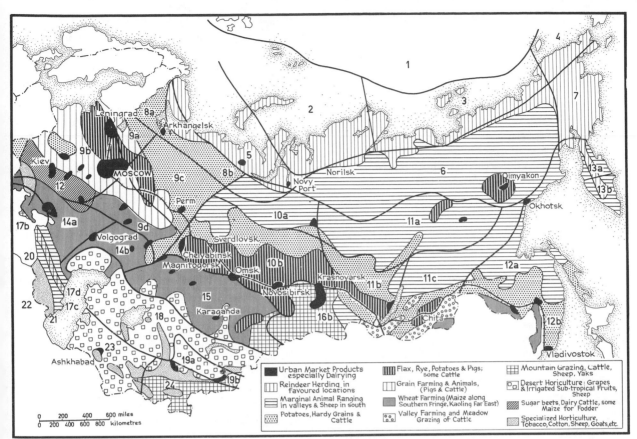

FIG. 8.1   Soviet Agricultural Zones.

KEY TO FIG. 8.1

The following climatic type regions for the USSR, corresponding to agricultural zones, are based on B. P. Alisov's classification. (Cf. B. P. Alisov, Climate of the U.S.S.R., University of Moscow, 1956 (in Russian, trans. *in* A. A. Borisov, *op. cit.*, London, 1965, facing p. 89).

Zone	Region	Sub-region	Zone	Region	Sub-region
I Arctic	1. Sub-polar			15. Continental steppe of Western Siberia	
	2. Atlantic			16. Montane type of the Altai and Sayan	a. Forest
	3. East Siberian				b. Alpine
	4. Pacific			17. North Caucasian Montane type	a. Continental
II Sub-Arctic	5. Atlantic				b. Black Sea
	6. Siberian				c. Caspian
	7. Pacific				d. Alpine
III Temperate	8. Arcto-atlantic	a. Western		18. Continental desert type of Central Asia	
		b. Eastern			
	9. Atlanto-continental forest type	a. Northwestern		19. Montane type of the Tien Shan	a. Forest
		b. Southwestern			b. Alpine
		c. Northeastern			
		d. Southeastern	IV Sub-Tropical	20. Western Trans-caucasian	
	10. Continental forest type of W. Siberia	a. Northern		21. Eastern Trans-caucasian	
		b. Southern			
	11. Continental forest type of E. Siberia	a. Northern		22. Montane type of the Trans-caucasian uplands	
		b. Southwestern			
		c. Southeastern		23. South Turanian Desert type	
	12. Monsoon forest type	a. Northern		24. Montane type of the Pamir and Altai	
		b. Southern			
	13. Pacific forest type	a. Northern			
		b. Southern			
	14. Atlanto-continental steppe type	a. Western			
		b. Eastern			
		c. Black Sea			

Mensheha (1967) states that there are 143 million acres (57·9 million hectares) with adequate water supply available for irrigation in the Soviet Union. By 1964 only one-eighth of the potential irrigation land had been taken up. These subsurface reserves of water are often available in areas where water shortages are serious agricultural problems, as in Kazakhstan and the North Caucasus. In the unirrigated lands of Kazakhstan, wheat yields may fall as low as 3·5 bushels per acre, whereas irrigated lands of the southern Ukraine, the Povolzhye and North Caucasus averaged over a run of years yield 60–70 bushels of winter wheat per acre. Alternatively, 5000 lbs of rough rice per acre are obtained.

Again, about 66·8 million hectares of new land with agricultural potential are available if drainage and reclamation works are carried out. Only one-sixth of this area has been recovered so far. In 1966, the area of drained land in Belorussia, Leningrad, Pskov Regions and the Karelian A.S.S.R. covered 7·3 million hectares. By 1975, another 15–16 million hectares are to be added.

Taken together, measures of agricultural improvement will somewhat ameliorate the worst rigours of climatic capriciousness. Crop and animal yields will not then fluctuate so greatly between drought and optimum conditions.

In 1965, Belorussian reclaimed lands yielded 60 bushels of barley, or 24 bushels of rye, or 12 tons of potatoes per acre. It should be recognized, however, that these new lands can be won only at great cost, and some Soviet leaders believe that better results can be achieved by intensive production on existing lands.

The existence of these quite enormous areas of usable but unused agricultural lands are an apt comment on the relative stagnation of Soviet agriculture. It also points to the urgent need for a vigorous investment programme and a review of state procurement prices in the light of inflationary pressures, so that adequate incentives exist for agriculture improvements. As things now stand, those crops that secure most rewarding prices achieve much better investment and labour-application levels. These are particularly cotton, sugar-beets, maize and rice – all crops that have shown steadily improving physical yields over the past years (Table 8.1).

Agricultural policy changes have led to a lessening importance of the low-key cropping patterns; fallowing, hay, oats, rye, and even wheat in some

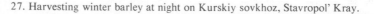

27. Harvesting winter barley at night on Kurskiy sovkhoz, Stavropol' Kray.

areas, have been replaced by high-status agriculture in which corn-for-silage, green fodder crops, dry legumes, and sugar-beets for sucrose and silage production, and often concomitant livestock industry are gaining strength. This represents a decided shift from the 'hay and grains' agricultural economy of pre-revolution Russia to a much more sophisticated, multi-strand agriculture with beneficial results for collective farmers, produce markets and land conservation practices.

Undoubtedly, while crop and land-use diversification is taking place in the Soviet Union, there are equally important moves to take advantage of potentials for regional specialization. A correct reading of Soviet policies in agriculture at the present time suggests a two-fold but interlocking pattern. On the one hand, the Soviet Union intends to make maximum use of inherent regional resources on bases of comparative advantage leading to specialization on the most suitable crops, while on the other hand, it seeks to retain flexibility within the farming system for each region to produce a group of diversified crops including even sub-environmental crops, awarding higher than average price incentives if necessary, so that the needs of the regional community are adequately served. At present, the use of drought-resistant crops, such as cotton, sunflower, safflower, and grain sorghums for fodder are making headway in semi-arid zones, often at the expense of the former wheat monoculture.

Agricultural Productivity

Soviet agricultural productivity trends are difficult to assess because meaningful indices are not easy to calculate. It is not easy to establish parameters, such as crop acreage per farm family, or labour and land productivity for specific kinds of agricultural produce. Soviet statistics provide some insights, however. As shown above, they give acreage under particular crops, acreage yields and the labour component for certain types of farm in some instances. Since 1958, it has not been possible to obtain correlates to support region by region analysis of agriculture. Nevertheless, researchers have managed to make some assessments of farm typologies, even allowing for the quite marked changes in organizational structure of Soviet agriculture and also for quality improvements inherent in certain branches of production.

Until recently, labour usage in the Soviet Union's agriculture was generally quite inefficient, especially on collective farms. Labour costs on collectives are between 50 to 100 per cent greater than on state farms in the comparable lines of production; they amount to one-third to a half of all production costs, whereas on state farms labour accounts for no more than one-fifth of production costs.

Field (1963) estimates that farm population densities in the Soviet Union relative to its land resources and its productive capacity are, on the average, about four times greater than those in the U.S.A. The factors that operate conjointly to produce this result are differences in man-power efficiency (Table 8.2), differences in physical endowment of agriculture, differences in the technological apparatus of farming and differences in the historical antecedents of farming in the two countries. In the Soviet Union, small-scale peasant farming gave way to high-density, directed collective farming by the 1930s; while the U.S.A. has retained a private ownership–tenancy system of agriculture throughout the period. Basically, for these reasons, farm productivity per farm worker in the Soviet Union is only one-fifth that of his American counterpart. Such a statement, however, conceals some important qualifications. First, the

TABLE 8.2

Labour Used per Centner of Output (man-hours)

Produce	Soviet Collective Farms 1956–7	Soviet State Farms 1956–7	U.S.A. Farms 1956
Grain	7·3	1·8	1·0
Potatoes	5·1	4·2	1·0
Sugar-beets	3·1	2·1	0·5
Cotton	42·8	29·8	18·8
Milk	14·7	9·9	4·7
Beef	112·0	52·0	7·9
Pork	103·0	43·0	6·3

Source: U.S. Congress, *Comparisons of the U.S. and Soviet Economies, Part I*, p. 215; quoted by P. E. Lydolph, *Geography of the USSR*, Wiley, New York, 2nd Edition, 1970, p. 404.

Soviet farm system is far less sophisticated than the American, so that many operations are carried on by farm workers in the Soviet Union, such as preparation of produce for market and off-farm transport which would be within the realm of non-farm activity in the U.S.A. Secondly, recent technological improvements in the Soviet Union agriculture have perhaps rendered an index of machine–man-hours in food production rather more comparable, thus lessening the discrepancy in a crude test of relative efficiency in Soviet–U.S. farming.

Thirdly, the physical constraints in Soviet agriculture operate much more severely than in the American case. In aggregate terms, Soviet farm production is some 75 per cent of the U.S. level, and since crop acreage is 50 per cent greater, postulated yields per unit area are only half the U.S. level. Whatever the Soviet authorities do or do not do, the inescapable fact is that Soviet environmental resources have lower production potential than so-called analogous lands in the U.S.A. A Canadian–Soviet analysis would provide a fairer and more rational comparison. Two-thirds of Soviet crop acreage lies in regions with less than 20 inches of precipitation, much of it received in the least desirable seasons of the year. Again, short and over-cool growing seasons predominate, and soils generally, but with a few notable exceptions, are podzolized and infertile. The range of yields between the least

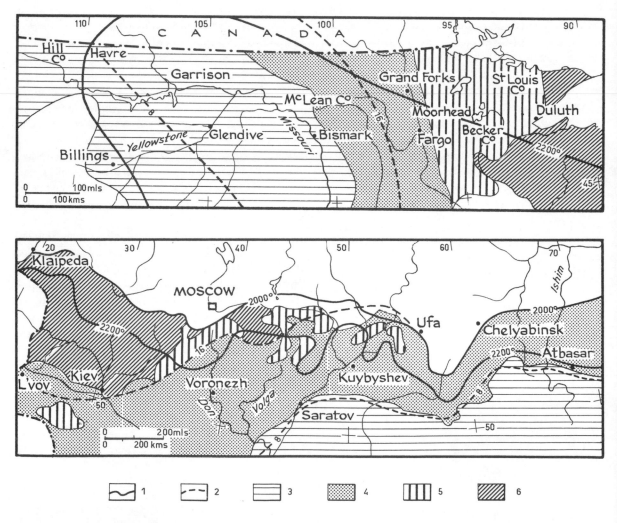

FIG. 8.2   Comparison of the Main U.S. and Soviet Agricultural Belts.

productive zones and the most productive zones for a given crop in the Soviet Union is far greater than that of a comparable crop in the U.S.A. (Fig. 8.2).

It is a paradox in Soviet agriculture that lands which have the most productive capacities from the environmental standpoint, i.e. the Chernozem Belt, are among the most impoverished communities merely because their very fertility has led to rural over-population in the past. On the other hand, areas like Northern Kazakhstan and Western Siberia, inferior in physical capacity, nevertheless have high rural income levels due to their relatively small farm population organized on state farms, and this despite the marginal dry-farming characteristics of many regions within the Virgin and Long-fallow Lands.

The Soviet government recognizes the problem of securing adequate voluntary rural depopulation in the most densely settled farm lands of the Soviet Union. Experience over the last decade has shown that, as efficiency and mechanization increase, farm labour is bound to be displaced. However, since the land belongs to the collective (ultimately to the State), any family leaving to take up urban employment cannot realize any part of the assets that they have in the past helped to create. In the Soviet Union the displaced person literally has to make a fresh start so that rural conservatism is very marked. In consequence, collectives are over-staffed, average shared-income is low, and much disguised rural unemployment exists in the sense that removal of farm labour would not adversely affect production.

Two facts are quite evident: (1) that in general eastern regions have considerably more sown area per farm worker than do the western regions where agriculture is long established, and (2) generally, state farms work commensurate sown acreages with far fewer farm workers than do the collectives.

This lends substance to Khrushchev's and other officials' statements on the relatively higher efficiency of state farms compared with the collectives although the comparison has been much disputed in recent years. The move over the last decade towards consolidation of collective farms into larger units and their transformation in many instances to state farm status have underscored the understandable desire of the authorities to raise agricultural productivity (Table 8.3). Labour displaced from collectives can be directed to state farms. Transformation into state farms added about 24 million hectares (60 million acres) of cropland between 1960 and 1970 at the expense of former collective holdings. Undoubtedly, there are several areas of intensive labour application within the overall farm system which have not been corrected and which divert effort away from collectives. Notably among these is the place of the individual plot in the agricultural ethos of the Soviet system (Fig. 8.3). The effort put into cultivation of private plots undoubtedly diverts many man-hours away from collective farming. In terms of product this may well be economically justified. Then there are unaccountable leakages of production between expected or biological yields of the fields and produce actually received into barns and storage places.

Under the New Lands programmes of the 1950s most augmented acreage that became available was developed as state farms and, indeed, the organization of farming in all new areas was through state farms. Total farm area in the Soviet Union of 388 million hectares at the time of Stalin's death rose to 505 million in 1961, 510 in 1966, and 546 million hectares in 1970. In 1953, 87 per cent of the total sown acreage was in the hands of collectives, in 1963 about 52·5 per cent, and in 1970, 47·8 per cent. By 1959 the crop area of state farms increased by over 40 million hectares, while collectives hardly increased their sown area at all. Between 1960 and 1970 state farm sown area rose by 24·5

KEY TO FIG. 8.2

1. Isolines of 'Growth Period' Temperature Summation (2000 °C and 2200 °C as noted)
2. Isolines of Moisture Coefficients (Equivalents of 8 and 16 inches of precipitation)

3. Chestnut Soils
4. Chernozem Soils
5. Grey Forest Soils
6. Turf-Podzolic Prairie Soils

After. A. Ye. Granovskaya, *op. cit.*

TABLE 8.3

Sown Acreage per Farm Worker in 1961

(1) Regions in which total crop acreage in collective farming *exceeds* 60%	Percentage of total crop acreage in collectives (1961)	Sown acreage per farm worker (in acres)	
		Collective	State
Northwest, Central, Volga–Vyatka	70	13·8	14·6
Baltic S.S.Rs	74	12·9	12·9
Belorussia	67	7·5	11·4
Moldavia	91	6·5	10·1
W. Ukraine (SW)	91	8·7	10·4
E. Ukraine (Donets-Dnieper + S)	76	14·9	17·5
Central Chernozem	72	17·8	23·1
Trans-Caucasus	87	4·8	5·5
Central Asia	72	5·7	7·8
(2) Regions in which total crop acreage in collective farms is *less than* 60%			
North Caucasus	59	18·5	27·2
Volga and Urals	54	26·0	39·0
West Siberia	37	36·3	42·0
East Siberia–Far East	35	26·5	33·3
Kazakhstan	18	31·0	66·2
U.S.S.R.	56	14	29

Source: After N. C. Field (1963), *op. cit.*, Table 2, p. 470 (re-arranged by author).

million hectares to 91·7 million while collectives decreased by 23·9 million hectares, falling to 99·1 million hectares. This is a useful measure of the switch to state farm ascendency in the Soviet system (Table 8.4).

Despite the shifts into state farming, collectives retain control of about one-half of the entire agricultural output, largely due to their more intensive cropping made possible by the fact that they possess about two-thirds of the nation's farm-

TABLE 8.4

Types of Farm in the Soviet Union (million hectares)

	Total Agricultural Areas			Arable Lands Under Cultivation		
	1954	1963	1970	1954	1963	1970
Personal plots (not on collective farms)	1·1	2·5	3·4	1·0	1·9	2·5
Household plots (on collective farms)	6·9	5·0	4·8	5·0	4·4	4·0
Collective farms	389·7	241·9	204·5	169·6	116·9	105·7
State farms (Sovkhoz and others)	88·7	283·1	333·1	28·0	101·0	111·3
Total Land Use in Agriculture	486·4	532·5	545·8	203·6	224·2	223·5

Sources: *Narodnoe Khozyaistvo, 1963*, Moscow, 1965, *and* for 1970 *Narodnoe Khozyaistvo, 1970*, Moscow, 1971, p. 290.

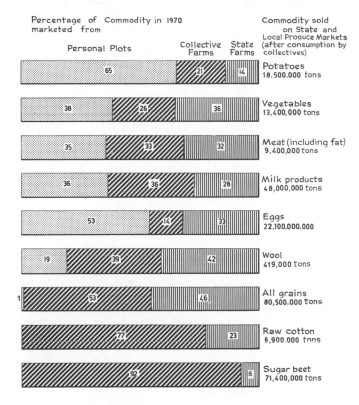

FIG. 8.3   Percentage of Various Commodities Sold from Sovkhozes, Kolkhoes, and Personal Plots, 1970.

working population. Private producers – mainly from personal plots on collectives – control about one-tenth of the agricultural output. This goes partly to household consumption but much of the surplus output is sold on local markets.

Rural population has declined in the Soviet Union by around 20 per cent since 1913. At the same time, about 84 million hectares of sown land have been added to the Soviet agricultural area. Allowing for the lower acreage productivity of

TABLE 8.5

Percentage of Specific Crop Types Grown on Stated Type of Farm Enterprise

	All Agricultural Production		Grain		Cotton		Sugar-beet		Potatoes		Vegetables	
	1950	1963	1950	1963	1950	1963	1950	1963	1950	1963	1950	1963
Private plots*	24	16	2	—	—	—	—	—	61	50	24	13
Collective farms	62	50	87	59	96	81	97	92	31	28	55	34
State farms	14	34	11	41	4	19	3	8	8	22	21	53
	100	100	100	100	100	100	100	100	100	100	100	100

Source: *Narodnoe Khozyaistvo, 1963*, Moscow, 1965.

* Private plots include household plots on collective farms and personal plots not connected with collective farms.
N.B. The 1970 situation is shown on Fig. 8.3.

TABLE 8.6

Rural Population and Acreage in Crops

	Rural Population (in millions)			Farm Acreage (in million acres)		
	1959	1962	1970	1959	1961	1970
U.S.S.R.	108·8	107·9	105·6	485·0	505·4	552·0
R.S.F.S.R., total; of which:	56·0	53·9	49·1	284·2	300·5	330·5
Mixed Forest and Wooded Steppe	25·2	23·4	22·2	81·0	87·2	93·2
Volga–Urals–Siberia	24·0	23·5	20·4	164·5	173·9	183·3
North Caucasus	6·8	7·0	6·5	38·7	39·4	54·0
Ukraine	22·7	22·2	21·4	82·0	84·0	84·0
Belorussia	5·6	5·4	5·1	13·9	14·5	15·3
Baltic Republics	3·1	3·1	2·9	11·4	11·9	12·1
Moldavia	2·2	2·3	2·4	4·88	4·7	4·7
Trans-Caucasus	5·1	5·4	6·0	6·5	5·7	5·3
Central Asia	8·9	9·6	12·4	13·2	13·5	15·6
Kazakhstan	5·2	6·0	6·3	69·0	70·6	84·5

Sources: Field, op. cit., 1963 (Table 3), p. 472 and *Narodnoe Khozyaistvo, 1970*, Moscow, 1971, for 1970 figures added. Re-arrangement by the author.

much of the new dry farming areas, and the countervailing increase in irrigated acreage, the amount of sown land per rural resident has about doubled. Higher average yields per worker and per unit area from Soviet agriculture have been the means by which the State has partially financed urban growth and the industrialization programme.

In Field's (1963) assessment, '. . . Future changes in the density of the farm population of the Soviet Union will depend to a much greater extent than in the past on the rural depopulation process and less on the expansion of the cultivated acreage'. These trends must severely affect the Ukraine which holds some 20–25 per cent of the country's total farm population. Rural depopulation here and in the mixed-forest zone of the European R.S.F.S.R. has been most rapid. The rural–urban flow can be attributed to the 'push' forces of collective farm mechanization and also the general intensification of agriculture, but also, perhaps quite as importantly, to the 'pull' forces of the burgeoning of industrial job opportunities in the cities of these regions. This city-ward flow substantially exceeds rural natural increase rates in the most densely settled parts of western R.S.F.S.R., Belorussia and the Ukraine.

Field concludes by suggesting a solution to rural impoverishment. 'Depopulation of the countryside would have to be established as a national goal similar to other economic objectives, and policies formulated to deal specifically with the complex of factors that impede it. Whether this could be accomplished through the collective farm system employing some form of material incentive to induce migration, or whether it would require an element of compulsion more readily exercised through the State farm system is open to debate'.

To reach U.S. levels of farm occupancy would require a shift of some 50–60 million persons off the land in the Soviet Union. With current rapid urban growth and problems of housing and services due to natural increase alone, such a deployment appears to be feasible only in the longer term. Nevertheless, the new Model Statutes for Collective Farms introduced in April, 1969, give more responsibility to farm management to find their own methods of obtaining production and allocating their land between specific kinds of crop or land-use, and by implication, to use labour efficiently.

CHAPTER NINE

CHANGES IN AGRICULTURAL STRUCTURE

Soviet authorities are now endeavouring to raise the status of agriculture. Belatedly they have realized that it is matters of sophisticated food supplies, adequate diet and quality of living that really challenge the government's claim to superiority over the capitalist system. Soviet consumers are now demanding a better standard of life with the trappings of an affluent society such as private vehicles, TV sets, washing machines, and holidays abroad. Essentially the standard of living can be most easily improved by making available an abundance of high quality agricultural commodities and semi-durable consumer goods in the varieties demanded and at low prices.

Soviet agriculture has been the Cinderella of economic activity for over three decades. This was partly a legacy of the harshness under which the collective farming system was set up by the Old Bolsheviks and the subsequent entrenchment of low priorities accorded to agriculture by successive Soviet governments. Under Soviet Communism, power developments and growth of heavy industries became the hallmarks of national prestige, so that few unused resources of capital, man-power, materials and planning expertise remained for some sectors of the economy such as agriculture.

Khrushchev envisaged a 'new order' of agricultural planning involving a rational distribution of agricultural production by growing those crops which in the regional environment would yield maximum production per hectare with a minimum expenditure of labour and materials. It is also clear that this new direction in agriculture moved away from the bureaucratic planning system where the state could demand less than optimum land-use to one where revenue—output of land and production costs become measures of the effectiveness of agricultural production and land-use allocation.

Experiments have been made in agricultural planning with price zonation and regionalization for various crops. Essentially this permits the central planning authorities to determine what is to be produced where, while at the same time compensating for environmental disadvantages of particular regions. Also it permits the distance of production centres from the principal markets for the commodity to be taken into account. These innovations in Soviet agricultural planning are discussed at length in Jensen's article on the subject (1968) noted in the bibliography.

During the early 1960s, new priorities promoted hitherto neglected lines of Soviet endeavour, including transport, consumer goods manufacture, and agriculture. The sudden surge in plans for agricultural development arose from two types of government decision. First a re-assessment of the role of agriculture in the overall Soviet economy, involving a belated realization that the pre-1953 system was not only socially inadequate, but could not provide sufficient foodstuffs in adequate variety nor enough industrial raw materials of farm origin to support the planned rise in consumption standards. Secondly, changes in the administrative and organizational structure affected agriculture as well as other branches of the Soviet economy. Under Khrushchev, collective political leadership led to the devolution of the powers of the Moscow Ministries for various industries and also for agriculture. Authority was then given to 104 Regional Economic Councils (Sovnarkhozes) whose rise and fall have been discussed in Chapter 7 above.

Agriculture was profoundly affected by this decentralization process and the new economic guidelines. Each Sovnarkhoz was allocated a production target embracing each specific agricultural commodity for which its physical environment was adjudged suitable. In aggregate, the Sovnarkhoz targets for each crop equalled the All-Union budget for that commodity. This planning envisaged achievement of the best use of agricultural resources, while at the same time allowing for differences in consumption levels of the various

regions, transport requirements, need to move surpluses to deficit areas, and the ideological motive
which ascribed 'balanced and proportional growth'
to under-developed regions, particularly the
National groups. Multi-objective planning for
agriculture of this sort has been described by
Mikheyeva (1966).

Within the boundaries of each Sovnarkhoz the
authorities allocated the total production target
between state farms and collective farms. Both at the
national and local levels care was taken to secure
adequate specialization and economies of scale in
farming, while at the same time allowing each unit a
range of crop diversification to meet immediate and
local needs. The central aim seems to have been to
create a farming system that was self-sustaining and
yet provided maximum surpluses for inter-regional
markets. State contracts and bonus payments for
production in excess of quotas were strong incentives to collective farming.

The Sovnarkhozes appointed agricultural inspectors who combined the roles of overseers and extension officers. Inspectors ensured best and most
up-to-date cultivation practices, recorded land-use
allocation on state and collective farms, and
promoted the use of fertilizers, high-quality seed,
and agricultural weedicides and other biological
controls. In livestock management, inspectors controlled veterinary and advisory services for breeding, artificial insemination, and development of new
animal technology. This considerably tightened
'grass-root' administrative control of the Soviet
agricultural system, compared with the ineffectual
but normally authoritarian bureaucracy of the
Moscow Ministry of Agriculture of the Stalinist
period. It became clear, however, that many did not
welcome the new drive towards efficiency
represented by the Sovnarkhoz system of control.
Collective farmers in particular resented interfer-
ence in their time-honoured Soviet or communal
management system, especially when enforced
amalgamation of collective farms and displacement
of labour became necessary in the interest of efficiency. Also, as many collective farms were converted to state farms, the feeling that nominally
independent farmers were becoming subordinate
state employees gained prominence. A measure of
the intensity of change in farming organization is
given by the decrease in numbers of collective

farms. There were 252,000 immediately after
World War II, only 37,100 by 1966 and 33,600 in
1970. At the same time there was a rise in the
number of state farms and area farmed by them
(Table 9.1). State farms are concentrated, for the
most part, in Kazakhstan, Central Asia, North
Caucasus, Volga, and the West Siberian economic
regions.

Despite opposition, the new Soviet farming
system did much to improve both output and yields
and also correct some defects that were glaringly
apparent. Machinery and operating personnel available from the former Machine Tractor Stations
(MTS), greatly improved the material basis of collective farming. The former three-tiered commodity
price system that enshrined state procurement
price, contract price, and 'free' market price at
successively higher levels for any given agricultural
product was replaced by a system of fixed commodity prices for each region. Variations in these
prices were determined by the authorities to

28. Virgin Lands grain farming helps to support a population
of 3 million round the sovkhozes of northern Kazakhstan. Here
grain cleaning is in progress on the threshing floor of the Berlik
sovkhoz, Kokchetav oblast, Kazakhstan.

provide incentives in agricultural production. Another reason for higher commodity prices was to encourage production in areas that were less favourable for a particular crop which nevertheless had a high priority on the national scale. In effect, this subsidized production in those regions where crop diversification was considered desirable or where there were environmental constraints on the success of production. One example of these regional pricing systems was the case of sugar-beets. The price in the core production area of the eastern Ukraine was 210 roubles per centner (100 metric pounds), while in the western areas (L'vov, Kishinev) and Baltic Republics prices in the same season ranged from 230 to 250 roubles per centner, while far away in the Volga–Urals Sovnarkhozes on the margin of climatic feasibility, sugar-beet price was set at the incentive level of 320 roubles per centner. For all crops, the regional price differential from core to margin was of the order of plus 50 per cent. Only partly could such a variation be justified in terms of transport cost saving; a large element of administratively determined locational incentive payment remains. In a true free market economy such incentives would not be possible because products grown in low-price zones would be transported to high-price zones, quickly eroding local output-price relations. But, of course, no such equalization of market forces is possible in the Soviet Union.

Under the collective farming system, the physical productivity of land, man, and machine has been very low indeed in the past. As recently as 1958, before rationalization of agriculture got under way, collective farms had nearly three times more workers per 1000 hectares sown in crops than state farms, even excluding MTS personnel normally attached to collectives. Despite the heavier labour-content of collective farming, crop yields were considerably below those of state farms in areas of

TABLE 9.1
Changes in the Organizational Structure of Soviet Agriculture

	1940	1950	1960	1965	1970
Collective Farm System					
Number of Farms (Thousands)	126·9	123·7	44·9	36·9	33·6
Farm Families (Millions)	18·7	20·5	17·1	15·4	14·4
Farm Workers (Millions)	29·0	27·6	21·7	18·6	16·7
Families per Farm (Number)	81·0	165·0	383·0	421·0	431·0
Farm Sown Area (Millions hectares)	117·7	121·0	123·0	105·1	99·1
Number of Tractors (Thousands)	401·0*	405·0*	621·0	772·0	961·0
Number of Tractor Units (Thousands) (in terms of 15 H.P. units)	494·0	609·0	1050·0	1398·0	2015·0
State Farm System					
Number of Farms (Thousands)	4·2	5·0	7·4	11·7	15·0
Farm Workers (Millions)	2·3	3·3	5·8	8·2	8·9
No. of Workers per Farm (Number)	547·6	660·0	783·8	700·8	593·3
Farm Sown Area (Millions hectares)	11·6	12·9	67·2	89·1	91·7
Number of Tractors (Thousands)	129·0*	190·0*	403·0	681·0	803·0
Number of Tractor Units (Thousands) (in terms of 15 H.P. units)	189·0	326·0	751·0	1325·0	1838·0

Source: *Narodnoe Khozyaistvo, 1970*, Moscow, 1971, p. 298; p. 383; p. 397 and p. 404.

For Collectives and State Farms, farm workers includes those directly engaged in agriculture and also auxiliary workers, machine operators, etc.

* Since the years 1940 and 1950 involved the servicing of Collective Farms by Machine Tractor Stations, no official statistics of tractors on farms are available. The author has distributed the total known tractor 'park' – all tractors used in agriculture – for those years between collectives and state farms on a rational basis for purposes of series comparison.

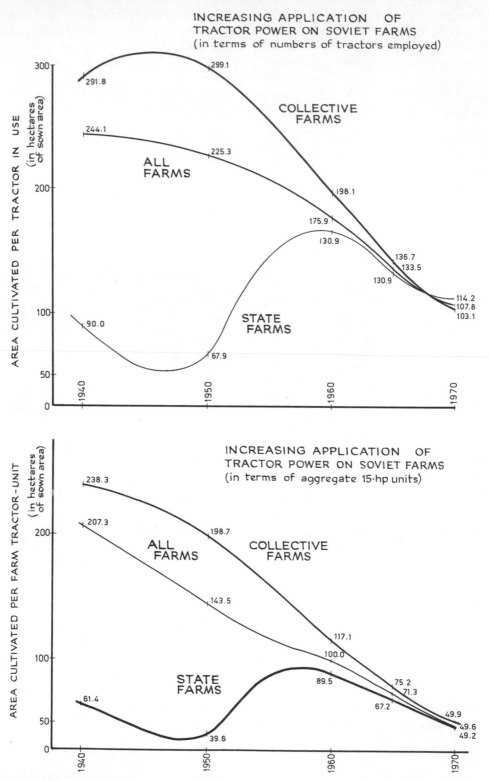

FIG. 9.1   Changes in Tractor Application to Soviet Farming.

29. This grain elevator with a capacity of 65,000 tons is located at Timashevskaya in the Kuban, Krasnodar Kray. The Kuban alone required nineteen new elevators to handle its growing output between 1966 and 1970. Other grain regions of the country are similarly increasing storage capacity consequent upon a rise in national grain output from 137 to 167 million tons annually.

comparable physical conditions. The inefficiency of the collective farm rested on their historical antecedents. Inevitably, the kolkhoz has had to support under-employed workers. In many instances, this amounted to disguised rural unemployment, especially in the most densely populated regions. The reforms of the 1960s insisted on productivity norms and introduced money wages for collective farmers instead of the traditional share-income based on the farm's total income and the man-hours of work contributed. These measures then considerably reduced the number of workers needed per 1000 hectares of farm land. From 1965 greater personal commitment has arisen due to the breaking up of the larger production brigades into small teams of 5–6 men (zvenos) who receive bonuses for good production levels.

The decline in the number of collective farmers and their dependents has been dramatic in post-war years. This trend is continuing (Table 9.2). A loss of 12·3 million collective farmers – or 4·3 million families – has been experienced over the three decades to 1970. Over the same period, state farming has gained 6·6 million workers and auxiliary employees.

In the earliest reform period (1954–56) the Soviet government's first thoughts were to convert all kolkhozes into the demonstrably more efficient sovkhozes. Since over 120,000 farms were involved, the transition was planned for a number of years. Over a four-year period about 20 million hectares of kolkhoz land were transferred to sovkhozes either by permitting sovkhozes to absorb neighbouring kolkhoz land or by combining a number of kolkhozes (usually the least efficient) and then converting the units into a new sovkhoz. Opposition in the countryside slowed down but did not entirely prevent the consolidation process. Nevertheless, in general, the trend towards the sovkhoz in farming is continuing (Table 9.2). In the early 1960s, the 'troika' system, embracing sovkhozes, kolkhozes, and sovnarkhozes was represented as an essential element in the gradual socialization of agriculture. For all practical purposes, however, the existing collective farms have since been completely

TABLE 9.2

Percentage Breakdown by Type of Agricultural System 1940–70

Percentage of Sown Area	1940	1950	1960	1965	1970
Collective Farms	78·1	82·7	60·6	50·2	47·9
Personal Plots (Collectives + others *)	13·1	6·4	3·3	3·2	3·3
State Farms (includes State enterprises)	8·8	10·9	36·1	46·6	48·8
	100·0	100·0	100·0	100·0	100·0
Total Sown Area (million hectares)	150·6	146·3	203·0	209·1	206·7

Source: *Narodnoe Khozyaistvo, 1970,* Moscow, 1971, p. 298.
  * Personal plots include collective farmers' household plots and plots of other workers.

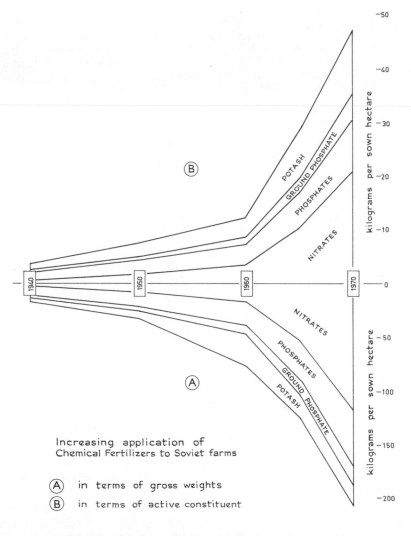

Increasing application of
Chemical Fertilizers to Soviet farms

(A) in terms of gross weights
(B) in terms of active constituent

FIG. 9.2   Changes in Fertilizer Application to Soviet Farming.

30. Spray irrigation of market garden crops on the Pobeda kolkhoz, Sunzhensky area, Checheno–Ingush A.O.

transformed to sovkhozes in everything but name. First, the collective worker is remunerated by money wages, the Soviet management committee operates under the guidance of a government-appointed manager and officials upon whom rest such decisions as 'hire and fire' and capital expenditure. Such investments may be drawn from indivisible funds of collectives; the mandatory accumulated profits derived from 10 per cent of a kolkhoz's annual net revenue. Thus collective farm managements may now invest in farm machinery and improvements, such as irrigation, drainage, farm roads, barns, buildings, and processing plant, subject only to the retention of 10 per cent of net revenue each year; the minimum that the State insists each collective farm must retain against a rainy day.

In addition to changes in organizational structure, Soviet agriculture is changing its crop emphasis to a remarkable degree. Firstly, non-grain crops are assuming greater importance and secondly, livestock emphasis in the farming system is growing stronger (Table 9.3).

TABLE 9.3

*Livestock Numbers in the Soviet Union 1941–71
(as at January 1st of year; in millions of head)*

	1941	1951	1961	1966	1970	1971
Dairy Cattle	28·0	24·3	34·8	40·1	40·5	41·0
Other Cattle	26·8	32·8	41·0	53·3	54·7	58·2
Pigs	27·6	24·4	58·7	59·6	56·1	67·5
Sheep	80·0	82·6	133·0	129·8	130·6	138·1
Goats	11·7	16·4	7·3	5·5	5·1	5·4
Poultry	255·7	292·8	515·6	490·7	590·3	652·7

Source: *Narodnoe Khozyaistvo, 1970*, Moscow, 1971, pp. 352–53, 396.

Despite a long tradition of grain farming, the Soviet Union is shifting quite swiftly to non-grain crops and animal husbandry. Historic grain-growing areas of the Ukraine and the Central Chernozem regions (mainly winter wheat) and Belorussia (mainly rye, oats, and barley) have shifted to industrial crops, fodder crops, vegetables, potatoes, and maize. These more intensive forms of land-use make better use of available labour. Much grain farming (mainly spring wheat) has shifted

31. Harvesting road-side silage and hoeing-up sugar-beets near Khar'kov. Note the fruit tree plantings along the verge. (Photograph by the author.)

eastwards to the steppe regions of Kazakhstan, the Urals, and Western Siberia (Fig. 10.1). These areas now have 67 per cent of the area sown to wheat (not production), whereas the share of the Ukraine, Volga, and North Caucasus decreased from 43 to their present 25 per cent of the wheat acreage. The move to even more extensive grain growing has raised problems in maintaining production, especially in circumstances in which early yields from virgin soils have been difficult to maintain.

Throughout the Soviet Union, the area sown in grain has increased about 12 per cent since 1950. In the same period, however, grain production increased by 58 per cent thus indicating a greater than two-fold increase in yields per hectare.

As a short-term solution to augmenting production, Soviet agriculture turned first to an extension of area. Only during the last two decades has the intensification of production in the existing area played any significant role in increasing output. This has unlocked a considerable potential. Improvements in yields per hectare are very marked (Table 8.1 above), especially during the decade 1960–70.

The cultivated areas under cotton, flax, hemp, sunflower, rape seed, sugar-beet and tobacco, have increased remarkably over the past two decades.

Maize, potatoes and fodder crops, associated with more intensive animal husbandry, have also increased. Maize-growing for grain and/or 'milkwax' stage for silage, has over-stepped all bounds, especially with the introduction of the prolific hybrid varieties once the anti-Mendelian theories of the Soviet geneticist T. D. Lysenko [1] had been overcome in the post-Stalinist period. At the height of Khrushchev's 'maize cult', the area planted in that crop in the Ukraine was half of the area planted in all grain crops. It is still grown for grain and as a fodder in the Ukraine, in Belorussia and even the Baltic Republics. In the latter zones, it has to some extent replaced hardier fodder grains such as rye, oats, and barley, because of its bulk and nutritional value. In particular, with the extension of irrigation agriculture, the late summer drought areas of the Ukraine and the Russian South have become important maize-for-grain areas.

---

[1] Academician Lysenko broke with Mendel's genetic principles and asserted that environmental influences could induce changes in genetic characteristics that would be inherited by succeeding generations of grain. His views on organic fertilizers also prevented the widespread development of the mineral fertilizer industry until well after his dismissal in February, 1965.

Soviet Livestock Industries

On some farms of the Ukraine, Belorussia and the Baltic Republics, mixed farming practices have developed, combining beef or dairy-cattle or pigs with some form of intensive cropping, frequently sugar-beet or potato growing. Such systems are quite alien to earlier patterns of Soviet agriculture and indicate well the innovative forces now at work. The general growth of the livestock industries is shown (Tables 9.3 and 9.4).

General improvements in the level of livestock management are the result of better nutrition and grazing efficiency. Between 1951 and 1971 the percentages shown in Table 9.4 indicate a resurgence of collective farmers' household plots in animal husbandry. Despite larger animal populations, percentages have been maintained or improved, in all cases except beef cattle and pigs.

The role of state farms in all fields of animal enterprise has increased markedly. Some specialized animal collectives have grown in importance.

Measures of livestock yields – such as milk per dairy cow, carcass weight of animals, and wool clip, have without exception improved during the last 20 years. Average milk production per dairy cow rose from 1370 kilograms annually in 1950 to 1853 kilograms in 1965 and 2110 kilograms in 1970. Pig-raising has received great emphasis in the Soviet Union simply because of the rate of progression possible in stock numbers and annual production rates with this quick-breeding animal. On average, piglets reared from a single sow yield around ten times more edible meat in a year than a calf from a beef cow. The distribution of particular kinds and breeds of livestock is shown (Fig. 10.2).

32. Harvesting flax by combine on the Verny Put kolkhoz near Uglich, Yaroslavl' oblast. The Soviet Union grows two-thirds of the world's flax. Linen cloth is a favoured material for clothing as a washable, hard-wearing, hygienic and warm fabric. The advent of synthetic fibres has had no appreciable affect on flax production.

TABLE 9.4

Changes in the Structure of Livestock Industries (Percentage of Total by Farm Organization)

Livestock	State Farms *		Collectives		Personal Plots		Total (No. of Livestock)	
	1951 %	1971 %	1951 %	1971 %	1951 %	1971 %	1951	1971 (Millions of Head)
Dairy Cattle	5·3	27·6	28·9	34·6	16·1	15·5	24·3	41·0
Other Cattle	8·8	35·7	64·4	47·3	26·8	17·0	32·8	58·2
Pigs	14·8	31·7	50·4	43·7	34·8	24·6	24·4	67·5
Sheep	10·9	40·4	73·6	38·8	15·5	20·8	82·6	138·1
Goats	1·9	7·4	45·7	11·1	52·4	81·5	16·4	5·4

Source for base statistics: *Narodnoe Khozyaistvo, 1970*, Moscow, 1971, pp. 352–53.

* Includes both State Farms and other government establishments, e.g. research stations, experimental farms, etc.

The Technological Factors

Soviet agricultural developments have received immense assistance in recent decades from technological innovation. In particular, greater amounts and technically more elaborate forms of machinery – tractors, cultivators, combines, specialized harvesting machines like cotton and tea-pickers – have played their part. Moreover, rural electrification to the extent where all state and most collective farms – 99·8 per cent in 1970 – now receive electrical supplies, and the increased 'chemicalization' of agriculture (to use the Soviet term) have proved to be innovations of immense value. The role of new irrigation and drainage works has been referred to in Chapter 4; again it has been significant in promoting the intensification of agriculture.

Another factor which should not be forgotten is the increased application of science to agriculture. In 1971 over 35,000 specialist scientists were engaged in research in agricultural and veterinary colleges, and there were more than one hundred higher agricultural schools training specialists for farming activities. In consequence, the vast majority of state and collective farm managers are now technically qualified, in marked contrast to the pre-war situation.

Essential to an understanding of Soviet agricultural development is the part played by technological innovation. During the last twenty years, virtually all farms have received rural electrical supply. This has been greatly aided by the merging of scattered hamlets and villages into larger nucleated settlements, frequently small towns or *agrogorods*, that can be provided with modern infrastructure and amenities more conveniently.

Tractors and other farm machinery have greatly improved in power and efficiency. The mean drawbar capacity of tractors has risen from 39 h.p. to 60 h.p. over the past fifteen years. In 1972, the aggregate horse-power of the two million farm tractors then in existence amounted to 124 million h.p. and other farm machinery (combines, etc.) to 212 million h.p. All of this represents a very significant level of 'co-operating' investment in the Soviet Union's agricultural system (Fig. 9.1).

There is some evidence, nevertheless, that the Soviet Union's need for agricultural machinery is not completely met at the present time (Table 9.5). It appears from this table, however, that the gap between machinery requirements and annual supply of specific machines is becoming narrower, even allowing for obsolescence between 1960 and 1970. Within a period of two or three years Soviet agriculture will have enough tractors, drills, ploughs, cultivators, and various types of combines to meet its perceived requirements. The categories of machine that are in short supply are sugar-beet-lifting, potato-lifting, cotton-picking and flax-pulling machines, but the current Five-Year Plan will increase the rate of production for these items.

An excellent indication of the increase power application to farming is given by the sown area served per 15 h.p. tractor unit (Table 9.6). In recent

TABLE 9.5

Soviet Farm Machinery Supply

	Situation 1960		Situation 1970			
	Farm Inventory c. 1960	Total New Requirement	Supply of New Units 1970	Farm Inventory 1970	Deficit from 1960 Requirement	Years Needed to Close Supply Need
	In Thousands of Units					
Tractors (Physical Units)	1442	2696	309	1977	719	2·3
Tractor-drawn						
Sowing machines	1066	1628	187	1278	350	1·9
Ploughs	833	1180	207	940	240	1·2
Cultivators	813	395	205	1144	+749	—
Self-Propelled Combines						
Grain	517	845	97	623	222	2·3
Ensilage	184	251	33	139	112	3·5
Maize	61	111	48	33	78	1·7
Beets	48	251	10	57	194	19·4

Sources: 1960 Situation, N. S. Khrushchev's speech on agriculture, reported *Izvestiya*, 6.3.1962 (quoted by Braekhus, *op. cit.*, p. 50). 1970 situation, *Narodnoe Khozyaistvo, 1970*, Moscow, 1971, p. 377; p. 381.

years the difference in power available between state farms and collectives has been completely closed.

The chemicalization of Soviet agriculture has been very pronounced in the last two decades (Fig. 9.2). In 1971, the Soviet Union produced 61·4 million tons of various fertilizers. In consequence, mineral fertilizer application has been greatly improved. In just one decade to 1970, the use of nitrogenous fertilizers increased six-fold, and that of phosphatic-types three fold. Recently more complex fertilizers such as double- and triple-superphosphates, urea, and compound fertilizers have been used to a far greater extent than previously (Table 9.7).

Although very much greater amounts of fertilizer have been invested in agriculture, the regional usage pattern has been very uneven. For example, Uzbekistan's irrigated agriculture used 125 kilograms per hectare; the Baltic Republics about 80 kilograms, while Kazakhstan's more extensive-type of grain farming received only 3 kilograms per hectare.

TABLE 9.6

Soviet Tractor Power Applied to Agriculture, 1940–70

Year	State Farms			Collective Farms		
	Sown Area (million hectares)	Tractor Units (15 h.p.) (thousands)	Area per Tractor (hectares)	Sown Area (million hectares)	Tractor Units (15 h.p.) (thousands)	Area per Tractor (hectares)
1940	11·6	189	61·4	117·7	494	238·3
1950	12·9	326	39·6	121·0	609	198·7
1960	67·2	751	89·5	123·0	1050	117·1
1965	89·1	1325	67·2	105·1	1398	75·2
1970	91·7	1838	49·9	99·1	2015	49·2

Source: Derived from Table 9.1 above.

TABLE 9.7

Soviet Chemical Fertilizer Application, 1940–70
(*in kilograms per sown hectare*)

Type of Fertilizer	1940	1950	1960	1965	1970
Nitrogenous	4·1	8·6	17·3	50·4	101·9
Phosphatic	7·1	13·7	20·4	36·4	53·6
Phosphates; ground	2·5	2·7	6·4	14·7	23·2
Potash	2·8	5·9	8·5	20·6	28·1
All Types	16·5	30·9	52·6	122·1	206·8

Source: Derived from *Narodnoe Khozyaistvo, 1970*.
Moscow, p. 342 and Table 9.1 above.

Throughout the Soviet Union, rising levels in crop yields rest mainly on fertilizer application, but nevertheless, the greater use of herbicides, weedicides, insecticides, and trace-elements has been an additional factor in rising agricultural standards. Also, since the early 1960s advances in veterinary medicine in the Soviet Union and improved animal husbandry have resulted in quite dramatic flock and herd innovations – rising numbers of animals; better yields of meat, milk, eggs, and wool; artificial insemination for sheep as well as cattle, and higher progeny rates.

To conclude this section, the following points should be emphasized:

1. Soviet agriculture has recently undertaken wide-sweeping structural and economic changes. These render the current production system very much more flexible and responsive to consumption requirements than was the earlier post-war system.

2. The variety of crops and quality of agricultural produce have improved immensely under the new measures, and the same is true of animal husbandry.

3. The regional dispersion of various types of agricultural activity has moved toward locational specialization while permitting a degree of diversification under properly adjusted price incentives.

4. Last, but by no means least, Soviet authorities have rendered the social conditions and living standards of collectives and state farm workers much more acceptable than was physically possible in the Stalinist era. Indeed, improving qualities of rural life have for the first time since the revolution made the Russian countryside both a happier and healthier place in which to live and work. Nevertheless, the authorities acknowledge that much remains to be done to secure an even brighter future.

CHAPTER TEN

AGRICULTURAL LANDSCAPES

Soviet agriculture presents a number of distinct agricultural landscapes which are devoted to:

1. Grain farming; in particular, winter and spring wheat, but also oats, barley, maize, rice, and buckwheat.
2. Vegetable and potato-growing.
3. Fibre-yielding plants: flax, hemp, cotton, and others.
4. Oil-bearing plants; sunflower, linseed, safflower, soya bean, castor-oil bean, mustard, and others.
5. Sugar-beet farming.
6. Fruit-growing and orcharding.
7. Sub-tropical crops, makhorka, tobacco, and koksagyz.
8. Animal husbandry.

1. Grain Farming. In 1970 the Soviet grain harvest was 186·8 million tons and of this more than half — 99·7 million tons — was spring or winter wheat cultivated on 65 million hectares. Thus the Soviet wheat harvest is greater than the combined output of the United States, Canada, Australia and France.

Wheat. Wheat falls into two categories; winter wheat, grown dominantly in the southwestern parts of European Russia from the Central Chernozem region to the North Caucasus and the southern Ukraine (maturing in 110–30 days), and spring wheat (maturing in 85–110 days) which dominates the agriculture of central and eastern regions of the steppe lands. Most Russian wheat is of the hard red variety. Spring sowing and harsher climatic conditions render the average yields of spring wheat much lower than those for winter wheat — 12·3 centners per hectare on average against 22·8 centners.

In terms of area sown to wheat, there has been a progressive shift from the old wheat lands to the new (Fig. 10.1). In the west, former wheat lands are being turned over to maize-growing, sugar-beet and animal husbandry based on rotation pastures. The new wheat lands comprise the Volga region, the Urals, Tselinnyy Kray (Virgin Lands Kray), other parts of Kazakhstan and both Western and Eastern Siberia (Table 10.1).

The western and eastern wheat zones — broadly corresponding with the distribution of winter and spring varieties — contrast strongly. The western is based on intensive wheat farming in association with other crop rotations, whereas the eastern relies on extensive monoculture of wheat over vast areas and, as noted, has much lower productivity. In Tselinnyy Kray for instance, yields of spring wheat in the worst years have been as low as 3·7 centners per hectare (1957) and 2·8 (1963), thus only one-tenth of the yields common from the chernozem lands.

The principal varieties of wheat grown in the Soviet Union are: Odesskaya, Bezostaya, and Stepnaya. Together these varieties and their progeny occupy 60 per cent of the winter wheat areas. In the spring wheat varieties, Al'bidum, Lyutestens and Mil'turum are most common, taking up to 70 per cent of the sown area.

To a degree wheat-farming problems are being overcome by better varieties. Bezostaya I and Mironovskaya-808, are high-yielding varieties with high germination capacities; others are Aurora, Kavkaz, and Odesskaya-51. On irrigated lands in the south and Central Asia, these winter varieties have given phenomenal yields, up to 90 centners per hectare. Some nominally winter wheat varieties are being bred for spring sowing — Yershovskaya-68 is one such strain — yielding 32 centners per hectare in regions where 20 centners would be considered normal.

Durum wheat is grown along the southern margins of the spring wheat belt. Under proper management durum gives higher yields than common spring wheats; it can survive semi-arid conditions well and is high in protein content. In the Soviet Union, durum is not much used for pasta products (macaroni, etc.), its chief use in other parts of the world. Both spring wheat and durum are frequently grown under the *perelog* system, in which the land is fallowed every two or three years to restore humus

TABLE 10.1
Soviet Spring and Winter Wheat Production by Economic Region (in millions metric tons)

	Mean Annual 1958–61			Production 1970		
	Spring	Winter	Total	Spring	Winter	Total
Russian Federation	28·0	10·7	38·7	41·3	21·6	62·9
Northwest	0·1	...	0·1	0·1	0·1	0·2
Centre	0·2	0·6	0·8	0·2	1·6	1·8
Volga–Vyatka	0·4	0·1	0·5	0·8	0·3	1·1
Central Chernozem	0·6	2·0	2·6	0·5	3·1	3·6
Volga	5·2	0·7	5·9	8·4	5·6	14·0
North Caucasus	0·2	7·3	7·5	0·3	10·9	11·2
Urals	8·1	...	8·1	11·9	...	11·9
West Siberia	9·9	—	9·9	13·6	—	13·6
East Siberia	2·9	—	2·9	4·8	—	4·8
Far East	0·4	—	0·4	0·7	—	0·7
Ukraine and Moldavia	0·1	13·0	13·1	0·2	16·1	16·3
Donets-Dnieper	0·1	4·9	5·0	0·1	8·1	8·2
Southwest	...	4·1	4·1	0·1	4·6	4·7
South	...	3·2	3·2	—	3·0	3·0
Moldavia	—	0·8	0·8	—	0·4	0·4
Kazakhstan	14·8	0·7	15·5	15·8	1·4	17·2
Tselinnyy Kray	11·3	0·1	11·4	12·5	0·2	12·7
Other Kazakhstan	3·5	0·6	4·1	3·3	1·2	4·5
Other Regions	0·4	1·4	1·8	0·3	3·0	3·3
Baltic and Belorussia	0·2	0·2	0·4	0·1	0·7	0·8
Trans-Caucasus	...	0·7	0·7	—	0·9	0·9
Central Asia	0·2	0·5	0·7	0·2	1·4	1·6
Soviet Union	43·3	25·8	69·1	57·6	42·1	99·7

Sources: Commonwealth of Australia, Bureau of Agricultural Economics, *The Economics of the Soviet Wheat Industry*, Canberra, 1966, Appendix V, p. 78, for 1958–61 production figures, and *Narodnoe Khozyaistvo, 1970*, Moscow, 1971, for 1970 production figures by Republics and aggregate for Economic Regions, pp. 301; 312–13 (calculated from area and yields). Breakdown for winter and spring varieties by row and column balances and estimates from actual 1964 regional percentages of total Republican production. The signs: — no production ... insignificant production.

and moisture in the soil. In the absence of *perelog* farming yields fall off disastrously, a prime reason for some of the disappointing results once the initial fertility of the Virgin Lands became exhausted.

Other Grains. Apart from wheat the Soviet Union has a considerable production of other grains. Maize for grain is confined to moist warm areas of the South Ukraine, Moldavia, and the North Caucasus. Elsewhere, maize is used in the milk-wax stage or as green feed as it does not fully mature. Production – 9·4 million tons in 1970 – and yields have improved very considerably since the introduction of American hybrid strains. Plans are afoot to double output by 1975.

Rye is grown in Belorussia and adjacent areas which are too humid for successful wheat culture.

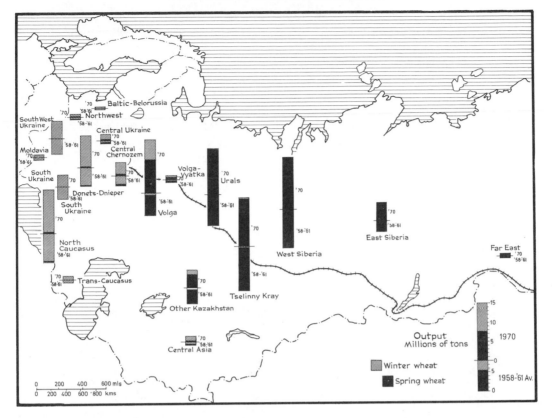

FIG. 10.1   Changes in the Output of Spring and Winter Wheat by Regions, 1958–61 Average and 1970.

However, with the introduction of more fodder roots and rotation pastures and the drainage of marshy soils, less rye is now grown than formerly. This also corresponds to smaller demand for black bread, the main end product for rye flour, in the Russian diet. Oats has suffered a similar fate with the virtual elimination of draught animals from Soviet farming and again a dietary change away from gruels. Barley, however, is one small grain that has improved its position. Production in 1970 was 34·5 million tons. It now figures largely as a feed grain. The main growing areas correspond to the winter wheat belt, but minor extensions occur in the spring wheat belt and in the dry farming areas of south Central Asia. In the Moslem areas, barley is widely used as a bread-grain, but its chief use — other than as feedstuff — is in malting and brewing.

Millet and buckwheat are minor grains in the Soviet farming system. Output in 1970 was 5·1 million tons. Millet is concentrated in the im-

mediate environs of Tambor Oblast, but buckwheat is widely grown throughout Western R.S.F.S.R., Belorussia, and in the Ukraine where it has for centuries been a staple diet.

Rice production has increased phenomenally in the Soviet Union due to new irrigated areas and the draining of brackish or saline lagoons, the so-called *liman*. In 1970 just under 1·3 million tons of rice were produced from some 350,000 hectares. Somewhat less than half of this came from southern Russia – the Colchis Lowland, Kuban and the Don – while the remainder came from the irrigation areas of the South Ukraine, Kazakhstan, and Central Asia. Overall, yields have improved dramatically; from 14·6 centners per hectare in 1950 to 36·5 centners in 1970.

2. *Vegetables and Potatoes*. Soviet production of vegetables more than doubled between 1950 and 1970, while output of potatoes increased by 11 per cent. These crops now (1970) occupy less area

(10·1 million hectares) than they did in 1950, and higher output is due entirely to tremendous improvement in yields: from 72 to 138 centners per hectare for vegetables and from 104 to 120 for potatoes. Potatoes are grown mainly in the cool, moist areas of the forest-steppe and forest-zone marshlands of the west. Vegetables, depending on variety, are grown throughout the Soviet Union. Cabbages of enormous size are grown in the extreme north while peas, beans, cucumbers, and other curbis are found in favoured areas of the south.

3. *Fibre Plants.* The Soviet Union cultivates more than 30 types of industrial crop and prominent among these are the fibre-plants: cotton, flax, hemp, kenaf and jute.

Cotton production reached 6·9 million tons in 1970 and 7·3 million in 1972. This placed the Soviet Union in first world rank, surpassing the United States and overhauling India's production two-fold. Raw cotton yields have increased substantially in the past twenty years, reaching 25·1 centners per hectare in 1970.

Cotton is grown under irrigation in Central Asia and Trans-Caucasia, dominantly on the basis of

33. An efficient potato-picking machine developed by Soviet engineers is here seen lifting the crop on Lyubanskiy sovkhoz, Belorussia.

collective farming. Important areas are the Fergana Basin, the Tashkent district, the lower Amu-Darya, and the Zeravshan Valley. Uzbekistan ranks as the chief cotton producing republic – 4·7 million tons in 1972 – and currently nearly one-half of its investments in agriculture are being devoted to irrigation works, especially trunk canals and control headstocks. This will add 40,000 hectares of irrigable land. Other large investments are in fertilizer plants and the Tashkent agricultural machinery factory. Recently this factory began batch production of a new type of four-row cotton-picker.

Flax cultivation is concentrated in waterlogged soil areas of Belorussia, the Baltic Republics, in the southern margins of the Northwest, and in areas north and west of Moscow favoured by a cool, moist climate. The present harvest of flax fibre – all of which goes to linen manufacturing plants – exceeds 460,000 tons annually.

Hemp (which requires more warmth than flax fibre) is another fibre crop (needed by the rope-warping industry) which is grown in Belorussia and southern parts of the Centre (Kursk and Penza Oblasts). Due to the Soviet Union's need for jute for

34. Vineyards of the Alazan Valley, Georgia, produce grapes for some of the Republic's renowned vintage wines.

35. The Soviet Union has vast areas of hothouses or glass-houses for the cultivation of a wide range of crops, especially in the northern areas where the growing season is too short for outside farming. Shown here is the 36-hectare Moskovskiy sovkhoz near the capital – the largest single hothouse in the country – which supplies an aggregate of about 12,000 tons of tomatoes, cucumbers, radishes, and lettuces to the metropolis annually.

its grain industries it has made every effort to establish cultivation, especially following erratic supplies from India after the partition in 1947. Jute is now grown around Tashkent where a modern mill was set up in 1952. Recently new mills have been opened in Tadzhikistan, and these too are supplied with locally grown jute. Kenaf, another fibre crop, has been widely used in the Soviet Union as a jute

substitute. Hemp (for oil-seed) and kenaf are grown in the Chu Valley along the border between Kazakhstan and Uzbekistan.

4. *Oil-bearing Crops.* The chief oil-seed crops in the Soviet Union are sunflower, soya bean, linseed (southern flax = kudryash), castor-oil bean, mustard seed, ground-nut, sesame, and rape. In addition, the tung tree is widely cultivated in the sub-tropical Caucasus for its oil-bearing nuts. These yield an inedible oil widely used in industry, especially for steel hardening and paint-making.

Sunflower oil is used both for culinary and industrial purposes in the Soviet Union. It is planted in the drier steppe areas of the South Ukraine and North Caucasus and further east to Karaganda and Pavlodar. Altogether, some 5 million hectares are under sunflower; a five-fold increase since the early years of cultivation. Plant geneticists have succeeded in raising the oil-content of the sunflower seed to 50 per cent, thus effectively doubling the yield of oil per hectare. In 1971 the sunflower harvest exceeded 5·6 million tons – over two-thirds of the world production of this oil-seed.

Soya bean is grown in the sheltered valleys of the Far East where the crop is naturally acclimatized. Linseed, hemp for oil-seed, and the castor-oil plants are cultivated in the drier margins of the steppe lands and even in the semi-arid regions of the North Caucasus and Central Asia. Similar conditions are needed for the production of sesame seed, although yields are greatly improved under ground irrigation methods. The Soviet Union is not ideally suited to the cropping of ground-nuts but small quantities are grown in the summer rains areas of the sub-tropical south. Mustard and rape-seed are grown in substantial quantities in the northern temperate areas of European Russia. They are extremely useful to build up fertility and soil structure, and as a rotation crop in the agricultural system of small grains, a leguminous crop or fallow, followed by sugar-beet for some years, before being returned to a short-term grassland rotation.

5. *Sugar-Beet.* It might be surprising to learn that the Soviet Union ranks first in the world's production of sugar. In 1971, the sugar-beet harvest was greater than 72 million tons and this yielded in excess of ten million tons of raw sugar. Of this amount, 64 per cent came from the Ukraine

36. Cotton-picking machines harvest the crop on the '30th Anniversary of the October Revolution' kolkhoz in Surkhan-Darya oblast, Uzbekistan.

37. Storage stacks of cotton at the Gagarin centre, Surkhan-Darya oblast, Uzbekistan.

38. Newly established cherry orchards on the chestnut soils of Poltava oblast. (Photograph by the author.)

where numerous raw-sugar mills and refineries have been set-up since the war. Other important beet-growing areas are the Central Chernozem region, the Middle Volga lands and the Kuban in the North Caucasus. Moldavia west of the Ukraine has become a significant producer in post-war years. Production has even been pushed into the southern margins of Belorussia, but far more success has attended irrigated sugar-beet farming in Kazakhstan and Kirghizia.

6. *Fruit-Growing and Orcharding.* The Soviet Union for many years neglected the cultivation of fruit-bearing crops being content to leave this type of activity to individual collective farmers. This became an important use of their personal plots in consequence. In recent years, however, great effort has been expended in 'industrializing' the cultivation of all types of fruit-growing and orchards.

The collectives are now involved in the growing of citrus fruits – tangerines, mandarines, lemons, and oranges – in the sub-tropical areas of the Caucasus. Dates, figs, and olives are also well established on small areas of suitable land, especially around the oases of Kazakhstan and the Central Asian republics.

Again, in a twenty-year period the area planted in small fruits – strawberries, raspberries, currants, and gooseberries – has almost trebled. Cultivation is dominantly in areas of warmer temperate climate, and involves some four million hectares at the present time. Vineyards have also expanded very considerably, more than three-fold in fact, to give a total area under vines of more than 2 million hectares. Between 1961 and 1969 Soviet wine production increased from 8·5 million hectolitres to 24·0 million. Of this latter quantity, 6·1 million hectolitres came from the Ukraine, 6·5 million from Belorussia (Trans-Carpathia) and the balance from Moldavia, and the Trans-Caucasian republics in the main. Because the Soviet Union is not yet self-sufficient in orchard fruit – citrus, apples, pears, cherries, plums, apricots, and peaches – great effort is being made to expand the area planted. In the temperate areas very large orchard enterprises are being established, and urban labour and students are encouraged to participate in harvest fruit-picking as a part of their holiday programs. In the sub-tropical areas and in favoured locations in Kazakhstan, Central Asia, and the Crimea orchards of apricots and peaches have been established. The cooler sub-montane areas of the Altai and similar areas of Central Asia have many new plantings of pome-fruits.

7. *Sub-Tropical Crops.* A number of sub-tropical crops have been mentioned already, but there are others that merit attention. These include tea, tobacco, makhorka, sericulture, and rose cultivation. Kok sagyz and tau sagyz are latex-bearing plants cultivated to yield natural rubber, but the impact of the Soviet synthetic rubber industry is now diverting the semi-arid lands formerly used for sagyz cultivation to other crops and pastoral activities.

Tea plantations are located in favoured hill areas of Trans-Caucasia, especially along the Black Sea coasts and the Lenkoran coast of the Caspian Sea. Here, between 1940 and 1970, the area under tea plantation expanded from 55,300 hectares to 74,400 hectares. These yield high quality tea-leaf that is now entirely mechanically harvested. Each year about 240,000 tons of leaf are produced, processed into black or green tea in factories that dot the hills of the growing areas, and bulk-shipped to Soviet markets through Black Sea or Caspian ports.

Since natural conditions for tea-growing in the Soviet Union are not comparable with those of India or China, Russian plant breeders have given much attention to breeding varieties of tea suitable for the harsher Soviet climatic character. In tea, as in other crops, the names of I. V. Michurin and T. D. Lysenko are permanently linked with indefatigable trials to improve crop strains for Soviet conditions, although their genetic theories have been rejected by most of the world's leading geneticists.

Tobacco-growing in the Soviet Union is mainly confined to warmer areas of the south, Moldavia, the Crimea, the Black Sea Ukraine and the Caucasus, especially the Kuban and eastern coast of the Black Sea. Minor areas are found in the irrigated oases of Central Asia. Makhorka, a coarser variety of tobacco widely used in the Soviet Union, can tolerate cooler conditions and is grown along the steppe-land margins of the sugar-beet belt. The pungent, strong-flavoured makhorka is a robust flue-cured type of tobacco, while elsewhere Soviet tobacco is prepared as dark or light air-cured leaf. In the Central Asian areas and in some parts of the Trans-Caucasus, the leaf is cured in oriental style to yield a bright yellow aromatic tobacco favoured in some cigarette blends.

Trans-Caucasia and the North Caucasus are traditional areas for sericulture – the growing of white mulberry groves to support a silk-worm industry. Despite the dramatic growth in cellulose-based and synthetic fibre production in the last decade, the Soviet Union has retained its traditional silk-spinning and weaving industries; a prime example of historical inertia. The cacoons are first boiled to kill the larvae and then the silk filament is reeled preparatory to spinning into yarn composed of several filaments.

Another ancient industry of Trans-Caucasia is the cultivation of roses for the manufacture of attar and distillation of rose oil. These are primary ingredients in the perfume industry and the Soviet Union has developed a long-established and wide-ranging export of these commodities.

As suggested in the previous paragraphs, Soviet agriculture, although so significantly grain-oriented, really has an extremely diverse structure ranging as it does through industrial crops of many kinds.

8. *Animal Husbandry.* The post-war growth of the animal industries in the Soviet Union has shown a remarkable upward swing. In early 1972, the Soviet Union had 102·4 million head of horned cattle (including 41·3 million dairy cows and 61·1 million beef-type cattle) (Fig. 10.2). It also had at that time 71·4 million pigs, 140 million sheep, and 5·4 million goats. These figures may be compared with those given for earlier years in Table 9.3 above.

The current (ninth) Five-Year Plan (1971–75) calls for very sharp increases in animal products and will involve specialized and regionally concentrated branches of animal husbandry. Currently 1170 large state enterprises are being built for this purpose, and these will supplement the existing animal enterprises on state and collective farms to produce more beef, pork, milk, and milk products.

Between 1961 and 1970, cattle numbers increased by 23·5 million, including 8 million more

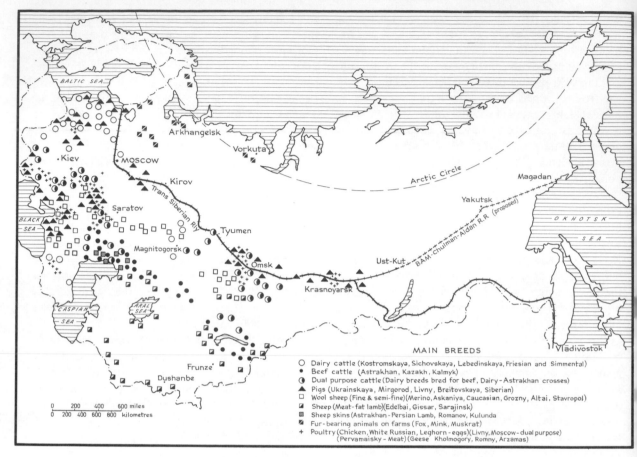

MAIN BREEDS

○ Dairy cattle (Kostromskaya, Sichovskaya, Lebedinskaya, Friesian and Simmental)
● Beef cattle (Astrakhan, Kazakh, Kalmyk)
◑ Dual purpose cattle (Dairy breeds bred for beef, Dairy-Astrakhan crosses)
▲ Pigs (Ukrainskaya, Mirgorod, Livny, Breitovskaya, Siberian)
□ Wool sheep (Fine & semi-fine)(Merino, Askaniya, Caucasian, Grozny, Altai, Stavropol)
◪ Sheep (Meat-fat lamb)(Edelbai, Gissar, Sarajinsk)
▨ Sheep skins (Astrakhan-Persian Lamb, Romanov, Kulunda)
◩ Fur-bearing animals on farms (Fox, Mink, Muskrat)
+ Poultry (Chicken, White Russian, Leghorn - eggs)(Livny, Moscow-dual purpose)
    (Pervamaisky - Meat) (Geese Kholmogory, Romny, Arzamas)

FIG. 10.2   Animal Husbandry in the Soviet Union: Main Breeds of Animals.

dairy cows. The main areas undergoing intensive developments are the western Russian Federation, Belorussia, the Ukraine, the Baltic Republics (both for dairying and beef cattle) and Kazakhstan (for beef cattle). The non-chernozem zone of European Russia is famous for various breeds of dairy cattle – the Kostromskaya, Kholmogorskaya, Yaroslavskaya high milk-yield breeds. While very considerable improvements in milk yields – 2300 kilograms per cow – have been made in the Soviet Union, improvements in beef-cattle breeding have been much less spectacular.

Pig-raising has been stepped up in the Russian Federation and the Ukraine; together rearing half of the current pig population of the Soviet Union. Other pig-raising areas are the Baltic Republics and Belorussia which together boast 40 per cent of the Union's pig population. Throughout these areas

modern piggeries with mechanized feeding and litter removal have been established. The main lines of future growth in pig-raising are to take place in these already established areas, with a consequent intensification of associated farming – fodder crops, roughage, etc. The raising of baconer pigs on the Danish model has been most spectacularly developed in the Baltic Republics. With their emphasis also on egg-production and poultry the Baltic zone of the Soviet Union is rapidly becoming a little Denmark.

Sheep-farming is confined to the drier areas of the Soviet Union. Kazakhstan, with about one-quarter of the Soviet Union's sheep population, and Central Asia are the most important regions. The Volga region and North Caucasus also have very substantial sheep numbers. The indigenous sheep of these regions yield poor-quality coarse wool, but they have considerable stamina and ability to subsist on poorer pastures. With the introduction of fine and semi-fine wool breeds – as indicated in Chapter 9 above – cross-breeds now have very much improved productivity. Merino-crosses are now suitable for the severe conditions of Siberia and northern Kazakhstan. Astrakhan sheep, indigenous to Uzbekistan and Turkmenistan, are now raised under considerably different climatic conditions in Moldavia without deterioration in the quality of sheepskins produced.

Stavropol sheep bred in the Ukraine and North Caucasus are notable for their fine wool and heavy fleeces. Whereas the mean fleece-weight per sheep in the Soviet Union was, until recently, only 3·3 kilograms, the Stavropol breed yields a super-fine fleece of up to 25 kilograms. Present wool production in the Soviet Union is 419,000 tons, thus placing it in second world rank after Australia.

Poultry farming is another branch of animal husbandry that has experienced vigorous growth in the last decade or so. The poultry population now exceeds 650 million head. The main areas are the Ukraine (more than 25 per cent of all poultry), the Baltic Republics, Belorussia, Moldavia, and the North Caucasus. The Centre also has a well-established poultry industry.

Among the hens the dominant breeds are the introduced Leghorn, and the Soviet breeds, Russian white, Pervomayskaya, and Moskovskaya. Ducks are also very popular in the Soviet Union with the indigenous breeds, the Zerkal'naya, Moskovskaya, and Ukrainskaya as the most common. The considerable goose populations are based on Soviet breeds, the Barkovskaya, Barovskaya, and Kholmogorskaya.

In addition to the collective and state poultry farms there are now two types of highly specialized farms: the large industrial poultry farms run on mechanized farming principles and the state-run suburban poultry farms geared to large metropolitan markets. The Brattsevo and Tomilino poultry farms near Moscow are excellent examples of the suburban type. These supply not only fresh farm eggs, but also refrigerated and frozen poultry to the Moscow markets. The large industrial poultry farms are usually state enterprises geared to egg and poultry–meat production for nationwide markets.

Minor branches of animal husbandry worthy of

39. The large dairying and fodder-growing enterprise at Olaine, Latvia. Here farm-produced green maize, fodder roots, small grains, and grass are converted to silage to support 2000 Latvian brown cows over the long winter months.

40. The Naberezhnye sovkhoz dairy-farm in Kustanay oblast, Kazakhstan. The farm is the production centre of a complex with 4500 Friesian dairy cows which yield more than 120 centners of whole milk and much butter daily.

passing mention are bee-keeping and fur-bearing animal farming. The use of apiaries has had a long and successful history in the Soviet Union. Main honey-producing areas are the southern steppes and forest steppes where natural vegetation and crops such as sunflowers and orchard fruit are associated with bee-keeping. Fur-bearing animal farming has developed rapidly since the 1960s. Breeding-minks of various mutations have been imported from Canada, Finland, and the Scandinavian countries to such an extent that there are now fears that the Soviet Union will become the dominant mink-farming nation. Since the fur trade is in large measure based on scarcity, Soviet motives have been suspected by other fur-farming countries, particularly those of Scandinavia. Similar, although less weighty fears, are held for other species of fur-bearing animals now bred in captivity in the Soviet North's farming system: various species of fox (blue, silver, red, and arctic), marten, sable, ermine, nutria, and kolinsky.

It is evident that the Soviet Union has a strong and powerful agricultural system, or rather series of land-use systems, which make effective, if not always the best, use of its climatic, soil, and vegetation resources. In recent years, these systems

have undergone rapid change, sometimes amounting to re-birth and re-vitalization of older, less well-formed systems. Such transformations, it would appear, must assist the country to serve the objectives of raising the standard of living for a growing population and also provide the necessary agricultural raw materials for burgeoning industry.

41. An apiary on the Michurin kolkhoz, Krasnodar Kray. The many mountainous areas of the southern Soviet Union produce honey for domestic and export markets.

42. Mechanized tea-picking on the Gal sovkhoz, Georgia. The farm produces about 1200 tons of fresh tea leaf annually.

43. The pig-fattening complex at Gatchino, south of Leningrad. It feeds 50,000 pigs and produces over 17,000 tons of pork annually. A dual organic-chemical fertilizer plant attached to the factory yields about 200,000 tons of complex fertilizer annually.

44. The pig-fattening complex at the Zavolzhskiy sovkhoz, Kalinin oblast. It runs 25,000 pigs and yields over 4500 tons of pork annually. Seen are the senior veterinary surgeon and two pig tenders discussing their charges.

45. Mechanized feeding on the Zakharovskaya poultry farm, Ryazan' oblast. It handles 240,000 hens which produce 35,000 eggs daily for Moscow and other markets of the Centre.

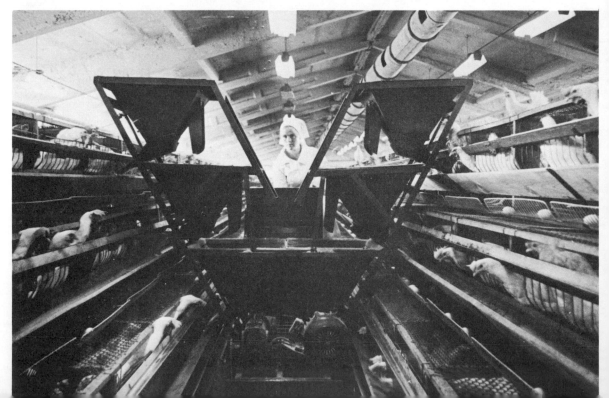

SOVIET INDUSTRIAL POLICIES

Soviet industry is the bell-wether of the whole national economy. Without a progressive development of heavy industry which creates the means of production and the power resources to project the economy forward, the Soviet Union could not have achieved its main aims. Also, in recent years, the industrial economy has rendered possible the implementation of policies for greater quantities and more variety of products from light industries thus improving the Russian standard of living immensely. If this has not yet placed the Soviet Union in the front-rank position among the world's leading industrial nations, it has at least created a strong and resilient structure to do so in the near future.

Some idea of the degree of progress over a thirty year period, 1940–70, is given in the following Table 11.1. Other indicators are given in the tables and discussion of succeeding sections of this chapter. In the five chapters that follow Soviet industry is discussed under the following headings:

Chapter 11   Soviet Industrial Policies
   „   12   Fuel, Power, and Energy Resources
   „   13   Metal Mining and Associated Industries
   „   14   Soviet Heavy Industries
   „   15   Light Industries and Consumer Markets.

Soviet industrial policies have shown some remarkable changes of emphasis during the 50 years of Soviet rule.

The basic problem facing the Soviet government and planning authorities is the fundamental differences between the western and eastern parts of the Soviet Union. In general, the European part of the country, containing 65 per cent of the population at present, is heavily settled. Its resource-base, however, is under strain and grossly over-extended. Many resources show signs of depletion after centuries of vigorous use. The Asian parts of the country on the other hand, and in particular, the Siberias, are virtually frontier lands with vast under-populated hinterlands rich in resources of many varieties. Oil and natural gas, coal (including coking coal), hydroelectric potential, iron-ore and non-ferrous metals have been found in great abundance. The planners' problem has been to marry the consuming potential represented by the dense populations and urbanization of the west with the production potential of eastern regions. A further problem concerns the distribution feasibilities of materials and products inherent in the remoteness of the eastern resource bases.

Over time, two contrary principles have become manifest. Stalin's government answered the east–west regional balance problem by encouraging, and sometimes forcing by means of compulsory labour, a west to east shift of population and industry. In part, this policy was a response to economic and strategic needs of the war years and their aftermath. These dictated a decentralization of consumption–production functions away from the European parts of the country and also attempts to ease a heavily strained transport system. In part also, the eastward shift was measured against time-honoured Communist doctrine; ideological–political decisions aimed at achieving balanced and proportional growth of industrial complexes and economic activities as a means of attaining equitable distribution for the benefit of the whole population. In the event, such a policy can rely heavily on the directed or quasi-forced movement of labour to those remote but resource-rich areas which the authorities wish to develop.

Since Stalin's time, however, strategic and ideological criteria in the redeployment of productive forces have become less important. Forced migration has now all but ceased, and the free interplay of market forces – albeit greatly modified to be acceptable to Soviet planners and theoreticians – has now arisen as a determinant in the location of production in relation to ultimate

TABLE 11.1
Soviet Heavy Industries Output, 1940–70

Industry	1940	1950	1960	1970
Iron-Ore (million tons)	29·9	39·7	106·2	195·5
Crude Oil (million tons)	31·1	37·9	148·0	352·6
Electric Power Generated (1000 m kWh)	48·3	91·2	292·0	740·4
Mineral Fertilizers (million tons)	3·0	5·5	13·8	55·4
Machine Tools (thousands)	58·4	70·6	154·0	202·3
Steam and Gas Turbines (1000 kW capacity)	972·0	2,381·0	9,200·0	16,191·0
Oil Industry Equipment (thousand tons)	15·5	47·9	92·8	126·6
Diesel Locomotives (thousand)	5·0	125·0	1,303·0	1,485·0
Electric Locomotives (thousand)	9·0	102·0	396·0	323·0
Lorries and Buses (thousand)	136·0	294·4	385·0	571·8
Tractors (thousand)	31·6	108·8	238·5	458·5
Looms (thousand)	1·8	8·7	16·4	19·8
Excavators (units)	274·0	3,540·0	12,290·0	30,974·0
Timber (hauled million m³) *	117·9	161·0	261·5	298·6
Cement (million tons)	5·7	10·2	45·5	95·2

Source: *Narodnoe Khozyaistvo, 1970,* Moscow, 1971.
  * Excludes farm production.

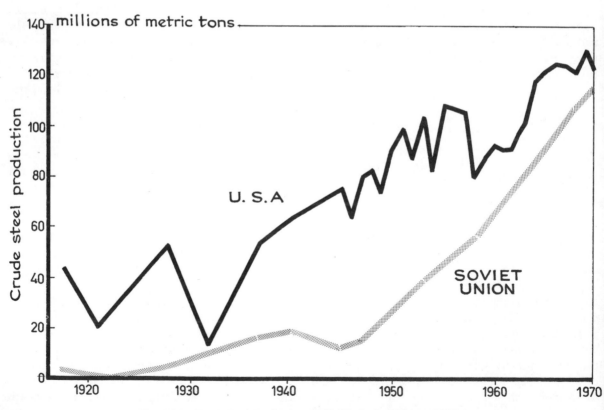

FIG. 11.1   Crude Steel Production, 1920–70, Soviet Union and U.S.A.

markets. For the future the growth of industry and economic activities in eastern areas will be increasingly organized on capital-intensive lines so that energy producing and raw material exploiting activities will concentrate on the most economic and most easily transported resources. Emphasis is to be given to improved transport technology, particularly pipelines and central-traffic-controlled diesel or electric railway systems. This, it is hoped, will permit energy, materials, and semi-manufactures to be transported efficiently from east to west. Under such an industrial policy the European parts of the Soviet Union will retain and expand their labour-intense branches of the economy, particularly light industries, agricultural processing, and the whole gamut of tertiary administrative activities almost indispensable to the smooth operation of centralized or command economies.

The development of the power resources of the Soviet Union is marked by a continuous increase in the production of coal, oil, and natural gas. It also embraces the widespread extension of a network of electricity generation in hydroelectric and thermal stations and the transmission of petroleum products through an inter-regional pipeline grid system. The emphasis on the use of electrical energy gives effect to the views held by Lenin and Stalin on the over-riding importance of this source of energy in promoting industrial advance and ultimately converting the country to Communism.

Before the 1960s, Soviet power resource policies were based on political and strategic criteria and never on strictly economic considerations. In its fuel policies the Soviet Union at first emphasized coal- and peat-fired electricity generating stations. But since World War II, oil and natural gas have become increasingly vital in the growth of Soviet energy production and capacity. These have now overtaken coal and hydroelectrical energy in terms of growth rates. The relatively late development of the petroleum branch in the Soviet Union, despite the fact that oil-working began at Baku, is due to many factors, but perhaps the most significant ones are: (1) Outmoded government priorities of the Stalinist period which relied on the exploitation of all fuel deposits irrespective of their quality and production cost status. (2) A somewhat feeble technology in petroleum mining and especially

distribution before World War II. Only during the 1960s has Soviet oil refinery and pipeline development matched that of other technically advanced countries such as the high-capacity oil and natural gas industries of the U.S.A.

Soviet authorities made the excuse that they had no need to develop petroleum resources early, since these are situated mainly in the eastern parts of the country. It was said that coal production under the control of a powerful Moscow Ministry was adequate to support the country's main industrial bases. While such rationalization has a measure of truth, the greater economy of oil and natural gas due to higher calorific values and ease of pipeline shipment were largely ignored until fairly recently. This is yet another example of the Soviet Union's failure to apply rational economic criteria to the underlying processes of its natural growth.

It is without question that the Soviet Union retained heavy emphasis on coal mining and often developed many too small, low-grade fuel production operations for far too long. The government policy of utilizing rather poor local resources of coal, brown coal, peat, and oil-shale in an effort to decentralize industrial growth and, at the same time, reduce transportation costs on fuel from major mining areas and thus relieve an overtaxed railway system, has proved an altogether unfortunate policy. Nevertheless the policy of using small and marginal fuel resources has had the effect of spreading industry to outlying areas served by a local fuel base.

The reliance on coal production in the Soviet energy economy was also partly motivated by the desire to promote the larger metallurgical centres, such as the Donets Basin (Donbas), the Urals, and the Kuznetsk Basin whose iron and steel industries needed coking coal for their blast furnaces. The coal-consuming industries are concentrated in a relatively small number of major mining centres. Notable industries are steel and chemicals. Soviet railways have always been involved in major coal movements. Of the Soviet railways' total freight movements of 1504 billion ton-kilometres in 1960, shipments of coal were its major component at 333·8 billion ton-kilometres, or 22 per cent of all traffic. In 1970 total freight movements rose to 2495 billion ton-kilometres of which coal was 449 billion or 18 per cent.

The re-assessment of the role of various power industries in the Soviet economy began in the mid-50s. The rise of Khrushchev to authority proved a catalyst in the decision-making that revamped the fuel policies of the Soviet government (Table 11.2). Widespread geological exploration following the opening up of the east during the war, revealed tremendous new resources of oil and natural gas. At the same time, Soviet planners became much more conscious of economic rationale. The local fuel policies of the past, often involving high-cost production, were abandoned as the relative advantage of transporting low-cost fuels to distant consumption points was realized. Also it was realized that the strategic dispersal of industry became less significant in an age of probable nuclear and ballistic missile warfare. Moreover, Soviet industry and particularly heavy industry had reached new and merit-worthy technological levels (Fig. 11.1).

TABLE 11.2
Fuel Balance Table*
(Percentage of Total Production)

	1932	1940	1950	1960	1970
Coal	49·6	58·3	64·5	50·7	35·5
Oil	28·7	18·5	17·0	28·7	36·6
Natural Gas	0·9	1·8	2·3	7·4	19·8
Peat	5·2	5·7	4·6	2·7	2·5
Oil-Shale	0·1	0·2	0·4	0·7	0·7
Firewood	15·0	14·2	8·8	6·8	2·3
Hydroelectric Power	0·5	1·3	2·4	3·0	2·6
	100·0	100·0	100·0	100·0	100·0

Sources: *Narodnoe Khozyaistvo, 1970*, Moscow, 1971, p. 183.

* Conversion to Standard Fuel units of 7000 kilogram calories (12,600 B.Th.U) for non-coal fuels, and kilowatt equivalent for hydroelectric power. Data for 1960 and 1970 hydroelectric power percentage added by author. The role of atomic power, now significant, is excluded.

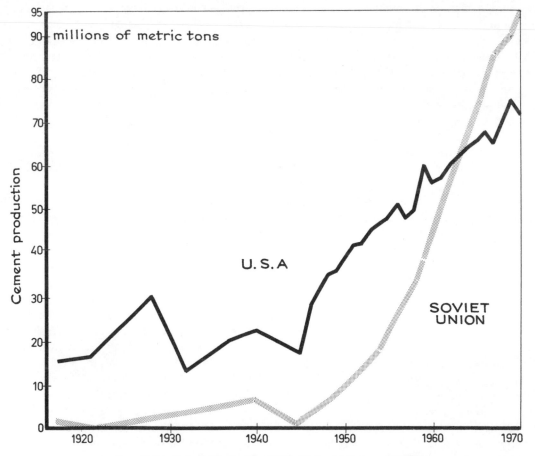

FIG. 11.2   Cement Production, 1920–70, Soviet Union and U.S.A.

Advances in the iron and steel industry rendered it capable of turning out large diameters of steel pipes required for the transmission of oil and natural gas. Also the new oil fields proved to be so rich that they quickly became industrial nodes in their own right. These new economic regions are referred to in the discussion of the Soviet oil industry in the regional chapters of this book. The construction industries too have experienced an upswing as evidenced by cement production (Fig. 11.2).

Another innovation of great significance is the swing to more capital-intense methods of production. Soviet industrial mechanization as well as automatic machine control are now adopted for all kinds of industrial plant. Such controls now manipulate virtually all of the blast furnace and steel furnace operations in the Soviet Union. Similarly all larger hydroelectric plants have automatic control. Open-cut coal-mining is also fully mechanized. Underground coal-mining and haulage, peat-cutting, timber-cutting and jinkering are also similarly highly mechanized.

In continuance of an earlier Soviet policy from the second Five-Year Plan onwards, far greater emphasis has been placed on industrialization of the Eastern areas of the country. In 1970 the eastern parts of the country (Urals, Central Asian Republics, Siberia, and the Far East) accounted for 51 per cent of all coal production, 25 per cent of the crude oil, 37 per cent of the pig-iron, 41 per cent of the steel and 41 per cent of the electrical energy produced, but they had only 35 per cent of the country's population.

CHAPTER TWELVE

FUEL, POWER, AND ENERGY RESOURCES

The industrial growth and transportation mobility of any country ultimately depends on its fuel, power and energy resources. Without these the intensification of production is just not feasible. The Soviet Union has experienced a three-and-a-half fold gain in its energy output between 1940 and 1970.

Coal. Coal production has continued to increase in the Soviet Union in absolute terms, although it has become relatively less important in the country's fuel economy (Table 12.1).

Coal production remains important in those branches of industry in which the direct use of coal is a vital component, such as in the iron and steel and other metallurgical industries and in some branches of the chemical industry, particularly the manufacture of dyestuffs. Whereas non-coking coal

output has been increasing at an average rate of about 3 per cent annually, coking coal has averaged nearly treble that percentage increase over the last two decades (Table 12.2). Further advances in coking-coal production, consonant with the expanding needs of iron and steel plants and non-ferrous smelters, are planned for the future. The distribution of Soviet coalfields is shown in Fig. 12.1.

The capacity of the coal-mining industry was raised by 13·3 million tons during 1969. This includes 9·5 million tons from R.S.F.S.R. mines, mainly those of the Kuznetsk Basin, and Kizel Basin in the Urals; an additional 0·9 million tons from the Donbas, and 2·7 million tons from Karaganda, and the new and rapidly expanding mining centre of Ekibastuz in Kazakhstan. Coking

TABLE 12.1
Coal Production (Black Coal) by Republics
(millions metric tons)

Coalfields *	1940		1950		1960		1965		1970	
R.S.F.S.R.	72·8		160·3		294·6		325·9		344·8	
European		21·6		58·1		90·2		91·9		99·0
Urals		12·2		33·0		61·3		61·6		46·8
Siberia		39·0		69·2		143·1		172·4		199·0
Ukraine	83·8		78·0		172·1		194·3		207·1	
Uzbekistan	...		1·5		3·4		4·5		3·7	
Kazakhstan	7·0		17·4		32·4		45·8		61·6	
Georgia	0·6		1·7		2·8		2·6		2·3	
Kirghizia	1·5		1·8		3·5		3·7		3·7	
Tadzhikistan	0·2		0·4		0·8		0·9		0·9	
Armenia	...		—		—		—		—	
Turkmenistan	...		—		—		—		—	
Total U.S.S.R.	165·9		261·1		509·6		577·7		624·1	

Sources: *Narodnoe Khozyaistvo, 1970*, Moscow, 1971, p. 188. Breakdown for R.S.F.S.R., *Soviet Geography*, various issues; for 1970, *S.G.*, **13** (5) 1972, p. 326.

* R.S.F.S.R. Europe includes Pechora, Moscow Basin, and Rostov Oblast sector of the Donbas; Urals includes Kizel, Chelyabinsk, Serov, and Bashkiria, and Siberia includes Kuznetsk, Eastern Siberia, and Far East.

Ukraine includes most of the Donbas, L'vov-Volynian, and Dnieper Basins; Kazakhstan includes Karaganda and Ekibastuz; Uzbekistan includes Fergana Valley and Angren.

coal production was augmented by the opening of Kazakhstan's No. 1 Tentek vertical shaft in the Karaganda coalfield.

In terms of tonnage capacity the Donets Basin, striding the Ukraine–Rostov Oblast border, still remains the most important source of coking coal in the Soviet Union; 79 million tons in 1969 against about 50 million from the Kuznetsk Basin and 17·4 million from Karaganda (see also Table 12.1). New bituminous coal mines were opened in 1970 in L'vov, Sakhalin, Voroshilovgrad, and Dnepropetrovsk, bringing total production to 624·1 million tons and 641·0 million tons in 1971. This level of production is about one-quarter of the total world output.

Since the late 1960s, open-cut mining of coal, using huge walking draglines to remove the overburden and coal, has become extremely common.

Such mines are located at Yerunak, Ekibastuz, Tash-Kumyr and Cheremkhovo (bituminous) and Irsha-Borodino, Raichikhinsk, and Aleksandriya (brown coal). At this stage about 25 per cent of all coal output is obtained by open-cut methods with consequent economies in production costs.

It is noteworthy, however, that the eastern centres are becoming more and more important for the production of coking coal with the passage of time; especially the Karaganda and Ekibastuz coalfields.

The same shift to the east is apparent for coal production in general (Table 12.1). Future plans for the year 1980 envisage a dramatic role for the eastern coalfields. For example, expansion plans announced in 1970 (*Pravda*, 9.3.1970) for the Kuznetsk Basin stipulate 180 million tons by 1980 against a 1969 output of 107 million tons. The

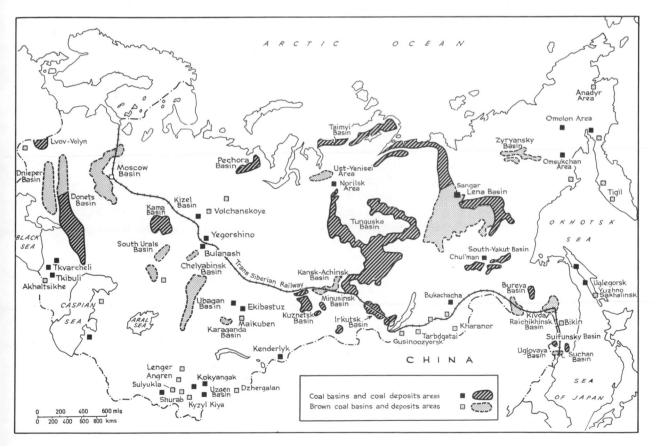

FIG. 12.1   Major Bituminous and Brown Coalfields.

46. The Bogatyr open-cut coal deposit at Ekibastuz, Kazakhstan. Here a giant 3000-tons per-hour rotary coal cutter works continuously 24 hours a day.

main capacity increase is to be achieved by opening up the Yerunak coking-coal deposit on the Tom' River, 20 miles northeast of Novokuznetsk. This will have two shaft mines and two open-cut mines with a total capacity of 32 million tons. The infrastructure for this project requires a new city of about 130,000 persons near the mine location. Following a world-wide trend, the Soviet coal industry is now paying increasing attention to open-cut mining even at considerable depths. Modern walking draglines of huge capacity make it possible to remove huge masses of over-burden quite economically.

Underground mining during the past few years has began hydraulic mining of coal. Powerful water jets break the coal from the seam and the mixture then passes to underground crushers. The coal-slurry is continuously pumped to the surface where the coal settles out ready for coking.

Modernization programmes are important, too. Many of the Soviet Union's older mining centres have adopted advanced forms of mechanical cutting, haulage, and winding in coal-mines. The Donbas has closed numerous older, difficult-to-work and depleted mines, more than compensating for the resulting loss of production by building modern, deeper mines further to the northwest where the coal lies deeper, concealed under younger strata. Similar action has been taken in the Vorkuta Basin where the harsh sub-Arctic environment has always rendered mining difficult and costly. Consolidation of the old No. 5 and No. 7 mines in the Ayach–Aga suburb of Vorkuta nearly doubled mine capacity to 2 million tons. The arc of mines running from Ayach–Aga north and west, 10 miles distant from Vorkuta, yields 14 million tons of coking and steam coal annually. This coal is transported 1000 miles by rail to the iron and steel

TABLE 12.2
Coking Coal Production by Location
(*millions metric tons*)

	1940	1950	1960	1965	1970
R.S.F.S.R.					
European (Kizel, Noril'sk)	0·7	2·7	2·6	2·7	2·9 (e)
Pechora Basin	—	0·2	3·8	4·7	5·0 (e)
Rostov Oblast	0·1	1·1	2·9	3·6	4·4 (e)
Ukraine	27·3	27·3	62·0	77·0	80·7
Kuznetsk Basin	5·9	14·9	28·5	38·0	53·0 (e)
Karaganda	1·3	5·5	8·3	11·0	16·9
Georgia	—	—	2·2	2·0	1·8
U.S.S.R.	35·3	51·7	110·3	139·0	164·7

Source: *Narodnoe Khozyaistvo, 1970*, Moscow, 1971, p. 188. R.S.F.S.R. breakdown added by author; 1970 estimated (e).

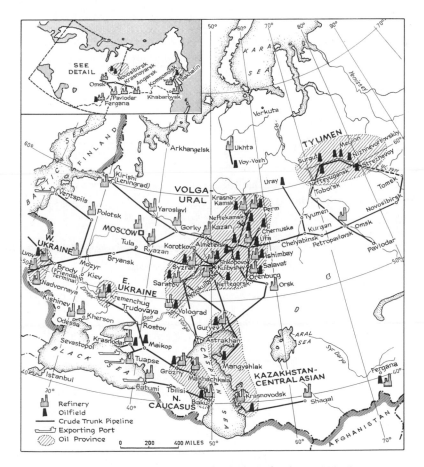

FIG. 12.2   Major Oil Provinces, Oil-fields, Refineries, and Pipelines.

centre of Cherepovets and also to Leningrad. Other outlying mines of the Vorkuta coalfield are at Khal'mer-Yu and Yun'yaga (Fig. 12.1). Expansion to take in the Vorgashor deposit is now under construction (1970) and will produce 4·5 million tons annually. A portion of the Vorkuta production is used in district heating; and a power station at Severnyy, 10 miles north of Vorkuta, supplies industrial and domestic electricity.

Another example of sub-arctic coal-mining is the Inta Basin coalfield, 150 miles southwest of Vorkuta. Here seven mines produce about 6 million tons of steam coal annually.

As in the case of black coal production, brown coal output has grown considerably over the last two decades. Principally this has been to serve coalfield power stations and sometimes on-site chemical complexes.

The West Bogoroditsk open-cut brown coal mine in the Tula Basin near Moscow has greatly increased its capacity in recent years. Essentially this is the result of a recovery programme designed to reconstruct the old Tula–Lipetsk brown coal-mining district. A peak production of 47 million tons was reached here in 1958, but thereafter declined as pipeline supplies of oil and natural gas reached Moscow and its satellite towns, thus causing a deliberate shift away from costly, low-grade brown coal won from underground mines. Now, however, a modernization programme involving complete mechanization of mining and haulage operations is planned for the brown coal areas of Tula, Ryazan', and Kaluga Oblasts. A start has been made by constructing new underground mines at Belkovskaya and Lipkovskaya resulting in a five-fold increase in the capacity of these mines. Overall district production for the coalfield power stations is to be stabilized at some 35 million tons annually. New plant includes two washeries (capacity 10 million tons each) to prepare the coal for efficient use in the power stations. Formerly operations were adversely affected by the high ash (32 per cent) and sulphur (3·6 per cent) content of Moscow district brown coals.

In the eastern regions also high priorities are given to the mining of brown coal. In Irkutsk Oblast the Azey open-cut mine, 10 miles east of Tulun, has reached an output level of 3 million tons annually. On completion of the planned coalfield power station, capacity will be increased fourfold. The Azey brown coal is an extension of the sub-bituminous coals of the Cheremkhovo coalfield now yielding 17 million tons of open-cut coal annually.

Another development, again characteristic of the U.S.S.R.'s on-going fuel requirements, is the Sakhalin brown coal open-cut mine at Vakhrushev, south of Poronaysk. The Lermontov mine here feeds a 750,000 ton-capacity washery that in turn feeds the South Sakhalin power station, the largest electricity works on the island. Altogether, Sakhalin Island produces about 5 million tons of coal annually, almost equally divided between black coal and brown coal.

Oil Developments. Oil developments in the Soviet Union have created a remarkable and swift redeployment of energy sources and contributed significantly to industrial growth (Fig. 12.2). As late as the mid-1940s Soviet oil production was still concentrated mainly in Azerbaydzhan and other regions of the South Caucasus. But during and immediately following the war, a dramatic shift in oil production eastward ensued (Table 12.3).

The Second Baku or Ural–Volga oil-fields between the Volga River and Ural Mountains greatly

TABLE 12.3
Crude Oil Production by Region
(millions metric tons)

	1940	1950	1960	1965	1970
Ukhta	0·1	0·5	0·7	2·2	3·1
North Caucasus *	4·6	6·0	12·1	20·7	24·2
Volga–Urals †	1·8	11·0	104·0	173·7	223·0
Azerbaydzhan	22·2	14·8	17·8	21·5	20·2
Ukraine-Belorussia	0·4	0·3	2·2	7·6	18·1
Kazakhstan	0·7	1·1	1·6	2·0	13·2
Central Asia ‡	0·8	3·4	7·4	11·8	16·8
Others §	0·5	0·6	1·6	3·4	34·0
U.S.S.R.	31·1	37·7	147·4	242·9	352·6

Source: *Narodnoe Khozyaistvo, 1970*, Moscow, 1971, p. 184;
   Breakdown R.S.F.S.R. 1940–65, *Soviet Geography*, March 1968: 223–24; *idem*, April, 1969, p. 210, *idem*, May, 1972, p. 324.

   * Groznyy, Krasnodar, Stavropol', Dagestan.
   † Tataria, Kuybyshev, Saratov, Volgograd; Bashkiria, Orenburg, Perm.
   ‡ Turkmenia, Uzbekistan, Kirghizia, Tadzhikistan.
   § Tyumen', Sakhalin.

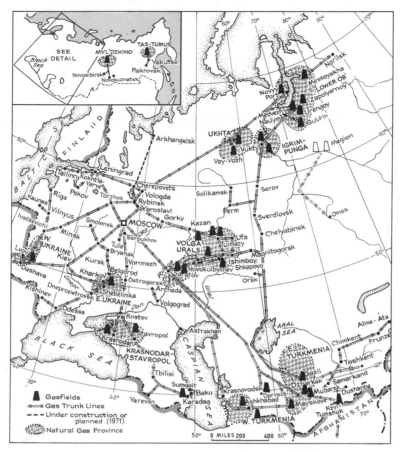

Fig. 12.3   Major Natural Gas Provinces and Pipelines.

accelerated production from insignificant pre-war levels. This province embraces four separate oil-fields: Samarska Luka (Kuybyshev), Tuimazy and Ishimbay (both Bashkir A.S.S.R.), and Perm' oblast. During the 1950s immense oil-rich provinces in Devonian and Carboniferous strata were opened up as new production oil-fields along the middle Volga, first in the Tatar A.S.S.R., then Bashkir A.S.S.R., and finally the treasure-trove of the Kuybyshev oblast (Table 12.4).

Soviet crude oil production reached 243 million tons by 1965, placing it in second rank as a world oil producer. Production for 1970 was 352·6 million tons. Over three quarters of the present production is contributed by the eastern regions, particularly the Volga–Urals oil-fields and the new Western Siberian oil-fields.

Even the vast resources of the Volga–Urals oil provinces, however, are now undergoing partial eclipse as tremendous developments take place in the Tyumen' Basin and around the city of Surgut on the middle reaches of the Ob' River in Western Siberia as well as the Mangyshlak oil-fields in the deserts of western Kazakhstan. Both of these petroliferous provinces occur in Mesozoic formations that have proved such prolific producers in the Middle East.

The various shifts to new oil-producing regions have meant that concomitant developments in refinery locations have occurred. It was also necessary for the Soviet planners to create an entirely new, high-capacity pipeline network. This network was constructed to link new oil-fields with refining complexes and also final markets for products. Crude oil production at first outstripped both Soviet refining capacity and also the means of transporting oil to market locations. As a short-term measure, Volga tankers and rail tank cars permitted excess

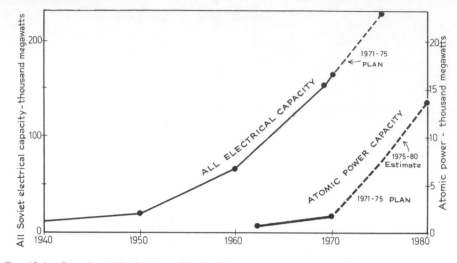

FIG. 12.4   Growth and Projections of Soviet Electrical Capacity and Atomic Energy, 1940–80.

TABLE 12.4

Crude Oil Production in the Volga–Urals District
(millions metric tons)

	Tatar A.S.S.R.	Bashkir A.S.S.R.	Kuybyshev Oblast	U.S.S.R. Total
1950	0·9	5·7	3·5	37·9
1955	14·5	14·2	7·3	70·8
1960	45·0	25·3	22·0	147·9
1965	76·5	40·7	33·4	242·9
1966	83·0	43·4	n.a.	265·1
1967	89·1	45·3	n.a.	288·1
1968	93·3	44·4	n.a.	309·0
1969	97·0	41·0	n.a.	330·0
1970	100·0	39·2	n.a.	352·6

Source: *Soviet Geography: Review and Translation,*
1970, p. 217; *ibid.,* 1972, p. 329.

refining capacity in Azerbaydzhan, particularly in
the Baku and Groznyy refining complexes, to
process shipments from the new sources.

By the mid-1950s a new and somewhat am-
bivalent policy in oil refinery location was begun.
Hitherto oil had been refined near the oil-fields, and
the products shipped to market areas by pipeline or
tank car. After several years, however, a conscious
decision by planners resulted in refining capacity
being built in or near major markets although substantial and large capacity refineries were built in
the Volga–Urals oil-source areas also (Table 12.5).
Crude oil brought in through large-diameter long-

distance pipelines proved much more efficient than
rail tank car shipment. Thus pipeline shipment has
proved a sensible and economical alternative following the new Soviet policy in refinery location
which replicates a world-wide trend to market
orientation. In consequence of these changes there
are few product pipelines in the Soviet Union, and

47. The Novopolotsk oil refinery and petrochemical plant,
Belorussia. The photograph shows the hydro-refining
installation.

those that remain are small in size and capacity, serving only the immediate environs of the refining centre. This is especially evident in the Volga–Urals oil-fields where major petro-chemical plants are now concentrated.

At present, Soviet refining capacity is limited despite recent growth. The lack is essentially in the more complex forms of refinery equipment needed for reforming, catalytic cracking and similar advanced processes. This shortage of refinery equipment affects not only the yields from crude oil of most useful fractions, but also the flow of supplies to the growing petro-chemical industries of the Soviet Union. This, in particular, affects styrene production, required for the synthetic rubber industry, as well as various plastic branches. Volga crude oils are especially in need of cracking to remove harmful sulphur impurities from products

TABLE 12.5

Distribution of Soviet Petroleum Refineries with Capacities in 1970 (millions of tons crude throughput per annum)

Region and City		%	Region and City		%
Volga–Urals		*30·5*	*Central Regions*		*7·6*
Kuybyshev ⎫	18·0	7·6	Moscow (Lyubertsy)	3·4 (e)	1·4
Novokuybyshev ⎭			Gor'kiy (Kstovo)	4·6 (e)	1·9
Ufa	18·0	7·6	Ryazan' (1960)	2·5 (e)	1·1
Novo-Ufa	5·0 (e)	2·1	Yaroslavl' (1961)	7·5	3·2
Ishimbay-Salavat	7·0	3·0	Novoyaroslavl'	n.a.	
Syzran'	7·0	3·0			
Perm'	6·6	2·8			
Krasnokamsk			*Western–Northwestern*		*10·2*
Saratov	3·6	1·5	Polotsk (1963)	8·0	3·4
Volgograd	5·0	2·1	Mozyr'	8·0	3·4
Orsk	1·8	0·8	Kirishi (Leningrad) (1966)	8·0	3·4
			Yurbarkas	n.a.	n.a.
Caucasus		*17·3*	*Ukraine*		*4·6*
Baku	21·0	8·8	Drogobych	1·0	0·4
Batumi	3·6	1·5	Kherson	1·0	0·4
Groznyy	12·3	5·2	Odessa	1·0	0·4
Krasnodar	1·2	0·5	Kremenchug	8·0	3·4
Tuapse	3·1	1·3	*Komi A.S.S.R.*		*0·4*
			Ukhta	1·0	0·4
Kazakhstan–Central Asia		*11·9*			
Gur'yev	4·9	2·1	*Siberia–Far East*		*17·5*
Krasnovodsk	6·7	2·8	Novosibirsk	1·0 (e)	0·4
Fergana	6·6	2·8	Omsk	22·0	9·5
Vannovskiy	1·8	0·8	Krasnoyarsk	2·0	0·8
Pavlodar	5·0 (e)	2·1	Angarsk	13·2	5·6
Chimkent	3·0 (e)	1·3	Irkutsk	1·0 (e)	0·4
			Khabarovsk	1·0	0·4
			Komsomol'sk-on-Amur	1·0	0·4
Sub-total	141·2	59·7		95·2	40·3
			U.S.S.R. Total	236·4	100·0

Source: L. Dienes, *The Soviet Chemical Industry*, Univ. of Chicago, Geography Research Paper, No. 119, 1969, pp. 90–91; up-dated by author.

that otherwise provide good quality diesel and distillate fuel oils.

Distances between oil-fields and market locations have meant that large-diameter pipelines have virtually replaced rail transport for crude oil in the Soviet Union. By 1971 trunk pipelines installed amounted to 38,400 kilometres; half of these began operation after 1960.

Crude oil production in the Soviet Union has increased by 15·7 million tons per annum over the last twenty years. The U.S.A. with a first rank production of 475 million tons in 1970, has increased at 10·4 million tons annually. Major new output in the Soviet Union is arising from the development of new resources of the Tyumen' oil-

fields of Western Siberia and the Mangyshlak oil-field of Kazakhstan. Production from the latter field rose 2·5 million tons to 8 million tons in 1969. Production at Mangyshlak now accounts for about 80 per cent of Kazakhstan's output.

A pipeline was built to connect the field with the Gur'yev refinery, since greatly expanded to handle the additional throughput. Currently the same pipeline is being extended to the Kuybyshev refining complex. In addition to the new distillation plant at the Gur'yev refinery, straight-run and reforming capacity now operates in refineries at Angarsk near Irkutsk in Siberia, Perm' in the Urals, at Kirishi in Leningrad Oblast and at Kremenchug in the Ukraine. Refinery expansion at Ryazan' and Yaroslavl' in European Russia is now completed. Further refinery extensions are currently taking place at Ufa in Bashkiria, at Kherson in the Ukraine, and at Polotsk in Belorussia (Table 12.5).

When the Psyol River refinery near Kremenchug was first built in 1961, it was intended to receive crude oil from the Volga–Urals oil-fields using a southern branch of the Friendship pipeline that supplies crude oil to Eastern Europe. The discovery and drilling of the oil-fields of the Dnieper-Donets Basin, however, provide an alternative source to serve the Kremenchug refinery complex without tapping Volga–Ural crude supplies. The Dnieper-Donets oil region produces nearly 70 per cent of the Ukraine's crude oil, the balance coming from the Dashava or western fields on the flanks of the Carpathians.

With the continuing expansion of production from the West Siberian and Mangyshlak oil-fields, a 650-mile, 40-inch pipeline has been built from Nefteyugansk, the main production centre in the Ust'-Balyk oil-field, via Demyansk on the Irtysh River to the Omsk refinery.

The Kirishi refinery completed in 1966 first used crude oil brought in by tank car from the Ukhta oil-field, but is currently served from the Tatar oil-fields by the recently completed Novoyaroslavl'–Kirishi pipeline.

The major pipeline link in the Soviet Union's entire network is the 2500-mile system transporting crude oil from the Tatar and Kuybyshev fields to East European refineries and serving Russian complexes *en route*. The main trunk, a 4500 kilometres long, 40-inch diameter link, is called the Trans-

48. The Novopolotsk oil refinery and petrochemical plant, Belorussia. Photograph shows the gas fractionating towers in the petrochemical combine.

49. The Perm petrochemical plant, western Urals, makes intermediates (propane, isobutane, and isopentane) destined for other Soviet plants making synthetic rubbers, plastics, and man-made fibres.

European Friendship (Druzhba) pipeline. It was opened in 1964 and crude oil now flows from the Volga oil-fields to refineries at Bratislava (Czechoslovakia), Szazhalombatta (Hungary), Pløck (Poland), and Schwedt (East Germany). Exports of 15 million tons of Soviet crude are made through the Soviet terminal at the Brody pumping installation near L'vov each year, and this will be raised to 50 million tons by 1975. Within the Soviet Union, the Friendship trunk line passes from Kuybyshev through Pensa, Michurinsk, Lipetsk, Bryansk, Unecha, and Mozyr'. In this last town it branches west and south. A northern link reaches the Baltic Sea at Ventspils (Latvia) via the Polotsk–Unecha extension from Mozyr'. The Friendship

system is now being expanded by adding a parallel pipeline. At the moment the network carries about 15 million metric tons of crude oil to Eastern Europe, virtually the whole of Soviet exports to the four countries concerned. But this is small compared with Soviet internal shipments of 340 million tons in 1971. In 1970, the Soviet Union exported a total of 95·8 million tons of crude oil or petroleum products.

An oil pipeline, 1760 kilometres long, now connects the Mangyshlak oil-field of western Kazakhstan to a refinery complex on the Volga at Kuybyshev. It has a throughput of about 12 million tons. Formerly Uzen', the main production point on the Mangyshlak oil-field, fed a pipeline to the

Caspian Sea port of Shevchenko. Here the crude was trans-shipped either to Volga-bound tankers or into rail tank cars for transport to the Gur'yev refinery via the new Shevchenko–Beyneu–Makat railway.

Oil production in Perm' oblast has greatly expanded with a noticeable shift away from the older northern portion of the oil province. New fields to the south, astride the Sverdlovsk–Kazan' railway, were recently opened up, especially around the town of Chernushka. Output from these fields quadrupled to 13 million tons in a period of five years to 1967. Production rose to 17 million tons in 1970.

Crude is transported over a 75-kilometre pipeline from Chernushka to Kaltasy in the neighbouring Bashkir A.S.S.R. Here it links into the existing network of pipelines from the new oil-fields of Neftekamsk in northeastern Bashkir A.S.S.R. Crude from these areas is refined at Ishimbay and Salavat.

The Arlan oil-field with a production of 11·5 million tons annually or nearly one-quarter of Bashkiria's output (46·8 million tons in 1968), is located near the Tatar A.S.S.R. The Arlan oil-field serves the Karmanovo electric generating plant (1·2 million kW) in northwest Bashkiria. Another oil-powered station at Zainsk reached 1·4 million kW with the existing seven generators and will eventually expand to 2·4 million kW when five new generators are installed as demand warrants. The oil-field's own thermal station at Novyy Zay southeast of Zainsk also has a capacity of 1·2 million kW.

With the discovery of oil in the Mesozoic strata underlying the Tertiary layers previously worked, the old oil-producing centre of Groznyy in the Northern Caucasus has undergone substantial revival. Both Groznyy and the oil centre of Malgobek have shared in the new exploitation, raising production from a low point of 2 million tons annually to about 16 million tons in 1968. New pipelines built from Malgobek terminal of the Groznyy fields serve the Donbas and Black Sea ports at Novorossiysk via Tikhoretsk and Rostov-on-Don. The new refineries in the Lisichansk district use crude oil from this source.

In addition to the transmission of crude oil, the Groznyy refinery itself has recently completed a new catalytic cracking unit, providing high-grade fractions for a developing petro-chemical industry.

The plant also yields hydrogen that is then recycled in the hydrogenation and other desulphurizing processes required to upgrade diesel and other heavy fuel oils for which the Groznyy crudes are particularly suitable.

The Volga–Urals oil-field terminal of Tuymazy (Bashkiria) formerly transported oil to refineries at Omsk and Angarsk near Irkutsk. With the opening up of the Western Siberian oil-fields in the middle Ob' Basin, however, the flow in this pipeline has now been reversed west of Omsk. Since 1967, this crude flows first to Omsk, then west to Petropavlovsk and Ufa, or east to the Novosibirsk and Angarsk refineries. It is planned that westward flows will provide considerable surpluses for transmission further west into the Central Region. Before the construction of the Siberian network, refineries at various points had to depend on tank car shipments which greatly congested the Trans-Siberian railway system.

The discovery and rapid development of the Ob'

50. The Gazli gas-field, Uzbekistan, has 122 wells which serve four collection–distribution points, one of which is shown in the photograph.

TABLE 12.6
Natural Gas Production by Region
(1000 million cubic metres)

	1940	1955	1960	1965	1968	1970
R.S.F.S.R.	1·4	4·5	24·6	64·3	78·4	83·3
European	1·4	1·7	14·6	62·5	65·3	70·0
Urals	...	2·4	9·4	1·2	4·0	2·3
Siberia	...	0·4	0·6	0·6	9·1	11·0
Ukraine	0·5	2·9	14·3	39·4	50·9	61·0
Azerbaydzhan	2·5	1·5	5·8	6·2	5·0	5·5
Uzbekistan	—	—	0·4	16·5	29·0	32·1
Turkmenia	...				4·8	13·1
Other*	...	0·1	0·6	1·2	1·0	2·1
U.S.S.R.	4·4	9·0	45·7	127·6	169·1	197·1

Source: *Narodnoe Khozyaistvo, 1970*, Moscow, 1971; 1965 and 1970, *S.G.*, **13** (5) 1972, p. 325.
   *Other: Kazakhstan, Tadzhikistan, Kirghizia.
   ... insignificant.
   — no production.

Basin's three separate oil-fields of West Siberia [1] made improved transport facilities essential. A 40-inch, 650-mile oil pipeline links the oil town of Nefteyugansk (formerly Ust'-Balyk) in Tyumen' oblast southwest of Surgut to the Omsk terminal and refinery. The pipeline runs southwest to Demyansk, across the Irtysh River to Vagay, south-east to Abatskiy on the Ishim River, and onwards to Omsk. Another 20/28-inch, 270-mile pipeline links Shaim and Tyumen'. A railway serving the oil-fields runs to Tobol'sk and Surgut.

Natural Gas Developments. Natural gas development in the Soviet Union makes it the pre-eminent industrial and domestic fuel in the country at the present time (Fig. 12.3). The use of natural gas for industry and domestic equipment has actually caused oil surpluses. Crude oil is thus increasingly available for export to Eastern Europe, Austria, Italy, Yugoslavia, France, Western Germany and Finland; a fact of considerable importance in the current world energy crisis. Of the Soviet total gas production of 181 billion cubic metres in 1969, 159 billion was dry natural gas, 20·5 billion cubic metres was oil-associated gas (condensate), and 1·7 billion was manufactured gas obtained from coal and oil-shale. Natural gas production rose from a mere 45·7 billion cubic metres in 1960 to 197·1 billion in 1970 (Table 12.6).

Official development plans given by the Ministry for the Gas Industry call for further expansion to a phenomenal 680/720 billion cubic metres by 1980. Such an enormous growth is premised on the known reserves of newly discovered and now developing natural gas-fields of Western Siberia (Tyumen' oblast mainly), Turkmenistan and the Ukraine. These account for more than half of the recoverable gas, estimated at 7·75 trillion cubic metres. The economic transmission of gas from these remote areas of Siberia to the central European parts of the Soviet Union and beyond requires large-diameter pipelines of 1220 mm–1420 mm (49 to 56 inches) diameter; new pipelines of twice this diameter are envisaged to secure very great economy of transmission costs. The balance of production will come from the Ukraine, western and southeastern North Caucasus, Tadzhikistan and Uzbekistan, already significant producing areas.

[1] (a) Shaim on the Konda River – production 4·7 million tons in 1970; (b) Nefteyugansk on the Ob' River – production 11·6 million tons in 1970; (c) Megion on the Ob' River (Surgut) – production 15·1 million tons in 1970; thus together producing 31·4 million tons of crude annually, nearly 9 per cent of the Soviet output. By 1971 production from this oil-field was 44·2 million tons.

Ross Guest (1967) indicates that plans call for the completion of 26,000 kilometres (16,250 miles) of gas pipelines. Although the problem of provision of large-diameter pipes has been overcome, so that the 1959–65 Plan goals were achieved, the Soviet Union now faces bottlenecks in the design and supply of compressors and control machinery. Nevertheless the gas pipeline network amounted to 67,500 kilometres in 1970, and this conveyed 181,500 million cubic metres of gas.

The Central Asian–Moscow–Leningrad natural gas 40-inch pipeline, completed in 1967, covers a distance of 2640 kilometres (1650 miles) and has a capacity of 10,500 million cubic metres per annum. This augments supplies already received by a 28-inch pipeline from North Caucasus. The pipeline, which opened in Moscow in October, 1967, and Leningrad some months later, transports gas from the Achak gas-field (northeastern Turkmenistan) and from Gazli (western Uzbekistan) in the Amu-Darya Basin. The Gazli gas-field, supplying about 80 per cent of Uzbekistan's total production, also supplies the Urals region by two pipelines opened in 1963 and 1965 respectively. To this was added the Bazay (Kazakhstan) gas production of about 1500 million cubic metres as it lies on the pipeline's routeway. Kazan receives natural gas by pipeline from Minnibayevo (Tatar A.S.S.R.) for a new petro-chemical plant concerned with organic synthesis.

In Western Siberia the sub-arctic natural gas-fields of the Punga-Igrim district were heavily dependent on the construction of pipelines to make their vast resources viable. The Punga-Igrim gas-fields south of Berezovo are now linked to Serov and Ivdel' in the northern Urals. Other gas-fields at Shaim, Okhteur'ye and Tazovskoye are undergoing rapid development.

Gas-fields in the eastern Ukraine at Shebelinka and Yefremovka, southeast of Khar'kov, and Vuktyl' field of the Komi A.S.S.R., 120 miles east of Ukhta, are also connected by pipelines with the Centre. The Shebelinka gas pipeline network is linked with Odessa, Kiev, Bryansk, and Ostrogozhsk. The two latter nodes connect into the Moscow gas pipeline network. A new 32-inch, 120-kilometre gas pipeline from Shebelinka links Slavyansk in the Donbas. It transports 4000 million cubic metres annually and supplements the 10,000 million cubic metres that the Donbas receives from Kuban in the Caucasus. The Yefremovka gas-field, 24 kilometres west of Shebelinka, is linked to Kiev through a 40-inch, 480-kilometre pipeline which was opened in December, 1969. This parallels the 28-inch line from Shebelinka, opened in 1962. Both pipelines together have increased capacity five-fold, providing Kiev with about 12,300 million cubic metres of natural gas annually. Altogether the gas transmission network for the Shebelinka–Yefremovka gas-fields has a capacity of 45,000 million cubic metres annually. Some gas is transported to Austria and Italy, thus representing the first gas exports, in contradistinction to oil exports, from the Soviet Union.

The Vuktyl' gas-field is the richest in the northern regions – reserves are put at 220,000 million cubic metres – and current production is about 8000 million cubic metres annually. Since 1968 Vuktyl' gas has been transported by a 56-inch to 48-inch, 1600-kilometre pipeline linking Ukhta–Rybinsk–Torzhok. At Torzhok this pipeline links into the northwest-bound Moscow–Leningrad trunk line, and then continues westward to Belorussia. A parallel 56-inch duplicate pipeline from Vuktyl' to Torzhok, now under construction, is a mark of this system's importance. A further mammoth 100-inch trunk line is planned for the future. This will connect with the Moscow–Leningrad gas network at Torzhok, and then continue eastward to Minsk. This 100-inch gas trunk line is due for completion in the early 1970s.

A 28-inch diameter, 300-kilometre natural gas pipeline has been built to serve the Noril'sk and Talnakh nickel–copper–cobalt–platinum complex (Fig. 12.3). This pipeline transports gas from the Messoyakha gas-field of northern Siberia. This energy source together with the Snezhnogorsk hydroelectric station on the Khantayka River is now beginning to replace the use of local bituminous coal in Noril'sk.

Since 1967 natural gas has been brought by the 20-inch, 400-kilometre pipeline from the Tas-Tumus gas-field on the Vilyuy estuary to the 100,000 kW gas-turbine generating plant at Yakutsk. The pipeline, which carries 500 million cubic metres annually, has now been extended to Pokrovsk. Such gas pipelines greatly assist the opening up of the Soviet Union's Far North.

51. The Novovoronezh atomic power station on the Don river has four nuclear reactors with an aggregate capacity of 1·5 million kilowatts.

The Achak gas-field in Turkmenia has greatly augmented Soviet production of natural gas. In December, 1969, a 20-inch, 480-kilometre gas pipeline linked the Mayskoye gas-field near Mary in Turkmenia to the city of Ashkhabad and also Bezmein. In Ashkhabad the gas is used in a new glass factory, and at Bezmein a 170,000 kW turbo-electric generating plant and a cement factory use the gas. The Mayskoye gas-field also powers a newly built 1,370,000 kW thermal power station at Mary. These developments supplement the Achak gas-field of northeastern Turkmenia to supply the Central industrial region through a gas trunk line opened in 1969.

The Oil-Shale Industry. The oil-shale industry at Kohtla-Järve in Estonia is now of little more than local importance. In 1968 the Kohtla-Järve to Leningrad, 20-inch, 330-kilometre pipeline formerly transporting oil-shale gas, had its flow direction reversed. Now natural gas flows from the Leningrad terminal to a synthetic ammonia-nitrogenous fertilizer plant located in Kohtla-Järve. Natural gas received by trunk pipelines in Leningrad has a much higher calorific value than oil-shale gas. The latter, however, will continue to be produced; then, admixed with natural gas from Leningrad, it will be transported eastward by double pipelines to Tallin on the Baltic.

Minsk in Belorussia receives gas by pipeline from the northwestern gas-fields of Siberia. This greatly supplements supplies obtained from the Dashava (Ukraine) gas-fields since 1960. In the larger cities, especially Minsk and Gomel', natural gas and liquefied petroleum gases have become important generating and domestic fuels. They are now displacing the local peat-fuel and long-haul bituminous coal, previously the mainstay of industrial and domestic usage. Throughout Belorussia as a whole natural gas now supplies 20 per cent of the energy requirements, and this proportion is likely to reach 60 per cent in the 1970s.

Atomic Energy. The Soviet Union has made considerable progress in the development of atomic energy (Fig. 12.4). Nuclear power stations have been built at many different locations, and some are very large capacity plants (Table 12.7). The Soviet

52. The Beloyarsk atomic power station, Sverdlovsk oblast. This plant has recently commissioned a 600,000-kilowatt fast breeder reactor bringing aggregate capacity to 900,000 kilowatts.

Union also has atomic-powered ice-breakers including the 'Lenin' that keeps the Northern Sea Route free of ice-blockage and open for navigation for some five months of the year. The Soviet Navy has numerous atomic submarines also, and reportedly nuclear propulsion for surface vessels, military aircraft and rockets are under investigation.

The Novovoronezhskiy nuclear power plants, situated on the Don River just south of Voronezh in the Central Region, added a second reactor unit of 375,000 kW capacity in December, 1969 and two 440,000 kW units in 1971. These, like their predecessors, are of the pressurized light water type. Over the years, the Soviet Union has accumulated sufficient technical experience so that the authorities have now standardized a satisfactory design for a 440,000 kW nuclear reactor unit that can be batch-produced. These are now being built to supplement hydroelectric and thermal power stations in the Soviet's growing electrical power system. As indicated, two such standard units have

been added to the central Novovoronezh atomic power plant, giving a total capacity of 1·5 million kW, thus making it the largest single nuclear power station in the Soviet Union. Since the date of the above table, the Leningrad nuclear power station (one million kW capacity) and new atomic power stations at Yerevan, Armenia, and on the Kola Peninsula have been commissioned. Other nuclear power plants are being constructed at Kursk (Russian Federation) and also at Chernobyl, north of Kiev, in the Ukraine. The Siberian multi-unit atomic plant, believed to be in the neighbourhood of Irkutsk, is not indicated in Russian sources as it produces plutonium used in the manufacture of nuclear missiles. Another new atomic power station is located at Ust'-Kamenogorsk in the Altai mountains and there are plans for yet others at Smolensk and in the Ukraine at a site yet to be selected under the current 1971–75 Five-Year Plan. Two small atomic power stations are now operating at Melekess (Volga) (50 MW) and Bilibino in the northeastern Siberian goldmining centre (48 MW). Uranium, suitably enriched for use in atomic power plants is obtained from Taboshar, southeast of Tashkent; Andizhan in the Tynya-Muyan mountains; Slydianka near Lake Baykal; the Kolyma River, from Krivoi Rog (Ukraine) and southern Armenia.

Electric Power Generation. The rate of growth of electric power generation in the Soviet Union has been nothing less than spectacular. Between 1960 and 1970 the quantity of power generated rose from 292,000 million kWh to 740,000 kWh and reached 800,000 million by 1971. Such an achievement has been made possible by the continuing installation of new power stations – thermal, hydroelectric and atomic – and the upgrading of existing plants by installing new generating capacity.

In 1970 alone, new power stations were commissioned at Grodno (Belorussia), in Estonia, in Murmansk oblast, in Stavropol' Kray and in Vladivostok (Far East). Some of the largest thermal power stations have a rated capacity of 2·4 million kW, comprising eight turbo-generators of 300,000 kW each. Mammoth generators of 500,000–800,000 kW capacity and even a single unit of 1,200,000 kW have been installed or are currently under construction. At the present time, thermal

TABLE 12.7
*Major Soviet Nuclear Power Stations (as at June, 1970)**

Location	Output MW†	Type	State
Siberia	600	PW	operating
Novovoronezh-1	240 (280)	PW	operating
Novovoronezh-2	365 (375)	PW	operating
Beloyarsk-1	94	BW	operating
Beloyarsk-2	200 (600)	BW	operating
Shevchenko BN 350 (Desalination)	150 (350)	F	under construction (op. 1971)
BN 600 (site undisclosed)	600	F	under construction (op. 1971)
Kola	400 (440)	PW	under construction (op. 1971)
Novovoronezh-3 + 4	880	PW	committed (op. 1971)
Oktomberyan-1 + 2	880	PW	under construction

* These are all large 'commercial' type stations; numerous smaller capacity nuclear stations, mainly for experimental purposes, exist.
† 1974 figures in parenthesis.

PW = Pressurized light water type
BW = Boiling light water type
  F = Fast breeder type

Total capacities by type (June, 1970):

(6) PW 3365 MW (operating, under construction or committed)
(2) F   750 MW (under construction)
(2) BW 294 MW (operating)

Source: Australian Atomic Energy Commission. *Annual Report, 1969–70*: 21–25.

power stations account for 80 per cent of all electricity production, and utilize various raw materials for their fuel sources: coal, oil, natural gas, peat, and combustible shale. Examples of thermal plants recently commissioned are given in Table 12.8.

From the foregoing discussion it is apparent that the Soviet Union is capable of harnessing power resources at a very considerable rate (Fig. 12.4). During 1971 a total generating capacity of 12·3 million kW was commissioned giving the Soviet Union an aggregate operating capacity of 190 million kW from all electrical energy sources. Most of the growth in power generation has occurred in the European parts of the Russian Federation, the Ukraine, and the Urals (Table 12.9).

Hydroelectric power in the Soviet Union is mainly developed on the Dniester, Western Dwina, Neman, Volga, Irtysk, Ob', Angara, Yenisey, and on the rivers of Trans-Caucasia and Central Asia. On the Volga, there are now seven giant hydroelectric

TABLE 12.8
Major Recent Generating Plants in the Soviet Union

Name	Location	Units Added (No.)	Unit Rating (kW)	Present Capacity (million kW)
Kirishi	Leningrad	1	300,000	1·35
Kostroma	Centre	1	300,000	1·5
Karmanovo	Bashkiria	1	300,000	1·2
Novocherkassk	Rostov	1	300,000	2·1
Iriklinskiy	Orenburg	1	300,000	0·9
Reftinskiy	Sverdlovsk	2	300,000	0·9
Ladyzhin	Ukraine	5	300,000	1·8
Slavyansk	Ukraine	1	800,000	2·0
Tripol'ye	Ukraine	1	300,000	1·5
Lukoml'	Belorussia	2	300,000	1·5
Kishinev	Moldavia	1	200,000	1·6
Tbilisi	Georgia	1	n.a.	1·12
Narva	Estonia	1	n.a.	1·0
Kaunas-Vilnius	Lithuania	1	300,000	1·5
Tashkent	Uzbekistan	1	160,000	1·92

Source: *Soviet Geography*, **13** (5) 1972, pp. 326–27.

TABLE 12.9

Geographical Distribution of Electricity Output

(1000 million kilowatt-hours)

	1940	1950	1960	1965	1970	Growth 1950–70(%)
R.S.F.S.R.	30·8	63·4	197·0	333·0	469·0	639·7
of which:						
European	21·6	35·2	104·0	170·0	250·0	610·2
Urals	6·1	18·1	49·0	76·0	87·0	380·7
Siberia	3·1	10·1	44·0	87·0	132·0	1206·9
Ukraine	12·4	14·7	54·0	95·0	138·0	838·8
Moldavia	...	0·1	0·7	3·1	7·6	7500·0
Belorussia	0·5	0·7	3·6	8·4	15·1	2057·1
Baltic	0·3	1·1	4·8	12·4	21·7	1872·7
Trans-Caucasia	2·9	5·2	13·0	19·3	27·1	421·1
Kazakhstan	0·6	2·6	10·5	19·2	34·7	1234·6
Central Asia	0·7	3·3	8·9	16·8	26·8	712·1
U.S.S.R.	48·2	91·1	292·5	507·2	740·0	712·3

Sources: *Narodnoe Khozyaistvo, 1970*, Moscow. 1971, p. 180; *S.G.*, **13** (5) 1972, p. 326; Shabad, *Basic Industrial Resources of the U.S.S.R.*, p. 32.

power plants – some multi-purpose in that they provide not only power, but also irrigation systems for agriculture and improved navigation. The 'Lenin' and '22nd CPSU Congress' Hydropower Stations of 2·3 million kW and 2·5 million kW capacity respectively are the largest situated at Kuybyshev and Volgograd. Another at Cheboksary is under construction (1·4 million kW capacity).

In Asia, the two stations on the Angara river, the Bratsk and Ust'-Ilimsk Hydropower Stations of 5 million kW and 4·5 million kW respectively are among the world's largest, far surpassing the United States' Grand Coulee dam on the Columbia river (1,947,000 kW capacity). But even the Angara scheme is to be overtaken by Soviet hydroelectric power developments on the mighty Yenisey river. Here the Krasnoyarsk hydroelectric station (6·0 million kW capacity) has recently opened and two further plants, the Yenisey and Sayan – each again of 6·0 million kW capacity – are planned.

All of the electrical power developments in the Soviet Union would not make sense were it not for the construction of immense high-voltage grid networks to link together the various generating plants and the main industrial regions. The unified network of transmission lines of the European Soviet Union links into a single system over 600 thermal, hydropower, and atomic stations, with an aggregate capacity of about 110 million kW. Power plants in the Urals, Western Siberia, and Trans-Caucasus are being progressively linked to the European power grid. Other unified power networks are also being established in Siberia and Central Asia. Ultimately the aim is for a unified power grid to embrace the whole of the country from the western frontiers – and from the COMECON countries beyond – to the Far East.

CHAPTER THIRTEEN

METAL MINING AND ASSOCIATED INDUSTRIES

The Soviet Union is fortunate in having a number of important metallogenic provinces most of which occur in proximity to crystalline shields deep within the earth's crust. The principal provinces are:

(1) The Kola–Karelian Shield (iron-ore, nickel),
(2) The Southern Ukraine and Centre (iron-ore, uranium and manganese),
(3) Caucasus (copper, molybdenum),
(4) The Urals (iron-ore, copper, chromium, nickel, aluminium, titanium, gold),
(5) Kazakhstan (iron-ore, copper, lead-zinc-silver, aluminium, tungsten, molybdenum),
(6) The Far East (gold, tin, lead and other poly-metallics).

Iron-Ore

The Soviet Union's iron-ore resources are calculated at around 100,000 million tons. They are located mainly in the European part of the country. The Centre and Central Chernozem districts account for 24·5 per cent of the total known reserves; the Ukraine for 29·5 per cent, and the Northwest for 3·6 per cent, making up about 60 per cent of total industrial-quality iron-ore reserves. The Urals (16·4 per cent), Kazakhstan (15·5 per cent) and Siberia and the Far East (10·5 per cent) account for the balance. Distribution of these iron-ore resources together with those of coking coal and manganese – all inputs for the iron and steel industry – are shown (Fig. 13.1).

Estimates of these resources are based on four categories of reserve: A, B, C_1, and C_2. These range from detailed geological information usually based on mining operations (A), through less detailed data for categories B and C_1, to inferred reserves of type C_2. It is therefore probable that lesser explored areas of Siberia, the Far East, and Central Asia may yet hold substantial treasures of iron-ore and other metals. Geological prospecting and modern geochemical explorations are considerable in the remoter, under-surveyed areas of the Soviet Union at the present time.

The European Iron-Ores

The European production of iron-ore comes mainly from the Krivoy Rog Basin, the Kursk Magnetic Anomaly (KMA); the Kerch Peninsula, and various newly exploited areas (Table 13.1).

Krivoy Rog has two qualities of iron-ore. The rich, high-quality ores are won by shaft-mining at around 300 metres' depth, although some mines reach 1000 metres. The leaner ores of magnetite-quartzites are produced from open-cuts, and are then concentrated ready for sintering plants. Most of this production comes from shaft mines.

The Kursk Magnetic Anomaly embraces several centres in the Central Chernozem region: Belgorod, Orel, Bryansk, Voronezh, and Kaluga. The main mining areas in the 600 kilometre by 40 kilometre wide KMA deposit are the Orel–Valniki zone and the Volchansk–Shablykino zone. The thickness of the ore-body varies from 40 metres in the north central part to 350 metres in the southern part. The rich ore contains 55–62 per cent iron, while the quartzites yield 32 per cent iron. Production is currently around 12·0 million tons annually.

The historic Tula–Lipetsk iron-ore deposits are now of comparatively little importance having been over-shadowed by the KMA workings.

Kerch Peninsula in the Crimea has large reserves of low grade hematite iron-ore. These ores, located at Kamysh-Burunskoye, contain 28–39 per cent iron and considerable manganese, vanadium, phosphorus, and arsenic. They therefore require dressing and concentration before they can be used in steel-making. The phosphorus slag by-product is used as a fertilizer.

Newer Iron-Ore Workings

Yena-Kovdor, Kirovogorsk, and Olenegorsk magnetite deposits are located on the Kola Peninsula near the Murmansk railway. Other iron-ore deposits (ferruginous quartzites) occur at Pudozhgorsk, Mezhoyorskoye and Kostamukshskoye in Karelia. Although low-grade, these

TABLE 13.1

Soviet Iron-Ore Mining by Regions (millions metric tons)

	1940	1950	1960	1965	1970	Growth 1960–70 (%)
R.S.F.S.R.	9·7	18·7	39·7	54·1	64·7	63·0
of which:						
European*	1·1	1·0	6·4	18·4	25·7	301·6
Urals†	8·1	15·5	27·3	27·5	26·2	−40
Siberia‡	0·5	2·2	6·0	8·2	12·8	113·3
Ukraine§	20·2	21·0	59·1	84·1	111·2	88·2
Azerbaydzhan	—	—	1·3	1·5	1·4	7·8
Kazakhstan‖	—	—	5·8	14·1	18·2	213·8
U.S.S.R.	29·9		105·9	153·8	195·5	84·6

Sources: Shabad, *op. cit.*, p. 36; *S.G.*, **13** (5) 1972, p. 322.

* Includes: Kola, Tula-Lipetsk, and Kursk Magnetic Anomaly.
† Includes: Magnitogorsk, Beloretsk, Kachkanar, Lys'va, and others.
‡ Includes: Kuzbas area and Zhelenogorsk.
§ Includes: Krivoy Rog and Kerch (Crimea).
‖ Includes: Rudnyy and Karazhal.

ores are easily dressed and, like the Kola Peninsula ores, now serve the Cherepovets iron and steel mills.

The Dashkesan magnetite iron-ore workings of Azerbaydzhan are located 35 kilometres southwest of Kirovabad and serve the Rustavi iron and steel mills. Cobalt lenses are disseminated in these iron-ore beds and yield a useful joint product. Mining is by open-cut methods.

The Iron-Ore Deposits of the Eastern Areas
The Urals. Numerous deposits of iron-ore are found in the Ural Mountains, the oldest iron-working centre in the Soviet Union. Stretching along the flanks of the Urals, major deposits occur at Bogoslovsk and Severniye Rudniki in the north; at Kachkanar, Tagil-Kushva and Alapayevsk in the centre, and at Bakal, Zigazino-Komarovskoye, Orsk-Khalilovo and the Magnitnaya groups in the south (Fig. 13.1).

The northern Urals or Sverdlovsk District deposits are magnetite-hematite iron-ores with a 37–58 per cent iron content. The upper beds of these deposits are worked by open-cut methods. The Bogoslovsk sector, however, involves both shaft and open-cut mining at Auerbakhovskoye, Vorontsova, and Pokrovskoye. Recently new

deposits were opened up at Severo- and Novo-Peschansk. These iron-ores, like other northern workings, supply lump ore or concentrates to the Serov iron and steel mills.

The central Urals, or Tagil-Kushva District deposits, include ores with 32–55 per cent iron content. The major mining areas, using open-cut and shaft mining, are at Blagodat, Vysokaya, and Lebyazhiya, while to the north, the Kachkanar group of deposits are poor quality vanadium–titanium–magnetites. However, these occur in huge volume so are easily mined by open-cut and massive blasting methods and provide first-rate sintering material when adequately dressed before shipment. Careful milling and concentration is necessary, however, to remove excessive amounts of sulphur and phosphorus. The central Urals iron-ores serve the Nizhniy Tagil, Kushva, Nizhnyaya-Salda, and Chusovskoy iron and steel centres.

The Alapayevsk ores are brown hematites which have been worked for centuries and are now facing exhaustion. To a degree, the Alapayevsk ores are being replaced by the dressed vanadium–titanium–magnetites from the Pervouralsk, Visim, and Kusa mining areas. These too serve the Chusovskoy iron and steel works.

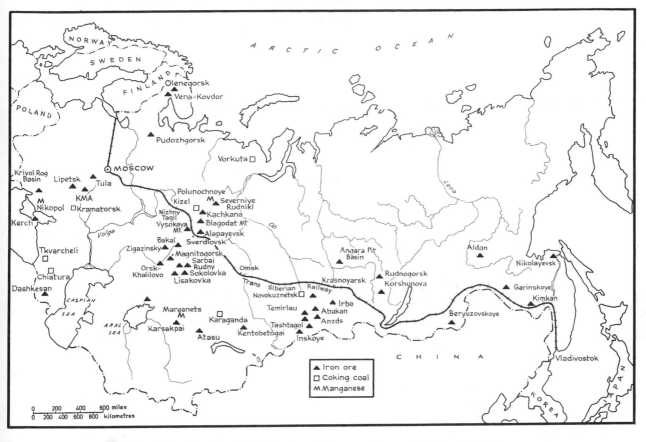

FIG. 13.1 Iron-Ore, Coking Coal, and Manganese Sources in the Soviet Union.

The Bakal group iron-ores include both siderites and brown hematites, averaging 32 per cent and 45 per cent iron respectively. The manganese content of these ores is good, and they are also low in deleterious impurities. They serve the Chelyabinsk iron and steel works as well as the Satka and Asha plants.

The best-known Ural iron-ore deposit is that at Magnitogorsk in the southern Urals because of its long association with the Urals–Kuzbas iron and steel Kombinat. The complex, high-quality ores are now practically exhausted. Although production in 1970 was still running at some 15 million tons annually, output will be phased out shortly. In future, the ore requirements of the Magnitogorsk iron and steel works will come from the Kustanay District (Ayat and Lisakovka deposits).

The Orsk-Khalilovo group of iron-ores occur at Novo-Kievskoye and Akkermanovskoye. These are

characterized by their high content of chromium, nickel, and cobalt, and consequently high-alloy steels are produced in the Orsk-Khalilovo iron and steel works.

Newer Eastern Areas. Extensive deposits of iron-ore occur in Kazakhstan, the Siberias and the Far East. Some have been of considerable importance in the Kuznetsk iron and steel industry for about 40 years, but others are the outcome of recent and more intensified prospecting. The most important iron-ore mining districts are: Lisakovka (Kazakhstan), Atasu (Karaganda), Auzas (Krasnoyarsk Kray), Abakan (East Siberia), and South Aldan (Southern Yakutia). These are shown in their appropriate groupings on the distribution map (Fig. 13.1).

Non-Ferrous Metals

The distribution of non-ferrous metal ores in the

53. A test drilling rig on the Kursk Magnetic Anomaly (iron-ore body) near Belgorod. (Photograph by the author.)

Soviet Union is of the greatest importance. First, modern industrial technologies demand greater and greater quantities of base metals like copper, lead, zinc, tin; the light metals, aluminium, magnesium, and titanium, as well as modern requirements of the steel industry, such as the ferro-alloys, manganese, tungsten, nickel, chrome, cobalt, and molybdenum. In addition to requirements of these metals, somewhat lesser quantities of rare metals have become essential to certain special technologies: tantalum and columbium for space-flight; radium and other radio-isotopes in medicine and scientific research.

Secondly, the actual geographical distribution of all of these non-ferrous metals is important in relation to the existing centres of industry. Sometimes ores contain only 2–3 per cent of the wanted metal, and in disseminated-type ores, often less than 0·5 per cent. Thus economic working of physically remote deposits, or even of deposits not convenient to an existing transport network, may be impossible. Frequently, to be viable, deposits need concentration; sometimes smelter operations in the immediate vicinity of the mines are essential. The Soviet Union has an enviable record both in the use of remote ore-bodies and also in the creation of beneficiation, concentration, or pelletization plants established near deposits to reduce transport costs to a minimum.

Sulphuric acid, obtained as a by-product of smelting, and always difficult to transport, is sometimes used directly in nearby superphosphate plants, as in the case of the Krasnoural'sk and Revda smelters in the Urals and the Almalyk plant in Central Asia. However, those plants are exceptions, for the trend to higher strength phosphatic fertilizers is having the effect of drawing fertilizer plants towards the sources of apatite rock in the Kola Peninsula and also towards the market-oriented copper smelters which ship out acid to fertilizer plants in tank cars.

Ferro-Alloy Metals. The Soviet Union has perhaps the greatest endowment of ferro-alloying materials of any nation in the world. Metals such as manganese, chromium, nickel, vanadium, tungsten, molybdenum, cobalt, antimony, and other ferro-alloys add variously strength, hardness, resilience, toughness, rust-resistance, magnetism, and other useful properties to steel. In general, each alloying metal is required in relatively small quantities, but since Soviet ingot steel production is now running at some 91·0 million metric tons annually (1965) – 121 million tons in 1970 – ferro-alloys are needed in considerable tonnages.

The main locations for the production of ferro-alloy ores in the Soviet Union are shown below (Table 13.2). These have been grouped under principal metallogenic provinces of the Soviet Union; the western regions, the Caucasus, the Urals, Kazakhstan, and certain outlying prospects and mines.

Ferro-alloy metals such as ferro-manganese, ferro-chromium, ferro-nickel, ferro-tungsten and others are often made in specialized smelters, virtually small blast furnaces, such as those located at Monchegorsk (Kola Peninsula), Pobugskoye (Ukraine), Orsk (South Urals) and Verkhniy Ufaley, and Rezh (both Central Urals). These smelters produce the metal required either in the form of matte, often in combination with iron, or as a metal-bearing slag. Such crude ferro-alloys require further treatment in electric furnaces not infrequently associated with cheap hydroelectric or gas-fired

TABLE 13.2
Location of Major Ferro-Alloy Deposits, 1970
(Note: Specific mine or concentrator plant locations are given rather than general district locations.)

Ferro-Alloys (Estimated Production in 1970 of Beneficiated Ore, in Thousand Tons)	Main Ferro-Alloy Metal Locations			
	Western Regions (W) Caucasus (C)	Urals (U) Siberia (S)	Kazakhstan (K) Central Asia (A)	All other Regions (Specified)
Manganese (6,841)	Nikopol' (W) Chiatura (C) Pobugskoye (W) Bolshoi Tokmak (W)	Polunochnoye (U) Marsyaty (U) Yurkino (U) Novo-Beryozskoye (U) Usinskoye (S)	Dzhezdy (K) Karazhal (K)	Malyy Khingan (Far East)
Tungsten (8)	Tyrnyauz (C)	Dzhida (Buryat A.S.S.R.) (Zakamensk) Khapcheranga (S) Sherlovaya Gora (S)	Gornyy Altai (K) Akchatau (K) Almalyk (A) Ingichka (A) Chorukh-Dayron (A) Pendzhikent (A)	Vostok (Far East) Iul'tin (Chukchi N.O.)
Nickel (90)	Monchegorsk (W) Pobugskoye (W) Zhdanovsk (W) Kaula (W) Nittis-Kumuzhya (W) Zapolyarnyy (W)	Svetlyy (U) Rezh (U) Orsk (U) Vishnevaya Gora (U) Novotroitsk (U) Yelizavetinskoye (U) Noril'sk-Talnakh (S)	Batamshinskiy (K) Novo-Taiketkentskoye (K)	
Chromium (1·4)		Novotroitsk (U) Sarany (U)	Khromtau (K)	
Cobalt (2)	Nikel' (W) Zapolyarnyy (W) Deshkesan (C)	Yelizavetinskoye (U) Cheremshanka (U) Buruktal (U) Noril'sk-Talnakh (S) Khovu-Aksy (S)	Novo-Taiketkentskoye (K)	
Molybdenum (6)	Tyrnyauz (C) Agarak (C) Kadzharan (C) Dastakert (C)	Zakamensk (S) Davenda (S) Khapchcranga (S) Sorsk (S) Vershino- Shakhtaminskiy (S)	Akchatau (K) Dzhambul (K) Almalyk (A) Chorukh-Dayron (A) Kounradskoye (K) Bozshakul (K)	Iul'tin (Chukchi N.O.)
Vanadium (1)	Zaporozh'ye (W) (as by-product)	Kusa (U) Pervoural'sk (U) Kachkanar (U)		
Antimony (1)	Nikitovka (W)	Aktash (S) Razdolinsk (S)	Khaidarkan (A) Turgay (K)	
Columbium-Tantalum (1)	Revda (W)	Vishnevogorsk (U) Orlovsk (S) Yuzhnyy (U) Miass (Chita Ob.) Belogorskiy (S)		
Zirconium (1)	Irshansk (W) Volnogorsk (W) Sedovo (W) Kovdor (W)			

Sources: D. B. Shimkin, *Minerals: A Key to Soviet Power*, Harvard U.P., Cambridge, Mass., 1953, and T. Shabad, *Basic Industrial Resources of the USSR*, Columbia U.P., New York, 1969, both up-dated by the author.

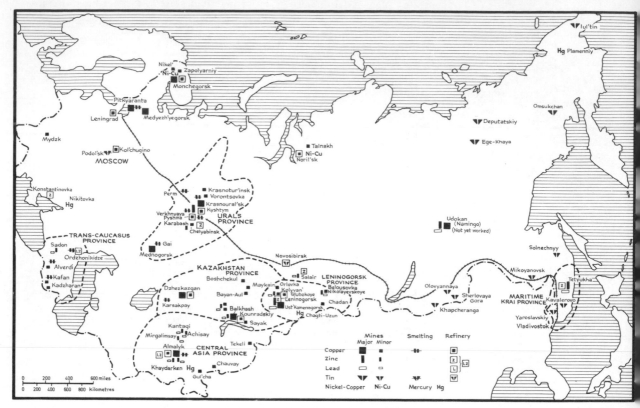

FIG. 13.2   Non-Ferrous Base Metals in the Soviet Union.

thermal power stations. This process yields the ferro-alloy as a combination of iron and non-ferrous metal, such as manganese or chromium, suitable for charging into steel mill furnaces along with the molten iron.

Ferro-alloy electric furnaces are located for the most part in or near iron and steel centres. Examples are those at Tula, Lipetsk (Centre); Nikopol', Zaporozh'ye, Kadiyevka (Ukraine); Zestafoni (Caucasus); Aktyubinsk (Southern Urals); Chelyabinsk, Chusovoy and Serov (Urals); Yermak (Kazakhstan); Chirchik (Uzbekistan); Novokuznetsk (Western Siberia) and Ust'-Kamenogorsk (Kazakhstan).

As can be seen from Table 13.2 the principal sources of ferro-alloys are the Kola Peninsula, the Dnieper–Donbas areas of the Ukraine, the Trans-Caucasus, and the southern and central Urals. However, increasingly in post-war years new mines and prospects have been opened up in Kazakhstan

and in the border mountains with Mongolia and China.

In many instances ferro-alloy metals occur in ores as joint products; nickel and cobalt with copper; tungsten with tin and molybdenum, or molybdenum alone; antimony with mercury, vanadium with iron and titanium, and so on. Frequently therefore the mining of iron-ores and basic non-ferrous metals will yield ferro-alloys as by-products recoverable from smelter slag or furnace dross.

In addition to the main ferro-alloys, valuable and rare metals of great significance in the nuclear and space-age are sometimes recovered in electrolytic processing. Such metals are tantalum, columbium, selenium, tellurium, hafnium, and metals of the platinum group: rhaetium, osmium, palladium, iridium, and germanium. Secondary recovery of the latter group of rare metals has now become especially significant since platinum bearing placer deposits in the Soviet Union are now all but ex-

54. The Sukharino iron-ore deposit, Kuznetsk Basin. Ten-ton lorries carry ore from the Samarskiy open-cut to the nearby concentration plant at Sukharino.

hausted, and rare metal production from the new Arctic prospects is difficult and costly.

Base Metals

One group of metals of overwhelming economic significance to Soviet progress is the base metals, copper, lead–zinc, tin; with these might be included mercury – a metal of far greater importance than the mere weight of output would imply (Fig. 13.2).

Copper Deposits. The Soviet Union ranks second in the world as a copper producer. Current annual output (metal content) is about 900,000 metric tons according to the United States Bureau of Mines statistics. Another 120,000 tons of copper are recovered from scrap metal.

The chief occurrences of copper ores in the Soviet Union are in the Urals, Kazakhstan, Eastern Siberia, Uzbekistan, and Armenia.

In the Urals, old copper mining centres such as Karabash, Kirovgrad, and Baymak have become

depleted. During World War II, however, new mining and smelting centres were opened up and the copper refining centres were modernized. The electrolytic refineries were at Verkhnyaya Pyshma (built 1934) and Kyshtym (pre-1917) while mining centres such as Krasnoural'sk, Revda (Sredneural'sk) and Mednogorsk had concentrators and smelters reducing the ores to blister copper. Other electrolytic refineries were located in the main copper market areas: Leningrad, Moscow and the neighbouring Kol'chugino.

The Ural copper ore-bodies at Degtyarsk, Sibay and Uchaly – a new ore-dressing complex opened in 1972 – in the Bashkir A.S.S.R. and at Gay (Orenburg oblast) are exceptionally rich in copper. The Gay deposit yields 10 per cent metal. Since 1961 Gay has served its concentrator with both underground and open-cut copper ore and its immediate area of the southern Urals is now one of the Soviet Union's principal copper-working regions.

55. The Kachkanar iron-ore deposit, Central Urals, is also rich in vanadium. Here at the Gusevogorsk open-cut an 8 cubic metre bucket excavator loads 800-ton ore trains bound for the ore-dressing mill.

Kazakhstan's copper deposits are chiefly low-grade disseminated copper–porphyry ores. Large open-cut workings are located at Kounradskoye (Lake Balkhash), Bozshakul, Karsakpay and Dzhezkazgan near Karaganda. A lode-deposit occurs at Uspenskoye. Copper refineries exist at Kounradskoye, Dzhezkazgan, and at the new integrated centre of Almalyk in Uzbekistan.

The old smelting centre at Glubokoye in eastern Kazakhstan recently opened electrolytic refining operations. The complex treats local ore and copper–zinc ores received from the Orlovka and Nikolayevka mines.

The Uzbekistan copper ores at Almalyk are of the low-grade disseminated type, but fortunately can be worked by cheap open-cut methods.

The Chita region of Eastern Siberia has copper–lead–zinc ores at Udokan but these are so remote that they are not yet worked. The Altay deposits at Nikolayevskoye and Belousovka are of the pyrites-type.

Armenia has disseminated-type copper ores and these are worked at Kadzharan and Agarak. Lode deposits occur at Zangezur and Alavardi; the latter has an integrated copper cycle with a mine, concentration plant, smelter and refinery.

Other Soviet copper-sources are found in Krasnoyarsk Kray at Kialykh, Uzenskoye and Glafirniskoye (Khakass A.O.), and Noril'sk in the Far North; in the Caucasus at Khudes and Urup; and at Kaula and Nittis-Kumuzkya on the Kola Peninsula.

In recent years Soviet authorities have suggested that it may be more economic to locate copper-smelters in the market areas rather than near the mines. This is because of the higher metal content of concentrates now being produced, the higher economies of scale at large smelters, and the recovery of valuable by-products thus made possible. In 1965, nearly one-half of smelter concentrates was subject to the long hauls to market-oriented smelters. This caused a six-fold increase in freight volume handled, but nearly 40 per cent of this was attributed to the great production of copper. Most of the country's concentrators now match the high concentrate ratios of 35 per cent copper per ton reached at the Dzhezkazgan concentrator in Kazakhstan, yielding one ton of metal for about three tons of concentrate.

The more modern mills also permit extraction of zinc, selenium, tellurium, and nickel metals as well as sulphur or sulphuric acid from the concentrates,

whereas formerly only the more valuable gold and silver were recovered.

Polymetallic Deposits. Lead, zinc, and silver are frequently combined in one ore-body and are therefore referred to as polymetallic deposits. Sometimes major copper mineralization is also associated with polymetallic occurrences and not infrequently minor amounts of such metals as gold, cadmium, selenium, tellurium, and other metals of this group. Soviet lead production is currently about 450,000 tons annually; zinc 610,000 tons.

The principal locations of polymetallic ores in the Soviet Union are in Kazakhstan, Central Asia, the Caucasus, in the two Siberias, and the Far East (Fig. 13.2). The Kazakhstan mines are at Ust'-Kamenogorsk, Belousovka, Leninogorsk, Kentau, and several neighbouring mining centres such as the Tishinka lead–zinc deposit. In Central Asia, the Almalyk (Altyn–Topkan) mine in Uzbekistan is notable, while the North Ossetian region of the

56. The Dzhezkazgan copper mine (No. 55) in Kazakhstan. This mine is typical of the fully mechanized working of the new mining districts.

Caucasus has the Sadon lead–zinc mine. Concentrates are sent to lead and zinc refineries at Ordzhonikidze. In Siberia, the Salair (Kuznetsk Basin) and Nerchinsk (Chita oblast) mines are the most important polymetallic sources. The Tetyukhe complex in the Far East is one of the few large non-ferrous metal enterprises in this region.

In recent years, the Soviet authorities have greatly extended the scope of polymetallic mining. New and technically much more efficient means of mining, concentration of ores, smelting, and metal refining have been introduced. Formerly retort smelting was used in the Soviet Union and, as this required heat from coal or coke, the smelters were sited in coalfield areas. Examples are the older existing smelters at Konstantinovka in the Ukraine, Belovo in the Kuzbas, and Chelyabinsk in the Urals.

Since World War II, however, new techniques of metal recovery have been adopted. Each of the mining areas now has modern concentrating plants, smelters, or metal recovery plants. Concentrates then move to neighbouring lead-smelting plants such as those at Leninogorsk, Ust'-Kamenogorsk and Chimkent (Fig. 13.2), served by natural gas, or to electrolytic zinc refineries based on abundant supplies of hydroelectric power, now readily available by high-voltage transmission grids. The process involves the leaching of zinc concentrates with sulphuric acid – a by-product of lead-smelting. This leaching process forms zinc sulphate which is then passed to an electrolytic cell to separate the zinc metal. As a consequence of this development, new smelter-refinery complexes have been set up at the mine sites. It is therefore no longer necessary to freight metal concentrates over long rail hauls. New combined lead smelters and zinc-refineries are located at Leninogorsk, Ust'-Kamenogorsk, and Almalyk. There is a zinc refinery at Tetyukhe in the Far East. The old Konstantinovka plant (Ukraine) has also been rebuilt following war damage and converted to the new electrolytic process.

Zinc refineries have considerable electrical energy requirements. With the building of large hydroelectric power plants in eastern Kazakhstan, zinc refineries have been established near the mining operations. The Ust'-Kamenogorsk refinery was built in 1947 and this was followed by the Leninogorsk refinery (1966) and Almalyk refinery (1970) in Uzbekistan. Construction of the zinc refineries and lead smelters in the Asiatic parts of the Soviet Union will completely eliminate the need to transport concentrates to the market areas in European Russia. Henceforth only ingots and semi-finished products will need to be shipped and this will represent an immense saving in freight costs.

Tin Deposits. Tin has been a metal of acute scarcity in the Soviet Union. Imports could be obtained from Southeast Asia, but only at the expense of scarce foreign exchange. In consequence, the Soviet Union has made every effort to develop and maintain its own tin-mining industry. Present production is about 20,000 tons annually.

Early mining was based on local placer deposits in Chita oblast, particularly at Sherlovaya Gora

57. At the Dzhezkazgan mine a 25-metre boom prepares for drilling at the working face.

58. Drilling driftways in the Leninogorskiy combine in Kazakhstan. This mine has two horizontal ore-bodies: silver–lead–zinc in the upper level and copper–zinc below.

and Khapcheranga, but these were quickly depleted. Mining then shifted to larger lode or placer prospects in the Yakut A.S.S.R. (e.g. Ege-Khaya, Deputatskiy) and the Kolyma River deposits inland from the Magadan coast. Operations here were very much hampered by the inclement Arctic climate, but useful tin production resulted. From the 1950s onwards, new tin-mining areas such as those of the Primorskiy Kray (e.g. Tetyukhe and Yaroslavskiy), Gornyy, Khingansk and Solnechnyy in the Amur Basin, were opened up. Also the earlier centre of Omsukchan in the Kolyma gold-mining district survived as a significant producer. In 1959 the Iul'tin

59. The Leninogorskiy combine has two open-cuts in addition to its underground workings; one at Tishinskiy (shown here) and another at Andreevskiy.

molybdenum–tin mining operation began. This was situated in far northeastern Siberia in the Chukchi National Okrug, beyond the Arctic Circle (Fig. 13.2).

Tin smelters are located at Podol'sk south of Moscow, and at Novosibirsk. Thus concentrates must be moved thousands of miles before processing to recover the metal.

Aluminium Group Metals

Metals in the aluminium group include aluminium, magnesium, titanium and tantalum; they are sometimes known as the light metals. Their high strength-to-weight ratio makes them extremely important in aircraft and other transportation industries. Their role in space-vehicles, nuclear power, transmission lines and building construction have also expanded greatly in the Soviet Union in post-war years.

Aluminium. Although the Soviet Union lacks adequate resources of bauxite, the ore from which most of the world's aluminium is obtained, it has pressed into service other aluminiferous minerals such as nephelite, alunite and kaolin. Since the first two aluminium reduction plants were opened at Volkhov (Leningrad district) and Zaporozh'ye (Dnieper district) in 1933 – and these used the low-grade bauxite ores of Boksitogorsk, near Volkhov – there has been continued growth of the Soviet aluminium industry (Fig. 13.3). The Kamensk (Urals) alumina (aluminium oxide) and reduction

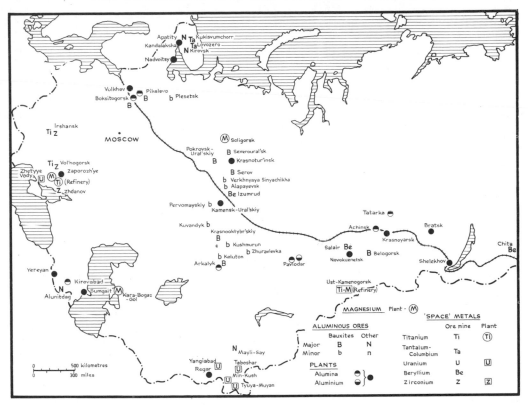

FIG. 13.3   Non-Ferrous Light Metals in the Soviet Union.

plant was opened in 1939. The West Siberian aluminium reduction plant at Novokuznetsk was opened in 1943 and another integrated alumina–aluminium metal plant was set up at Krasnoturinsk (Urals) two years later. All three plants obtained their raw materials, directly or indirectly, from the Severoural'sk bauxite deposit in the Urals.

After World War II the aluminium industry has shifted towards the Eastern Siberian hydroelectric-power plants because of the high power component needed in the electrical reduction of alumina to aluminium metal. Also at the same time a necessary search for, and development of, other aluminium-bearing ores attracted the industry eastward – a fortuitous advantage. New reduction plants in Siberia were set up at Shelekhov near Irkutsk in 1962, at Krasnoyarsk in 1964 and Anzeb near Bratsk in 1967. The Bratsk aluminium plant is located in the western suburb of Chekanoskiy close to the Anzeb railway station. The Shelekhov plant had six electrolysis units in operation in 1967 and the

Anzeb plant four units. Eventually each of these aluminium plants will have 24 such electrolysis units.

In 1970 the four Siberian aluminium plants accounted for about 1·3 million tons of the Soviet aluminium output of 2 million tons, or 65 per cent. Aluminium exports have increased considerably over recent years. The main areas importing Soviet aluminium, apart from the COMECOM countries, are the Netherlands and Great Britain.

Although there has been a substantial shift of aluminium production to the east, efforts have been made to upgrade the older centres of the west. The Volgograd reduction plant was open in 1959 and utilized hydroelectric power from the Volga. Other plants were built at Yerevan in Armenia and Sumgait in Azerbaydzhan.

The Nadvoitsy aluminium plant in Karelia has recently expanded output by 30 per cent with the addition of a fourth electrolysis unit. In order to supply this and other aluminium plants with raw materials, new resources have been opened up.

Northwestern R.S.F.S.R. uses Kola Peninsula nephelite in its aluminium industry, conversion to alumina taking place at Pikalevo and Volkhov. The final-stage reduction of alumina to aluminium metal takes place at Volkhov, Nadvoitsy in Karelia and Kandalaksha on the Kola Peninsula. Although these areas were very important at the inception of the Soviet aluminium industry, they have been superseded by the larger resources of ores and hydroelectric power of Siberia as indicated above.

A new bauxite development was set up at Plesetsk in the marshy and forested terrain of the Iksa tributary of the Onega River. A railway link from the Vologda–Arkhangel'sk main line extends the present spur line from Plesetsk to Oksovskiy, a timber shipping point on the Onega River. At present the land is drained and overburden stripped, and mining is thought to have begun in 1970. The bauxite is a complex ore of bochmite and kaolinite, containing 53 per cent alumina, 18·5 per cent silica, and 7 per cent iron oxide. The deposit is large and compact and therefore easily worked by open-cut methods. In consequence it contrasts with the Boksitogorsk workings which occur in numerous small deposits that are now virtually worked out.

At first, Krasnoyarsk used alumina from the Urals (Kamensk and Krasnoturinsk) which also supplied other Western Siberian plants at Novokuznetsk and Shelekhov, near Irkutsk. The Pavlodar alumina plant, opened in 1964, now provides the main source for all four Siberian reduction plants. Pavlodar uses the low-grade bauxite (high silica content) from the Almalyk and Krasnooktyabr'skiy areas of Kustanay oblast, Kazakhstan. Ore mining operations have been set up at Krasnooktyabr'skiy as well as at Almalyk. Eastern alumina production is now about 2·5 million tons annually, enough for over 1·2 million tons of aluminium metal.

Alumina production is now no longer concentrated in the Urals. Supplies as indicated, are obtained from Pavlodar (Kazakhstan), based on the Almalyk bauxite deposits of Kustanay oblast, or from Kirovabad in Azerbaydzhan which uses a local source of alunite from the Alunitdag mine. The Razdan nephelite deposit in Armenia is also used for alumina production. The Pavlodar and Kirovabad alumina plants began production in 1964 and 1966 respectively. Other alumina facilities are located at Achinsk, Western Siberia, open since 1969. The Achinsk plant uses the Kiya-Shaltyr' nephelite deposit near Belogorsk in Kemerovo oblast, 145 rail miles from Achinsk.

The Achinsk plant consists of two 600-foot rotary kilns which treat nephelite concentrate and limestone to yield alumina with cement clinker, soda-ash and potash as by-products. The planned capacity of this plant is one million tons of alumina and 4·5 million tons of cement. The Achinsk plant will reduce the length of haul of alumina to the aluminium plants at Krasnoyarsk, Bratsk, and Shelekhov, hitherto supplied from the Urals and Pavlodar alumina centres.

Magnesium. Magnesium when alloyed with aluminium produces extremely strong, stress-resistant, and light metals useful in the aircraft and space-vehicle industries, including intercontinental ballistic missiles.

Magnesium metal in the Soviet Union is derived principally from magnesite and carnallite and similar magnesium-bearing minerals. The first magnesium metal plants were located at Zaporozh'ye (1935) in the Dnieper Basin and at Solikamsk (1936) and nearby Berezniki (1943) both in the Urals. A fourth magnesium refinery was set up in Ust'-Kamenogorsk (1965) in eastern Kazakhstan (see Fig. 13.3). This modern plant is linked with titanium metal production since this requires the great heat generated by magnesium in the reduction process. Berezniki and Zaporozh'ye also produce titanium as well as magnesium metal using the same process.

In the Carpathian piedmont the Kalush chemical and metallurgical complex extracts magnesium metal, using local kainite and langbeinite deposits as its raw materials. These minerals are complex potassium magnesium sulphates remaining after the extraction of a sylvite – a potassium chloride – deposit. Since 1967 the Dombrovskiy open-cut has provided the Kalush complex with potassium sulphate fertilizer-making material. Magnesium metal is a by-product of the hydrolysis process used.

The Soviet Union currently produces about 45,000 metric tons of magnesium metal annually. New capacity at the Ust'-Kamenogorsk reduction plant doubled production in 1966 and further expansion for the industry is planned.

Titanium Metal. The Soviet Union derives its

titanium metal from two distinct sources: from titano-magnetite lodes such as those at Kachkanar and Kusa in the Urals, and from heavy mineral sands dredged from river valleys of the Ukraine, notably the Irsha and Samotkan' Rivers.

The Ural deposits yield iron-ore, vanadium slag, and a titanium dioxide concentrate. The latter is converted to a titanium slag and then shipped to one of the four reduction plants. The heavy mineral sands from river valleys are worked at Irshansk and Vol'nogorsk, while the Sedovo beach mineral sands on the Azov Coast in the Ukraine, yield the titaniferous minerals, rutile and ilmenite, as well as zirconium, hafnium, and monazite, sources of various rare metals.

Titanium, long used in its dioxide form as a white pigment in the paint industry, was first produced as a metal in the Soviet Union in 1954. The main reduction plants producing magnesium and titanium metals as joint products are at Podol'sk, south of Moscow, Zaporozh'ye on the Dnieper River, Berezniki (Urals) and Ust'-Kamenogorsk.

Other Light Metals. Nuclear energy and astrospace developments in the Soviet Union have created demands for lithium and beryllium, two light metals used as coolants in nuclear reactions, and also tantalum and columbium. All are rare metals found in granitic mica-pegmatites of Chita Oblast, Eastern Siberia, and Karelia. Extraction of these metals is frequently a by-product of smelting or reduction processes performed on other metals.

Other Mining Operations

Other mining operations worthy of brief mention are those employed in the recovery of mercury, uranium, gold, diamonds, and asbestos.

Mercury. Mercury has a widespread occurrence in the Soviet Union. The chief mining areas are Nikitovka in the Ukraine; Shorbulag in the Trans-Caucasus; Khaydarken (Fergana Basin) in Central Asia, and Plamennyy in Chukchi National Okrug in the far north of Siberia. In Nikitovka, near Gorlovka in the Donbas, mercury ore is associated with antimony. This is also the case at Aktash (Altay Kray), Western Siberia, Turgai, Northern Kazakhstan, and Razdolinsk (Krasnoyarsk Kray) where, however, antimony is the dominant metal.

In Trans-Caucasia, a mercury-mining centre and smelter were set up at Shorbulag. This centre in Azerbaydzhan, under development since 1967, is near Kel'badzhar on the Terter River, southeast of Lake Sevan. The Shorbulag smelter uses ore from mines at Agyatag, Levskiy, and Sarydash as well as local ores.

The Chukchi National Okrug in northeastern Siberia's Palyavaam Range has a mercury mine and mill that have operated since 1967. In winter it is serviced by sledge trains from the Arctic port of Pevek, 200 miles to the northeast, and also by air lift.

Soviet production of mercury was about 40,000 flasks (each of 76 pounds weight) in the mid-1960s.

Uranium. Uranium mining in the Soviet Union is located at Zheltyye Vody (Ukraine); Sillimaë (Estonia); Tynya-Muyan and Min-Kush (Kirghizia); Taboshar (Tadzhikistan) and Yangiabad (Uzbekistan).

The Krivoy Rog iron-ore district has now become a very important producer of uranium ore although the exact significance of the Central Asian workings is not known. At Zheltyye Vody and Terny within the environs of Krivoy Rog, the uranium ore-body has been worked since 1957. It is in physical contact with the famous iron-ore occurrence that trends north–south. The Sillimaë uranium is obtained as a by-product of oil-shale workings. No reliable figures are available on Soviet uranium production.

Gold. One of the principal gold producers in the Soviet Union is Uzbekistan, which gained a new open-cut gold mine and concentrator in 1969. The gold-bearing lode is situated at Altynkan on the southern slopes of the Kurama Mountains flanking the Fergana Basin. The Altynkan complex includes the Guzaksay open-cut working the Chadak deposit, and the Pirmirab adit mine. Another lode occurs at Kochbulak, also in the Kurama Mountains. Another gold centre is at Zarafshan in the middle of the Kyzyl Kum desert.

Kazakhstan too has its gold-mining centres. Anezov (formerly Bakyrchik) in the Kalba Mountains of eastern Kazakhstan, is another lode deposit which has been under development for some years, and compares with similar projects at Zod, near Lake Sevan, in Armenia. It seems probable that the traditional placer gold deposits of the Lena tributaries – Bodaybo and Vitim Valley – and Aldan and Kolyma district of eastern Siberia, are now so depleted that a shift to more expensive lode mining is a necessity. Modern mechanization however may render new placer deposits such as those of Bilibino (Chuckchi N.O.) much more economical to work.

Diamonds. The supply point on the northern highway leading to the Mirnyy diamond mines in Yakutia is Lensk, formerly Mukhtuya. It is situated on the Lena River. Lensk also channels materials northward to Vilyuy hydroelectric station at Chernyshevskiy, northwest of Mirnyy.

Another diamond mining concentrator is at Udachnaya on the Daldyn River in Yakutia. Like the other mines, it is based on a kimberlite pipe which yields gem-stone quality and industrial diamonds. It ships material to the mill at Novyy which is 40 miles northeast of Aykhal, another diamond centre. The Aykhal–Novyy diamond-mining area is near the Arctic Circle in the Far North of Siberia, about 250 miles north of Mirnyy, the Soviet Union's chief diamond mining location.

Cutting and polishing of gemstones is carried out at Smolensk, the 'Amsterdam' of the Soviet Union.

Asbestos. In 1967 Soviet asbestos production was 28 million tons of fibre-rock, yielding 1·8 million tons of asbestos fibre. This is about half of the world's total production. The main producing centres are Asbest (formerly Bazhenovo) in the Urals; Dzhetygara in northwestern Kazakhstan; Ak-Dovurak in the Tuva A.S.S.R.; and a recently opened centre at Yasnyy in eastern Orenburg Oblast.

Improved technology at the Asbest mill will more than double the present capacity and can work economically low-grade rock containing less than 3 per cent fibre. Production from the three open-cuts amounts to some 15 million tons of rock annually, estimated to yield just under 1 million tons of fibre based on the 5–7 per cent rock usually mined.

The Dzhetygara asbestos deposit in northwestern Kazakhstan and also that at Ak-Dovurak in Tuva went into production in the mid-60s. Total production from these mines and the old asbestos centres of the Urals exceed 1 million tons. Dzhetygara has a production of some 200,000 tons.

This discussion of the Soviet Union's metal mining and associated industries is essential groundwork for the following section which deals with the country's heavy industries.

CHAPTER FOURTEEN

SOVIET HEAVY INDUSTRIES

Throughout the fifty or so years of the Soviet régime it is the heavy industrial branches of the economy that have developed most and received the greatest investment of financial and human resources. The Soviet Union's motivation in this regard has been to overtake levels of production in the western world and thus, it is argued, show the superiority of the Soviet system of economic management.

As far as heavy industry is concerned the Soviet Union can claim a fair measure of achievement in closing the gap between the industrial output of the United States and its own. Comparing the ratio of the United States to Soviet production in various heavy industries on a *per capita* basis — necessary because of differences in population size of the two countries — it is quite evident that the successful closing of the gap is a real phenomenon and not just a hollow propaganda claim.

If the level of Soviet production *per capita* in a given heavy industry is taken as 1, then the following table indicates the relative United States–Soviet position at various dates (Table 14.1).

Thus in 1937 the United States produced 4·8 and 7·8 times more coal and oil respectively *per capita* than did the Soviet Union. By 1960 the ratios had changed to 0·9 and 2·8 for these same products; and in 1970 to 1·0 and 1·6. Consequently, in the case of coal output *per capita* the United States and Soviet Union were on a par. In cement production *per capita* the Soviet Union was superior to the United States and in pig-iron, crude steel, oil, and mineral fertilizers the gap was closed to a considerable degree in a matter of two or three decades. Pre-eminently the reason for the Soviet approach to United States' levels of heavy industry has been through the rate of growth achieved. This postulates a commanding ability to mobilize resources quickly and efficiently.

In the absence of any remarkable upturn in the United States before 1975 – such an upturn could perhaps only result as the outcome of global war – then the current Ninth Five-Year Plan (1971–75) will render all Soviet heavy industry comparable in output status with that of the world's first-ranking industrial nation. Many economic geographers,

TABLE 14.1

Ratio of U.S. Output per Capita *to Soviet Output Equal 1*

Production	1937	1950	1960	1970	Relative Soviet Growth 1950–70 (%)*
Coal	4·8	2·7	0·9	1·0	170
Oil	7·8	8·4	2·8	1·6	425
Electric power	5·2	5·1	3·6	2·8	82
Pig Iron	3·3	3·7	1·6	1·2	208
Steel	3·7	3·8	1·6	1·4	171
Metal Cutting Lathes	n.a.	4·4	1·0	1·4	214
Cement	4·7	4·6	1·4	0·9	411
Mineral Fertilizers	2·0	3·8	2·8	1·7	123

Source: R. Belousov, *USSR Heavy Industry*, Novosti Press Publishing, Moscow, 1972, p. 8; except growth calculated by author.

* The relative Soviet growth 1950–70, indicates the degree to which the gap has been closed in specific lines of production *vis-à-vis* the U.S.A.

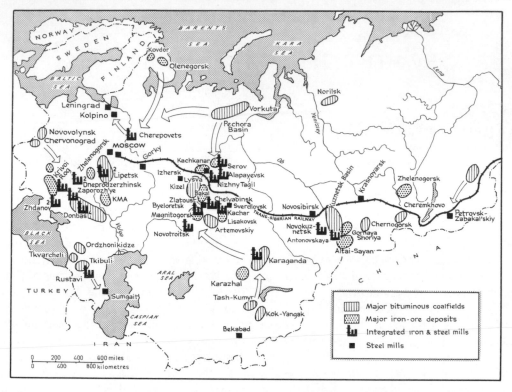

FIG. 14.1   Iron and Steel Industries: Integrated Plants and Steel Mills.

however, have reservations concerning the qualitative aspects of the two countries' performances. For instance, it seems unlikely that the Soviet Union can immediately match the variety and detailed technological specification of many branches of heavy industry – the range of steel shapes and specifications, the variety of heavy and organic chemicals, etc. – that are currently produced in the United States.

At the beginning of 1970 the Soviet Union had nearly 50,000 individual industrial enterprises, some large and some small, comprising industrial plants, factories, mines, quarries, and power stations. The aggregate fixed assets of these enterprises was estimated at 227,000 million roubles (257,000 million U.S. dollars) as at January 1, 1970 (Belousov, op.cit., p. 8).

Discussion of some of the Soviet Union's heavy industry branches follows:

Iron and Steel Industry
At the present time the Soviet iron and steel industry accounts for about one-fifth of the world's

steel production; more than is produced in West Germany, France, Britain and Italy taken together. In 1971 the Soviet Union produced 121 million tons of crude steel and the United States 122 million tons in 1970. The growth in Soviet pig-iron, crude steel, and rolled-steel products is shown in Table 14.2.

The Soviet Union now has 28 integrated, or full-cycle, iron and steel mills capable of producing in excess of one million tons a year (Fig. 14.1). Each of these embraces blast-furnaces, steel-making open-hearth and/or converter furnaces, sometimes B.O.S. (oxygen) furnaces, blooming and rolling mills, and sometimes continuous casting plants and similar installations of modern iron and steel technology.

A list of the equipment and capacities of major integrated mills is shown (Table 14.3). Only those iron and steel mills with an output in excess of one million tons of pig-iron or crude steel are shown. Altogether there are 70 iron and steel or steel-only mills in the Soviet Union. A breakdown of all mills by region and capacities is given below (Table 14.4).

TABLE 14.2

Growth of the Soviet Iron and Steel Industry

Soviet Iron and Steel Production (in million metric tons) 1913–1970							
	Pig-iron	*Ingot Steel*	*Rolled Steel*		*Pig-iron*	*Ingot Steel*	*Rolled Steel*
1913 (Russia)	4·2	4·2	3·5	1955	33·3	45·3	35·3
1928–29	4·0	4·8	3·9	1960	46·8	65·3	50·9
1932	6·2	5·9	4·4	1965	66·2	91·0	61·7
1940	14·9	18·3	13·1	1968	78·8	106·5	74·1
1946	10·0	13·4	9·6	1969	81·6	110·0	76·3
1950	19·2	27·3	20·9	1970	85·9	115·9	80·6

Source: *Narodnoe Khozyaistvo, 1970*, Moscow, 1971, p. 190.

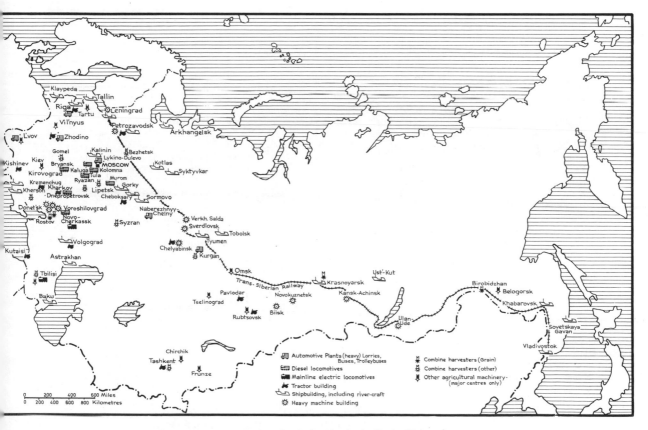

FIG. 14.2   Engineering Industries in the Soviet Union.

TABLE 14.3

Integrated Steel Mills in the Soviet Union with Crude Steel Capacities exceeding one million tons annually

Region and Locality of Iron and Steel Mill	Crude Steel Capacity Thousand metric tons	Pig-iron Capacity Thousand metric tons	Blast-Furnace No.	Open-Hearth Units No.	Other Major Facilities (See abbreviations below)
UKRAINE					
Donets Basin					
Donetsk	1000	1500	4	8	R. Mill; Cont. Casting
Makeyevka	3000	2700	5	18	1 Elect. Merch.; Wire.
Yenakiyevo	1500	2000	6	n.a.	Plate + Rail; Bessemer
Kommunarsk (formerly Voroshilovsk)	2600	2200	5	10	Plate + Heavy Mill
Dnieper Bend					
Zaporozh'ye	3500	3200	6	12	66″ H + C Strip: 20″ tinning
Zaporozh'ye	(1200)		—	—	20 Elec. Alloy + special steels
Dneprodzerzhinsk	3500	4500	13	21	H. Sect. R. Mill; Pipe Mill
Dnepropetrovsk	1000	3800	7	10	Plate, H. Sect. R. Mill; 3 Oxy. C.
Krivoy Rog	3000	5500	7	2	Sect + Wire; Coke + Sint; 8 Oxy. C.
Nikopol'	—	—	—	—	Seamless Tube; Extrusion Tube
Sea of Azov					
Zhdanov	3400	3500	6	12	1 Oxy. C.; Merch.
Zhdanov	2500	2500	4	18	1 Oxy. C.; Cont. Strip
URALS					
Nizhniy Tagil	3200	3000	5	18	Plate + H. Sect.; 2 Oxy. C.
Serov	700	1000	7	9	Plate, Sheet + Sect.; Special S.
Chelyabinsk	2500	3300	6	11	12 Elec. 1 Oxy. Plant.
Magnitogorsk	8500	6500	10	32	Plate + H. Sect.; Elec. tin.; Casting
Novo-Troitsk	2000	1400	4	7	Plate; 3 Bessemer; Special S.
Kamensk-Ural'skiy	—	—	—	—	Tube Mill
Zlatoust	1300		—	9	20 Elec. 1 Oxy. Plant. Alloy + Ball-bearing S.
NORTH AND CENTRAL					
Tula		2300	3	n.a.	Sintering; Cont. Casting.
Novo-Lipetsk	6500	2000	2	—	4 Elec.; Strip Mill; 2 Cont. Cast.
Cherepovets	1200	1000	3	6	Plate + Sect. Mill
SOUTHERN AND EASTERN					
Volgograd				16	2 Elec.; Plate; Wire; Alloy
Rustavi	1500	800	2	8	Struct. M.; Tube M.; Forging
Begovat	1700			3	Bar Mill.
Karaganda	4000	3000	4	2	H & C Sheet M.; B.O.S. Converter
Antonovskaya (Kuzbas)	4000	3000	4/5	10	Hy. Struct.; Tube M.; Wire; B.O.S.
Novokuznetsk	5000	3500	5	20	Hy. Struct.; B.O.S. Converters.

Source: H. G. Cordero (ed.), *Iron and Steel Works of the World*, 4th edn., Metal Bulletin Books Ltd., London, 1965.

ABBREVIATIONS

R. Mill	Rolling Mill	Coke + Sint.	Coke Ovens and Sintering Works or Plant
Cont. Casting	Continuous Casting	Merch.	Merchant Section Mill
Elec.	Electric Steel Furnace	Cont. Strip	Continuous Strip Mill
Plate/Rail	Plate and/or Rail Mills	Special S.	Special Steel Plant (including High Alloy and Armour Plate Mills)
Bessemer	Bessemer Converter		
Plate/Heavy	Plate and/or Heavy Section Rolling Mills	Elec. Tin	Electrolytic Tin-Plate Line
H + C Strip	Hot and Cold Strip Mill	Oxy. Plant	Bulk Oxygen-Making Plant
Tinning	Hot Dip Tin-Plate Line	Ball-bearing S.	Ball-Bearing Steel Mill (High Alloy Steels)
Elec. Alloy	Electric Furnace making Ferro-Alloys	Struct. M.	Structural Section Rolling Mill
H. Sect.	Heavy Section Rolling Mills	Forging	Forging Presses and/or Hammers
Oxy. C.	Oxygen Steel Converters (Bessemer Converters, Oxygen Blown)	B.O.S.	Bulk Oxygen Steel Converters
		Hy. Struct.	Heavy Structural Section Mills
Sect. + Wire	Section Rolling Mills plus Wire Mills	Tube M.	Tube-Forming or Rolling Mills

Recent developments in the Soviet steel industry range from sintering and pelletizing plants which convert low-grade or fine iron-ore into a more efficient charge for blast-furnaces. Since the first Soviet pellet plant was opened at the Rudnyy mines (Sokolovka–Sarabay deposit) in 1965, over 80 per cent of all blast-furnace ore charges are in sintered or pellet form. Another innovation has been the increasing size of blast-furnaces. At present 16 of the Soviet Union's blast-furnaces have capacities of 2000 cubic metres or over, nearly half of the world total of these in 1971 (33). The two largest furnaces have capacities of 2700 and 3000 cubic metres and are capable of smelting 1·5–2·0 million tons of pig-iron yearly. Similarly, the largest open-hearth has a capacity of 900 tons, considerably larger than those commonly in use.

The overall pattern of the integrated and specialist steel-mills in 1970 is shown in Table 14.4. This illustrates, first, the number of steel mill plants in each size-class category in each of the five steel-making regions, and secondly, the percentage of the national steel output for which each size category and region is responsible.

It can be noted that nearly 60 per cent of the national steel output comes from the 15 plants with annual production in excess of 2·4 million tons each, and these plants are overwhelmingly situated in the Ukraine (Donbas and Dnieper Bend). Moreover, it is evident that the Ukraine and Urals together account for the lion's share of the national output; 41 steel plants (58.6 per cent of all steel plants) producing 71·3 per cent of all steel. It is also clear that nearly two-thirds of their output comes from the 14 larger plants (i.e. those with steel output in excess of 1·2 million tons annually).

Throughout the steel industry natural gas admixture with the air blast of furnaces and as a fuel in steel furnaces has improved performance, saving coke and labour costs. Blast-furnaces are in some

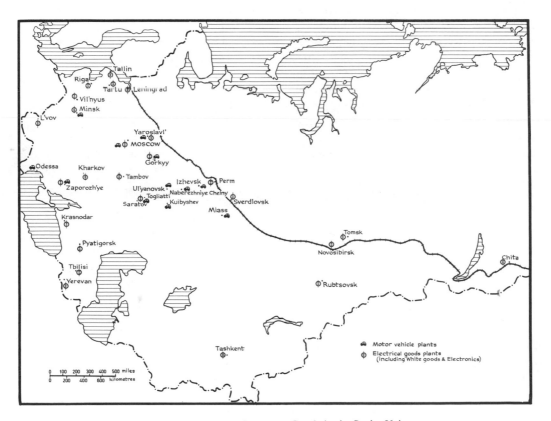

FIG. 14.3 Durable Consumer Goods in the Soviet Union.

TABLE 14.4

Soviet Steel-Making by Plant Size-Class and Percentage of National Steel Output, 1970

Capacity of Steel Plant (in thousands tons)	<300		301–600		601–1200		1201–2400		2401–4800		>4800		Total	
Regions	No.	%	No.	%	No.	%	No.	%	No.	%	No.	%	No.	%
Ukraine (Incl. Donbas)	4	1·0	2	4·5	6	5·2	1	5·8	7	18·6	1	5·2	21	40·3
Urals	7	1·3	4	1·9	4	4·6	2	5·5	2	7·4	1	10·3	20	31·0
Central and Northern	8	2·5	3	2·7	2	2·9	0	0·0	1	2·7	1	5·6	15	16·4
Southern	3	0·2	1	0·2	1	0·3	3	1·7	0	1·9	0	0·0	8	4·3
Siberia and Far East	2	0·3	2	1·0	0	0·0	0	0·0	2	6·7	0	0·0	6	8·0
Soviet Union	24	5·3	12	10·3	13	13·0	6	13·0	12	37·3	3	21·1	70	100·0

Sources: Base figures on steel-making capacities of plants; Cordero, *op. cit.*, 1965, updated by author. Percentages are calculated from *known* production of larger plants in 1970 plus *estimated* production of smaller plants. Consistency has been maintained against *known* regional production of steel for all plants and total national steel output, and also *known capacities* of smaller plants.

cases fully automated. B.O.S. or oxygen converters and oxygen lancing in open-hearth furnaces have greatly speeded up the steel-making process and continuous casting of steel, first introduced in 1953, has been adopted in the Donetsk, Magnitogorsk, Tula, and Novo-Lipetsk steel plants. The latter technology is also thought to be in operation at the new West Siberian Steel Works at Antonovskaya, first opened in 1968. Krivoy Rog has the world's largest blast-furnace, and steel industry authorities now plan to standardize this size and even larger units in other new installations. The Novo-Lipetsk mill has a blast-furnace of 3170 cubic metres capacity, i.e. 112,000 cubic feet. In 1970, some 173,900 tons of equipment were built for Soviet iron and steel plants plus another 140,100 tons of rolling mill equipment (Belousov, 1972, p. 25). This was more than double the equipment 'invested' in this industry in the year 1950.

Another aspect of the technological improvement of the iron and steel industry has been the continual upgrading of its efficiency. For example, the coefficient of use of blast-furnaces has been raised very significantly between 1950 and 1970; from a requirement of 0·98 cubic metres per ton of iron output to 0·597 cubic metres. Thus the same capacity furnace now yields some 63 per cent more metal than formerly. This has been achieved by such innovations as sintered or pelletized charges;

increasing the throat-pressure by 1·5 to 2·0 atmospheres (this reduces the volume of gases passing through the furnace and lowers their velocity so that iron-making materials can be substituted for coke), and the enrichment of the air blast with oxygen (or natural gas) and raising its temperature (to 900–1000° C) by moisturizing with superheated steam.

In the case of open-hearth furnaces, similar productivity improvements have been achieved. Between 1950 and 1970 the average daily yield of steel per square metre of open-hearth furnace sole rose from 5·36 tons to 9·15 tons; a gain of about 70 per cent. Again enrichment of the furnace fuel — often natural gas — with oxygen has been dominantly responsible for the improvement. However, the economies available by using the B.O.S. process (oxygen converters) have caused a rapid swing away from open-hearth furnaces in the newest steel mills. The capital cost of a B.O.S. plant is 40 per cent lower than that of an open-hearth plant of similar capacity, and it makes steel of improved quality at lower cost. Again the continuous casting of steel which teems molten steel through a vertical water-cooled mould so that it can pass directly to the rolling mills has rendered ingot-shops, soaking pits for re-heating the steel, and blooming and slabbing mill superfluous. This is an enormous saving of capital equipment, space, and cost.

60. The Rustavi iron and steel mill, Georgia. Teeming ingots in the open-hearth furnace section.

The current ninth Five-Year Plan (1971–75) will concentrate on qualitative improvements in steel-making now that the most difficult problems of attaining the gross amount of steel output have been overcome. The Plan calls for an output of 146 million tons of steel by 1975. This will however include a much higher proportion of alloy-steels compared to carbon steels than in the past. Currently a railway freight wagon built of low-alloy steel is four tons lighter than one made of ordinary carbon steel. This will save freight haulage costs and improve the pay-load. Such developments in the steel industry have only been made possible because of the growth of ferro-alloy supplies and power to supply electro-metallurgical plants.

The Regional Distribution of the Iron and Steel Industry

The regional distribution in the manufacture of pig-iron, crude steel, and rolled metal is shown in Tables 14.5, 14.6, and 14.7.

Iron and steel production rose substantially between 1950 and 1970. But while all regions increased their output some gained proportionately to others. The Ukraine (Donbas and Dnieper Bend) showed a remarkable increase in crude steel production from 8·3 million tons to 46·6 million tons. Between 1950 and 1970 it improved its share of the nation's steel output from 31·9 per cent to 40·3 per cent; once again emphasizing the re-birth of its steel industry after the devastation suffered during the last war. Virtually all of the Ukraine's gain in percentage terms was accounted for by a relative (not absolute) decline in steel production in the Urals; from 38·0 to 31·0 per cent of the Soviet output. This gives credence to the increasing difficulty of maintaining viable iron-ore and coking-coal supplies for the Urals's iron and steel plants at the present high level of output.

Another region of relative decline is Western Siberia. Between 1950 and 1970 its share of the national steel output declined from 12·4 per cent to 8·0 per cent – a fact easily hidden by an absolute

TABLE 14.5

Soviet Pig-Iron Production (in million metric tons)

	1940	1950	1960	1965	1970	Growth 1940–70 (%)
R.S.F.S.R.	5·3	10·0	21·6	31·2	42·0	692·4
Europe	1·1	0·9	3·1	7·6	11·8	972·7
Urals	2·7	7·2	15·1	18·8	22·9	748·1
Siberia	1·5	1·9	3·3	4·8	7·3	386·7
Ukraine	9·6	9·2	24·2	32·6	41·4	331·2
Kazakhstan	—	—	0·3	1·6	1·8	500·0*
Georgia	—	—	0·7	0·8	0·8	14·3*
U.S.S.R.	14·9	19·2	46·8	66·2	86·0	467·5

Sources: *Narodnoe Khozyaistvo, 1970*, Moscow, 1971, p. 191; *Soviet Geography*, **13** (5) 1972: 323; Shabad, *op. cit.*, p. 38.
* For period 1960–70.

increase of 6 million tons; from 3·4 to 9·4 million tons in 1950 and 1970 respectively.

All other regions have indicated a percentage gain in steel output; the southern region embracing Trans-Caucasia, Kazakhstan (Karaganda) and Central Asia improved its share of national output from 1·4 to 4·3 per cent in the twenty years to 1970. During this time output increased from less than 400,000 tons to 5·0 million tons of steel;

evidence of a growing self-sufficiency in meeting local steel requirements from local mills.

A correct reading of iron and steel production trends suggests a move to regional self-sufficiency with the exception of the two dominant producers, the Ukraine and the Urals, whose output is geared both to local outlets and the national market, and moreover, through COMECON, the East European market supplied from the Donbas.

TABLE 14.6

Soviet Crude Steel Production (in million metric tons)

	1940	1950	1960	1965	1970	Growth 1940–70 (%)
R.S.F.S.R.	9·3	18·5	36·6	50·1	63·9	587·1
Europe	3·4	4·4	9·2	14·0	18·5	444·1
Urals	4·0	10·7	21·9	29·4	36·0	800·0
Siberia	1·9	3·4	5·5	6·7	9·4	394·7
Ukraine	8·9	8·3	26·1	37·0	46·6	423·6
Kazakhstan	—	0·1	0·3	1·1	2·2	2100·0*
Georgia	...	0·1	1·1	1·4	1·4	1300·0*
Azerbaydzhan	...	...	0·6	0·8	0·7	16·7*
Latvia	...	...	...	0·1	0·4	300·0*
Uzbekistan	...	0·1	0·3	0·4	0·4	300·0*
Other †	0·1	0·2	0·3	0·1	0·3	200·0
U.S.S.R.	18·3	27·3	65·3	91·0	115·9	533·3

Sources: *Narodnoe Khozyaistvo, 1970*, Moscow, 1971, p. 191; *Soviet Geography*, **13** (5) 1972: 323; Shabad, *op. cit.*, p. 43.
* For period for which figures are available.
† All other republics' production plus amounts shown as insignificant in table.

TABLE 14.7
Soviet Rolled Steel Production (in million metric tons)

	1940	1950	1960	1965	1970	Growth 1940–70 (%)
R.S.F.S.R.	5·7	11·9	23·7	33·1	43·2	657·9
Europe	2·1	2·8	6·0	9·3	12·5	495·2
Urals	2·4	6·9	14·2	19·4	24·4	916·7
Siberia	1·2	2·2	3·5	4·4	6·3	425·0
Ukraine	5·6	5·8	18·0	26·0	32·7	483·9
Kazakhstan	—	0·1	0.3	0·4	2·4	2300·0*
Georgia	—	—	0.8	1·0	1·1	37·5*
Azerbaydzhan	...	...	0·4	0·6	0·6	50·0*
Latvia	...	...	0·1	0·3	0·3	200·0*
Uzbekistan	—	...	0·2	0·2	0·3	50·0*
Other †	0·1	0·2	0·2	...	...	n.a.
U.S.S.R.	11·4	18·0	43·7	61·6	80·6	607·0

Sources: *Narodnoe Khozyaistvo, 1970*, Moscow, 1971, p. 193; R.S.F.S.R. breakdown calculated by author from crude steel production.

* For period for which figures are available.

† All other republics' production plus amounts shown as insignificant in table.

The Engineering Industries

The Soviet engineering industries have made great strides in post-war years (Fig. 14.2). Production of tractors – agricultural and construction types – in the Soviet Union and also the output of diesel and electric locomotives, turbines, generators, coal-cutting machinery, oil-well turbo-drills and some classes of machine tool now exceeds rates of production of similar engineering products in the United States. Production figures for representative types are given below (Table 14.8).

In its technological levels the Soviet Union is second to none. It has for example, successfully built such sophisticated engineering products as space satellites, intercontinental ballistic missiles, nuclear powered electricity plants, ice-breakers and submarines, supersonic jet planes, and cybernetic computers.

The Soviet engineering industries now employ about one-third of the total industrial manpower and their enterprises account for one quarter of the country's fixed productive capital. The emphasis on producer-goods types of engineering (the means of production rather than consumer products) has meant that there has been substantial growth in the Soviet Union's fixed productive capital over time. In 1960 it was three times greater in terms of current roubles than it was in 1940; by 1970 it was 7·5 times greater. Such a rate of economic growth is unsurpassed anywhere in the world. The high growth rate of heavy engineering industries has made possible the introduction of automated equipment, modern technology, and substitution of outmoded methods of production long before the existing equipment was completely obsolete. For instance, open-hearth steel-making is now giving way to oxygen converter steel-making not only in new mills, but also in existing plants.

Another example is a new type of continuous steel-making process begun in Zaporozh'ye. This is really a four-in-one furnace. The first part melts pig-iron and scrap steel which then flows into the second part. This uses an oxygen stream to burn out superfluous carbon and then discharges the melt into the third-stage furnace in which steel conditioning materials, especially ferro-alloys, are added bringing the steel to an exact specification. The fourth part is a large 'holding' furnace that merely retains the steel received from earlier stages until enough is accumulated to begin teeming into a continuous casting mould. The whole four-in-one furnace cycle takes 40–50 minutes against the 4–6 hours required for a conventional open-hearth furnace. Moreover, the use of plasma-burners in the

TABLE 14.8

Production of Engineering Industries, 1940–1970 (Output in Stated Units)

	Units	1940	1950	1960	1970	Growth 1950–70 (%)
Soviet National Income	Index (1940 = 1)	1·0	1·6	4·4	8·7	443·7
Engineering Output	Index (1940 = 1)	1·0	2·3	11·8	37·1	1513·0
Turbines (steam, water, gas)	million kW	1·2	2·7	9·2	16·2	500·0
Generators	million kW	0·5	0·9	7·9	10·6	1077·8
Iron & Steel Ind. Equipment	thousand tons	23·7	111·2	218·3	314·0	182·4
Coal Combines	No.	22	344·0	881	1130	228·5
Petroleum Ind. Equipment	thousand tons	15·5	47·9	9·3	126·6	164·3
Bulldozers	thousands	0·1	3·8	12·8	33·5	781·6
Excavators	thousands	0·3	3·5	12·6	31·0	785·7
Diesel Locomotives	No.	5	125·0	1303	1485	1088·0
Electric Locomotives	No.	9	102	396	322	215·7
Motor Lorries	thousands	136·0	294·4	362·0	525·0	78·3
Agricultural Tractors	thousands	31·6	116·7	238·5	459·0	293·3
Grain Combines	thousands	13	46	59	99	115·2
Metal-Cutting Lathes	thousands	58·4	70·6	154·0	201·0	184·7
Forge and Press Machines	thousands	4·7	9·0	29·5	41·2	357·8

Source: R. Belousov, *USSR Heavy Industry*, Novosti Press Agency, Moscow, 1972, *passim.*

new furnace ensures that the steel produced is equal in quality to high-grade electric steel.

Power and Electro-Technical Engineering. This branch of heavy industry has been widely developed during the last five decades. Engineering plants making boilers, steam turbines, electrical generators, hydraulic turbines, diesel engines, electric motors, and railway locomotives are located mainly in the European parts of the Soviet Union: the oldest centres with long traditions of skilled workmanship and engineering expertise.

Boiler-making plants are situated at Podol'sk, Belgorod, and Taganrog. Two relatively new plants are in Altay Kray at Barnaul and Biysk. Turbine and generator works are located in Leningrad (three separate plants), Khar'kov, Kaluga and Kaunas. During the war the Novosibirsk turbine works was built and other power engineering plants were located in the Urals.

Diesel engine plants are found in Leningrad (Russkiy Diesel), Riga, Gor'kiy, and in the Ukraine at Khar'kov and Melitopol.

The aggregate capacity of all turbines – steam, hydraulic- and gas-operated – built in 1970 and

1971 was 16·2 and 16·8 million kW respectively. In 1958 the first Soviet turbine of 200,000 kW capacity was built, but now individual steam turbines of 500,000 kW and 800,000 kW are constructed in Leningrad and other plants.

Similarly modern super-heated boilers capable of producing 2,500 tons of steam per hour are currently built. Also high-voltage transmission systems of 400–500 kV are usual. Gas turbines are operating not only in power stations, but also in pipeline pumping stations, in locomotives and in turbo-prop–jet aircraft. Such power engineering developments are transforming the Soviet industrial scene and greatly stepping up the rate of production.

Since the opening of the first experimental nuclear power plant at Dubna in 1953 the atomic power industry has undergone rapid growth. During the current Five-Year Plan (1971–75) batch production of standardized nuclear power stations of one million kW capacity is to be undertaken. Andranik Petrosyants, Chairman of the Soviet State Committee for the Utilization of Atomic Energy, envisages growth of the atomic power capacity from its present 11·8 million kW to 18–20 million

61. Leningrad's 'Kirov' Tractor Works. Shipping 220-hp, K-700 tractors to the Soviet Union's western farming districts.

62. The Minsk Tractor Works, Belorussia. Here the light 'Belorus' MTS-50 tractors are being prepared for shipment. Since 1953 this plant has built over a million units on its mass assembly lines.

kW and 30 million kW by 1975 and 1980 respectively. He also anticipates a switch away from thermal neutron reactors (using Uranium-235) to fast neutron types (breeder reactors). These can use many different kinds of fuel such as standard uranium (U-238) and thorium and moreover 'breed' more fuel than they use in the process. The switch is already evident as noted in the previous statistics. Of a total atomic power capacity in 1971 of 11,820,000 kW about 750,000 kW was derived from the two fast neutron reactors then operating at Beloyarsk and Shevchenko.

Mining Engineering. The widespread development of underground and open-cut mining in the Soviet Union has necessitated new and improved types of mining equipment. This ranges from oil-field turbo-drills, to coal combines that 'plough' along the coal face, bucket excavators, walking draglines and rotary excavators for the removal of overburden, coal and ore materials.

The largest dragline built in the Soviet Union is capable of moving 7 million cubic metres of rock annually (boom length 100 metres, bucket load 25 cubic metres). Coal and ore transportation is now undertaken by 40- or 70-ton dump-trucks or 100-ton capacity, swing-bottom, dump-cars hauled by wheeled tractors.

Another example of advanced mining technology is the Soviet-invented turbo-drill. With this equipment oil or gas wells are drilled to depths of up to 10,000 metres without the normal rotation of the drill pipes. Instead, the vertical column of drill pipes supports a hydraulic turbine head which turns the drill bit. This is capable of boring through hard rock to great depths and since the whole drill string does not turn much less energy is required for the

63. The Ryazan' Combine builds potato-picking machines shown here in the storage yard.

64. Combined harvesters lined up at the Stepnoy sovkhoz ready to begin grain harvesting from 25,000 hectares.

operation. The improved efficiency attained is shown by the following data (Table 14.9).

Transport Engineering. This branch of heavy engineering has undertaken some quite revolutionary technological changes in post-war years. Soviet railways have now virtually completed the switch to diesel and electric locomotives. The last steam engine was built in 1956 and all currently operating steam locomotives are being progressively replaced by more efficiently powered locomotives. Details are given in Chapter 16 on transportation.

Diesel locomotives are built at Lyudinovo (Central Region), Kherson (Ukraine), Kolomna, Khar'kov, and Lugansk (Voroshilovgrad). Electric locomotives are built at Novocherkassk and Tbilisi. These works receive the electric motors and control gear from the Dynamo Works in Moscow.

Freight wagons have been redesigned. The 60-ton four-axle bogie-type open or closed wagon with automatic coupling has been introduced on many heavily used routes. Also a six-axle open wagon of 93-ton capacity and a new 73-ton refrigerator car are currently under batch production. For passenger rolling stock new light-weight all-metal air-conditioned carriages have been placed into service. All freight wagons and passenger cars are equipped with roller bearings.

At the moment some 45,000 freight wagons and 2000 carriages are being produced annually at works situated in the Urals, at Kaliningrad, Kremenchug, and Chesnokovka (Altay Kray). The Riga carriage works specializes in lighter types of

TABLE 14.9

Drilling Speed of Soviet Oil Wells (Depth drilled in metres per Operating Month) *

Type of Operation	1940	1950	1960	1970	Growth 1950–70
Exploratory Drilling	233	209	401	349	67·0
Operational Drilling	412	629	993	1127	79·2

Source: Belousov, *op. cit.*, p. 45.

* Drilling operations *include* all stages, boring, drawing drill strings to change bits, down-time, etc. Thus net drilling speeds are much higher than the figures given.

electric railway vehicles used on metropolitan systems. It also builds the power units.

The Soviet shipbuilding industry has grown considerably in post-war years – from very small beginnings. Present designs include 150,000-ton tankers, 100,000-ton dual-purpose, liquid-bulk freight vessels, merchant vessels, factory vessels for the fisheries and whaling, ice-breakers, passenger liners, and hydrofoils.

The early shipyards in Leningrad, Nikolayev, and river port slipways at Kherson, Kiev, Gor'kiy, Krasnoarmeysk, Astrakhan', and Tyumen', have all been modernized and improved since the war. New marine yards have been opened along the Baltic Coast and Vladivostok and river shipyards in Perm', Krasnoyarsk, Blagoveshchensk, and Khabarovsk. The Krasnoye Sormovo yards near Gor'kiy, specialize in hydrofoils, capable of speeds of up to 100 kilometres per hour.

In recent years, the Soviet motor vehicle industry has witnessed something of a political *volte face*. Formerly the manufacture of private passenger cars was a very low-keyed operation. The rationale behind this policy was to concentrate the use of scarce resources – basic steel sheet, rubber and other materials – into the production of tractors, motor lorries, and buses. However, the present greater availability of these materials and the new political viewpoint that cars are a legitimate element in a people's democracy,[1] have caused a tremendous burgeoning of private vehicle building in the Soviet Union (Fig. 14.3).

[1] Premier Aleksei N. Kosygin's speech to the State Planning Commission, March, 1965. In this speech Khruschev's idea that the private vehicle was a 'weakness' of the capitalist system was rejected and new guidelines for Soviet car manufacture were laid down.

65. The Elektrosila Works of Leningrad heavy industries. Assembling a 500-megawatt turbo-generator.

66. The Izhora plant of Leningrad heavy industries. Marking out the base frame for a caterpillar excavator shovel.

67. The 'Uralmash' heavy engineering plant at Sverdlovsk, Central Urals. Assembling the roll-stand for a heavy- duty H-section beam mill to be supplied to the Nizhniy Tagil iron and steel mill. Annual capacity 1·5 million tons.

As a result of the new policy, Renault of France were invited to modernize the Moskvich plant in Moscow raising its output to 200,000 vehicles per year, and in May, 1966, Fiat of Italy was commissioned to build an entirely new plant on the Volga at Stavropol. This city was re-named Tol'yatti (Togliatti) to honour the Italian communist leader and mark the contribution of Fiat. A consortium of Italian and Russian technologists and machinery and equipment purchased from Western European and United States sources established the 800 million rouble Volga Auto Plant at Tol'yatti. The first 'Zhiguli' car came off the assembly line in August, 1970, and production has since reached the designed capacity of 660,000 cars per year (1,360 cars per day).

Sheet steel for the Volga Auto Plant comes from Magnitogorsk and Karaganda. Tyres are manufactured in Tol'yatti from locally produced synthetic rubber.

Investment in the Volga Auto Plant represents two-thirds of the planned investment in the vehicle industry during the decade 1966–75.

Other vehicle manufacturing plants and their output (where known) are as follows: Moscow makes 'Moskvich' cars (200,000 units annually); Izhevsk (Udmurt A.S.S.R.; 300,000 units) assembles 'Moskvich' cars: Gor'kiy makes 'Volga' cars (1965, 50,000 units), Zaporozh'ye makes 'Zaporozhets' cars; Minsk and L'vov make lorries and buses; Zhodino (Belorussia) makes 75-ton, 950 bhp lorries, and Ul'yanovsk, north of Tol'yatti, makes UAZ cross-country vehicles, the equivalent of the British Land-Rover. Another plant in the Tatar A.S.S.R. manufactures lorries and specialized vehicles.

In 1970 the Soviet Union produced 916,118 motor vehicles (524,507 lorries; 344,248 cars and 47,363 buses). Thus the Plan target of 800,000 vehicles by 1970 was handsomely achieved. In 1971 vehicle production was 1,143,000 units. Despite these efforts, Soviet vehicle building remains substantially behind the United States, Japan, Germany and Britain in production levels. Moreover, the total Soviet vehicle inventory, estimated at 4 million vehicles currently in use, is far below that of the United States (70 million vehicles in use in 1970) despite its much larger population and territory.

Machine Tool Industries

Among the fastest growing heavy industries in the Soviet Union are the machine tool branches. In 1971 about 205,000 machine tools of all types were built. Lathes and metal shaping machines such as milling machines, planers, boring and drilling machines, metal presses and forging presses are built in many individual plants scattered throughout the country.

Automation of machine tools, using pneumatic, hydraulic, and electronic devices, and the building of specialized precision machines – such as transfer lines for the vehicle industries – to cope with mass production techniques has been developing rapidly over the last decade. The introduction of a transfer line in the Moskvich car plant cut the space required for machining cylinder blocks by half and reduced the overall machining time from 135 to 15 minutes. It also reduced the work-force from 180 to 3 transfer operators. The Soviet government has engaged in large-scale modernization of plants as it finds that the costs involved can be recouped within two years. This is an even quicker way of increasing production than building entirely new industrial plants from scratch and, moreover, it conserves capital resources.

Concomitantly with the expansion of machine-tool industries progress has been made in instrument making, measuring devices and precision control equipment manufacture. The manufacture of digital computers doubled between 1966 and 1970; output of computers, ancillary equipment, and spares in 1972 was valued at 1180 million roubles. At present the Soviet Union has begun production of the more sophisticated third generation miniaturized-circuit computers capable of 1000 million operations per second.

The Russian machine tool industries are located in Moscow (Ordzhonikidze and Krasnyy Proletariy Machine Tool works), at Leningrad, Khar'kov, Minsk, Vitebsk, Odessa, Kramatorsk, and Kuybyshev. Gorkiy makes automatic lathes and milling machines; Novosibirsk hydraulic metal presses, and Kolomna a variety of specialized machine tools. The Tula arms factory also produces machine tools.

Heavy Chemical Industries

In the post-war period chemical production has very considerably increased. The manufacture of sulphuric and other acids, caustic soda and other alkalis,

68. The Soviet Union's chief car manufacturing centre at Tol'yatti, Kuybyshev oblast. The main assembly line has an annual capacity of 660,000 units. The plant was built by a consortium of Russian and Italian engineers who used advanced technology and machines bought from Italian, United States, and British sources as well as from Russian specialist enterprises.

TABLE 14.10
Soviet Chemical Production (*Excluding Fertilizers*)
(*in thousands of tons unless otherwise stated*)

Chemical	1940	1950	1960	1970
Sulphuric Acid (monohydrate)	1587	2125	5398	12 059
Caustic Soda	190	325	765	1938
Soda Ash	540	750	1890	3850 (1972
Synthetic Dyes	34·3	46·2	84·1	98·0
Chemical Fibres	11·1	24·2	211·2	623·0
Synthetic Resins and Plastics	10·9	67·1	311·6	1672·0
Tyres (millions)	3·0	7·4	17·2	34·6

Source: Belousov, *op. cit.*, p. 72; figures for Soda Ash from Shabad, *op. čit.*, p. 81.

ammonia and mineral fertilizers have all shown vigorous growth trends. This expansion is even more apparent in the petro-chemical industries (Table 14.10).

The manufacture of sulphuric acid has shifted away from the older tower method to the modern contact method over recent years. This is consistent with the swing away from pyrites as a source of sulphur to brimstone (native sulphur), smelter and refinery gases, and hydrogen sulphide from natural gas as the main sources. In 1965 about 66·4 per cent of Soviet sulphuric acid was produced by the contact method; in 1970 some 77·7 per cent. In the current 1971–75 Plan the percentage is to rise to 87 per cent, although a renewed use of Urals pyrites is envisaged due to a shortfall in brimstone supplies.

In 1970 the Soviet Union produced 1·95 million tons of sulphur; some by the Frasch process (American) from the Yavorov deposit on the Dniester river and near Kuybyshev on the Volga. Changes in the sources of sulphur over recent years are shown below (Table 14.11).

While sulphuric acid goes dominantly into the mineral fertilizer industry, caustic soda and soda ash are used in the production of alumina, glass, dyestuffs, soaps, and detergents, and a wide range of cosmetic and pharmaceutical products.

The chief centres for the production of acids and strong alkalis are as follows: for acids, Voskresensk, Shcholkovo, Novomoskovsk and Chernorechensk in the Central Region; Odessa, Konstantinovka and Vinnitsa in the Ukraine, and

TABLE 14.11
Soviet Sulphur Sources (*in percentages of total*)

	1960	1965	1970	1975 Plan
Pyrites (Urals)	62·8	46·1	47·0	56·7
Brimstone (native sulphur)	17·9	26·3	19·0	13·5
Smelter gases	15·2	21·5	25·5	23·3
Hydrogen Sulphide	4·1	6·1	8·0	6·1
Others (including Frasch)	—	—	0·5	0·4
	100·0	100·0	100·0	100·0

Source: *Soviet Geography*, **13** (3) 1972, p. 185. (Figures adjusted from source to make 100%).

Perm', Berezniki and Kirovograd in the Urals. For alkalis produced from common salt and limestone, Donetsk and Slavyansk in the Ukraine; Berezniki and Sterlitamak in the Urals, and Yavan in Tadzhikistan are the chief centres.

Mineral Fertilizers. The intensification of agriculture is making pressing demands on the Soviet fertilizer industry. Fortunately production has increased substantially, but it still remains behind potential demand (Table 14.12).

Potash fertilizers are manufactured mainly in the Urals (Berezniki–Solikamsk), at Soligorsk in Belorussia and in the Carpathian foothills (Stebnik and Kalush). Production at these centres is shown in Table 14.13.

TABLE 14.12
Soviet Mineral Fertilizer Production
A = Total Production; B in Terms of Active Ingredient (both in thousand tons)

Fertilizer	1940		1950		1960		1970	
	A	B	A	B	A	B	A	B
Nitrogenous	972	199	1913	392	4892	1003	26 442	5423
Phosphatic	1352	253	2351	440	4878	912	13 370	2500
Ground Phosphate Rock	382	73	483	92	1492	282	5764	1089
Potash	532	221	750	312	2605	1084	9824	4087
All Fertilizers	3238	746	5497	1236	13 867	3281	55 400	13 099

Source: *Narodnoe Khozyaistvo 1970*, Moscow, 1971, p. 198. (Figures slightly adjusted to give correct totals.)

Major centres for the production of superphosphates are located at Voskresensk, Odessa, Vinnitsa, Konstantinovka, Leningrad, Perm', Aktyubinsk, and Dzhambul. Other superphosphate plants in the agricultural areas are Sumy (Ukraine), Riga, and Kedainyai. Plants located in the raw-material areas are those working phosphorite deposits – Samarkand, Kokand, and Chardzhou – whereas the market-centred plants mainly use Khibiny apatites or local supplies of Thomas slag as their raw materials. The Kola Peninsula apatites are costly to transport and a shift towards phosphorites is now under way (Table 14.14).

TABLE 14.13
Soviet Potash Fertilizer Production (in million tons in terms of 41·6% K_2O Units)

Centre	1970	1975 Plan
Berezniki–Solikamsk	3·8	10·8
Soligorsk	4·8	8·0
Stebnik–Kalush	1·0	1·0
Total	9·6	19·8

Source: *Soviet Geography*, **13** (3), 1972, p. 186.

69. The Kara-Bogaz-Gol sulphate workings near Bekdash, Caspian Sea. Here machines sweep the already evaporated salts into their holding bins.

70. Kara-Bogaz-Gol sulphate is loaded into lorries for transport to western Kazakhstan's chemical plants.

71. The ammonia installation at the Nevinnomyssk chemical mill, North Caucasus. This fertilizer plant, one of the largest in the Soviet Union, makes nitrogenous fertilizers.

72. The Kuybyshev synthetic rubber plant, Middle Volga.

73. The Kursk technical rubber goods plant. Rubber ball dividers used to separate different oil shipments in pipelines being fitted with isotope sensors.

74. The Berezniki potash deposit, Urals. Here mining cars are loaded with raw sylvinite from the higher level stopes.

TABLE 14.14

Soviet Phosphorus Sources (As Percentage of Raw Material)

	1965	1970	1975 Plan
Kola Pen. (Kirovsk Apatite)	86·6	81·7	69·6
Karatau Basin (Phosphorite)	13·4	18·3	27·5
Kingisepp (Phosphate rock)	—	—	2·2
Yegor'yevsk (Phosphate rock)	—	—	0·7
	100·0	100·0	100·0

Source: *Soviet Geography*, **13** (3) 1972, p. 185.

75. The Soligorsk Potash Works in Belorussia. Here concentrator tanks extract the crude potassium needed by the 1·2 million ton per annum fertilizer plant shown in the background.

The Kola Peninsula production of apatite was 11·3 million tons in 1970 and will increase to 14·5 million tons by 1975. Since its percentage share as a phosphatic source is to decline substantially, the other centres can be postulated to grow quite significantly.

The shift towards more complex and powerful fertilizers in the current (1971–75) Plan period is illustrated in Table 14.15.

In general, the ninth Five-Year Plan (1971–75) calls for mineral fertilizer output to be doubled and since there is to be a shift to more powerful ingredients the effect on Soviet agriculture will be considerably enhanced.

Chapter 15 on the light industries and consumer goods deals with other aspects of the chemical industries; chemical fibres, synthetic rubber, resins, and plastics as well as fine chemical and pharmaceutical products.

TABLE 14.15
Soviet Phosphatic Fertilizer Output (in million tons and percentage of total)

	1970		1975 Plan	
	Output	%	Output	%
Ordinary Fertilizers	11·58	88·5	13·63	61·7
of which:				
Simple Superphosphate	8·50	65·0	7·83	35·4
Double Superphosphate	2·83	21·6	5·57	25·2
Phosphate (Thomas) Slag	0·25	1·9	0·23	1·1
Complex Fertilizers	1·48	11·5	8·47	38·3
of which:				
Ammophos	0·46	3·5	4·16	18·8
Diammophos	—	—	0·05	0·02
Nitroammophoska	0·34	2·8	2·30	10·5
Nitrophoska	0·26	2·0	0·36	1·7
Nitrophos	0·42	3·2	1·60	7·3
Total Phosphate Fertilizer	13·06	100·0	22·10*	100·0

Source: *Soviet Geography*, **13**, (3) 1972, p. 185.
  * Excludes three million tons of feed phosphates, and therefore not used as fertilizers.

76. The Berezniki potash deposit (sylvinite), Urals, yields more than half of the country's potash fertilizers. Here pneumatic-tyred boring and hauling machines feed raw material to a conveyor belt.

CHAPTER FIFTEEN

LIGHT INDUSTRIES AND CONSUMER MARKETS

The slow development of light industries in the Soviet Union and equally the disregard of immediate consumer interests was dictated by government policy which placed greatest emphasis on the producer goods industries. The acute scarcity of many forms of essential products, like coal, oil, steel, and basic chemical materials, and also the need to build up strong foundations in the means of production, meant that few resources in capital, manpower, and raw materials were available to service light industry before the 1960s. In consequence, light consumer goods industries are still somewhat constrained in their development.

Over the last three decades, however, the Soviet Union has created a sufficiently powerful heavy industry base to permit renewed and, lately, more vigorous attention to the light industries. Moreover, those branches of heavy industry that manufacture durable or semi-durable consumer goods – motor vehicles, television sets, refrigerators, household appliances, etc. – have also received greater investment (Fig. 14.3 above).

The share of the heavy engineering industries in output value of these classes of consumer goods rose from 19 per cent in 1965 to 23 per cent in 1970. The Soviet Economic Development Plan for 1971–75 aims to increase this further to 29 per cent by 1975. Thus the 'plough-back' role of heavy industry (the so-called A-class industries in Soviet terminology) is decreasing relatively over time, although the expansion in absolute terms is planned to continue.

In the light industries catering for traditional consumer needs – food industries, tobacco, beverages, and alcoholic drinks, textiles, clothing, books, and many others – the expansion has been going on for the past decade or so (Fig. 15.1). During the current Five-Year Plan (1971–75) the growth rates planned for consumer goods industries will, for the first time in Soviet history, exceed those laid down for heavy industry. The aim is to improve the real income of the Soviet citizen and provide more choice than in the past in the range and variety of goods available for purchase. The 24th Party Congress thus shifted emphasis in the Soviet economy to a further raising of the Russian standard of living. The means selected is to increase the proportion of the national effort and funds channelled into agriculture, light industries, semi-durable consumer goods, and social services.

Recent changes in output levels in A-class and B-class industries in the Soviet Union – that is, in the heavy industries (durable consumer goods included) and consumer goods industries proper – clearly indicate the greater emphasis on the consumer goods component. During the period 1961–65 the output of heavy industries rose by 58 per cent and consumer goods by 36 per cent; in 1966–70 the respective percentages were 51 and 49, and in the 1971–75 Plan growth rates are expected to be 46·3 and 48·6 per cent respectively.

Closer examination of these figures, however, indicates that virtually all of the additional growth in the consumer goods sector came from the durable and semi-durable goods component in the heavy industries. In fact, there has been very little relative gain in the output of consumer goods proper, although in absolute terms these industries have all undergone considerable expansion. The relevant statistics are given below (Table 15.1). Since great confusion has been apparent in the past in the role of durable consumer industries, the author has attempted to divide the class-A industrial group given in Soviet statistics into two categories: viz., producer goods industries and consumer durables industries – something perhaps not attempted by Russian statisticians. Whatever the exact pattern of output in percentage terms of the consumer goods industries, there is little doubt that they have expanded very considerably in recent years. Further, as the percentage figures show (Table 15.1), there has been a very marked shift towards production of consumer goods, both

TABLE 15.1

Soviet Industrial Production by Categories (in Percentage of Total Rouble Value)

Year	Means of Production (Class-A)			Consumer Goods		
	Means of Production	I Producer Goods Proper (estimate)	II Durable Consumer Goods (estimate)	Consumer Goods (Class-B)	Including Durables	Total Industrial Production
	(a)	(b)	(c)	(d)	(c + d)	(a + d)
1940	61·2	60·5	0·7	38·8	39·5	100·0
1945	74·9	73·9	1·0	25·1	26·1	100·0
1950	68·8	66·6	2·2	31·2	33·4	100·0
1955	70·5	66·5	4·0	29·5	33·5	100·0
1960	72·5	64·7	7·8	27·5	35·3	100·0
1965	74·1	61·0	13·1	25·9	39·0	100·0
1970	73·4	56·6	16·8	26·6	43·4	100·0
1975 plan	71·8	51·0	20·8	28·2	49·0	100·0

Source: *Narodnoe Khozyaistvo, 1970*, Moscow, 1971; for Class A and Class B percentages only, 1940–70. Breakdown into Producer goods proper and Consumer Durables are author's estimates and from these are derived total consumer goods of all classes.

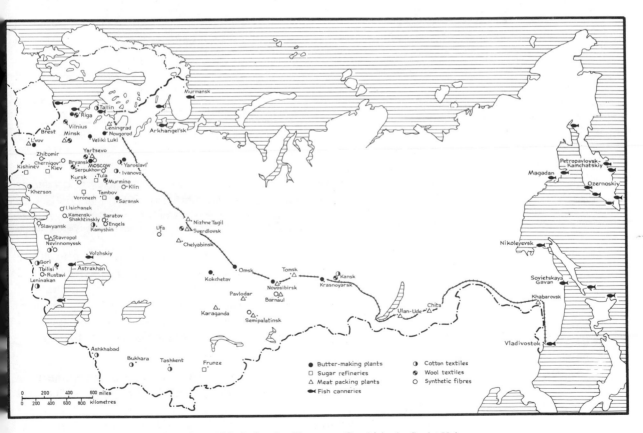

FIG. 15.1   Light Industries (Consumer Goods) in the Soviet Union.

TABLE 15.2
Consumer Goods Industries Output 1940–70 (Representative Selection)

Product	Units	1940	1950	1960	1965	1970
Meat, abattoir	thousand tons	1501	1556	4406	5245	7144
Butter, dairy	thousand tons	226	336	737	1072	963
Cheese	thousand tons	51	73	194	310	478
Vegetable Oils	thousand tons	798	819	1586	2770	2784
Margarine	thousand tons	121	192	431	670	762
Granulated Sugar	thousand tons	2165	2523	6363	11 037	10 221
Canned Foods	million tins	1113	1535	4864	7078	10 676
Wine	million hectolitres	1·97	2·38	7·77	13·39	26·80
Beer	million hectolitres	12·10	13·10	25·00	31·69	41·90
Tobacco products	billion units	100	125	245	304	323
Soap (40% fat basis)	thousand tons	700	816	1474	1926	1912
Cotton fabrics	million square metres	2704	2745	4834	5499	6152
Woollen fabrics	million square metres	152·0	193·0	439·0	466·0	643·0
Silk fabrics (natural & artificial)	million square metres	64·2	106·0	675·0	801·0	1146·0
Leather footwear	million pairs	211·4	203·4	419·0	486·0	676·0
Paper	thousand tons	812	1180	2334	3231	4185
Clocks and Watches	millions	2·8	7·6	26·0	30·6	40·2
Radio-Radiograms	thousands	160	1072	4165	5160	7815
Television Sets	thousands	0·3	11·9	1726	3655	6682
Bicycles and Mopeds	thousands	255	649	2783	3873	4443
Motor Cycles + Scooters	thousands	6·7	123	533	711	833
Refrigerators (domestic)	thousands	—	0·3	895	3430	5243
Vacuum Cleaners	thousands	—	6·1	501	800	1509
Washing Machines	thousands	175	502	3096	800	1400
Cameras	thousands	355	261	1764	1053	2045

Source: *Narodnoe Khozyaistvo, 1970*, Moscow, 1971; pp. 144, 148, 228, 238, 251, 254.

consumption goods and durables. It can be argued that the upswing since 1965 represents a fundamental change in Soviet basic ideology – a shift towards consumer 'sovereignty' – and, at the same time, an emergence of new social values in raising the standard of living of the Russian population.

The consumer statistics (above) show much the same conclusion expressed in the form of individual commodities and durable consumer goods (Table 15.2). Without exception, Soviet consumer production and with this, light industries, have undergone a growth phase, sometimes a remarkably vigorous growth phase, since 1940. The figures arbitrarily selected are necessarily limited because of space, but they are nevertheless representative of the whole range of consumer industries.

Even more emphasis is to be given to consumer industries in the ninth Five-Year Plan, 1971–75. According to the decision of the 24th Congress of the Soviet Communist Party:

The main task of the five-year plan is to ensure a considerable rise of the people's material and cultural level on the basis of a high rate of development of socialist production, enhancement of its efficiency, scientific and technical progress and acceleration of the growth of labour productivity.[1]

It should be noted, however, that some consumer goods industries got off to a bad start. As reported

[1] Quoted from, *USSR 1972*, Novosti Press Agency Year Book, Novosti, Moscow, 1972, p. 181.

in *Pravda*, 30.1.1973, the production statistics for 1972 presented by the Soviet Central Statistical Board stated that ready-made clothing, knitwear garments, and leather footwear had not met the annual plan targets. Substantially, the reason was an under-allocation of new technological equipment destined for these and other light industries. This points up a perennial problem in command-type planning: difficulties in one segment of the plan quickly affect other industries which, through inter-industry linkages, are transmitted widely throughout the economy. Newly commissioned enterprises are especially prone to difficulties in the initial period, as are those of their capitalist counterparts in the western world.

The Food Industries

In gross value of output Soviet food industries rank third in the national economy; after engineering–metal working industries, and the textile industries. Most branches of the food industries are concentrated in the European parts of the Soviet Union. These include grain products, milk products, fish, meat, vegetable and fruit canning, and many others. Only gradually is light industry spreading to the east and southeast. Thus many heavy industrial complexes are still without adequate production in light industry and food processing establishments. Frequently too, primary food production and the associated processing industries are geographically separated, especially in areas of recent agricultural development.

It is evident that the market-oriented branches of the food industries – grain milling, large bakeries, liquid milk processing, and abattoirs – suffer from the greatest inertia. Raw material oriented processing – sugar refining, oil-seed pressing, butter and cheese processing, starch and wine-making – have been much more resilient in locational shifts, moving as new centres of raw material production emerge. For example, the Ukraine area of sugar-beet agriculture once had 80 per cent of the sugar refinery capacity, while today it has a little over 60 per cent. New refinery capacity has emerged in the Kuban (15 large sugar refineries), the Volga, South Kazakhstan, and Far East among others.

Grain Milling. New grain milling industry has been set up in the Centre, Ukraine, the Volga,

77. At Besemyanka, Kuybyshev oblast, there is the Soviet Union's largest confectionery factory. The full automated plant turns out 27,000 tons of 'Rossiya' chocolates annually.

Caucasus, Urals, Siberia, and the Far East. Emphasis in establishing the fully mechanized roller-mills has been placed on economies of scale and the immediate market prospects for the output. Since it is easier and cheaper to transport grain rather than flour, all new mills are located in areas of large population.

During the last two decades there has been greater correspondence between milling capacity and population, but there still remains some rail transport of flour, including some uneconomic cross-haulage of grain and flour, particularly in Central Asia and Kazakhstan.

The larger cities all have large mechanized and automated bakeries, but most small centres have bakeries which are small, often costly to operate, and restricted in their market radius because it is not feasible to transport bread efficiently by road. The production of farinaceous foods such as macaroni and noodles has recently become an important branch of the food industries.

Dairy Processing. The Soviet Union lags behind countries like the United States, Denmark, and New Zealand in modern dairy technology. Nevertheless, attempts have been made recently to establish large modern dairy factories in the largest centres of population, for example at Torez (Thorez) and Krasnoarmeysk (Donetsk oblast). These factories concentrate on the manufacture of immediate milk products: pasteurized household milk, sour milk or cream – extensively used in Russian cooking – curds and kefir, an effervescent milk liquor popular in the Soviet Union. Russian *per capita* consumption of dairy products is now about 350 kilograms a year.

Butter-making and cheese-making plants, on the other hand, are dominantly located in the main dairy-farming areas, the Baltic Republics, Belorussia, the Northwest, and Centre. These products are more easily transportable than whole milk and there are substantial economies in setting up a large, modern dairy factory such as that at Kaunas. Plants manufacturing condensed milk and milk powder are similarly located, sometimes within the same complex. Modern dairy complexes have been established recently in the Ukraine, Azerbaydzhan and Georgia. New milk powder fac-

78. Eggs being automatically sized, graded and date-stamped at the Glebov egg plant near Moscow. Crates of eggs are dispatched to shops and works canteens throughout the Centre.

tories have been set up at Pugachev, and Kuybyshev.

Meat-Packing. The post-war development in the meat-packing industry has been one of the sagas of Soviet development. From a position of acute meat scarcity in the recent past, the country now undertakes the slaughter and packaging of all kinds of meat in large, modern abattoir-factories. Bacon processing plants are located at Melitopol, Poltava, and Kremenchug in the Ukraine. Others are at Leningrad, Voronezh, and Engel's.

As in the case of dairy product factories, meat-packing plants are located in both market areas and in the main areas of animal production. The Moscow, Leningrad, Vinnitsa and Bryansk factories are representative of the former, while the meat-packing plants located at Krasnodar, Leninakan, Sverdlovsk, Petropavlovsk, Ulan-Ude and Khabarovsk are representative of the great number in the beef and mutton producing areas. In both types of location, abattoir–freezer-plants and less frequently canning plants are involved. In Kazakhstan alone, nine meat-packing plants were set up under the eighth Five-Year Plan (1966–70). Elsewhere new plants have been set up in Grodno, Novgorod, Achinsk, and Naberezhnyye Chelny.

Sugar Refineries. In 1970, the Soviet Union produced over 10 million tons of granulated sugar, double the amount produced in the United States. Changes in the production of refined sugar from sugar-beet and sugar cane respectively are shown in Table 15.3.

Since 7–8 tons of sugar-beets are required to extract one ton of refined sugar, all beet refineries are located in the beet-growing areas. It would not be economic to transport sugar-beet over long distances. Moreover, the beet-pulp remaining – 85–90 per cent of the raw material input – yields a valuable dairy-cattle and animal feed.

As indicated earlier, some 60 per cent of the sugar-refining capacity is in the main areas of beet cultivation of the Ukraine and Voronezh, Belgorod, and Kursk oblasts. A new refinery at Znamensky (Tambov oblast) opened in 1972. In recent decades, however, new beet-growing areas, Kazakhstan, Central Asia, Georgia, Armenia, and Krasnodar Kray have set up sugar refineries. The main centres are at Frunze, Alma-Ata, Taldy-Kurgan,

TABLE 15.3
Soviet Sugar Refining Production of Granulated Sugar (thousands of tons)

Year	Derived from Sugar-Beet	Derived from Sugar Cane*	Total Output	Percentage from Beet
1940	2165	—	2165	100·0
1945	465	—	465	100·0
1950	2523	—	2523	100·0
1955	3239	180	3419	94·7
1960	5266	1097	6363	82·8
1965	8924	2113	11 037	80·8
1966	8295	1445	9740	85·2
1967	8453	1486	9939	85·0
1968	9030	1736	10 766	83·9
1969	9272	1075	10 347	89·6
1970	8139	2082	10 221	79·6

Source: *Narodnoe Khozyaistvo, 1970*, Moscow, 1971; p. 150–51 for Total and Beet Production.

* Raw cane sugar is imported from Cuba under trade agreements. This arose from the Soviet Union's desire to support Cuba once the United States and other western countries placed embargoes on Cuban sugar.

Novo-Troitsk, Biysk and Aleysk among others. In the Far East the refinery is at Ussuriysk. In the Kuban, refineries are located at Novo-Kubansky, Uspenskaya, Kanevskaya, and elsewhere; a total of fifteen refineries in all. Moldavia is a new sugar-refining area.

The Textile Industries

Soviet textile manufacture has undergone vital transformations in recent years. First, there has been a substantial re-location of the various branches of the industry away from the historic centres. Dominantly this has been a movement towards indigenous raw material sources; the cotton-growing areas of Central Asia, the wool-growing areas of Kazakhstan, Siberia, and the North Caucasus, and the chemical fibre centres of the Middle Volga and elsewhere.

Secondly, the scale of operations and organization of the mills have both changed. Modern integrated and large-scale mills (*kombinats*) engage in spinning, weaving, and finishing of fabrics under one roof whereas formerly these were specialized branches and geographically separated

phases of the textile industry. The new location and scale of operation secure very considerable economies in textile manufacturing.

Thirdly, the availability of oil and natural gas has given far greater flexibility to the setting up of textile mills. In the old centres it required one and a half tons of coal to provide the steam and energy to process every ton of textile material, cotton, linen, wool, or silk. It was then quite impractical to move energy to textile raw materials; a constraint no longer valid now that pipelines and high-voltage transmission lines criss-cross the country.

There has been a strong tendency for the cotton textile industry to gravitate towards market concentrations. First, there are important economies of scale for the integrated mills, or *kombinats*, since they are able to make many different varieties of goods and yet maintain economic output levels for each. Moreover, it is much cheaper to transport compressed cotton bales (500 kilograms/cubic metre) than to transport cotton fabric or finished goods, partly as a result of space saving – about 15 to 20 per cent – but also partly due to higher freight rates on finished goods ton for ton than on raw materials.

The Moscow–Ivanovo area of the Centre still maintains 67–68 per cent of the Soviet cotton industry. This is a major part of the national production, but over recent years the concentration in the centre has declined somewhat (Table 15.4).

TABLE 15.4
Regional Distribution of the Cotton Textile Industry (In percentage of total in terms of linear metres)

	1913	1940	1963	1970
Centre	91	87	74·1	67·5 (e)
Other Western R.S.F.S.R.	5	6	7·4	9·8 (e)
Eastern R.S.F.S.R.	0	1	3·7	4·8 (e)
Ukraine and Belorussia	...	...	2·5	4·5*
Baltic	3	1	3·0	4·2
Trans-Caucasia	1	2	3·9	3·9
Central Asia	0	3	5·4	5·3†

Source: Pryde, *op. cit.*, 1968, pp. 580, 586; For 1970, *Narodnoe Khozyaistvo, 1970*, Moscow, 1971, p. 240; calculations and estimate by author.

* Includes Moldavia.

† Includes Kazakhstan.

The earlier centres of the cotton textile industry are located at Moscow, Ivanovo, Shuya, Orekhovo-Zuyevo and many other industrial towns in the belt including Moscow oblast, Vladimir oblast, and Ivanovo oblast (Fig. 15.1). New *kombinats* have been constructed since the war at Donetsk, Kamyshin (Volgograd oblast), Cheboksary, Kherson, Gori, Barnaul, and Dushanbe. Others, including those built in the cotton-growing areas, are located at Tashkent, Bukhara, Samarkand, Fergana, Alma-Ata, Osh, and Kustanai. There are also new mills at Kemerovo, Leninsk-Kuznetsky, and Biysk in Western Siberia. Plants using a new technology developed to manufacture unwoven cotton textiles are dominantly in the long established enterprises of the Centre; in Moscow, Tula, and Tambov oblasts.

Woollen textiles have experienced considerable expansion in keeping with the greater availability of domestic wool supplies. The oldest centres of the industry are in the Baltic areas and Volga river ports of the Centre marking their earlier dependence on imported wool. With the swing to Soviet supplies of wool, new woollen mills were established in Chernigov, Khar'kov and Kremenchug (Ukraine); in Minsk, Grodno and Vitebsk (Belorussia); and Krasnodar and Nevinnomyssk (North Caucasus). Moscow oblast has been long renowned for mills weaving worsteds and fine woollens; the Lyubertsy and Monino woollen mills.

With the expansion of sheep numbers in Trans-Caucasia, Kazakhstan, Central Asia, Krasnoyarsk Kray and elsewhere, new woollen mills have been set up in raw material areas. Moreover, since the development of synthetic wool-substitute fibres, the older mills of the Centre and new mills in Estonia, Belorussia, and Azerbaydzhan, will concentrate on wool-synthetic fabrics.

The linen fabric industry of the Soviet Union, historically the oldest of all textile industries, has experienced rather less expansion than the other branches. The industry shows very considerable inertia and remains in the flax-growing areas. Retting is still carried on in the traditional manner, and fibre is sent to mills in Vladimir, Bryansk, Kostroma, Yaroslavl' and Ivanovo oblasts. Several modern mills have been built in Rovno, Pskov, Orsha, Smolensk, Kostroma, Molodechno, Vyaz'ma, Vologda, Panevezhis, and elsewhere. Out-liers of the linen industry occur in the Tatar A.S.S.R. and Altai Kray.

The Soviet silk industry is located partly in the raw material areas (early stages) and partly in the market areas (weaving and finishing). Silk reeling plants which wind the filament from the cacoons are located in Caucasia, Uzbekistan, Turkmenistan, and Kirghizia at numerous different centres. Silk twisting and/or weaving are located at Vitebsk (Belorussia), Kirzhach (Vladimir oblast), Kutaisi and Tbilisi (Georgia), Nukha (Azerbaydzhan), Namangan, and Margelan (Uzbekistan).

Artificial 'silk' fibres (principally cellulose rayon and acetate rayon) have substantially augmented the production of silk-type fabrics in the Soviet Union as they have done in every other natural silk producing country, such as Japan and India. Nevertheless the natural silk industry has proved more tenacious in the Soviet Union than elsewhere, due partly to official encouragement, and partly as a prestige fabric in a society for long inured to accept second-best in textiles. Some true synthetic fibres such as kapron (the Soviet equivalent to nylon) are now availabe due to the rise of the petro-chemical industry.

The earlier chief centres for rayon production

79. A cotton spinning mill at Dushanbe, Tadzhikistan.

are located at Leningrad, Kalinin, Klin, Mogilev, Gor'kiy, and Krasnoyarsk. Modern centres of the rayon industry (cellulosic fibres) are: Serpukhov, Mytishchi, Ryazan, and Shuya (Centre); Balakovo and Engel's (Volga); Kirovakan (Caucasus), and Kiev, Svetlogorsk, Sokal', Cherkassy, and Kaunas (European parts).

The synthetic fibre industries, rapidly emerging as a separate branch of the petro-chemical industries, are located at Kursk, Klin, and Novomoskovsk (Centre); Barnaul (Western Siberia); Ufa, Salavat, Saratov, Engel's, and Volzhskiy (Volga and adjacent areas); Yerevan, Rustavi, and Nevinnomyssk (Caucasus), and Kiev, Zhitomir, Mogilev, Chernigov, and Vilnius (European areas).

Rayon-type fibre production was about 440,000 tons in 1970, almost equally divided between staple fibre and continuous filament. Synthetic fibre production was just over 142,000 tons in the same year; somewhat less than a third of this was staple fibre and the remainder continuous filament. Since each ton of fibre represents an equivalent output to 350 sheep, the current output of man-made fibres can be thought of notionally, as more than doubling the present Soviet sheep population.

80. The weaving section of a cellulose rayon factory in Rustavi, Georgia.

Other Consumer Goods Industries

Footwear manufacture in the Soviet Union is almost conterminous with the garment-making industries. The main locations are within the Central and Northwestern R.S.F.S.R. and the Ukraine. In recent times modern mechanized footwear factories have been set up in Minsk, Kiev, Kuznetsk (Penza oblast), Simferopol' (Crimea), Tbilisi (Georgia) and in Novosibirsk.

Modern leather tanneries have joined the old-established plants in Leningrad, Moscow, and Berdichev. These are located at Ostashkov and Kirov as well as Melekess, Volsk, and Rechitsa. The last three plants also manufacture tannin extract.

Over the past decade, great effort has been made to spread the footwear industries more evenly. New factories have been opened at Kishinev (Moldavia), Rostov, Sarapul (Udmurt A.S.S.R.), and Raichikhinsk (Amur oblast). Artificial leather manufacture has become an important industry and significant amounts of this raw material are supplied for uppers and soles.

Consumer Markets

A clear indication of the rising standard of living in the Soviet Union is the increased use of durable consumer goods. The manufactured quantities of furniture, radios and radiograms, television sets, washing machines, refrigerators, and vacuum cleaners has increased sharply since 1960. Production levels in 1940 of many of these lines were insignificant. Again, the output of motorcycles, motor scooters, mopeds, and bicycles has shown a seven-fold growth since 1960. Clocks, watches, cameras, home movie cameras, gramophone records, musical instruments, sports goods, have also shown an upswing. There is however, no evidence to suggest that these consumer markets have yet reached saturation point.

It is very important to keep discussion of Soviet consumer markets in proper perspective. In the

81. The Slok cellulose and paper mill, Latvia. The calender shown makes high-quality card (150 tons per day) used for perforated computer cards.

82. The Kursk synthetic fibre plant makes 'lavsan' fibre in these rectification columns.

Soviet socialist system many things which make considerable claims on consumer spending in other countries – housing rentals, health, education, holidays, intra-city transport, cultural activities – are either provided free of charge or are heavily subsidized from the so-called State consumption fund in the Soviet Union. At present the average Soviet family has about one-quarter of its real income provided by the consumption fund.

In these circumstances the impact of consumer demand falls substantially in the free-choice areas of the total market – consumption goods, comparison goods, and consumer durables. The system of rationing for these purchases is through state-established market prices. Goods in short supply are deliberately high-priced to inhibit sales; at least until future production can keep pace with pent-up demand. Examples are cars, television sets, and some household appliances.

In terms of rate of growth, the consumer goods industries for decades lagged behind the growth of the means of production; a 'lead' of one to three per cent depending on the groups of industries compared was indicated. Now however, it appears that the situation is reversed, with the consumer segment, and particularly the durable goods segment, growing faster than producer goods industries.

One of the consequences of this change has been the planning methods now used to determine the level of production for any given consumer industry. Demand for given lines of production are officially assessed by groups of manufacturing enterprises, wholesale and retail outlets, and others concerned with the product. Moreover, in consonance with the present shift away from industry indicators in terms of physical outputs to targets for sales, costs, profits, and return on capital employed in the industry, there is a strong incentive to base production on aggregate sales revenue and so too on demand at current prices.

The new cost-accounting principles adopted by the Soviet Union for all sectors of its economy have been especially important in the consumer goods industries. As long as general national production directives are met, the decision processes and market mechanisms are left very much to enterprise groups. This has rendered the gearing of supply schedules and demand for products much more sensitive. In the past lack of knowledge of demand in the buyers market led to many anomalies; over-supply of goods not wanted and under-supply of goods for which demand was strong.

Another innovation of significance is the All-Union Demand Research Institute which carries out enquiries to assess the actual requirements for consumer products. Until the switch to consumer-oriented production, past planning tended to schedule production on a maximum-yield basis whether it was for agricultural or other resources and products that were contemplated. Once demand for given products becomes saturated such planning can lead to out-of-phase production. For example, in 1966, the total retail sales of sugar was 24 per cent less than the current production. With the new system, trade orders for all classes of goods, and so too production schedules, are based on retail outlets' assessments of demand. This is vital now that consumer industries are getting bigger allocations of funds, labour, equipment, and managerial talent. The essential role played by the Central Planning

83. A Minsk, Belorussia, electronic engineering plant makes black and white television sets (other plants make coloured sets). The set shown features a combined channel—selector—tuning knob and terminals for attachment of a videotape recorder. Thus videotape programmes can be used in schools, colleges, and industrial enterprises for instruction purposes.

Commission (Gosplan) in such a flexible production system is to set the overall parameters of production, investments and basic materials; more on the basis of economic opportunity costs, i.e. that if consumers choose to consume say more cars they must relinquish demands on household appliances, etc.

One enormous advantage that the Soviet Union has in this 'market perception' planning is the low density of retail outlets for consumer goods. Despite the enormous size of the country, the wide dispersal of urban centres, and the marked differences in consumer demand between regions, the Soviet Union has relatively fewer retail outlets than Britain or the United States. In the early 1960s, there were only 2·8 retail outlets per 1000 population in the Soviet Union compared to 9·3 in Britain. Also the work-force employed in the wholesale–retail section of total national employment was 4 per cent in the Soviet Union, but 15 per cent in Britain. Undoubtedly conditions have since improved – the Soviet Union's percentage had climbed to 7 per cent by 1970 – but retail trade deficiencies are still nevertheless apparent. Undoubtedly, however, the Soviet government's decision substantially to increase production of consumer goods and free many of the market constraints can be seen, in part at least, as a victory for the principle of consumer sovereignty. It is indeed a move towards the conscious betterment of the Soviet people's quality of life.

84. 'Music while you work' in a Tallin telephone instrument factory. Headsets are used rather than loudspeakers so that workers have a choice.

CHAPTER SIXTEEN

SOVIET TRANSPORTATION

Since transportation and trade are so closely linked together, this and the following chapter may be considered as complementary.

The Soviet transportation systems have undergone significant changes in recent years. First, there has been a great increase in freight movement of all types of goods and also in the number of passengers carried. In 1958 total freight turnover of the Soviet Union was 1604·8 billion (thousand million) ton-kilometres. By 1965 this had risen to 2764·0 billion ton-kilometres and by 1970 to 3825·0 billion indicating a vast increase of tonnages of freight handled, and concomitantly, a growing necessity of longer inter-regional hauls. Secondly, a marked feature of the Soviet transport system was a reallocation of freight to newer and more flexible modes of transport. In the event, railways and river transport both lost ground relatively while there was an upward trend in sea transport and motor freight haulage and quite a surge forward in the use of pipelines. Air freight, insignificant in 1960, had gained prominence by the 1970s, accounting for nearly 1·9 billion ton-kilometres.

According to official Soviet statistics (1971) the following changes between modes of freight distribution occurred (Table 16.1).

In consequence of important agricultural and industrial developments in regions east of the Urals, the aggregate inter-regional haulage of freights has increased very considerably (Fig. 16.1).

In absolute terms all modes of freight movement have increased throughout the Soviet period. Railway freight turnover, despite a fall in its relative share in total freight, is now six times greater than it was in the peak war years when movements were exceptionally heavy. In 1970 railway freight movements amounted to nearly 2500 billion ton-kilometres, indicating a 62·8 per cent rise in the decade.

Most of the growth in both railway and other modes of freight haulage can be attributed to growth in the agricultural and industrial sectors and more particularly to the geographical redistribution of the points of production relative to markets which now necessitates more circulation (Table 16.2).

For railways alone all classes of bulk freight in terms of tonnages hauled increased substantially in the decade 1960–70; indeed an acceleration of a long-continuing upward trend. In 1970, about 647 million tons of coal and coke were transported compared with only 492 million tons in 1960. At the same time average length of haul increased, marginally for coal it is true, but quite substantially for metallurgical coke. Other commodities also experience significant growth in tonnages the railways handled and also once again in most cases, in the mean length of haul. There was a reduction in length of haul of petroleum products as new long-distance oil and natural gas pipelines carried a bigger share of the long-distance movements leaving more of the shorter distribution hauls to the railways. Nevertheless, the tonnages of petroleum handled by the railways doubled and there was a 57·9 per cent increase in ton-kilometres of petroleum freight.

In the decade to 1970, there was a remarkable change in the relative share of various commodity groups handled by the railways. While coal and coke still dominated the total traffic, accounting for 18 per cent, petroleum, iron and steel, construction materials, and ore freight movements overtook grain and timber as the mainstays of railway transport. These switches are shown in Table 16.2 by the changes in percentage of ton-kilometres handled.

Construction materials such as bricks, stone, plasterboard, cement, tiles, and earthenware products, have generated much of the short-haul demands on railway freight services and are symptomatic of the vigorous growth of Soviet building and civil engineering construction. The lesser use of timber in construction, reducing the relative rate of growth in this sector of freight haulage, is in part at

TABLE 16.1
Total Freight Shipments by Mode of Transport, 1940–1970

	1940		1950		1960		1970	
	Billion ton-km	%	Billion ton-km	%	Billion ton-km	%	Billion ton-km	%
Railway	415·8	85·1	602·3	84·4	1504·3	79·8	2494·6	65·3
Marine	23·8	4·9	39·7	5·6	131·5	7·0	655·2	17·1
River	36·1	7·4	46·2	6·5	99·6	5·3	174·0	4·5
Pipelines	3·8	0·8	4·9	0·7	51·2	2·7	281·6	7·4
Motor Vehicle	8·9	1·8	20·1	2·8	98·5	5·2	217·7	5·7
Aircraft	0·02	...	0·14	...	0·56	...	1·89	...
Total	488·4	100·0	713·3	100·0	1885·7	100·0	3825·0	100·0

Source: *Narodnoe Khozyaistvo, 1970*, Moscow, 1971, p. 427.

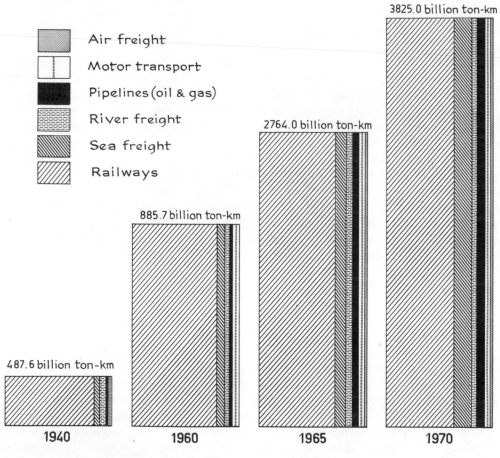

FIG. 16.1   Volume of Freight, 1940–70, by Mode of Transport.

TABLE 16.2
Commodity Components of Railway Freight, 1960 and 1970

Commodity	1960				1970			
	Million Tons	Billion Ton-km	%	Average Haul (km)	Million Tons	Billion Ton-km	%	Average Haul (km)
Coal	468	319	21·2	681	614	425	17·0	692
Coke	24	15	1·0	617	33	24	1·0	707
Petroleum	151	205	13·6	1360	303	354	14·2	1169
Iron & Steel	80	92	6·1	1163	142	192	7·7	1357
Construction materials	431	157	10·4	364	691	300	12·0	434
Timber	166	230	15·3	1387	179	295	11·8	1647
Ores	127	70	4·7	552	246	169	6·8	690
Mineral Fertilizers	20	24	1·6	1207	71	71	2·8	1000
Grain	81	94	6·3	1152	106	111	4·4	1050
Other Commodities	337	298	19·8	—	511	554	22·3	—
All Commodities	1885	1504	100·0	798	2896	2495	100·0	861

Source: *Narodnoe Khozyaistvo, 1970*, Moscow, 1971: pp. 431–32. Calculations by author.

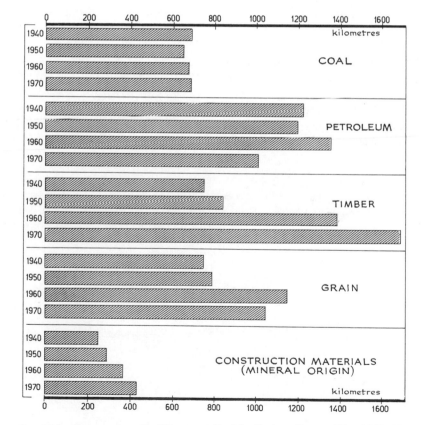

FIG. 16.2   Average Length of Transport Haul for Various Commodities, 1940–70.

least the result of the very lengthy hauls now needed to obtain this material. The mean haul is increasing year by year as shown in the graph (Fig. 16.2).

In those industrial sectors of the economy where the Soviet Union had a comparative late start – as, for example, in chemical fertilizers, synthetic fibres, plastic materials, etc. – there has been a marked effort to gear together production location and the chief market location, thus reducing the need for lengthy transportation. The development of numerous fertilizer plants in or near agricultural markets and at the same time with reasonable access to raw materials of phosphorites, salt, and sulphuric acid has been a feature of recent Soviet effort. As a consequence, the average length of haul by railways for synthetic fertilizers has been progressively reduced. It was 1496 kilometres in 1940; 1307 in 1950; 1207 in 1960 and about 1000 kilometres in 1970. Thus despite the very substantial gains in tonnages handled (Table 16.2) there has not been anything like the sustained pressure on the railways which is traditionally associated with movements of coal, petroleum, and iron and steel.

Soviet Railways. Soviet railways have a very high utilization rate. The extension of new railway lines (discussed in greater detail below) has to a large degree masked the great improvements in railway capacity through technological innovation. Light rail sections have been replaced with heavier ones, double tracks replace single line working; also centralized traffic control is now common and the introduction of greater numbers of more powerful diesel and electric locomotives, electrification of regional services, and the building of modern automatic marshalling yards, have all contributed to an increased potential of Soviet railways.

At present Soviet single-track lines are capable of handling more than 10 million tons of freight annually in a single direction, less if two-way traffic alternates. The modern double-track line has a capacity of 25 to 50 million tons annually depending on whether centralized traffic control, automatic blocking and express freight train speeds are available on the system.

Total mainline railway mileage in the Soviet Union increased substantially in the post-war period (Table 16.3). Aggregate mileage in 1970 was somewhat greater than 135,000 kilometres, nearly double the operating length existing in 1913. Really significant growth has occurred as the Soviet authorities endeavoured to spread railway networks into regions hitherto without this means of transport or with completely inadequate railway services. In the eastern parts of the Soviet Union spectacular advances were made in pre-war years. Entirely new networks were grafted on to the existing Trans-Siberian line which spread tenuously from the Urals to the Far East. The Asiatic part of the country, three times the size of the European part, rose from a mere 15 per cent in the country's railway mileage to about 34 per cent by 1940. Since then further

85. The Moscow 'Metro' intra-urban railway system has 37 miles (60 kilometres) of 5-foot gauge track – the same as Russian railways – and serves some sixty-two stations. In 1972 it carried about 5 million passengers daily. Other intra-urban railways operate in Leningrad, Kiev, Khar'kov, Tbilisi, and Baku; another is under construction in Tashkent.

TABLE 16.3
Railway Mileage in the Soviet Union, 1940 to 1970
by Regions (Thousands of Kilometres)

Regions	1940	1950	1960	1970
Western	23·9	23·1	23·5	23·4
Southern	22·5	24·7	26·0	27·7
Central and Volga	13·1	14·8	15·9	17·2
Northwest and Northern	9·8	11·4	11·9	12·9
Urals	6·5	7·6	7·9	8·6
Kazakhstan and Central Asia	10·7	12·9	16·6	19·5
Western Siberia	10·3	11·7	12·5	13·5
Eastern Siberia ⎫ Far East ⎭	9·3	10·7	11·5	12·4
Soviet Union	106·1	116·9	125·8	135·2

Source: Calculated by author from *Narodnoe Khozyaistvo,
1970*, Moscow, 1971, p. 430.
Notes: Figures for R.S.F.S.R. distributed between Economic
Regions according to author's estimate of track mileage in
respect of the 44 specific railway administrative regions,
derived from the State Railways timetable.
Mainline track length includes Soviet broad-gauge *and* narrow-gauge (a small proportion of the total) operated by the
Ministry of Transport. Thus spur-lines, mining and industrial site railways and track operated by industrial
Kombinats and other economic organizations are excluded
from the above totals. In 1967 these non-Ministry lines
amounted to 115,000 kilometres according to Lavrishchev,
op. cit., p. 327.

TABLE 16.4
*Railway Locomotive Types (as Percentage of Ton-
Kilometres of Net Freight Haulage)*

Year	Steam	Diesel/ Diesel-Electric	Electric	All Types
1940	97·8	0·2	2·0	100·0
1950	94·6	2·2	3·2	100·0
1960	56·8	21·4	21·8	100·0
1965	15·5	45·0	39·5	100·0
1970	3·5	47·8	48·7	100·0

Source: *Narodnoe Khozyaistvo, 1970*, Moscow, 1971,
p. 434.

advances have been made, especially in the far
north and eastern parts of the country (Table 16.3).
Between 1940 and 1970 some 29,000 kilometres of
new railway lines have been brought into operation.

Major new railway constructions are the important 3000 kilometres of extension to the South
Siberian Railway which began before World War
II. These include the Barnaul–Novokuznetsk–
Abakan and Tayshet sections. At Tayshet the line
joins the Trans-Siberian Railway. From this point
too the new Lena Railway taps areas to the northeast, and there are proposals for extension of this
line to reach the Pacific.

A new line from Magnitogorsk connecting the
Trans-Siberian at Chishmy near Ufa, via
Beloretsk, has given better access to the South
Siberian Railway at its western end. The short
radial, completed in 1970, has connected this line
with Chishmy thus obviating the need for trains to
run over the Trans-Siberian at all.

The Central Siberian Railway (2500 kilometres)
runs parallel to and between the Trans-Siberian and
South Siberian Railways. It leaves the latter line
at Tobol to connect Kustanay-Kokchetav and
Altaiskaya near Barnaul where it rejoins the South
Siberian Railway. An extension line from Abakan
to Tayshet on the Trans-Siberian goes on to Bratsk
and the Lena Railway.

Lines to the South of the Trans-Siberian are very
important, bringing transport to new coalfields and
metallurgical resources. They also serve the grain-
growing areas of the Virgin Lands. The Central
Siberian Railway which is now standard broad-
gauge, has in parts replaced the temporary narrow
gauge lines built in the early years of agricultural
development in northern Kazakstan. Lines north of
the Trans-Siberian are opening up oil and timber
provinces of great importance.

In Central Asia the Chardzhou to Astrakhan'
Railway is currently completing vital sections.
These are the Kungrad–Beineu line across the
Ust'-Yurt Plateau where it will link up with two
lines both built along the Caspian Depression; one
to Astrakhan' via Gur'yev (334 kilometres) and the
other southwards to the Mangyshlak oilfields. These
new lines total some 1600 kilometres.

During the eighth Five-Year Plan (1966–70) the
following extension lines were completed Ivdel–Ob'
(318 kilometres); Tavda–Sotnik (186 kilometres),
and the Tyumen'–Tobolsk–Surgut (650 kilometres)
line. These lines give access to new oil- and gas-
fields of the Middle Ob' and the timber resources of
Western Siberia.

Railways scheduled for construction follow the
trend of opening up new resource-rich areas already

evident in recent railway building. In Eastern Siberia new railways giving access to industrial areas are planned for the Khrebtovaya–Ust'-Ilimskaya line and the Reshety–Boguchany (Angara River) line.

The most progressive and imaginative future construction is the long proposed Baykal–Amur Railway, an entirely new line considerably north of the present Trans-Siberian Railway. This is perhaps sorely needed because of the strategic vulnerability of the latter line running as it does near the Chinese border. In recent years, vigorous Chinese claims to Soviet territory would, if successful, appropriate most railways of the Soviet Far East. The proposed new line would leave the present Lena Railway at Ust'-Kut, pass eastwards north of Lake Baikal then through Angarsk, Tyndinskiy, and Zeya to reach Komsomol'sk-on-Amur, there to join the existing line to Sovetskaya Gavan on the Tatar Strait.

An alternate suggestion would take the line from Tyndinskiy through the depression between the Stanovoy Mountains and the Khrebet Dzhagdy to reach the Sea of Okhotsk coastal plains at Chumikan and so to the Amur at Nikolayevsk. These proposed lines, in addition to their strategic value, would permit the opening up of the Markovo oil-field, the aluminium ores of the Vitim valley, and also the copper deposits of Udoken. There is some evidence that joint Soviet–Japanese ventures may build these lines to give Japan access to copper, coking coal, and timber.

Throughout the Soviet Union the most heavily utilized railways are being progressively electrified. Between 1966 and 1970 some 10,000 kilometres of existing line were converted to electric haulage. In addition to the heavy traffic areas of the West, Centre and Urals, the Trans-Siberian Railway has during this period been further electrified. The Sluydyanka–Karymskaya section has now been converted to electric traction (Table 16.4).

Marine Transport. Soviet Marine transport has increased very rapidly since World War II, involving both international and coastal shipments. Total freight shipments by all modes of transport, including marine, are shown in Table 16.1 above.

A five-fold increase in marine transport occurred in the decade to 1970. In that year 162 million tons of sea freight were shipped including 9·3 million tons of coal, 10·6 million tons of timber, 13·6 million tons of ores and concentrates, and 13·5 million tons of construction materials (mineral origin). The balance was made up of grains, metals and semi-finished metals, salt, fish and fish products, and a wide range of manufactured goods. The latter made up slightly less than half of the total tonnage handled by sea freight.

With the increasing importance of sea freight, Soviet ports have undergone expansion. The twenty most important ports are listed in Table 16.5. Some ports such as Kherson, Berdyansk, Petropavlovsk-Kamchatsky, and Nakhodka, have grown at an extremely fast rate since 1959. Unfortunately, official

TABLE 16.5
Soviet Marine Ports (Exceeding 100,000 persons in 1970)

Area	Population (in thousands)			% Increase 1959–70
	1959	1967	1970	
Black Sea				
Odessa	664	776	892	34
Nikolayev	235	331	342	45
Kherson	158	235	261	65
Novorossiysk	93	123	133	42
Batumi	82	100	101	23
Sea of Azov				
Rostov-on-Don	600	757	789	31
Taganrog	202	245	254	26
Zhdanov	284	385	417	47
Berdyansk	65	87	100	53
Kerch	98	118	128	30
Baltic				
Leningrad	3321	3706	3950	19
Riga	580	680	732	26
Tallin	282	340	363	29
Kaliningrad	204	270	297	46
Klaypeda	90	131	140	55
White Sea				
Arkhangel'sk	258	310	343	33
Barents Sea				
Murmansk	222	287	309	39
Bering Sea				
Petropavlovsk-Kamchatka	86	123	154	80
Sea of Japan				
Vladivostok	291	397	411	52
Nakhodka	64	96	104	64

Source: population figures for 1959, 1967, 1970: *Narodnoe Khozyaistvo, 1970*, Moscow, 1971: pp. 37–45.

Soviet statistics do not provide figures on tonnages of cargo handled by various ports, but some indication of their growth is given by the continual rise in sea freight and the expansion of each port's population. Coastal shipping no less than international marine freight has grown tremendously over the last two decades.

The most serious inhibiting factor with Soviet sea and river transport is their closure by ice in winter. Ports of the Arctic coast and the great northern rivers are open for only a few months of the year being closed during the long winter season and a variable part of autumn and spring also (Fig. 3.3 above). At the other extreme ports like Murmansk and Odessa enjoy more equable climatic conditions and are open for 85–90 per cent of the year. Murmansk is indeed kept open for the whole year by ice-breaking for 50 days. While the Baltic coastal ports of Klaypeda, Liyepaya, and Ventspils, remain ice-free, those in bay-head situations like Riga and Leningrad are closed for a period of three months in winter. Ice-breakers operate to extend the open season. On the Pacific coast too, Vladivostok and Nakhodka are kept open by ice-breakers for the whole year.

86. Timber loading at Port Vanino, Soviet Far East, destined for the Japanese market.

TABLE 16.6
Soviet Merchant Shipping (Thousands GRT)

Year	Merchant Fleet		Oil Tanker Fleet		Bulk Carrier Fleet	
	Tonnage (thousands GRT)	Per cent of world tonnage	Tonnage (thousands GRT)	Per cent of world tonnage	Tonnage (thousands GRT)	Per cent of world tonnage
1953	2292	2·46	176	0·80	—	—
1960	3429	2·65	693	1·68	—	—
1961	4066	2·99	957	2·19	—	—
1962	4684	3·35	1196	2·65	—	—
1963	5434	3·72	1356	2·88	—	—
1964	6958	4·56	1716	3·39	116	0·70
1965	8238	5·14	2118	3·74	116	0·62
1966	9492	5·46	2484	4·14	135	0·56
1967	10617	5·84	2739	4·27	116	0·40
1968	12062	6·22	2936	4·24	116	0·33
1969	13705	6·47	3171	4·10	198	0·47
1970	14832	6·52	3460	4·02	207	0·44

Source: Lloyd's Register of Shipping, London.
Note: Soviet ships engaged on trade within the Caspian Sea excluded from totals.

Since the early 1950s a rapid increase in the size of the Soviet merchant fleet has occurred. There has been an even more spectacular growth in the oil tanker and bulk carrier fleets, although these still remain small by world standards. By 1970, Soviet merchant vessels of all classes made up somewhat more than ten per cent of the world's gross registered tonnage (Table 16.6). Also the Soviet Union has consistently improved its position over the last two decades providing more merchant tonnage to carry its own expanding overseas trade, and to satisfy the growing demand for domestic coastal shipments.

Soviet shipping statistics of its seaborne trade, and those provided by Lloyd's Register of Shipping in London, confirm a very significant growth in Soviet exports by its marine fleet, while imports in Soviet vessels remain quite small (Table 16.7). The Soviet fleet carries over 100 million metric tons of freight each year, or roughly one-quarter of the tonnage handled by the United States merchant marine.

The Northern Sea Route operates for five months each year with the help of the atomic ice-breaker 'Lenin' providing an Arctic seaway from Murmansk to Vladivostok via the Bering Strait. This carries cargoes of timber, metal concentrates,

gold, diamonds, and furs from the Soviet northlands. In recent years the Soviet Union's cargo liners, such as the Balt–Pacific Line, run between Leningrad, Australia, and the west coast of Latin America. Another line operates in the Atlantic and Indian oceans. In consequence of these developments the Soviet Union seeks 'peaceful passage' of all international sea routes.

The steady relative decline in river traffic in the Soviet Union is due to the increasing efficiency of other modes of transport in terms of capital and operating costs. Whereas rivers can handle slow-moving bulk cargoes of grain, coal, and oil quite well, there are natural disadvantages of inland transport such as sinuosity and that the mainly north–south flow of river traffic runs counter to the main transport requirements of the country. Sinuosity more than doubles comparable rail distances on many rivers of the Soviet Union, and average haulage speeds are only one-third that of rail. Paradoxically, construction works intended to improve the navigability of rivers, involving locks and dredged channels, have slowed down transit times. Finally, the lack of flexibility of river transport has been a severe impediment to its further development in the Soviet Union.

Road Haulage. Historically Soviet road construction and the extension of highway networks have lagged behind the rates of most advanced countries. In consequence much road traffic meets only short-haul requirements and intra-city freight. Except in the developing far northern areas and Kazakhstan, where feeder roads run northwards or southwards respectively from the main east–west railway systems, there has been little incentive for the planning authorities to encourage long-distance road haulage.

The Soviet Union has 1·36 million kilometres of motor traffic roads, but less than a third of these (511,600 kilometres in 1970) are hard surface roads suitable for heavy vehicular traffic. The use of dirt roads rather than concrete and bitumen roads places a heavy toll on vehicle wear and tear in the Soviet Union, and operating costs are consequently high.

During the 1966–70 Five-Year Plan, three important highways were built. These are the Moscow Ring Road (109 kilometres); the Moscow–Kuybyshev Highway (1000 kilometres) and the

TABLE 16.7
Soviet Seaborne Trade (excluding transit traffic)

	Goods Loaded	Goods Unloaded	Total Trade	Soviet Union as % age of U.S. Seaborne Trade
	(Millions of Metric Tons)			
1960	38·8	5·9	44·7	14·6
1961	51·2	7·3	58·5	19·6
1962	60·0	6·9	66·9	20·6
1963	66·7	8·9	75·6	21·7
1964	71·5	12·2	83·7	21·8
1965	79·1	12·7	91·8	22·8
1966	90·3	12·4	102·7	24·1
1967	98·4	10·3	108·7	25·8
1968	100·8	11·1	111·9	24·3
1969	105·0	11·1	116·1	25·1
1970	106·9	14·4	121·3	23·7

Source: Lloyd's Register of Shipping, London, 1970; *U.N. Statistical Yearbook, 1972*, pp. 426–27.

87. A heavy-duty roller re-building the Kiev–Khar'kov highway. Such road improvement programmes are gradually helping the development of long-distance road freight haulage, especially in areas devoid of railways or convenient navigable rivers. (Photograph by the author.)

88. A new road linking Dushanbe, the capital of Tadzhikistan, to the Nurek hydroelectric and chemical complex.

89. Unimproved dirt roads, that still make up the vast majority of roads in the Soviet Union, suffer most during periods of summer downpour, while in winter they are hummocky wastelands. Recently greater availability of heavy road-building machinery is considerably ameliorating the situation. (Photograph by the author, 1961.)

90. A 3425-kilometre gas pipeline under construction in Turkmenistan linking the new Karakum gas-fields to the Centre. Shown here is a bitumenized-paper wrapping machine in operation.

Frunze–Osh Alpine Highway (600 kilometres). The latter has great strategic value given Chinese pressure in western Sinkiang. Other roads have been built or re-constructed in the Ukraine, the Urals, the Volga district, and Siberia. It appears certain that conditions in heavily trafficked areas are gradually improving.

Despite the paucity of modern highways, the Soviet Union has nevertheless expanded motor freight traffic more than ten-fold since 1950. In 1970 some 218 billion ton-kilometres of motor freight were achieved. In great measure this was due to the augmentation to the Soviet lorry fleet (Table 16.8).

Air Transport. Air transport has grown significantly in the Soviet Union in the post-war period. Air cargo rose near fourteen times between 1950 and 1970 reaching 1886·7 million ton-kilometres in the latter year. Or, stated in tonnage terms, slightly more than 1·8 million tons of cargo were carried by air, nearly half of this was airmail articles.

Passenger kilometres increased even more rapidly by 65 times between 1950 and 1970. In that year 71·4 million passengers were carried attaining 78·2 billion passenger-kilometres, giving a mean journey distance of 1095 kilometres. Clearly air transport has come of age in the Soviet Union. As in so many other fields, Soviet air transport

TABLE 16.8
Soviet Motor Transport

Freight Transport	1940	1950	1960	1970
Freight carried (million tons)	858·6	1859·2	8492·7	14,622·8
Freight (billion ton–kilometres)	8·9	20·1	98·5	217·7
Average Haul (kilometres)	10·4	10·8	11·6	15·1
Length of Roads				
Hard Surface (thousand kilometres)	143·4	177·3	270·8	511·6
of which:				
Cement/Asphalt/Bitumen/Macadam-Surfaced	7·1	19·2	77·1	207·0
Passenger Traffic				
Passengers (No. per Seat available annually)	4999	6577	7811	5713
Passenger–kilometres (thousands)	28·8	32·5	42·1	43·0
Average distance travelled (kilometres)	5·7	4·9	5·4	7·5
Production of Heavy Vehicles				
Lorries and buses (thousands)	136·0	294·4	385·0	571·8

Source: *Narodnoe Khozyaistvo, 1970*, Moscow, 1971, pp. 451, 455. *Statesman's Yearbook*, 1972–73, p. 1409.

91. Before the construction of oil pipelines Soviet railways were often hard-pressed to provide sufficient tank car services to carry long-distance oil shipments. (Photograph by the author, 1961.)

experiences very high utilization of capacity: 76·5 per cent in cargo traffic and 74·9 per cent in passenger flights (1970).

Aeroflot carries about 80 million internal passengers annually. In 1956 the TU-104 ('Academician A.N. Tupolev') started making regular flights. Other batch-produced aircraft are the IL- series ('S. Ilyushin'), AN- series ('O. Antonov'), MI- helicopter series ('M. Mil'), and KA- helicopter series ('N. Kamov'). Aircraft of these series now make up the bulk of the Aeroflot fleet, although newer planes of the TU- series are increasing their relative share of the total passenger capacity. Since 1961 the TU-114, carrying 170 passengers, has been used on the Moscow–Khabarovsk; Moscow–Delhi, Moscow–Havana, and Moscow–Tokyo flights. The newer TU-134, TU-154, and TU-144 and IL-62 airlines are now operating both internal and overseas services. Also the YAK-40 jet plane has been put into regular service recently.

The TU-144 swing-wing supersonic passenger plane flies at 2500 kph and is the Russian equivalent of the Franco-British Concorde. Mass production of the TU-144 has commenced.

Nikolai Bykov, the Deputy Minister of Civil Aviation in the U.S.S.R., has stated that 63 international airports are now served by Soviet flights and also that the internal flight lines now total 225,000 kilometres.

The use of aircraft in agriculture and forestry is another example of the growing role of this mode of transportation in the Soviet economy. In 1960, 20·08 million hectares of land were serviced by aircraft, spreading fertilizers, weedicides, and pesticides. This area increased to 55·4 million hectares and 83·28 million hectares in 1965 and 1970 respectively. About 45 per cent of these services (37·9 million hectares) were performed in the R.S.F.S.R. The Ukraine (16·0 million hectares) and Kazakhstan (14·4 million hectares) were the two other dominant republics serviced by agricultural aviation.

Pipeline Transportation. Oil and natural gas pipelines, one of the fastest developing modes of Soviet transport, have been already detailed in Chapter 12, on the petroleum industry. In 1970 nearly 340 million tons of crude oil and products were transported by pipeline. As indicated in Table 16·9, pipeline traffic has accounted for an increasing percentage of the total ton-kilometres of freight in the Soviet Union, ranking third after

railway and marine transport. Natural gas transport by pipeline has been especially important in these developments, since the liquefaction of gas for transport by rail tank-car or alternatively river or ocean tankers requires costly capital equipment.

In consequence of Soviet policy to relieve the hard-pressed railways, pipeline construction in recent decades has expanded considerably, especially large-bore, long-distance pipelines that are most economic to operate.

TABLE 16.9

Oil and Natural Gas Pipelines

	1940	1950	1960	1970
Length, Oil (thousand kilometres)	4·1	5·4	17·3	37·4
Length, Gas (thousand kilometres)	—	2·3	21·0	67·5
Shipments, Oil (million tons)	7·9	15·3	129·9	339·9
Shipments, Natural Gas (billion cu. metres)	—	1·5	32·8	181·5
Total Freight, Oil (billion ton–km)	3·8	4·9	51·2	281·6

Source: *Narodnoe Khozyaistvo, 1970*, Moscow, 1971, p. 450.

CHAPTER SEVENTEEN

SOVIET FOREIGN TRADE AND OVERSEAS AID

Soviet foreign trade is dominated by three principles: (*a*) the acquisition of needed raw materials, essential consumer imports, and certain specialized producer goods on most favourable terms, (*b*) the selection of trading partners mainly from neighbouring communist countries or the developing 'Third World' countries to which the Soviet Union has granted aid involving trade credits, and (*c*) the sale of gold, diamonds, furs, and caviar to acquire foreign exchange. Agricultural products figure prominently in Soviet external trade (Fig. 17.1).

The degree to which communist and 'Third World' trade dominates Soviet exports and imports is shown below (Table 17.1).

Under the Council for Economic Mutual Aid agreement (generally referred to as the COMECON pact) between East European countries, Soviet trade was able to benefit greatly. Member states of COMECON include the Soviet Union, Bulgaria, Czechoslovakia, Hungary, East Germany, Poland, Rumania, and significantly, Mongolia. In July,

1971 the 25th Session of COMECON adopted a plan for Socialist economic integration for 1971–75. Czechoslovakia and East Germany are already important suppliers of technical goods to the Soviet Union. Imports from these sources include machine tools, press forge equipment, complete rolling mills, food processing plants, and a high proportion of the Soviet Union's requirements of precision instruments. In return these and other COMECON countries received raw cotton, coal, oil, natural gas, electrical energy, ores, and some classes of machinery and equipment.

Under COMECON, trade between the Soviet Union and its partners is worked out, frequently by bilateral negotiations, between the respective State trading corporations. The Soviet Union has thirty specialized trade corporations; one importing for the Union of Co-operative Societies. Member countries of COMECON seek to ensure regional specialization on goods for which particular countries have a comparative cost advantage, but

TABLE 17.1
Soviet Trade Statistics by Trading Areas (in million roubles)

	1960				1970			
	Exports		Imports		Exports		Imports	
	million roubles	%	million roubles	%	million roubles	%	million roubles	%
Eastern Europe	2809	56·1	2538	50·1	7530	65·4	6880	65·1
Other Communist Countries	866	17·3	902	17·8				
Western Europe	876	17·5	892	17·6	3990	34·6	3685	34·9
Developing Countries	325	6·5	572	11·3				
Rest of World	130	2·6	162	3·2				
Total	5006	100·0	5066	100·0	11520	100·0	10565	100·0

Sources: 1960, *Mitteilungen der Bundesstelle für Aussenhandelsinformation*, No. 147, Köln, 1961 (converted to current roubles). 1970, *Narodnoe Khozyaistvo, 1970*, Moscow, 1971, p. 615.

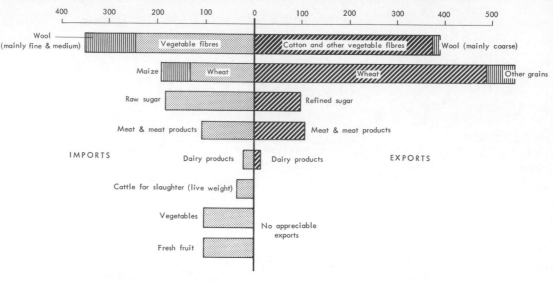

FIG. 17.1   Soviet Foreign Trade in Agricultural Products, 1971.

difficulties have arisen in heavy industrial goods considered to be of strategic importance which are thus over-supplied. Purchasing agreements are commonly determined one year ahead of requirements to give sufficient time for Gosplan to integrate internal production plans with supplies to be received from outside sources.

In practice, there is a strong tendency for the Soviet Union to acquire balanced trade with COMECON and other communist countries on a bilateral basis. Frequently negotiations are almost barter operations, with the parties ensuring they purchase only as much as they sell. This minimizes foreign exchange requirements, but sometimes has the undesirable effect of forcing half-wanted commodities and products into the schedules merely to balance trade.

In the immediate post-war period, COMECON has had to combat serious material and product shortages experienced by the Communist countries. In essence COMECON first functioned as a type of Marshall Plan and subsequently as a sort of Common Market. Neither of these Western European arrangements applied to the Eastern Bloc and consequently the COMECON countries developed their own trading arrangements.

In the late 1950s the COMECON countries met 75–80 per cent of their trade requirements by inter-

nal arrangements, usually bilateral trade agreements. However, with the passage of time more and more trade has drifted outside the bloc countries, mainly to the 'Third World' countries for imports of raw materials against capital goods or towards a varied trade with Western European countries. In consequence, trade within COMECON has dropped to about 50 per cent of total trade, leaving Soviet–Western world trade as a growing influence. Increasingly this trade is composed of imports of essential raw materials and commodities not produced within the Soviet Bloc, some fuels, capital plants, and equipment – sometimes with important technological 'know-how' attached, e.g. British Nylon Spinners, Dunlop Rubber and Fiat Motor plants supplied complete plants and technology to the Soviet Union – and frequently a range of manufactured goods which it was advantageous for the Soviet Union to import rather than make for itself (Fig. 17.2). At the moment Soviet exports to communist countries are 5 per cent greater than its imports and this is, in a sense, a measure of the counter-flow of goods in triangular trade from Western sources into the Soviet Union.

Some indication of these trade elements is given in the following table (Table 17.2).

Over the last two decades there have been very significant changes in the structure of Soviet

TABLE 17.2

Major Exports and Imports, 1970

Exports			Imports		
Machinery and Equipment	(d)	2482·0	Machinery and Equipment	(d)	3707·0
Rolled Steel	(b)	7·0	Rolled Steel	(b)	1·5
Cellulose	(a)	448·0	Cellulose	(a)	298·0
Paper	(a)	474·6	Paper	(a)	420·0
Cotton Flock and Yarn	(a)	517·0	Cotton Flock and Yarn	(a)	258·0
Woven cotton	(c)	307·0	Woven cotton	(c)	155·0
Sugar	(a)	1079·0	Raw Sugar	(a)	3003·0
Newsprint	(a)	259·6	Staple Filament	(a)	79·0
Coal	(b)	24·5	Knitted goods	(d)	202·7
Crude Oil	(b)	66·8	Tobacco	(a)	70·0
Oil Products	(b)	29·0	Cacao beans	(a)	100·0
Iron-ore	(b)	36·1	Coffee beans	(a)	41·5
Manganese ore	(a)	1243·0	Tea	(a)	29·0
Pig-iron	(b)	4·8	Meat and meat products	(a)	165·0
Potash	(a)	3147·0	Grain Concentrates (for feed)	(a)	323·0
Sulphate of Ammonia	(a)	883·0	Fruit, fresh	(a)	680·0
Photographic Apparatus	(e)	621·0	Fruit, dried	(a)	129·0
			Margarine, vegetable	(a)	65·0

Source: *Narodnoe Khozyaistvo, 1970*, Moscow, 1971, pp. 616–17.

(a) Thousand tons.
(b) Million tons.
(c) Million sq. metres.
(d) Million roubles.
(e) Thousands.

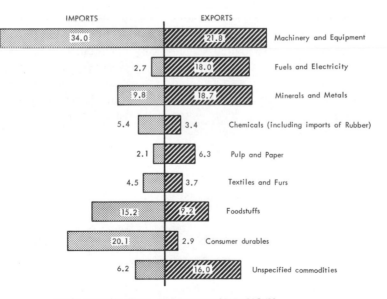

SOVIET EXTERNAL TRADE, 1971 BY COMMODITY GROUPS
(In percentage of total Exports or Imports by rouble value)

FIG. 17.2   Soviet External Trade by Commodity Groups, 1971.

TABLE 17.3

Soviet Trade by Commodity Groups, 1950 and 1970 (in Terms of Percentage of Rouble Value)

	1950		1970	
	Exports	Imports	Exports	Imports
Machinery and Equipment	11·8	21·5	21·5	35·1
Fuels and Electrical Energy	3·9	11·8	15·6	2·0
Ores, Concentrates, Metals	11·3	15·0	19·8	10·5
Chemicals, Fertilizers, Rubber	4·3	6·9	4·2	5·6
Wood and Paper Products	3·1	3·8	6·5	2·2
Textile Fibres and Fabrics	11·2	7·7	3·4	4·8
Foodstuffs	20·6	17·5	8·4	15·0
Other Goods (n.e.s.)	33·8	15·8	20·6	24·8
Total	100·0	100·0	100·0	100·0
Total Value (Million Roubles)	1615·0	1310·0	11 520·0	10 565·0
of which:				
Trade with Communist Countries (million roubles)	n.a.	n.a.	7530·0	6880·0
Percentage of Trade with Communist Countries	n.a.	n.a.	65·4	65·1

Source: *Narodnoe Khozyaistvo, 1970*, Moscow, 1971, pp. 615–18.

exports and imports. First, total trade has experienced a steep rise; almost an eighteen-fold increase since 1950 (Table 17.3). During this period exports of fuels and electrical energy (via transmission lines) have greatly increased, as have ores, concentrates and metals and items in the machinery group. At the same time Soviet imports have shifted significantly to high priority classes of machinery and equipment, commodities, and manufactured products, especially consumer goods. Despite the Soviet domestic production of raw sugar, large quantities of Cuban raw cane sugar are imported to give ideological support to that country (Cf. Table 15.3 above).

Not infrequently Soviet trade with the outside world can be very unstable from year to year. Not only are questions of Soviet production involved which affect, for example, imports of grains and foodstuffs in drought years in the Soviet Union, but also short-term shifts in Soviet demand. Imports of wool from Australia over the past twenty years are symptomatic of this type of fluctuation (Table 17.4). Such unbalancing of trade had led some Western trading partners to characterize Soviet sales as unreliable; in some instances, indeed, it is

thought ideological questions may well influence particular trading commitments. Such swings in Soviet trade affect the Western world far more than that country's trade with communist and 'Third World' countries, which enjoy more stability in exports to, and imports from, the Soviet Union.

Nevertheless Soviet trade with the 'Third World' countries, the uncommitted developing countries of Asia, Africa, and Latin America, is usually unbalanced with an excess of Soviet imports which,

TABLE 17.4

Soviet Imports of Australian Wool
(million lbs, greasy basis)

Year		Year		Year	
1952–53	3·3	1958–59	0·3	1964–65	50·7
1953–54	56·5	1959–60	38·7	1965–66	29·5
1954–55	0·4	1960–61	1·2	1966–67	29·2
1955–56	—	1961–62	40·7	1967–68	46·1
1956–57	—	1962–63	49·4	1968–69	62·0
1957–58	0·1	1963–64	45·6	1969–70	67·4

Source: *Commonwealth of Australia Yearbook* (various years), Canberra.

in effect, is counterbalanced by loans and credits to support the developing country's security and economic growth. Only rarely is such foreign aid given as outright grants (Table 17.5). More frequently Soviet military or industrial equipment supplied has to be paid for by the recipient country over a period of 10–12 years at low rates of interest (2 to 2·5 per cent p.a.) on outstanding balances. Repayments of loans and interest are almost inevitably in terms of the produce and commodities of the recipient country exported to the Soviet Union.

Mainland China and Albania have been loudest in their condemnation of this Soviet practice, alleging that materials sent to repay loans are really needed in their own countries.

Whatever the merits of the Soviet foreign aid system, it seems clear that it has grown into an extreme world force, reminiscent of the old imperialist tag reversed that 'flag follows the trade'. Between 1955 and 1967 there was a ninefold increase in Soviet exports to 'Third World' countries; from $140 million to $1330 million (U.S.).

Over the same period Soviet imports from these underdeveloped countries nearly quadrupled; from $195 million to $700 million.

Because some exports represent long-term Soviet aid under general or specific bilateral aid agreements, only about $650 million in exports in 1967 were the result of genuine unfettered demand for Soviet goods. The rest was the aggregate of each 'Third World' country's use of Soviet credits to obtain imports serving specific projects, about half of which relate to military equipment. Concomitantly in 1967 it was estimated that about $150 million of 'Third World' country exports to the Soviet Union, or some 20 per cent of their total exports to that country, were repayments in kind against aid previously granted.

Soviet 'Third world' trade, excluding the effects of foreign aid, amounted to about $1230 million in 1967. This was then about 7–8 per cent of Soviet total external trade, but there seems every prospect that it has risen further in recent years. Even ignoring the direct and spin-off effects of Soviet aid programmes to developing countries, there is little

TABLE 17.5
Soviet 'Third World' Aid Programmes, 1954–1970 (Estimates in millions roubles*)

Country	Date of First Aid Agreement	Amount	Country	Date of First Aid Agreement	Amount
India	1955	8840	U.A.R. (Egypt)	1956	6300
Afghanistan	1954	2780	Iran	1963	1400
Indonesia	1956	1923	Syria	1957	920
Pakistan	1961	720	Turkey	1957	920
Other Asia	—	380	Algeria	1963	920
			Iraq	1959	1310
Total Asia	—	14643	Other	—	720
Ethiopia	1959	800	Total Middle East and N. Africa	—	12490
Guinea	1959	540			
Ghana	1960	380			
Other	—	1300	Argentina		400
			Cuba		400
Total Tropical Africa	—	3020			

Source: Todd, 'Soviet and East European Aid to Developing Countries' *in* Schöpflin, *op. cit.*, pp. 313–14 to 1967; updated to 1970 by author.

* Values throughout are expressed in 'old' roubles current between 1950–60. At this time, before the 1961 devaluation, the rouble was equivalent to $0.25 U.S.

doubt that the Soviet Union is determined to become a more influential trading country in the 1970s. This is quite different to the autarky practised so frequently during the Stalinist régime. The decade to 1970 placed the Soviet Union in one of the foremost world positions as a creditor nation, mainly through the twin agencies of trade and aid. Altogether, the period 1955–70 marks the burgeoning of the Soviet Union as a forthright con-tributor to other countries' economic development, although never approaching the level of the United States aid programmes or those of the United Nations agencies. Some indication of recent Soviet aid programme is given above (Table 17.5). Under these programmes communist countries received economic aid for some 1593 industrial and agricultural projects, while 'Third World' countries benefited to the tune of about 700 projects.

PART FOUR

SOVIET ECONOMIC REGIONS

CHAPTER EIGHTEEN

THE WESTERN REGION

Reference	Appendix 1 for details by administrative region of population, area, density and urbanization
Area	707·8 thousand square kilometres
Population	about 41·4 million
Average Density	58·4 persons per square kilometre
Urbanization (Per cent)	52
Largest Cities	1970 Population (in thousands)

Baltic		*Belorussia*		*S.W. Ukraine and Moldavia*	
Riga	732	Kiev	1632	L'vov	553
Vilnius	372	Minsk	917	Kishinev	356
Tallin	363	Gomel'	272	Vinnitsa	212
Kaunas	305	Vitebsk	231	Chernovtsy	187
Kaliningrad	297	Mogilev	202	Zhitomir	161
Klaypeda	144	Bobruysk	138	Chernigov	159
		Grodno	132	Cherkassy	158
		Brest	122	Rovno	116
		Orsha	101	Khmel'nitsky	113
		Polotsk	64	Ivano-Frankovsk	105
				Tiraspol	105
				Ternopol'	85

The Physical Environment

The Western Region includes the following major economic regions: the Baltic Republics (Estonia, Latvia, and Lithuania), Belorussian S.S.R., South-West Ukraine, and Moldavian S.S.R. It also includes Kaliningrad (formerly Königsberg) oblast on the Polish border, now administered by the Russian Federation (Fig. 18.1).

The physical divisions of the Western Region comprise:

(1) The low glacial plains of the Baltic (with numerous polder-like embayments almost cut off from the sea by long-shore spits);
(2) the middle plains and hill country;
(3) the Podolian Plateau;
(4) the Carpathian Mountains;

and (5) the Black Sea low coastal plains.

Agricultural development faces many physical constraints. The northern plains are covered by extensive areas of glacial lakes and marshlands — e.g. the Pripyat marshes. There are also boulder-strewn and scrub-covered fields, sluggish, low-gradient rivers that flood seasonally, and sandy, outwash soils of low fertility. Elsewhere conditions for agriculture are somewhat better, expecially in the richer soil areas of Southwest Ukraine and Moldavia, but the Podolian dissected country and the Carpathians are barriers to efficient farming systems.

Throughout history, man has adapted these lands to agriculture only by prodigious effort. In recent times, the Soviet authorities have paid great attention to ameliorative works; coastal reclamation, ditching and drainage of both the marshlands and the richer alluvial soils of the post-glacial *Urstromtäler*. Moreover, the adaption of the region to mixed farming systems has been undertaken. Mechanical ditch-diggers, and the application of agricultural lime and fertilizers have done much to

FIG. 18.1   Economic Development: Western Region.

improve the farming standards of the Western Region.

Agriculture in the Western Region

The varied physical environment, and also the latitudinal extent of the Western Region give it a diverse agricultural pattern.

The Baltic Republics. Immediately following World War II the Soviet government broke up the large land-holdings to permit landless peasants and small-holders to form collective farms (kolkhozes). Numerous state-run farms (sovkhozes) were also set-up. In 1970 there were 2389 collective and 701 state farms and these together cultivated nearly 4·6 million hectares of land, virtually the whole of the farmed area.

Mechanization and the provision of electricity to farms has improved agricultural productivity. All Baltic Republic state farms now have electricity from the regional grid, while supply to collectives varies from 70 per cent of farms in Estonia to nearly 100 per cent in both Latvia and Lithuania. Ploughing, seeding, and cultivating are mostly mechanized. The three Republics had a total of 147,000 tractor units in 1970 (measured in 15 h.p. units, thus a 30 h.p. tractor would count as 2 basic units). They also had 18,000 combine harvesters for grain farming.

With the draining of Baltic marshlands – over a million hectares have been reclaimed in Latvia, 0·8 million in Estonia, and 1·6 million in Lithuania in the post-war period – cultivation of the peat-soils for potatoes and sugar-beet expanded considerably. Associated with this was an upsurge in dairy farming based on beet pulp availability. Egg production and poultry rearing (especially geese) is another facet of Baltic agriculture. Frequently pigs are run in the potato fields to harvest the crop. This is a boon since currently labour-intense harvesting is expensive and there is a shortage of root-crop lifting machinery — only about 60 per cent of the potato harvest in the Soviet Union is mechanically lifted.

The two most important industrial crops of the Baltic Republics are flax and sugar-beet. Flax, barley, and rye are moisture-tolerant crops and can be grown successfully on undrained areas. Sugar-beet farming, although somewhat near the northern climatic margin, has increased substantially. The crop is planted mostly on drained, friable peaty soils of the Baltic Republics, especially in Lithuania.

The Baltic Republics have vast areas under these crops and also potatoes, root crops, and maize for silage. The hardy grains — barley, oats, and rye — are also cultivated. By 1970, Lithuanian collective farms had about 500 hectares of reclaimed land each on average. With fertilization, these drained lands were significant in grain production and yields were raised from 1·8 to 2·8 tons per hectare between 1966 and 1970.

Dairying is now highly developed on coastal pastures and marshland water-meadows. Frequently it is associated with sugar-beet and fodder crops. Simmenthal, Latvian brown, and Friesian cattle are favoured breeds. There is a heavy concentration of dairying near larger cities where milk and milk products are processed. In areas distant from the larger towns, mixed farms are common. These graze beef cattle, and raise pigs and poultry as well as engage in row-crop cultivation. Sheep for meat production are locally important. Many state and collective farms supply store-cattle and calves — both beef and dairy cattle — for dispatch to all parts of the Soviet Union.

The Baltic Republics have considerable areas of coniferous forests which yield significant quantities of softwood timber. In Estonia about 80,000 hectares have been afforested since the war. About 1·7 million hectares of State forest and collective-farm forest in Latvia produced 7·3 million cubic metres of timber in 1970, more than double the 1938 yield. In Lithuania forestry is less developed, but nevertheless covers 1·5 million hectares, 70 per cent in conifers, mainly pines. This again indicates the lower key of Lithuania's development compared with that of Estonia and Latvia.

The whole of the Baltic Coast is dotted with important fishing ports, many organized as collectives. Larger centres like Tallin, Riga, and Kaliningrad support deep-sea fisheries of all-Union importance. From these, modern stern-ramp factory trawlers put to sea for several months, fishing in the North Atlantic or on the West Coast of Africa, and only returning when their refrigerated holds are full. Chief landings at the fishing ports are fillets of cod, deep-sea bass, and other 'white' fish; eels, herrings, and sprats, occasionally Atlantic salmon. The factory ships process fish offal on board to make fish-meal, fish protein solubles, and liver oils.

Belorussian S.S.R. Belorussia had a cultivated area in 1970 of some 6 million hectares. Of the 1·7 million hectares drained subsequently to World War II, 572,000 hectares have been turned over to arable cultivation; the rest to improved pastures. The peaty soils need heavy applications of agricultural lime to reduce acidity, mineral fertilizer, and sometimes trace elements, but are then stated to be as rich as the chernozems. They give good harvests of grain, fodders, potatoes, and the rubber-yielding kok-sagyz in Belorussia.

Collective farms number 2206 and there are 820 state farms. These have at their disposal over 132,000 tractor units and 24,500 combine harvesters. Agricultural potential has improved dramatically in the post-war period. Formerly a Republic in which flax, hay, rye, and oats and potatoes were the dominant land-use systems, the area has swung into the cultivation of sugar-beets, and maize for silage or green feed. Even greater quantities of potatoes are now harvested.

Animal husbandry has grown in importance, particularly the rearing of dairy and beef cattle, the breeding of pigs (many for 'export' to other parts of the Soviet Union) and the intensive rearing of poultry. The consolidation of collective farms into larger units, frequently engrossing several villages, has done much to rationalize Belorussian farming and make the best use of some of the country's agriculturally least favourable environmental resources. Not infrequently the State farms carry on specialized activities such as flax-growing or dairying, while many of the enlarged collectives are taking on the aspects of mixed farming, until recently novel in the Russian farming scene.

Grain crops include rye, winter wheat, buckwheat — for which Belorussia is famous — barley and oats. The dense farming communities of the

92. A kolkhoz dairy farm at Berezino, Belorussia, indicates the tremendous improvement in herd quality that has been made possible by kolkhoz or sovkhoz control of animal husbandry. Productivity has also greatly improved.

93. Deep ploughing of drained lands at Soligorsk, Belorussia, preparatory to the cultivation of flax, potatoes, or rotation pastures.

central area also grow many varieties of industrial crop, particularly flax, hemp, sugar-beet, and makhorka. The chief concentration of flax-growing is the Vitebsk–Mogilev–Minsk triangle. Hemp is grown on drained peat-bogs in the south–central areas.

The Southwest Ukraine. The Southwest gained two eastern provinces of Poland after the war – Galicia and Volhynia – and also the small enclave of Ruthenia, formerly in Czechoslovakia. The Southwest Ukraine is a region of agricultural diversity. Pre-eminently the land-use pattern is based on varying soil conditions. These range from the infertile podzolics of the upland sandy country to the rich southern chernozems of the Black Sea steppes.

The higher areas of the Carpathians and Podolian plateau are covered with coniferous forest, dominantly pines. The Carpathian piedmont abounds in forests of fir and spruce. The best forest-steppe farming area is the broad belt of oak and beech forest which runs eastward from Ternopol to the middle Dnieper and beyond. These are the main winter-wheat growing areas, located in Ternopol', Khmel'nitskiy, Zhitomir and Vinnitsa oblasts, although both wheat and other grains are grown throughout the region.

Other major land-use systems of the Southwest Ukraine are sugar-beet, flax, maize for grain and fodder, and sunflower for oil-seed. Potatoes and vegetables are grown in Chernigov, Kiev, and Vinnitsa oblasts. Potatoes provide raw material for vodka distilleries and starch-hydrolysis plants. Some vegetables are destined for the many canneries in the Southwest which serve nation-wide markets.

Although dairy-farming is not so important as in the Baltic Republics and Belorussia, some milk production is available to serve the larger cities such as Kiev and L'vov. Pig-raising is the chief form of animal husbandry·of the Southwest, especially in the Pol'esye. Feed is usually vegetable wastes, beet pulp, and occasionally maize, produced on the collective farms.

On the hill-slopes of the Carpathians and central plateaux, sheep-breeding for wool and meat has expanded greatly in post-war years. In the past goat-herding was an important use of marginal country, but long-established over-grazing has caused erosional problems on the steeper slopes. Controlled grazing of sheep has been an effective ameliorative measure.

Moldavian S.S.R. Moldavia is a small republic flanked on three sides by the Ukraine. It includes two former Rumanian provinces – Bukovina and Bessarabia – annexed by the Soviet Union after the war.

In the south, Moldavia has chernozem soils of typical steppes while in the north it has wooded steppe soils and grey-brown forest soils. With its warm and moist climate, Moldavia is highly suited to intensive agriculture and horticulture. Over the centuries it has developed as one of the most densely populated rural landscapes, with Kishinev the capital as the only large city. Large, neat villages are strung along the rivers Prut and Dniester and a dense settlement network exists in the hill country. In particular, the loess-covered limestones of the Kodry Hills and the chernozem lowlands of the Budzhak and Beltsy Steppes are areas of intense land-use.

In 1971 Moldavia had 551 collective farms and 145 state farms. These use some 73,500 tractor units and 3,400 combine harvesters. Main land-uses include maize and winter wheat-growing, sugar-beet cultivation and sunflower for oil-seed as well as fruit growing. Moldavia is one of the pre-eminent wine-making areas of the Soviet Union having about one-third of the country's viticultural area. Beef cattle and sheep grazing are found mainly in the hill country, while large numbers of pigs (nearly 1·6 million) and poultry are sustained on the valley farms. Horticulture on small plots include the cultivation of makhorka, tobacco, opium poppy, mustard and caraway seed, and herbs of various kinds. All of these crops need large amounts of farm man-power. This is amply available from the dense Moldavian rural population. Soil and climatic conditions are generally ideal for these crops, although in the south there is severe tendency to summer drought.

Transportation in the Western Region
Both the Baltic and Black Sea provide excellent harbour sites. Most of the western ports of the Baltic are ice-free for very long periods and consequently attract a great deal of transit freight in winter when Leningrad and Arkhangel'sk are closed by ice. The main ports are Kaliningrad, Klaypeda, Liepaya, Ventspils, Riga, and Tallin.

94. The Pre-Baltic power station, Estonia, is typical of the regional electric plants that have brought electrical energy to the countryside throughout the Soviet Union. This station's turbo-alternators operate on steam raised from a mixture of oil-shale gas and natural gas. Capacity is 1·6 million kilowatts.

The principal Black Sea ports of the region are Odessa, Nikolayev and Kherson. River navigation improved by the construction of dams at Kiev and Kanev connects the Dnieper – 3·65 metres draft to the Pripyat confluence – with distant hinterlands. The Dniester, Pripyat, Desna in the south, and Niemen in the north, also carry considerable industrial freight by river boats.

The whole of the Western Region is criss-crossed by a dense railway network. Major trunk lines connect the Centre and Northwest with Baltic and Black Sea ports. The Moscow–Brest railway links the capital with European countries, and serves major industrial nodes of the Western Region. Major elements in rail freights are coal, iron and steel, aluminium, cotton, wool, and grain.

In the period since World War II, oil and natural gas pipelines – including the important Friendship pipeline to Eastern Europe – cross the Western Region. All major industrial nodes of the region are now sustained by heavy in-shipments of these fuels.

The Moscow–Warsaw motorway via Smolensk and Minsk is the most notable, heavy-duty highway.

Industry in the Western Region

The power resources of the Western Region although not inconsiderable are nevertheless inadequate to support the present degree of industrialization. In consequence coal, oil, and natural gas are brought in from other regions and a major 1000-megawatt atomic power station is being built near Chernigov to forestall a threatened power shortage.

At present major power stations are located at Narva (oil-shale fired), Kaunas (Niemen), Daugava (hydroelectric), Molodechno, Belgres, near Orsha, Grodno, Minsk, and two peat-fired stations at Vasilevichi and Smolevichi. These plants and the new Burshtyn, Dobrotvor and Kishinev thermal power stations, and hydroelectric plants at Kiev and Kanev (Dniester Cascade), are all linked together in a regional grid network. This serves not only the Western Region, but also the COMECON countries through 500-kilovolt transmission lines.

The Baltic Republics. In the post-war period the three Baltic Republics have been transformed into thriving industrial centres. In Estonia and Latvia, industrial activities now exceed agriculture in terms of gross domestic product. They now provide many more opportunities for skilled and well-paid employment. A notable aspect of this industrialization process is the growth in specialist workers – meaning those with higher technical qualifications – as a percentage of all industrial and office workers; many are in-migrant workers of Russian origin. Two distinct types of industries are evident: (1) those requiring a high degree of skill and technical expertise, and (2) those which are labour-intense forms of manufacturing but require little special skills.

In 1970 Estonia produced 18·9 million tons of high-grade oil-shale from deposits of Kohtla-Järve. A 208-kilometre pipeline connects the Kokhtla-Järve gas generators to Leningrad and Tallin. The Baltic Republics' industries, however, now receive a reversed flow of natural gas through new pipelines.

Peat-fired power stations, and a number of hydroelectric schemes on the Narva, Western Dvina, and Niemen Rivers, provide useful amounts of electrical energy. A wide scatter of small thermal power stations, many based on peat or low-grade coal fuel, gives a wide dispersion to industries. The heaviest concentrations of industry occur in the cities of Tallin, Riga, Kaunas, and Kaliningrad. These industries include railway passenger rolling stock, buses, shipbuilding, heavy engineering such as peat-digging, agricultural, and construction machinery. Electric motors are manufactured at the 'Volta' plant in Tallin.

Tallin has specialized precision-measuring instrument plants as well as plywood plants and a paper-mill. Riga has a steel plant which in 1970 produced nearly 443,000 tons from scrap metal, a factory manufacturing telephone exchange equipment of national importance, and various radio and television set factories. It also has textile mills making woollen, cotton, linen, and natural silk fabrics. Other plants make digital computers and ancillary equipment.

Throughout the Baltic Republics, the manufacture of cement and mineral fertilizers has grown in importance. By 1970, cement production was 3·0 million tons, and fertilizers output, largely based on Tallin phosphorites, expanded to meet the growing needs of agriculture.

Port industries include sugar refineries using im-ported Cuban raw cane-sugar as well as local beet-sugar. Canneries deal with fish landings and timber mills process both local and distant water-borne log supplies. Footwear manufacture, expanded substantially as Baltic tanneries provided more materials and Soviet production programmes swung more towards consumer goods. The Baltic Republics produced nearly 30 million pairs of footwear in 1970, all in modern mass-production factories which, like the textile, weaving and knitting mills, were heavy employers of female and juvenile labour.

Chemical industries are prominent in the Baltic zone. These include plants making nitrogenous fertilizers, lacquers and dyestuffs from natural gas brought in from the Dashava gas-fields of the Southwest Ukraine. Other factories make oil-shale derivatives, pharmaceutical preparations, plastics, and synthetic fibres (especially kapron for the hosiery and knitwear industries).

Among the food processing industries are bacon-curing, smoked pork fat – a speciality of Lithuania – pickled or smoked herrings and sprats, meat canning and dairy product factories.

Belorussian S.S.R. The most significant branches of industry in Belorussia are the manufacture of

95. Drilling in progress at one of the newly discovered oil districts in the southwest of the Latvian Republic.

96. The new industrial town of Novopolotsk, Belorussia. Shown here are blocks of flats laid out in open space setting and featuring mosaic panel of 'Soviet realistic art'.

97. Control valves in one of the Carpathian, Southwestern Ukraine, pumping stations serving the 'Friendship' oil pipeline to Eastern Europe.

motor vehicles, tractors, agricultural implements, and machine tools.

Grodno makes heavy-duty and tip lorries. Minsk manufactures the 'Belorus' wheeled tractor and many other types of farm implements. Lida makes flax-scutchers and potato-lifting machines. Other agricultural machinery centres are Gomel' (silage harvesters) and Slutsk.

Mogilev builds construction industry plant and materials handling equipment; Zhodino, ditch-digging machines, drag-lines, and road-making machinery. Several centres manufacture peat-cutting machines – Gomel', Orsha, Minsk, and Mozyr.

Precision engineering is represented by machine tools, transfer lines and automatic equipment. Such products are manufactured in Minsk, Orsha, Vitebsk, Molodechno, Baranovichi and Gomel'.

Belorussia developed early a wood chemical industry. This makes turpentine, resins, ethyl alcohol, xanthates and similar products. It also produces tannin extract and cellulosic fibres from its timber resources. The fibre plants are at Sokal' and Svetlogorsk and there is a match factory supplying the national market at Borisov. The Soligorsk potash deposit is vital for agricultural chemicals.

A modern petro-chemical industry using Dashava natural gas and oil brought in from other regions makes sulphuric acid – a by-product of refining – nitrogenous fertilizers, ethyl alcohol, polyethylene, detergents, plastics, lacquers, dyestuffs, and synthetic rubber and tyres. Grodno and Gomel' are important centres for these industries, as is the republic's capital, Minsk.

Light industries in Belorussia include flax-spinning and linen-weaving, dairy factories, and fruit and vegetable processing plants. A modern beet-sugar refinery is located at Grodno.

Southwest Ukraine. The emergence of the Dashava gas-fields has given rise to many new industrial activities in the Southwest Ukraine. In 1970 these gas-fields produced nearly a million cubic metres of natural gas and condensate – not much it is true compared to other Soviet gas-fields – but a vital fuel supplement in a fuel-poor region. The associated West Ukraine oil-field yielded 13·9 million tons of crude in that year.

The potash deposits of Stebnik, like those of near-by Soligorsk, support a fertilizer industry. Also native sulphur is extracted from a deposit at Rozdol. Rock Salt is obtained from near L'vov and Khust. These raw materials gave rise to a glass-making chemicals industry (soda ash, etc.) which, combined with local, good quality glass-making sands, has sustained plate-glass and hollow glass-ware factories of national significance. As noted, the heavy chemicals industries also support fertilizer plants needed to supply the region's agriculture. Other chemicals manufactured include toxic sprays for agriculture.

Engineering industries of the Southwest Ukraine are extremely important in the regional economy. Kiev and L'vov are major industrial centres, but there are many small centres with special attributes in engineering production. Electrical equipment, radio and electronic engineering, optical products including cameras and medical equipment, are among the most specialized types of product.

The building of river vessels, buses at L'vov, motorcycles, and many kinds of agricultural machines also figures prominently in the region's industrial output.

Food-processing industries are intimately associated with the region's agriculture. Pig-meat processing, fruit and vegetable canneries, flour-milling, vegetable oil pressing and distilleries are among the chief activities. Concentrated in the sugar-beet growing areas – from Khmel'nitsky to Kiev oblasts – are numerous sugar refineries. These have an aggregate production of about three million tons of granulated sugar annually; nearly a third of the national production.

Moldavian S.S.R. Until recently Moldavia was one of the most backward regions in the Soviet Union. In consequence, it has not yet experienced great development of industry and remains essentially a rural economy. Nevertheless, industries based on agricultural produce and meeting the immediate needs of rural activities have shown a strong tendency to emerge during the 1966–70 Plan. Moreover, with government encouragement traditional industries of the area such as silk-throwing (dependent on Moldavia's silk-worms and mulberry groves), survivals of an earlier era, have been revitalized. Wood-working and wineries also owe much to the Moldavian heritage. Wine production in 1970 was 24·5 million decalitres. Moldavian wine has a great reputation and serves the national market. Modern industrial innovations of recent years include a sugar refinery, a tobacco factory, and several food canneries using local materials, particularly peaches, apricots, and stone fruits. Meat packing and dairy products are also growing industries. These utilize the increasing quantities of farm output made possible by greater numbers of cattle and pigs now apparent in the general farming scene. Local deposits of phosphorites and gypsum give rise to a small fertilizer industry geared to supply the Moldavian market.

Conclusion

In general character the Western Region bears the imprint of its historical antecedents. It has an agricultural economy of great stability upon which have been superimposed many elements of careful innovation and new technology. For all the growth of industry evident during the eighth (1966–70) and current (1971–75) Five-Year Plans, the Western Region remains somewhat underdeveloped compared with the Centre and the Donets–Dnieper economic regions. Modern industrialism is but a thin veneer on an agrarian economy.

CHAPTER NINETEEN

SOUTH UKRAINE–
DONETS-DNIEPER REGION

Reference	Appendix 2 for details by administrative region of population, area, density, and urbanization
Area	326·3 thousand square kilometres
Population	about 26·5 million
Average Density	81·2 persons per square kilometre
Urbanization (Per cent)	62
Largest Cities	1970 Population (in thousands)

Donets-Dnieper		Kadiyevka	137
Khar'kov	1223	Melitopol'	137
Donetsk	879	Nikopol'	125
Dnepropetrovsk	862	Slavyansk	124
Zaporozhye	658	Kommunarsk	123
Krivoy Rog	573	Lisichansk	118
Zhdanov	417	Konstantinovka	105
Makeyevka	392	Krasnyy Luch	103
Voroshilovgrad	383		
Gorlovka	335	*South Ukraine*	
Dneprodzerzhinsk	227	Odessa	892
Poltava	220	Nikolayev	331
Kirovograd	189	Kherson	261
Sumy	159	Simferopol'	249
Kramatorsk	150	Sevastopol'	229
Kremenchug	148	Kerch	128

The South Ukraine–Donets-Dnieper Region comprises two distinct economic regions, the South Ukraine which is overwhelmingly agricultural in character and the Donets-Dnieper which is unequivocally industrial. This latter economic region is one of the pre-eminent industrial zones of the Soviet Union. The Donets-Dnieper produces one-third of the bituminous coal, one-half of the coking coal, 40 per cent of iron and steel, and has substantial elements of the country's heavy industries. The South Ukraine, on the other hand possesses an extremely rich agriculture with intensive land-uses in grains and other crops of great importance to the country's economy (Fig. 19.1).

The Physical Environment

The Donets-Dnieper and South Ukraine have the following physical divisions:

(1) The Middle Dnieper rolling steppe high plains (Black Earth Belt);
(2) The Prichernomorsk low plain (the raised portion of the former Sea of Azov–Black Sea Shelf);

and (3) The Crimean Peninsula.

The South Ukraine–Donets-Dnieper Region suffers from some physical constraints, particularly in its agriculture. In the south, the Crimea, like the neighbouring North Caucasus, suffers from

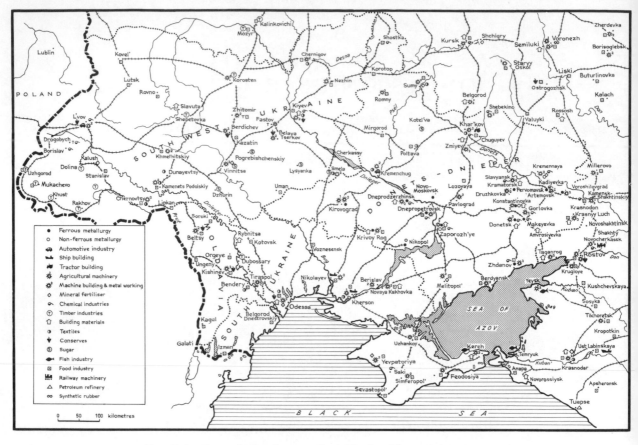

FIG. 19.1   Economic Development: South Ukraine–Donets-Dnieper Region.

summer droughts, periodically of great severity, which inhibit the cultivation of grains and other crops not well adapted to aridity. Moreover, the seasonal dry winds, the *sukhovey*, blowing in from the deserts of Central Asia cause desiccation of crops and sometimes great havoc.

The twin problems of general aridity and year-to-year fluctuations in summer high-temperature and hot-wind régimes, place much of the South Ukraine's and Crimea's agriculture under hazard. Severe droughts and disastrous crop failures are evident every four or five years. It is then that the Soviet Union becomes a net importer of wheat.

Agriculture in the Southern Region
The agricultural pattern of the Southern Region falls naturally into the two economic zones: The Donets-Dnieper, and South Ukraine.

Donets-Dnieper. This agricultural region owes its development to fertile and very productive chernozem and chestnut soils. The loess-cover, deposited by winds in the post-Pleistocene phase, has developed its pedological characteristics through long-term climatic action. Large amounts of humus are added annually by vegetable decay and biogenetic activity. In consequence, the wooded and grassland steppes have been the richest farmlands of Russia throughout history.

Although the central belt of meadow-grass steppe with its fertile chernozem soils is best known for its intensive industrial development between the Dnieper and Donets Rivers, it also has a very vigorous agriculture.

It is an area in which grain, especially winter wheat, sunflower, hemp, vegetables, berry fruit, and orchards thrive. Around the great industrial cities of the Donbas and Dnieper Bend, market gardening, intensive dairying, and such specialized crops as makhorka and tobacco find a ready inclusion in farming activities.

If the Donets-Dnieper Region is over-shadowed by the industrial image of the Donbas, it nevertheless ranks first in the Soviet Union for the production of winter wheat, maize for grain (i.e., maize grown to full maturity for its grain harvest), and sunflower seed; and second in rank for total grain output. This is a direct consequence of the intrinsic fertility of the chernozem-soil farmlands despite generations of use.

The sub-humid climate of the steppes is ideal for heavy-yielding grains like winter wheat. Annual rainfalls varies from 400 to 600 millimetres (16–24 inches), decreasing from north to south; mean winter and summer temperatures are 6°–20° C (21°–67° F) respectively – much like the northern prairie wheat-lands of the United States. While wheat cultivation has been the traditional main enterprise of Donets-Dnieper state farms and collectives, maize growing – both as maize for grain and as green fodder – has entered the field quite substantially since the mid-1950s.

Maize matures to milk-wax stage throughout the region, but the best location for fully mature grain – requiring greater warmth and sunshine – is the southern fringe of the Donets-Dnieper zone. The cultivation of maize amounts to 15–20 per cent of the farm area in this core zone. In the peripheral zones, however, a smaller percentage of farm area is devoted to this crop.

Sunflower cultivation is another activity which is widespread throughout the Donets-Dnieper Region. However, the drier steppe areas of the south are most favourable for this crop; indeed, the highest yields and richest oil content of sunflower seed are obtained from neighbouring economic regions, the South Ukraine and North Caucasus.

To the north of the wheat- and maize-growing farmlands of the Donets-Dnieper Region is the wooded steppe. This broad belt crosses the region from west to east; from the middle Dnieper to the Don. Here the soils are degraded chernozems; fertile, but subjected to some leaching due to the high incidence and intensity of summer rainfall. These soils are well-suited to the cultivation of sugar-beet, and consequently this becomes an essential element in the general farming system based on winter wheat. Maize for fodder or silage and sunflower remain important although the soils and climate are less suitable for these crops.

In the wooded steppe areas of the Donets-Dnieper Region mixed farming takes on a new and vital significance. State farms and collective farms, especially those engaged in sugar-beet cultivation, now pay more attention to beef cattle grazing, dairying, and pig-raising. Animals are fed on maize, green silage, and on beet pulp returned from the sugar refineries which dot the wooded steppe.

Despite the enormous demand for farm produce by the industrial areas of the Donets-Dnieper Region very substantial quantities are moved out of the region to serve national markets.

Market gardens, orchards, and small-area crops, such as tobacco and berries, as well as dairy-farming are found around the major conurbations. The Donets-Dnieper Region, it seems, would be an excellent 'laboratory' area for the testing of von Thünen's concentric circle theory of land rent.

South Ukraine. Agriculture in the South Ukraine is differentiated by increasing summer drought. The dry steppe grasslands developed on southern chernozem and chestnut soils are subject to frequent moisture stress and the incidence of the *sukhovey*. The soils are less fertile than the Donets-Dnieper soils to the north and because of lower rainfall generally, farming systems need to adapt.

On the Black Sea steppes and the dry-lands of the Crimean Peninsula, only xerophytic or semi-xerophytic plants are grown unless supplemental irrigation is available. In this adaptive land-use pattern, the common elements are: sunflowers grown for oil-seed, barley, and natural grassland farming of cattle, sheep (for wool production), and goats, each occupying a successively drier sub-stratum of the steppe landscape.

Nevertheless, despite the emphasis on pastoral activities, winter wheat and maize are also grown in the South Ukraine. The dry-land collective farms of the Prichernomorsk plain have a long history of adaptation to a hostile and capricious environment. In the South Ukraine crop diversity is the inevitable safeguard against economic annihilation practised by dry-land farmers throughout the world.

Inland, wheat and maize occupy the hollows in the plain while sunflower and other oil-seed crops –

98. Sugar-beet fields near Khar'kov. On this kolkhoz the beet pulp that remains after the extraction of the sugar is returned to the farm as animal feedstuffs. Note the silos in the background. (Photograph by the author.)

99. Ordzhonikidze manganese ore open-cut, Dniepropetrovsk oblast. The rotary cutter shown – made by the Novokramatorsk Machine Works – removes ore at the rate of 5000 tons per hour. The chernozem soil overburden is carefully stored (background) to rehabilitate farming once mining is completed.

100. Farm cottages on kolkhozes are warm, sturdy structures. Each individual farm family in the Soviet Union is guaranteed a home and a personal plot of land under the Constitution. Collective farm work is paid for on a time-plus-skill basis and the individuals also share in annual profits declared by their kolkhoz management. (Photograph by the author.)

caraway, linseed, poppy – are cultivated on the rises. For the South Ukraine region as a whole sunflower covers about two-thirds of the area planted in industrial crops. In favoured areas sugar-beets and tobacco are grown. The region has an excellent reputation for its high quality air-cured tobacco.

In the immediate vicinity of the coast, where moisture-bearing sea breezes ameliorate conditions, many types of intensive farming occur. Melons and other curbis are grown, especially on sandy low-lands of the Perekop Isthmus (Crimea). Early spring vegetables and salad crops as well as orchard fruit – peaches, apricots, and nectarines – and berries are grown in great profusion. Black Sea and Crimean vineyards produce both table grapes and vintage types.

On the cooler slopes of the Crimean Mountains, apple orchards and vineyards are sited according to air drainage and temperature inversion patterns, and also aspect, so that the fruit can catch the maximum sun. Throughout the South Ukraine irrigated rice is becoming ever more important. Along the *limans* of the Sea of Azov coast the cultivation of wet rice has become important in the last decade. The drainage of the brackish water of the *limans* (really lagoons separated from the open sea by long offshore spits) and the charging of these with fresh irrigation water, have allowed intensive rice culture, reminiscent of that employed in southern Spain or on the bayous coast of southern U.S.A.

On the high alpine pastures (or *yaila* as they are called) of the Crimean Mountains, cattle rearing and sheep grazing are the dominant forms of land-use. The mountains are imbricated – a three-fold *en echelon* series of range upon range with intervening valleys – and consequently each valley has a well-integrated agricultural system: livestock on the slopes and specialized land-uses in the protected valleys between. Tobacco, orchards, some dry cotton, and grain growing are typical valley land-uses.

Elsewhere in the South Ukraine beef cattle grazing and dairying, particularly for butter-making, have become important in post-war years, especially along the Sea of Azov coast. In the drier areas of eastern parts of the region, the breeding of fine-wool sheep is an established activity. Many state farms, as well as collectives, engage in this enterprise and there are substantial numbers of sheep in the hands of individual collective farmers also.

Transportation in the South Ukraine and Donets-Dnieper

The southern parts of the Ukraine and Russian Federation are marked by a wide disparity in its transport facilities. The Donets-Dnieper and South Ukraine are served by very dense rail and road networks, while in the North Caucasus and Trans-Caucasus railway lines are few and road networks elemental.

The Donets-Dnieper has many heavily used railway lines, including the electrified trunk lines, carrying coal, iron-ore, manganese ore and steel products within and beyond the region. Inter-regional lines connect the Donbas with Moscow by three separate routes: via Yelets, another via Khar'kov and a third via Ryazan'. The Yelets route in particular, is dominated by movements of coal, iron and steel, machines and heavy chemicals carried north, and by timber, machinery, and light manufactures carried south. Other through railway lines connect the Donbas with Zaporozh'ye, Krivoy Rog and the Sea of Azov ports, Zhdanov and Taganrog.

South Ukraine's railways connect to Moscow from Simferopol' (Crimea) via Zaporozh'ye and Nikolayev via Kiev. Lines from the Donbas lead to Kakhovka and the Crimea, then across the Kerch Strait by train ferry to Krasnodar. This is the quickest route used to haul freight and passengers between the Ukraine and the Caucasus. The trunk line from the north passes through Rostov to reach Baku on the Caspian. This line is now electrified. A branch from this railway (Groznyy–Astrakhan) connects Baku with the Volga system. The Black Sea route (Batumi–Tbilisi) from Rostov also reaches Baku so completing the circuit of Trans-Caucasia. Freight involves industrial products inwards and agricultural produce – grain, sugar, meat, wool, and fruit – and also cement, outwards.

The South Ukraine–Donets-Dnieper Region has one of the most intensely utilized shipping services of the Soviet Union. The Black Sea, Sea of Azov, and Caspian Sea with their associated navigable rivers (Dnieper, Volga–Don Canal and Volga navigation) link the manifold industrial and agricultural regions together.

The Black Sea also connects the Southern and Volga Regions with overseas markets and sources of imports. The international waters of the Bosphorus, Dardanelles, and Mediterranean carry a substantial proportion of the Soviet Union's cargo vessels, bulk-handling ships and oil tankers engaged in overseas trade. The modern, high mechanized port of Ilyichyovsk, near Odessa, has grown progressively in this trade. Odessa and Ilyichyovsk together now handle half of the country's foreign trade generated within the Black Sea and Volga Regions. Major out-bound cargoes include coal, oil, iron-ore, manganese, salt, and grain. These commodities also account for a substantial proportion of the coastwise trade with the notable additions of timber, tea, and fruit.

Industry in the South Ukraine–Donets-Dnieper Region

Industrial development in the South Ukraine–Donets-Dnieper Region has shown great advances in the post-war period. The southeastern Ukraine and, in particular, the Donets–Dnieper Bend–Sea of Azov territorial complexes, have been centres of heavy industry since Czarist times, although the development at an outstanding pace occurred only during the Soviet period.

Over the last twenty years or so great industrial changes have taken place, not only in the Donbas and associated districts, but also in the emerging North Caucasus and Trans-Caucasus industrial centres.

Power-engineering developments have been at the heart of these industrial transformations. New developments in the coalfields, the rehabilitation of the oil-producing industry, the growing network of oil and gas pipelines and high voltage transmission lines, and the use of new hydroelectric potential on the Dnieper and Don rivers have been outstanding, while in neighbouring Trans-Caucasia alone, hydroelectric power developments on the Rioni, Razdan, Kura (Zemo-Avachal), and other mountain streams, now provide about 6 per cent of the country's hydroelectric power output.

Donets-Dnieper Region. The heavy industries of the Donets-Dnieper Region include coal-mining, ferrous and non-ferrous metallurgy, engineering and chemical industries (Fig. 19.1). The overwhelming concentration of these industries reflects the excellent availability of steam and coking coal, iron-ore and manganese ore resources within the region.

Coal reserves of the Donbas amount to 240,000 million tons; 72 per cent in the Ukraine and 28 per cent in the Russian Federation's Rostov oblast. Coal-mining takes place in over 500 individual mines which supply not only local heavy industries, but the vast markets of the European parts of the Soviet Union too. Coal is mined to depths of 300–1000 metres. Tectonic movements have tilted, broken and contorted the coal seams and sometimes they are thin (average 0·93 metres). This makes mining difficult and expensive.

Recently oil and gas have replaced much of the market for steam coal, and consequently much greater attention is being given to the development of coking coals. These are found in the centre of the Donets Basin, while the steam coals and anthracite lie around the margins, particularly on the eastern and southeastern sides. Up to the present, large coalfield power stations have used these steam-raising coals, but over the last five years atomic power stations built at Novovoronezh, and now Kursk and Chernobyl' are taking over more of the load, particularly the peak load.

At present, mining is being re-vitalized by two methods: (1) the combination of adjacent mines into single larger enterprises which can be worked more effectively using modern coal-combines for cutting and handling the coal, and the provision of new high-speed haulage and winding gear, and (2) the sinking of new deep-mining shafts in the western parts of the concealed coalfields of Khar'kov oblast well northwest of the Donbas. The Donets-Dnieper Region's coal production now stands at 206 million tons, accounting for about one-third of the Soviet Union's bituminous coal and more than one half of its coking coal.

Donetsk and Voroshilovgrad (Lugansk) oblasts are the chief areas for coking coal production in the region. These embrace the following centres: Velikonadolsk, Donetsk, Makeyevka, Gorlovka (Tsentralny), Kadiyevka (Almaznom), Krasnodom, and several other smaller towns.

The Donets-Dnieper iron and steel mills produce 60 million tons of pig iron and steel annually. The major Donbas locations are Donetsk, Makeyevka, Voroshilovgrad (formerly Lugansk, but in 1971 reverted to its former name of Voroshilovgrad), and Kramatorsk. In addition there are six smaller integrated iron and steel centres in the Donbas; Konstantinovka, Almaznaya, Kadiyevka, Yenakievo, Kommunarsk, and Khartsyzsk. Almaznaya has recently opened a modern ferro-alloys plant which serves the whole region.

The Dnieper Bend group of iron and steel centres are located at Krivoy Rog, Zaporozh'ye, Dnepropetrovsk, Dneprodzerzhinsk and, a new centre, Novomoskovsk. These mills specialize in high manganese steel or various qualities of electric or alloy steels, especially chrome-, nickel-, and vanadium-steels.

Krivoy Rog's iron-ore deposits remain the most important source of blast-furnace material for all steel mills of the region. However, since its high grade ores are now nearly worked out, Krivoy Rog now concentrates on the lower grade quartzites (36 per cent iron) and supplies pellets of 65 per cent iron content. Other iron-ore pellets (from 25–45 per cent quartzites) and sintering iron ore fines (50–65 per cent ores) reach the Donbas from the Kursk Magnetic Anomaly ore-fields developed since World War II. Other new ore deposits have been opened up at Kremenchug and Dneprorudnoye (the high grade Belozerka deposit) on the south bank of the Kakhovka reservoir.

Kursk and Dneprorudnoye ores not only supplement the Krivoy Rog and Kremenchug ores directly in Donbas blast furnaces, but also allow the latter mining areas to export iron ore westward to the steel mills of Czechoslovakia, Poland, and East Germany. This iron-ore not infrequently returns to the Soviet Union transformed into technical equipment and machinery.

Nikopol' and Marganets manganese ores from the Donets-Dnieper Region and in-shipments from Chiatura (Georgian S.S.R.) supply essential manganese to the region's iron and steel plants.

In 1970 the Donets-Dnieper steel mills still ac-counted for 40 per cent of Soviet production de-spite a continuous relative decline since the 1930s when new centres of the Soviet iron and steel industry first began. Nevertheless, in absolute terms, expansion of the industry is not yet con-cluded. For instance, the eighth blast furnace installed at the Krivoy Rog plant has a capacity of 2700 cubic metres and is therefore among the largest in the world. Blast-furnaces of this size category are to be standardized for all future iron and steel centres in the Soviet Union.

Similar expansion is evident in the region's growth of ancillary facilities in steel mills. New billet and blooming mills have been added to all integrated steel plants and the region now has four specialized tube-mills capable of making oil pipes up to 40 inches in diameter. Bulk oxygen conver-ters (BOS) have been set up in the Krivoy Rog and Dnepropetrovsk steel mills, and Donetsk has introduced the continuous casting process.

Although coal-mining and the iron and steel industries dominate the scene in the Donets-Dnieper Region, other heavy industries are never-theless also important.

Non-ferrous metallurgy remains significant de-spite the rise of new smelters and refineries in the eastern regions. Konstantinovka has a zinc refinery of all-Union significance; Zaporozh'ye an alumin-ium refinery and Zheltyye Vody a uranium enrich-ment plant. Several other branches of non-ferrous processing – tin, nickel, and copper – are also found. Essentially these are examples of historical inertia leaving its imprint on the region's industrial make-up. The chemical industries too have this characteristic, although modern elements such as petrochemicals and cellulosic fibres have intruded in post-war years.

Formerly the chemical industries were based on coke-oven by-products, rock salt, and local phos-phorus slag. These yield ammonia, aniline dyestuffs, and nitrogenous fertilizers. Soda and var-ious strong alkalis emerged as a result of exploiting the brines of Slavyansk and rock salt deposits of Artemovsk. Other inorganic chemicals arose as de-rivatives of smelter by-products, and certain electro-chemicals – carborundum, tungsten-carbide, and explosives – arose due to the availability of cheap elec-tricity from the Dnieper hydroelectric schemes.

Now that Poltava–Shebelinka natural gas and oil from the Middle Volga are available in the region, the petrochemical industries have grown apace. Synthetic plastics and resins are made in Donetsk, Voroshilovgrad, and both Dnepropetrovsk and its neighbour Dneprodzerzhinsk.

The heavy engineering industries of the Donets-Dnieper Region involve heavy mining and iron and steel mill plant and machinery. The region also builds heavy machine tools. The major centres con-cerned are Donetsk, Kramatorsk, and Gorlovka. Voroshilovgrad, Novocherkassk, and Khar'kov build large diesel engines and railway locomotives, large-sized turbo-alternators, electric motors, and transformers. Agricultural machinery is built at Kirovograd and Rostov-on-Don.

Accompanying this profusion of producer goods industries, there are some examples of light and consumer-oriented industries in the Donets-Dnieper Region. These are based on the region's thriving agricultural–pastoral resources and its huge consumer markets. The chief light industries are salt processing, sugar refineries, vegetable oil processing (margarine manufacture), canneries, and fruit preservative plants. Such industries provide job opportunities for women and juvenile workers that cannot find employment in heavy industries; a useful balance in the region's employment structure.

The South Ukraine. This region, so far as indus-trial structure is concerned, is an appendage of the Donets-Dnieper Region. Both Zhdanov and Taganrog have small integrated iron and steel plants that have grown in response to the coking coal supplies of Rostov oblast and the self-fluxing, but low-grade, iron-ores of the Kerch Peninsula. These iron-ores contain not only lime gangue, but also phosphorus and sulphur, and consequently it is essential that they are beneficiated into pellets or sinter material before use. Because of the impurities contained, useful by-product plants making fer-tilizers, sulphuric acid, and basic slag cement (poz-zolan, quick-setting cement) are located in Kerch and Zhdanov.

Nikolayev and Kherson are important ship-building centres. Merchant vessels up to 44,000 tons' displacement have been built in these yards as well as oil-tankers, whale factory ships, trawlers, and passenger ferries and river vessels of many kinds.

Kherson is also a centre for the manufacture of agricultural implements; maize harvesters, tractor-drawn ploughs, oil-mill presses, and similar equipment.

Chemical industries in the South Ukraine comprise those making sulphuric acid, fertilizers, and agricultural toxic chemicals. Raw materials are local sulphur deposits extracted by the Frasch process, mineral salts obtained by solar evaporation of the Sea of Azov *limans* and vegetation cultivated locally for the extraction of essential oils and medical chemicals.

Light industries are important. They provide employment in cotton, wool, and silk (both natural and artificial) textiles; in the knitwear, hosiery and garment industries and in a wide range of food and tobacco industries based on local raw materials. The Crimean wineries produce internationally renowned 'massandra' vintage wines, shipped to both Russian and overseas markets.

As is evident, the South Ukraine–Donets-Dnieper Region is one of considerable importance. It is a region with a vital agricultural development as well as a long-established industrial growth which has made it the pre-eminent industrial zone of the Soviet Union.

CHAPTER TWENTY

NORTH CAUCASUS–
TRANS-CAUCASUS REGION

Reference Appendix 3 for details by administrative region of population, area, density, and urbanization

Area 616·7 thousand square kilometres

Population 27·2 million

Average Density 44·1 persons per square kilometre

Urbanization (Per cent) 50

Largest Cities 1970 Population (in thousands)

North Caucasus (R.S.F.S.R.)

North Caucasus (R.S.F.S.R.)			
Rostov-on-Don	789	Novoshakhtinsk	102
Krasnodar	464	Cherkessk	67
Groznyy	341		
Taganrog	254	*Trans-Caucasus Republics*	
Ordzhonikidze	236	Baku	1226
Sochi	224	Tbilisi	889
Shakhty	205	Yerevan	767
Stavropol'	198	Kirovabad	190
Makhachkala	186	Leninakan	165
Novocherkassk	162	Kutaisi	161
Nal'chik	146	Sumgait	124
Armavir	145	Sukhumi	102
Novorossiysk	133	Batumi	101
Maykop	110	Rustavi	98
		Dashkesan	62

The North Caucasus–Trans-Caucasus Region comprises the large and important southern agricultural zone of the Russian Federation – the North Caucasus so called – and the three republics of the Trans-Caucasus, Georgia, Armenia, and Azerbaydzhan, together with numerous autonomous republics in the mountainous fastnesses of the Caucasus. These Trans-Caucasian areas also possess a very rich and varied agriculture, sometimes with a high degree of specialized cropping (Fig. 20.1).

The Physical Environment

The North Caucasus–Trans-Caucasus embrace the following distinct physical divisions:

(1) The rolling plains of the northern North Caucasus;

(2) The Stavropol' Forelands and Plateau;

(3) The Great Caucasus Range;

(4) The Rioni–Kura Valleys and Syncline;

and (5) The Lesser Caucasus Mountains and Plateaux.

North Caucasus. Across the Don River from the southern Rostov oblast the Caucasian Foreland rises almost imperceptibly to the Stavropol' Plateau and the hills and rolling lowlands of Krasnodar Kray. This landscape, noted for its intensive agriculture, lies south of the Manych Depression, an ancient post-Pleistocene spillway that drained

FIG. 20.1 Economic Development: North and Trans-Caucasus Region.

the pro-glacial Caspian into the then much larger Sea of Azov–Black Sea Basin. This then included the drowned Prichernomorsk lowlands of the South Ukraine.

The North Caucasus lands are low-lying, semi-arid plains or sandy hills and plateaux that rise a hundred metres or so above the general elevation. The Foreland is under the influence of an extreme continental climate; summer thunderstorms and the cold *bora* winds of winter bring short-duration precipitation to these generally parched lands, especially in autumn and winter. Natural vegetation grades from sub-humid shrub forms along the western margins of the Foreland to arid grass steppe in the east. The saline soils support extensive types of grain farming or reasonably good grazing country, particularly for sheep and goats. Only the more favourable soils of the Kuma, Terek, and Kuban valleys are suited to more intensive forms of agriculture.

The Kuban Basin is famed for its chernozem-like soils, and has become one of the pre-eminent maize

for grain and sugar-beet producing areas of the Soviet Union, largely at the instance of Khrushchev's policies. But its traditional crops are still wheat and sunflower. Like the South Ukraine, the Kuban grows both spring and winter wheat in its agricultural system thus making possible dry-farming rotational patterns that utilize intensive crops like sugar-beet and cotton in conjunction with fallowing and sown grassland rotations as well as wheat culture.

In recent years, sugar-beet cultivation has grown very considerably. Rice has also become an established crop in the Kuban delta, Colchis lowland and Terek Valley. Again, the lower Kuban and Black Sea coastal plains are known for their sugar-beet farming, tobacco, citrus groves, and vineyards. The Adygey Autonomous Oblast, with Maykop (population 110,000) as its centre, has 22 state farms and 41 collectives. Cattle breeding is a dominant activity here, but farming typical of the drier Kuban lands is also common.

101. A ploughing competition in progress in Stavropol' Kray, North Caucasus, in 1971. Women as well as men tractor drivers participate in these competitions which do much to develop skills and pride of work.

102. Combines engaged in group harvesting of grain in the Kuban valley, Krasnodar Kray. Note the cruciform shelter belts of trees needed to combat wind erosion and maintain snow cover uniformity in winter.

A high proportion of the North Caucasus (about 80 per cent) is used for agricultural purposes; over one half of this area is in sown crops, the rest in meadows and pastures. While winter wheat, maize and sunflower are the dominant crops, favoured soil areas having warmer, moister conditions are planted in sugar-beet and tobacco with orchards and vineyards on the sandy slopes. Rice, millet, medicinal, and essential oil crops are grown on small areas.

Recent developments have added about two million hectares of cultivated land, much of it irrigated, in the North Caucasus. All of this was won from Virgin Land previously unused, even for nomadic grazing. The chief location for these developments are in Rostov oblast, and Krasnodar and Stavropol' Krays. These new lands now rival the Ukraine as the Soviet Union's top ranking agricultural area as far as physical productivity is concerned. Mechanized farming and the development of high-yielding strains of crops have resulted in very intensive land-use. In consequence, the North Caucasus now has the lowest production costs for most agricultural output in the whole of the Soviet Union.

The North Caucasus Foreland and piedmont slopes are ideally suited to fruit-farming. The collectives here, often quite small, grow pome and stone fruit, berries, and grapes. The apples, pears, plums, cherries, and small berries produced here account for nearly 40 per cent of the Russian Federation's total production. Many canneries have been set up, particularly in Rostov oblast and the Krasnodar and Stavropol' regions, and also in Dagestan.

The North Caucausus, although renowned for its crop agriculture, also has a well-developed animal husbandry. It is an important supplier of meat – beef, mutton, pork, and poultry. Butter, cheese, eggs, and wool are also freighted out of the area to the important markets of the Centre and Volga.

Frequently, there is transhumance of sheep between the high mountain pastures of the Great Caucasus Range and the winter pastures of the Nogay and Kalmyk Steppes. Both of these latter areas have capitalized on earlier traditions of nomadic herding, giving rise to a modern sedentary sheep-breeding industry. Most of the sheep are fine-wool sheep of first-rate stamina and quality, often the result of crosses between native breeds and the fine-wool merino.

Running across the Caucasian Foreland are a number of subordinate Soviet territories. These include the Karachay–Cherkess A.O., the Kabardino–Balkar A.S.S.R., the North Ossetian A.S.S.R., the Chechen–Ingush A.S.S.R., and along the central Caspian Sea, the Dagestan A.S.S.R. Towards the east these lands become increasingly arid and also suffer because of their inferior soils, especially the saline desert soils of the Nogay Steppe. These desert lands, often with ephemeral streams, yield only sparse pasturage for sheep and camels.

The Karachay–Cherkess A.O. (population 345,000), with Cherkessk as its centre, has benefited from the Kuban–Kalaussi irrigation scheme embracing some 200,000 hectares. Sugar-beet is an important crop sent to a local factory for processing. In the back-country livestock grazing and grain farming are long-established practices.

The Kabardino–Balkar A.S.S.R. (population 600,000), with its administrative capital at Nal'chik, is also engaged in livestock and grain farming, but some of its 35 state farms and 75 collective farms have dairy cattle or cultivate vineyards on the south-facing slopes of the Foreland hills.

The North Ossetian A.S.S.R. (population 560,000), lies on the northern flanks of the Great Caucasus Range. Its capital Ordzhonikidze was formerly called Vladikavkaz. It has a well-developed agriculture with 20 state farms and 45 collectives. Maize for grain is the chief crop; the maize-product factory at Beslan is reputedly the largest of its kind in the world. Other industries include distilleries, wood-processing, and food plants.

The Chechen–Ingush A.S.S.R. (population 1,084,000) has the oil centre of Groznyy as its capital. The Terek Valley, with 54 state farms and 51 collectives, serves food canneries, wood-working plants, and furniture factories. These last obtain softwood and hardwoods from the mountain forests of Caucasia.

The Dagestan A.S.S.R. (population 1,457,000) has its administrative capital Makhachkala on the Caspian coast. Despite its semi-arid climate it has a varied agriculture ranging from winter wheat to

103. The Leningradskaya cheese factory, Krasnodar Kray.

104. Unloading sugar-beet to stockpiles at the Leningradskaya sugar-beet refinery, Krasnodar Kray.

grapes. Sheep, beef cattle, and camels are significant activities on the Republic's 167 state farms and 376 collective farms. With the opening of the Sulak river hydroelectric power plant (capacity 2·5 million kW) many farms as well as industries are now served with electricity.

The Trans-Caucasus. The three Republics of Georgia, Armenia and Azerbaydzhan straddle the mountainous areas of the Caucasus. The Tertiary folding of the mountains left a complex pattern. The Great Caucasus Range runs from near Tuapse on the Black Sea coast to the Apsheron Peninsula, on which Baku stands, jutting out into the Caspian. To the south, the lower plateaux and ranges of the Lesser Caucasus run from Batumi to the Lenkoran coast of the Caspian. Separating the Great and Lesser Caucasus is the Caucasian syncline, drained by the Rioni and Kura rivers, although the low Sumari Range forms a knot linking the major ranges together.

Agriculture in these mountainous Republics has enormous variety, based on difference in elevation and micro-climatic conditions. They have a long growing season, a variety of fertile soils, high rainfall in their western parts, and abundant irrigation in the drier east.

Taking Georgia as an example, we find that agriculture has developed three distinctive systems: (1) the sub-tropical agriculture of the coastal slopes; citrus, tobacco, and tea, (2) the intensive wheat and sown crop agriculture of the plains, often under irrigation, and (3) the orchards, vineyards, and animal husbandry of the mountainous areas. In Georgia we see the agriculture of the moist Black Sea coast, the intensive agriculture of the Kutaisi district, and the orchards and vineyards of Kakhetia district developed along the Alazani tributary of the upper Kura river. Similar, although not quite so intensive, agriculture has developed in the Araks valley of Armenia and the Kura lowlands of Azerbaydzhan. These farming and horticultural districts are protected from cold northern winds by the Great or Lesser Caucasus ranges.

Lying northwest of Georgia along the warm Black Sea coast is the Abkhaz A.S.S.R. centred on Sukhumi. Here 26 state farms and 127 collectives specialize on sub-tropical or Mediterranean crops. Tea, grapes, tangerines, and lemons and fine quality tobacco are grown, while on the steep slopes backed by the forested mountains, hill farms graze cattle or sheep. Goats and pigs are also important. These farms also rear horses (14,000 in 1971) to supply the riding and recreation centres of the Black Sea health resorts at Sochi, Gagra, Sukhumi, Akhali-Antoni, Gulripsha, and Gudauta.

The Black Sea coastal hill slopes of Georgia also grow tea and citrus fruit. They also have many groves of tung trees. These provide nuts from which an important industrial oil is extracted, used in engineering works for steel hardening, and also in the paint-making industry.

The Kutaisi district in the mountainous areas on the Rioni river, specializes in vineyards and mulberry and silk-worm culture. Some of the celebrated Georgian wines come from here. In 1970 about 14·3 million decalitres were produced. The Republic also produce large quantities of silk each year, and there are no signs that modern synthetic fibre production in the Soviet Union has caused a falling off in production in contrast to experience in the Western World and Japan.

The Colchis lowlands along the Black Sea coast have been reclaimed adding 115,000 hectares of first-rate agriculture land, while drainage of marshes has also provided another 138,700 hectares. The Republic's 231 state farms (23 per cent of cultivated land) and its 1265 small-scale 'horticultural' collectives now farm a total of 737,000 hectares (1970) of which 347,000 hectares are irrigated. Maize has become an important crop in the Colchis lowland around the lower Rioni, while sugar-beet on reclaimed soils is a new and growing innovation. Extensive areas of hill slopes are planted in tea-gardens. Leaf-processing plants are widely scattered, shipping the green and black teas through the Black Sea ports of Sukhumi, Poti, and Batumi. Tea leaf production was 259,000 tons in 1970, yielding over 100,000 tons of dried leaf, satisfying most of the country's requirements.

The mountain-girt Alazani Valley in southern Georgia is renowned for its fruit orchards and also its vineyards. Like the Kutaisi district, it markets wines throughout the Soviet Union. The nearby headwaters of the Araks river system leading into Armenia's major agricultural district also have many orchards and vineyards. Here too, sugar-beet farming has been a recent innovation.

The main Araks valley, which forms the international border between the Soviet Union and both Turkey and Iran, is intensively developed for agriculture. Cotton is grown under irrigation in the Razdan valley south of Yerevan and in the Nakhichevan A.S.S.R. Armenia and Azerbaydzhan produce some of the best 'Egyptian' strain long-staple cotton. The Araks valley also grows large quantities of sub-tropical fruits – olives, figs, pomegranate, and almonds. Cork-oak, introduced from Portugal, is a recent innovation.

Apart from specialized irrigation crops, large areas of the Lesser Caucasus uplands are planted in winter wheat and barley. Cattle and sheep graze on the higher plateau surfaces. Pigs are important in the maize-growing areas of the valleys. Vineyards clothe the slopes and river terraces, particularly where insolation and aspect are favourable. In the Nakhichevan A.S.S.R. (capital Nakhichevan, population 35,000) there are 12 state farms and 68 collectives. These are chiefly concerned with ir-

rigated cotton, tobacco, vineyards, and fruit growing. Some sericulture is also practised.

Armenia has 409,000 hectares under cultivation and over half of this area is irrigated; 252,000 hectares in 1970. Altogether there are 261 state farms and 476 collectives; a few remnants of private farming still exist, but these now have only one-tenth of one per cent of the total farm area, an aggregate of less than 400 hectares. The whole of the farming system is served with electricity, principally from the Lake Sevan scheme, and tractors, grain combines and mechanical cotton pickers are widely utilized.

The agriculture of the Azerbaydzhan S.S.R. is characterized by irrigated cotton, grain, and sub-tropical fruit growing in the lowlands south of the Kura river and the lower Araks tributary. Another system distinguishes the northern part of the Caucasian syncline. Here vineyards and orchards are prominent on the south-facing slopes of the Great Caucasus Range, while along the left bank

105. Off-shore oil-well staging in the Caspian Sea at Neftyanye Kamni, Azerbaydzhan. Several such stages are linked together and the mainland at Cape Sangachaly by a 20-kilometre road.

tributaries of the Kura there are many farms engaged in sericulture and tobacco growing. Grayule, a latex-producing plant introduced some years ago from Mexico, and well adapted to desert régimes, is also extensively grown on interfluves. The city of Sumgait on the Caspian coast of Azerbaydzhan gained its early start in the rubber industry from grayule, although it has now largely switched over to synthetic rubber derived from petrochemicals. Yerevan also has a substantial synthetic rubber industry.

Over recent years, cotton cultivation in the Kura lowlands has expanded very substantially, due to additional irrigation water now available from the multi-purpose Mingechaur and the Samursky Canal schemes. These projects like those of the Sevan–Razdan Cascade and Araks Valley in Armenia, are typical of the massive improvement in irrigation in the Trans-Caucasian Republics.

In Azerbaydzhan over 70 per cent of the cultivated lands are irrigated. Egyptian and Sea Island strains of cotton and also rice and lucerne are grown on the best soils. The moist Lenkoran coast of the Caspian, favoured by warm, humid on-shore winds, grows citrus fruit, tea, sub-tropical nuts and fruit, and vegetables to perfection.

The Azerbaydzhan highlands and mountains are used extensively for grazing cattle and sheep, numbering nearly 1·6 million and 4·2 million head respectively. In recent times pasture improvements common to the whole of Trans-Caucasia, have increased meat production. This now supplements the Republic's agriculture income quite significantly. Also the development of a high-yielding winter wheat suitable for mountain climates has pushed cultivation well into the Caucasian piedmonts of Azerbaydzhan.

An example of sub-tropical agricultural production in Trans-Caucasia is given in the following table (Table 20.1).

Western Georgia produces about 90 per cent of the Soviet Union's processed tea. Another 8 per cent is obtained from production in Krasnodar Kray and on the Lenkoran coast which is currently expanding. Also many attempts are being made to foster tea cultivation in the Trans-Carpathian mountains, at numerous experimental locations in Central Asia and also in the Far East around the monsoon coast of Vladivostok. Currently Georgia

and Adzharia have the highest productivity for tea: some 2200–3900 pounds per acre, and unless productivity is substantially improved in other areas mentioned it seems doubtful whether they can survive as tea-growing localities in the long term. Nevertheless, the Soviet goal of being independent of imported teas seems capable of achievement. In 1972 Soviet production of processed tea was 109,000 metric tons against relatively insignificant imports.

Industry in the North Caucasus–Trans-Caucasus

The Caucasus Regions. The two regions of the Caucasus – North Caucasus and Trans-Caucasus – may be discussed together as they have comparatively little development of industry. It is indeed only during the last few years, dominantly since the mid-1950s, that serious attempts have been made to establish industries of national importance in these regions.

The three Trans-Caucasian republics are known for their mineral industries. The Chiatura manganese deposits, with reserves of some 250 million tons, spread in many pockets over an area of 360 square kilometres, now provide an output of three million tons of ore annually.

TABLE 20.1
Western Georgia: Sub-Tropical Crops (Per cent of Total Crop Area by Districts)

	Tea	Citrus	Tung
Zugdidi Foothills	32·6	5·9	28·9
Southern Foothills	21·8	17·8	20·9
Abkhazia	17·0	33·7	27·7
Interior (Imeretia)	12·3	0·1	0·9
Adzharia	11·2	39·7	19·4
Colchis Lowland	5·1	2·8	2·2
	100·0	100·0	100·0
Total Area (thousand ha)	74·4	10	2(est.)
Total Production (thousand tons) (1972)	109·0	n.a.	n.a.

Sources: For tea, R. M. Bone, *op. cit.*, quoting A. A. Mints, *Nekotorye Voprosy Geografii Subtropicheskogo Khozyaistva Gruzinskoy S.S.R.,* Izvestiya Akademii Nauk S.S.S.R., Seriya Geograficheskaya, No. 6, 1954, p. 63. For citrus and tung: R. G. Jensen, *op. cit.*, quoting A. A. Mints.

Other metal ores mined in Trans-Caucasia include copper, lead-zinc, molybdenum, tungsten, mercury, aluminium (alunite), and the precious metals. Gold is mined in Georgia. Azerbaydzhan's Dashkesan iron-ore is shipped to the Rustavi and Sumgait iron and steel plants.

The old oil-field areas of Maykop, Groznyy, and Baku have been given a new lease of life by water-pressurizing techniques developed by Soviet engineers. Moreover, entirely new oil- and gas-fields have been opened up along the Black Sea Coast (Kuban), in Stavropol' Kray, in Dagestan along the Kura River, and far out into the Caspian Sea off the Apsheron Peninsula.[1] These new fields have surpassed the old centres in their present production. Oil and natural gas pipelines transport raw materials to petrochemical plants throughout the two regions.

The Nevinnomyssk chemical *kombinat* makes nitrogenous fertilizers, plastics, and synthetic fibres from natural gas; Cherkessk, Yerevan, and Armavir make synthetic rubber and plastic products, and Sumgait also makes synthetic rubber, tyres, plastics, and heavy inorganic chemicals. An entirely new synthetic rubber plant based on natural gas has been set-up near Gudermes, east of Groznyy. Kamenskiy makes synthetic fibres and a large factory manufacturing synthetic fats has been built at Volgodonsk.

Engineering industries include plants manufacturing oil-drilling rigs and cement mixers (Groznyy); railway equipment (Armavir) and electrical measuring instruments (Krasnodar). Other industries include electric locomotives, motor lorries, oil-drilling plant, machine tools, agricultural machinery, and ball-bearings at various industrial centres of Trans-Caucasia.

Since World War II a small, but locally important, iron and steel plant has been built at Rustavi, Georgia (production 1·4 million tons in 1970). It obtains low-grade coal from the Tkibuli and Tkvarcheli coalfields (production 2·3 million tons in 1970) and iron-ore from the Dashkesan deposit in Azerbaydzhan. The steel output is used in oil pipeline manufacture and other Caucasian steel-user industries. Pipelines have been built to serve the oil ports of Batumi and Tuapse on the Black Sea.

Light industries include the Elista fish cannery processing Caspian sturgeon and packing black caviar for export and domestic markets; the Beslan maize-processing plant in the North Ossetian A.S.S.R., and various distilleries, textile mills — including the new integrated mill at Mingechaur — and furniture manufacturing plants, all using local raw materials.

Throughout the North Caucasian and Trans-Caucasus Regions the past two decades have seen the progressive promotion of new industries. In large measure this expansion has been made feasible by modern efficient technology. The spread of pipelines and electrical transmission lines no less than the emergence of efficient small-scale plants such as non-ferrous metal concentrators, small local steel plants, food-processing plants and all sorts of manufacturing enterprises, have permitted industry to spread far and wide away from the major industrial nodes. In particular, the autonomous republics no less than Georgia, Armenia, and Azerbaydzhan now benefit from much more diversified economies with a thriving agriculture and burgeoning industries well represented. This has given the population of these frontier lands of the Soviet Union much higher standards of living and more social amenities.

---

[1] Although Baku oil production has been transcended by newer oil-fields it nevertheless had an output of 20·2 million tons in 1970. Moreover, the once highly productive natural gas-fields of Karadag are now being used as reservoirs and replenished by natural gas piped in from Iran.

CHAPTER TWENTY-ONE

THE CENTRAL AND VOLGA REGION

Reference   Appendix 4 for details by administrative region of population, area, density, and urbanization

Area   1376·3 thousand square kilometres

Population   about 58·5 million

Average Density   42·5 persons per square kilometre

Urbanization (Per cent)   54

Largest Cities   1970 Population (in thousands)

Centre				*Volga–Vyatka*	
Moscow	7061	Elektrostal'	123	Volgograd	818
Yaroslavl'	517	Kovrov	123	Saratov	757
Tula	462	Orekhovo-Zuyevo	120	Astrakhan'	410
Ivanovo	420	Mytishchi	119	Penza	374
Ryazan'	350	Noginsk	104	Ul'yanovsk	254
Kalinin	345			Tol'yatti	251
Bryansk	318	*Central Black Earth*		Sterlitamak	185
Vladimir	234	Voronezh	660	Syzran'	173
Orel	232	Lipetsk	289	Volzhskiy	142
Kostroma	223	Kursk	284	Engel's	130
Rybinsk	218	Tambov	230	Novokuybyshev	104
Kaluga	211	Belgorod	151		
Smolensk	211	Yelets	101	*Volga–Vyatka*	
Podolsk	169	Michurinsk	94	Gor'kiy	1170
Lyubertsy	139	Borisoglebsk	64	Kirov	333
Kolomna	136			Dzerzhinsk	221
Novomoskovsk	134	*Volga*		Cheboksary	216
Serpukhov	124	Kuybyshev	1045	Saransk	191
		Kazan'	869	Yoshkar-Ola	166

The Central and Volga Region is one of the most densely settled and highly urbanized regions in the Soviet Union. The region, as defined for the purposes of this book, embraces four Soviet economic regions: the Centre around the capital, Moscow, the Central Black Earth, the Volga–Vyatka and Volga regions. Each has specific differentiating features and yet, as highly developed agricultural and industrial localities, they ' have certain common and inter-linked economies of great moment to the country as a whole (Fig. 21.1).

Agriculture in the Central and Volga Region

The Central and Volga Region presents differentiated agricultural landscapes resulting from climatic and soil conditions. The harsher climate and podzolized soils of the Centre and Volga–Vyatka divisions are not naturally propitious for agriculture, while the Central Black Earth and Volga divisions are among the best agricultural zones of the Soviet Union based as they are on the fertile chernozem and chestnut soils and much warmer climatic régimes.

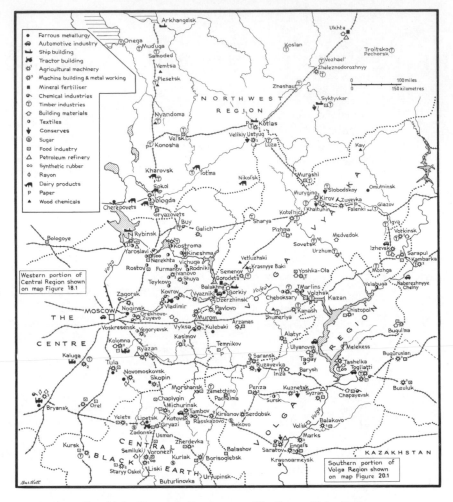

FIG. 21.1 Economic Development: The Centre–Volga Region.

The economic regions so differentiated may be discussed in turn.

The Centre–Volga–Vyatka. The chief crops grown in these regions are grains, flax and hemp for fibres, potatoes for household use but also as an animal feed, and industrial raw material, vegetables tolerant of infertile, podzolic soils, and, in marginal areas of the somewhat warmer south, small areas of sugar-beet.

Despite the physical constraints imposed on the regions about three-quarters of their cultivated land – about 40 per cent of total area – is under arable crops and one-quarter in meadows and pastures. Animals – cattle, pigs, and sheep – are a vital complement to intensive arable and meadow ley farming. The reason for the intense agricultural land-use in this far from propitious environment is the need to supply farm produce to the regions' many large cities and towns.

Grain crops include both spring and winter wheat, but more important are the hardy and soil-tolerant grains: buckwheat, rye, barley, and oats.

The Centre and Volga–Vyatka are the Soviet Union's pre-eminent potato and flax-growing areas; a belt famed for these crops extends from Kirov oblast westward to Smolensk and Bryansk. Hemp is grown somewhat to the south of this belt. Sugar-beet, not really typical of the two regions, is grown on better soils, especially in the south.

Throughout the area favoured meadow lands support diverse animal industries. Both collectives and state farms engage in this enterprise, as a part of their mixed farming system. This not only provides some diversity of output, but also returns organic manure to the soil. Nevertheless, because of the generally infertile soils, mineral fertilizer, and agricultural lime are liberally used also.

State farms have been prominent in dairying and pig-raising activities on a large-scale. Most of the regions' farms – both state and collectives – are well-equipped with farm machinery, mains water supply and electricity. Dairy farms have mechanized feed preparation, milking machines, and mechanical dung conveyors to keep the bails clean. The best developed dairy zone is the Lower Oka–Volga rivers confluence. Pig-rearing and sheep-farming (both meat and wool breeds) are especially found in Kirov oblast and south of the Upper Volga.

Over the past decade strenuous efforts have been made to increase agricultural output of these regions. The need to feed growing urban populations is becoming critical, for despite the recent mechanization and intensification of the regions' farming, it has not kept pace with demand. The Centre–Volga–Vyatka is far from self-sufficient in farm produce and consequently large 'imports' of grains and other commodities from the

Central Black Earth and Volga economic regions are necessary.

Central Black Earth–Volga. In contrast to the regions first discussed the Central Black Earth–Volga regions are among the best endowed agricultural regions of the Soviet Union. Both regions are favourable for wheat cultivation – winter wheat in the Central Black Earth and spring wheat in the Volga steppe lands.

Whereas the Central Black Earth has adequate rainfall the Volga region suffers greatly from recurrent summer drought. The incidence of drought causes considerable havoc to wheat farming in some years. For this reason ameliorative measures are well developed in the Volga region. These include irrigation, water, and snow retention in and on soil, shelter belts, and afforestation in selected areas. During the last decade alone nearly three million hectares of virgin and long-fallow lands have been ploughed and brought under grain cultivation. The Volga steppes give very high wheat yields under irrigation.

Because of critical water shortages in the growing season there are also long-term plans to divert the waters of certain northern rivers southwards into the Volga system, thus reversing their flow.

106. The Moscow stud-farm for Orloff horses (trotters) on the Moskva river floodplains.

This will provide even more irrigation potential in the Volga steppe lands.

Several autonomous republics within the region – Chuvash, Mari, Mordovian, and Tatar – also contribute substantially to its agriculture. Grains, fruit and vegetables, and flax as well as dairy cattle and sheep are raised to serve local and nationwide markets.

The Central Black Earth despite its emphasis on grain farming – winter wheat, barley, maize, and a little rye – has turned increasingly to industrial crops and mixed farming in recent years. The principal industrial crops are sugar-beet – grown especially in the Kursk–Belgorod–Voronezh triangle – sunflower, hemp, and tobacco. Sunflowers, adapted from high-oil-content North Caucasus strains, are produced more and more in Voronezh oblast. The Volga region also grows these crops together with mustard and coriander for their oil-seed. Some buckwheat and millet are grown on less fertile soils of southwest part of the Central Black Earth where summer drought becomes a special hazard. Maize used as a grain crop and also as a green fodder has taken up some of the area formerly occupied by spring wheat and rye in the Central Black Earth because of its high-yielding characteristics.

The great output of maize grain for fodder and silage and the introduction of leguminous plants and rotation grass leys into the farming system of these regions have stimulated animal husbandry. As a result, greater meat and milk production is now obtained from both the Central Black Earth and Volga regions. The Volga in particular has excellent hill-slope pastures and grazes six million head of beef cattle at the moment. It also has large flocks of wool sheep. The valley farmlands of both regions have many dairy herds, especially prevalent on state farms. Pigs and poultry are also in evidence.

The rich agriculture of the Central Black Earth–Volga regions ensures a sizable surplus of products to their own requirements. Meat, grains, milk, butter, lard and wool serve the Centre and other national markets.

Transport in the Central and Volga Region
This region is favoured by the densest and most heavily utilized railway network in the Soviet Union. Radial lines run in all directions from Moscow to all parts of the Soviet Union. The network embraces no less than 11 of the country's 43 individual railway systems. These carry inbound and out-bound freight in great volume and probably generate more than half of the total passenger journeys of the Soviet Union.

Railways are now completely electrified within the Centre and Central Black Earth regions, and major trunk routes such as the Donbas, Leningrad, and Trans-Siberian lines are also electrified. After World War II, new lateral river-side and cross-link railways have been built – Sviyazhsk–Ilovlinskaya, Astrakhan–Kizlyar and Surgut–Agryz lines for example.

Moscow has a well-organized suburban railway system carrying a large volume of commuter traffic. The system, underground in the city area, involves radial lines and two ring-lines: one around the periphery of the core area, and another farther out.

The region has excellent waterway facilities. From Moscow and Moskva–Oka and Volga links make the capital a 'port of seven seas'. Recent canal-building and renovation of existing canals has greatly increased Moscow's role as the country's pre-eminent inland port. Gor'kiy on the Volga has also enjoyed greater river traffic over recent years.

The Volga river – and the Volga–Don canal link to the Black Sea – are the Soviet Union's most vital waterway. These carry about 45 per cent of the country's total river-borne freight and some 30 per cent of the river-vessel passengers. Wherever railway lines crossed the river, considerable river ports have grown. Many of these are now important industrial centres with wharves, loading gantries, marshalling yards, and ferry terminals. Examples within the region are: Astrakhan', Saratov-Engel's, Kuybyshev, and Kazan'.

The major freight handled by the Volga waterway system includes grains, oil, Donbas coal, cement, salt (from Vladimirovka), cotton and fish products moving upstream, and milled timber – log-rafts are now no longer feasible because of lock-building – refined petroleum products, salt (from Baskunchak) and grain (bound for Black Sea and trans-Caspian destinations) moving downstream.

The Volga waterway and railway system is responsible for the region's excellent transport accessibility. Semi-manufactures are received from

107. Volgograd oblast is one of the country's main grain-growing areas. Here combines harvest winter wheat on the Zarya kolkhoz, Kotelnikovskiy district.

108. The 65-kilometre Gorodische irrigation canal in Volgograd oblast will water 27,000 hectares of wheatlands, orchards, and forest shelter belts and also create six fish-raising ponds totalling 766 hectares.

the Donbas, Urals, and elsewhere and the Volga region's own raw materials move easily to its major industrial centres.

New nodes are emerging, or old nodes reinforced, where oil and natural gas pipelines meet the Volga or east–west railways. Examples are Syzran', Novokuybyshev and Neftekamsk.

The whole of the Central and Volga Region is linked together by modern, high-voltage transmission lines.

Industry in the Central and Volga Region

The Centre. Traditionally the Centre has been a zone of light industries and consumer production, but during the phase of Soviet reconstruction large elements of heavy industry have been grafted on to its industrial structure.

Although the Centre suffered from inadequate energy resources for many years, this problem has now been largely overcome. The region's coal-mines have now developed highly mechanized mining and underground gasification of coal seams – all serving coal-field power stations.[1] Typical thermal stations based on coal are those at Novomoskovsk, Suvorovsk and Sovetsk; on peat (30 million tons mechanically extracted annually) at Ivanovo, Shatura, and Kalinin.

High voltage grids link these stations and bring in electric power from hydroelectric plants at Gor'kiy, Kuybyshev, and Volgograd and from the atomic power plants at Kursk and Novovoronezh.

But the energy sources which really cut the Gordian knot of the Centre's power supply problem are the pipelines which bring in oil and natural gas from all major fields of the Soviet Union.

Moscow has some twenty large-scale enterprises making machine-tools and instruments of all kinds. Satellite cities of the capital too have emerged as engineering centres of considerable importance. In the process old craft towns like Dimitrov, Kolomna, Yegor'yevsk, and others have been transformed.

Outside of the capital's environs cities such as Tula, Ryazan', and Vladimir have become manufacturing centres utilizing highly skilled labour.

Typical products of Moscow's satellites and the Centre's industrial nodes are control and radio-metering gear, optical instruments, computers, office machinery, and similar goods.

The iron and steel industries of the Centre are located in Moscow (The Hammer and Sickle and Elektrostal' works); at Novo-Tula and Novo-Lipetsk; and at Kosogorsk, near Tula. Novo-Lipetsk is a modern integrated iron and steel plant while the others are small or re-melting plants making special steels.

In electrical engineering and electronic products the region's excellent accumulation of skills and 'know-how' have borne fruit. It now manufactures lighting equipment (e.g. fluorescent tubes), transformers, electric motors, and radio and television receivers. Similarly, the Centre is well advanced in transport engineering. Motor vehicle plants are located in Moscow (Moskvich cars), Yaroslavl' (lorry engines), Bryansk (lorries), and Likino, near Moscow (buses). Diesel locomotives are built mainly at Kolomna, but also at Bryansk, Kalinin, Kaluga, Lyndinov, and Murom. River vessels are built at Rybinsk, Kostroma, and Moscow. Coal-mining equipment is made at Skopino and Novomoskovsk.

The Centre manufactures a wide range of farm machinery. The Lyubertsy plant makes self-propelled combine harvesters and wide-row hay-mowers. Tractors, grain harvesters, potato-digging and harvesting machines, and flax-pulling equipment are made variously at Vladimir, Tula, Ryazan', and Bezhetsk.

The Centre makes specialized industrial equipment for the textile, knitwear, footwear, paper, chemical, cement, and food processing industries. Textile machinery is built in Moscow, Ivanovo, Vladimir, Kalinin, and Shuya.

Chemical industries make organic and inorganic materials: nitrogenous fertilizers (Novomoskovsk and Shchekino) and phosphatic fertilizers (Voskresensk) on the one hand, and aniline dyes, synthetic rubber, synthetic fibres, resins, and plastics (at Vladimir, Kalinin, Klin, Orekhovo, Yaroslavl', Ryazan' as well as Moscow) on the other hand. Natural gas has been a major reason for these developments.

The light industries of the Centre have a long history and are particularly well developed. Textiles

---

[1] The Moscow–Tula Coal Basin contains many lenses of brown and bituminous coal extending over an area of some 25,000 square kilometres.

remain dominant in the zone despite the progressive construction of new spinning and weaving mills in the raw material areas of Central Asia and Trans-Caucasia. Linen, cotton and wool textile spinning and weaving, dyeing, finishing, and fabric printing are found throughout the Centre.

Cotton mills are especially prominent in Moscow, Ivanovo, Kalinin, and Vladimir oblasts; woollens in Bryansk and Moscow and its satellite centres; silk textiles in Moscow, Yaroslavl', and Klin, and linen in Kostroma, Yaroslavl', and Vladimir.

The Centre shows a marked survival of mills specializing on a single aspect of textile manufacture: spinning, weaving, or finishing. A few large integrated textile *kombinats* have been built, however, over the last decade or so.

It appears conclusive that many of the region's industries are connected with acquired scientific skills and technological expertise. This is no doubt due to the Centre's over-riding access to research facilities and institutions of higher learning: principally universities and polytechnics. For this reason alone, one may postulate a future high degree of geographical inertia for the high technology industries already established in the Centre.

Volga–Vyatka. This region is noted for its labour-intense industries and its material-oriented industries. Among the engineering–metal-working industries are mass-produced cars and lorries (Gor'kiy and Saransk), buses (Pavlov), and many small centres making vehicle components and vehicle electrical gear. The new Naberezhniye Chelny motor vehicle plant (Tatar A.S.S.R.) will shortly build 400,000 vehicles annually.

The Sormovo shipyards on the Volga make river vessels of all kinds: bucket and pump dredges, passenger hydrofoils and train ferries. Machine-tools are made in Gor'kiy and Pavlov and many oblast and autonomous republic capitals have engineering works.

The region is, however, better known for its

109. The entrained embankments of the Moskva River in Moscow. The Ministry of Foreign Affairs building (centre-background). (Photograph by the author.)

timber-based industries. Kirov and Gor'kiy oblasts and the Mari A.S.S.R. are the main forest areas. Recently production has been deliberately cut back in the interests of conservation, but nevertheless there is still a considerable output of milled timber, house frames, plywood, pulp- and paper-making, and match production.

A wood chemicals industry is also well established, using timber mill by-products. Main timber-milling centres are at Kozlovka, Krasnogorsk, Luza, Vyatskiye Polyany, and Novovyatsk. Balakhna and Volzhsk have pulp and paper mills and both Slobodskoy and Kirov make plywood and matches.

Other light industries based on local materials are linen textiles, leather working, footwear manufacture, and fur manufacture: Kirov, Gor'kiy, and Bogorodsk are the chief centres. Moscow is the Soviet Union's principal location for printing and publishing.

A wood–chemical industry arose at Vakhtan, Syava, and Shumerlya, but recently introduced raw materials – coal, oil, natural gas, and phosphorites – have broadened its base. The city of Dzerzhinsk is now one of the largest chemical complexes in the Soviet Union. It makes primary chemicals, inorganic acids, tar distillates, mineral fertilizers, insecticides, and raw chemicals for the cellulosic and synthetic fibre plants. The Gor'kiy refinery complex is also a petrochemical centre.

Central Black Earth. The energy supplies of the Central Black Earth have until recently existed dominantly outside the region. Industrial centres such as Voronezh, Kursk, and Lipetsk had to depend on the Moscow brown-coal basin and the Donets for their coal supplies but this soon became inadequate. In the post-war period therefore, transmission lines brought in Volga hydroelectric and Donbas thermal power. Also Stavropol' oil and Shebelinka natural gas serve the Central Black Earth. But perhaps the greatest innovation in the region's power supply situation is the building of four atomic power reactors at Novovoronezh totalling 1·5 million kilowatts capacity, and another at Kursk (under construction) of one million kW.

The relieved power status of the Central Black Earth has greatly assisted industrial development. In particular, the old iron and steel industry at Lipetsk has been given a new lease of life. Also the huge Kursk Magnetic Anomaly (K.M.A.) iron-ore deposit has stepped into the front rank as a supplier of pellets and ore concentrates, not only for the new integrated steel mill at Novo-Lipetsk, but also for the Tula, the Donbas, and the COMECON countries' mills.

The reserves of the K.M.A. deposit are estimated at 9000 thousand million tons of ore of all grades. The hematite–martite–siderite component of the ore-body contains 50–70 per cent iron, but the massive iron quartzites, greatest in total volume, contain only 30–43 per cent iron and must therefore be beneficiated before use. Ore-concentrating and pelleting plants are located at the Novo-Lipetsk mill and at the Svobodnyy Sokol' plant near the K.M.A. ore-body. The rich ores are worked by shaft mines to depths of 500 metres, but the surface, low-grade quartzites are worked to 80 metres' depth by open-cut methods, and at the moment, produce most ore.

Apart from these elements of heavy industry, the Central Black Earth manufactures a wide range of engineering equipment: mining machinery, building and construction equipment, lorries, machine tools, and plant for the agricultural, food, and chemical industries.

Other manufactures include: electrical components, radio, television, and instruments; asbestos products, tyres, and a wide range of organic chemicals. These latter involve potato alcohol (including vodka), fatty acids, acetylene, and many different pharmaceutical and toiletry products. A synthetic rubber plant is located in Voronezh and a synthetic tyre cord plant in Kursk.

Food industries include flour-milling, distilleries, butter factories, abattoirs, and tobacco processing in Tambov and Lipetsk. Sugar refineries are in the sugar-beet growing triangle, Belgorod–Kursk–Voronezh.

Volga. The Volga economic region has sprung into being to become a major industrial zone almost overnight. It is a narrow 1300-kilometre long zone stretching along the Volga from Kazan' to Astrakhan'. Kuybyshev (population 1,045,000) has grown tremendously since World War II and Volgograd (formerly Stalingrad), famous for steel and tractors, have become the chief industrial foci, basing their industries on oil, natural gas, steel, and engineering.

The region has developed its huge energy potential since World War II. Three hydroelectric power stations, each exceeding two million kilowatts capacity, have been built along the Volga (Kuybyshev, Saratov, Volgograd) and eventually twelve such stations will be operating. A 800-kilovolt D.C. transmission line links Volgograd to the Donbas and a 500-kilovolt line goes to Moscow. The stupendous 1500-kilovolt D.C. line from Saratov to Moscow and the Urals is under construction.

The Volga–Urals area also possesses one of the greatest oil resources of the Soviet Union. Oil-fields are located in the Tatar and Bashkir A.S.S.R.s, Kuybyshev oblast and smaller ones at Saratov and Volgograd. Pipelines serve not only Volga industries, but also the European areas and will extend to the Eastern Siberian terminals.

This oil province produces the cheapest oil in the Soviet Union – about one-third of the national mean cost per barrel. Water is pumped into the oil-bearing strata under high pressure, thus ensuring the release and maximum recovery of oil.

Oil and local salt brines recovered at Elton and Baskunchak are the bases for a thriving chemical industry in the Volga region. Products include chlorine derivatives, sulphuric acid, and synthetic alcohol (Novokuybyshev, Saratov, and Ufa), synthetic rubber (Sterlitamak and Tol'yatti) and synthetic fibres (Sterlitamak, Stavropol', and Kazan').

The earliest industries began in the Volga zone immediately before the war. Then the Volgograd tractor plant – one of the largest in the country – was set up; also the Ul'yanovsk motor vehicle plant, the Engel's trolley-bus works, and the Syzran' combine-harvester plant.

In the post-war period many new industrial plants have been built. Examples are machine-tool plants at Kuybyshev, Ul'yanovsk, Saratov, and Sterlitamak; agricultural machinery works at Kazan', Kuybyshev, Saratov, and Kamenka.

The region also has a number of precision engineering plants: computers, delicate scientific instruments, typewriters, and watches.

The food processing industries rank next to engineering in their contribution to the region's industrial output. The Volga and Caspian Sea have valuable fisheries: sturgeon, sevruga, and beluga; zander, shad, bream, and carp. Fish hatcheries have been set-up to rehabilitate the fisheries, since they have been greatly disturbed by over-fishing, the falling level of the Caspian Sea, and the construction of dams on the Volga. Astrakhan' is the most notable centre for fish canneries and freezing plants.

Other food industries include flour-milling at Volga ports and at railway break-of-bulk points. The main centres are Kuybyshev, Saratov, and Volgograd. Vegetable oil presses using locally grown sunflower, mustard, and coriander seed, are located at Saratov and Volgograd. Meat abattoirs and canneries as well as dairy product factories are widely scattered throughout the Volga region. Moreover, alcohol distilleries based on grain, tobacco-curing plants and vegetable canneries are well established, particularly in the autonomous republics.

Altogether the Central and Volga Region appears as the Soviet Union's pre-eminent industrial and urbanized province with many associated territorial production complexes based on the Centre, Central Black Earth, Volga–Vyatka and Volga economic regions. These serve not only the Central and Volga Region, but also the densely settled European part of the Soviet Union embracing nearly 154 million of the country's 244 million population (or 63 per cent).

CHAPTER TWENTY-TWO

THE NORTHWESTERN REGION AND NORTHLANDS

Reference	Appendix 5 for details by administrative region of population, area, density, and urbanization
Area	1662·8 (excluding Northlands)
Population	about 12·2 million (excluding Northlands)
Average Density	7·3 persons per square kilometre (excluding Northlands)
Urbanization (Per cent)	62 (excluding Northlands)
Principal Settlements	1970 Population (in thousands)

Northwest		*North of Arctic Circle*	
Leningrad	3950	Noril'sk	135
Arkhangel'sk	343	Vorkuta	90
Murmansk	309	Dikson	n.a.
Cherepovets	188	Dudinka	n.a.
Petrozavodsk	184	Igarka	n.a.
Vologda	178	Khatanga	n.a.
Novgorod	128	Novyy Port	n.a.
Severodvinsk	145	Pevek	n.a.
Pskov	127	Salekhard	n.a.
Syktyvkar	125	Srednekolymsk	n.a.
Volkhov	37[1]	Tiksi	n.a.
Tikhvin	18[1]	Uelen	n.a.
		Verkhoyansk	n.a.

[1] 1959 population, 1970 population n.a. (not available).

The Northwestern Region and Northlands comprise the Northwestern economic region as defined in Soviet statistical sources (i.e. embracing six oblasts, Pskov, Novgorod, Vologda, Leningrad, Arkhangel'sk, and Murmansk and the Karelian and Komi A.S.S.R.s) and also the whole of the Soviet Union north of the Arctic Circle. It is thought more appropriate to include the Northlands in the current discussion rather than in Western and Eastern Siberia and the Far East of which they are administratively a part because of the strong affinities these areas have in their physical attributes and problems of economic development (Fig. 22.1).

Agriculture in the Northwestern Region and Northlands

Agricultural potential in the region is distinctly constrained by the physical environment. Nevertheless, concerted effort has opened up even some of the areas north of the Arctic Circle to hot-house cultivation, and the raising of 'spring' vegetables during the short summer season.

The Northwest Region. This comprises a vast area in the northwestern portion of the Russian Federation, bordering on Estonia, Finland and Norway and stretching to the far north Barents Sea coast and eastward to the Ural mountains. An area

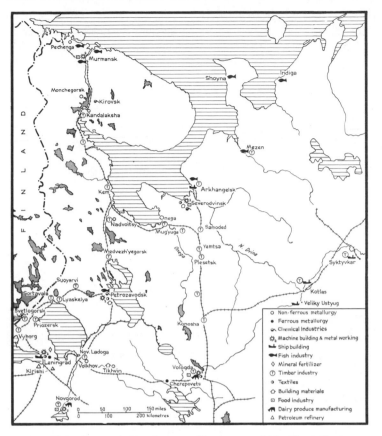

FIG. 22.1   Economic Development: Northwest and Northlands Region.

of tundra, forest tundra, and taiga, the Northwest has scant agricultural potential even in the best areas of the central–southwestern portion.

But the authorities have perforce made valiant attempts to foster economic development because the capital of the Northwest Region is Leningrad, second largest city in the Soviet Union, and cradle of the Bolshevik Revolution. The city sprawls over the Neva deltaic plain at the head of the Gulf of Finland; Peter the Great's celebrated 'window on the West'.

Throughout the agricultural areas of the Northwest podzolized soils of low fertility and severe limitations of climate – a short growing season, an over-abundance of precipitation, and sharp unseasonal frosts – render agricultural development hazardous. Less than 5 per cent of the area is under arable crops, 45 per cent is in pastures, and the remainder is unused wasteland of very low future potential.

Collective farming is essentially based on hay and dairying. Some areas are well-endowed with lush meadows where herds of hardy Kholmogorskaya and Yaroslavskaya dairy cattle graze. In 1971 the Karelian A.S.S.R. had a total of 56 state and 13 collective farms. Many of these tended cattle, pigs, sheep, and goats with considerable efficiency. These areas are noted for their butter-factories serving national markets. Pigs are raised also but are less in evidence except where pockets of arable farming are present, dominantly around the urban settlements. Further out sheep are grazed on the rough pastures which clothe the glacial landscape but they too are greatly restricted in their numbers due to the severity of winter cold and the impracticality of over-wintering very large flocks in stalls.

In a few favoured areas of the south, where micro-climates are suitable, there is a limited development of hardy grain cultivation. Spring wheat, spring rye, oats, and barley are sown. Flax, which is tolerant of lime-charged waterlogged soils, is grown in the Northwest, especially in the Vologda–Pskov–Novgorod triangle. However, the quality of the crop is inferior to the flax grown in the Central and Belorussian regions.

Throughout the region, farms are small and are little adapted to modern techniques of improvement: mechanization, consolidation, and crop specialization. Some ameliorative work has been carried out on the developing margins of farming, especially large-scale drainage of peat-podzols by the use of tractor-drawn moles fitted with baffle boards. These can cut V-shaped drainage ditches of about a metre depth and two metres' width at a rate of 1–2 kilometres per hour. When these bog-soils dry out they are used to establish pasture swards and small areas of fodder grain.

The forest industries of the Northwest rank first in Soviet timber production, followed by the Urals and Eastern Siberia. These resources have been exploited, and indeed, over-exploited, for very many years, and consequent production is gradually shifting eastwards as new and well-managed forest areas are opened up. Timber output of the Northwest is currently about 100 million cubic metres annually, compared to the newer East Siberian production of 50 million cubic metres.

In the Northwest, as in other lumbering areas of the northlands, production is moving inland from the waterways since bull-dozed logging roads and tractor-hauled log-jinkers have rendered the transport of logs on smaller local rivers unnecessary. Milling centres are located on rivers where very large rafts of logs can be received. Examples are Arkhangel'sk, Salekhard, and Igarka. The North Pechora railway now terminating at Novyy Port via Vorkuta has encouraged the development of forestry in new virgin areas and the locating of timber-mills along its route. Examples are those of Kotlas, Konosha, Syktyvkar, Velsk, and Zheshart. Unlike Petrozavodsk, Arkhangel'sk, and Igarka which serve overseas timber markets, the railway milling towns serve the Soviet Union's own markets.

Nevertheless, the growing scarcity of *accessible* forest in the Soviet Union, and a phenomenal growth in its own requirements for timber, pulp, paper, and cellulosic fibres (derived mainly from wood), have caused a marked change in the orientation of the Northwest's forest industries. Karelia, Arkhangel'sk, and Leningrad oblasts, now have many pulp, paper, and paperboard mills which currently sustain about one-third of the national production.

The Northlands. The Soviet northlands lying east of the Northwestern Region and beyond the Arctic Circle are little developed frontier landscapes at the moment. They run for thousands of kilometres from the Lower Ob' to the Bering Strait and embrace the spartan settlements strung along the lower courses of the Ob', Yenisey, Lena, Yana, and Kolyma rivers. Other settlements in sheltered embayments on Arctic seashores, or deep within broad estuaries, are ports of call along the Northern Sea Route from Murmansk to Vladivostok. These usually serve inland mining and timber-getting settlements, and the numerous prospecting parties which comb the Soviet north for ever more minerals.

Throughout the region, indigenous national (ethnic) groups – Nentsi, Komi, Yamolo-Nentsi, Evenki, Yakuts, and Chukots – herd reindeer. From time immemorial, these native peoples have used reindeer for their skins, meat, and local sleigh transport across the snow-covered tundra. The nomadic herding of the past is no longer practised, but instead, under Russian tutelage, the native groups have set up permanent settlements in which the fully domesticated reindeer are tended as cattle with veterinary services and all the other panoply of modern civilization.

The area between Igarka, Dudinka and Norilsk along the lower Yenisey has a reputation as being one of the most northerly agricultural areas in the world. It compares with the Matanuska Valley of Alaska in almost every climatic respect and grows much the same crops. Vegetables, especially cabbage, potatoes, fodder roots, and various glasshouse and hot-house crops of tomatoes, early vegetables and even roses are grown in great profusion. These are land-uses far beyond the expectation of the casual observer and indicate the ingenuity of man in adapting even the most unpromising environment to his needs.

In especially favoured areas dairy and beef cattle in small numbers are carefully tended and stall-fed. Elsewhere the ubiquitous reindeer provides milk and meat. Fish and wild game – bears, hares, badgers, and ducks in summer – are important sources of protein in the diet, and hunting is an essential part of domestic provision.

Hunting for fur-bearing animals in the tundra and taiga is a significant industry and currently produces 80 per cent of all 'wild' furs produced in the Soviet Union; dominantly sable, mink, squirrel, ermine, musk rat, Arctic foxes, and Siberian ferret. The industry is under the administrative control of Glavokhota (Chief Administration of Hunting).

Fur-farms breeding mink, silver and blue Arctic foxes are now becoming established in a few areas of the Soviet northlands. Like the products of hunting these pelts find ready markets in the international auctions held in Leningrad each year.

Transport in the Northwest and Northlands
The Northwest has a well-developed railway system considering its latitude. Ten railway lines funnel into Leningrad, six of major importance radiate in the direction of Helsinki, Murmansk, Vologda, Moscow, Vitebsk, and Tallin. These railway lines, and the fact that Leningrad is an important port, make it the chief nodal centre in the Soviet Union – in terms of freight turnover – after Moscow. Docks

110. Cultivation of green-house crops on the Industriya sovkhoz at Kirovsk, Murmansk oblast.

111. Logs stored on the sawmill pond at Volochak, Kalinin oblast. These will be used to saw construction scantlings. (Photograph by the author.)

and wharves handle in-bound freight for all destinations, while freight movements for Leningrad industries and export arrive mainly from the north and east. Largely this freight consists of logs and sawn timber, ores, chemical raw materials, and fish from the north; and non-ferrous metals, coal, oil, grain, and timber, as well as iron and steel (Cherepovets mills) from the east. A new northern line running near the international frontier in southern Karelia from Vyborg to Petrozavodsk and then north to Lendery has been completed. Another new line runs eastwards from Kandalaksha through Finland to the head of the Gulf of Bothnia.

Leningrad is the largest port engaged in international trade in the Soviet Union. With the opening of the deep-water White Sea–Baltic Canal system, merchant and naval vessels can now pass from the Baltic to the Soviet Far East via the Northern Sea Route in summer without leaving Soviet territorial waters. This has given Leningrad a further advantage as the main western naval base of the country.

Murmansk, kept ice-free by the warm Atlantic Drift, is the Soviet Union's chief northern fishing port. It is also the western terminal of the Northern Sea Route which links together the navigation of the Barents, Kara, Laptev, East Siberian, and Chukotsk Seas, and thus to the Bering Strait and beyond. Murmansk to Vladivostok is a distance of 10,500 nautical miles, considerably shorter than the route via Africa and southern Asia.

Arkhangel'sk is the chief timber port of the Northwest and loads logs and milled timber for overseas markets. The White Sea–Baltic and other deep-water canals connecting to the Volga navigation facilitate the inland exchange of timber, fish and building materials from the north for a reverse flow of coal, petroleum products, grain, and machinery.

In the Northlands the great rivers have been traditional routeways for many centuries. Now they are corridors of movement between the Trans-Siberian Railway and the Northern Sea Route. In Soviet times, the Ob', Yenisey, Lena, and Kolyma have been reinforced as outlets for timber, furs, metal concentrates, gold, and diamonds.

A proposal to develop a 300–350-kilometre far northern railway line from the present terminal at Tobol'sk via Surgut–Kolpashevo–Maklakovo–Boguchany–Ust'-Ilim is unlikely to come to fruition because of the on-going development of all-weather highways in the northlands. These are used to carry freight by multi-vehicle convoys of lorries or tractor-drawn road-trains which offer advantages in capital cost and flexibility compared with northern railway construction. Temporary roads are constructed along the ice-bound rivers each winter.

Air transport has also played a considerable role in both passenger and freight traffic in the northlands. Regular air services connect Leningrad and Moscow with Vorkuta, Noril'sk, Tiksi, and Nizhniye Kresty. Other routes lead to inland destinations like Pechora, Mirnyy, and Yakutsk.

Industry in the Northwest

The Northwest, essentially dominated by Leningrad and other industrial cities, ranks fourth in the value of industrial output. It ranks first in the number of persons engaged in manufacturing per 1000 population; a mark both of its limited agriculture potential and its transport nodality. Leningrad, Novgorod, Pskov, Cherepovets, and small industrial centres like Volkhov are noted for high-technology types of industry requiring highly skilled and adaptable manpower.

Power shortages in the Northwest have been overcome by oil and natural gas brought in by pipeline, coal from Vorkuta and the 2000-megawatt atomic power station now under construction in Leningrad.

Leningrad builds ice-breakers, refrigerator vessels, cargo ships, tankers, passenger liners, fishing and river vessels. The world's first nuclear-powered ice-breaker, the 'Lenin', was completed here in 1959. The city has also several power engineering works building turbines and alternators for thermal and hydroelectric power stations. Single units of 1000-megawatt capacity – very large by all world standards – have been built.

Other engineering products manufactured in Leningrad and other industrial centres include electric motors, welding machines, air compressors, computers, optical instruments, machine tools (automatic and programmed lathes, milling machines, die-sinkers, etc.), and a wide range of automated equipment for railways, metallurgical and fuel plants, and the textile, printing, footwear, paper, and tobacco industries.

112. The polar experimental station attached to the Soviet Institute of Plant-Growing at Lake Imandra, Khibiny mountains, near Murmansk. This station's work with vegetable crops introduced from Scandinavia and the mountainous areas of Afghanistan, Chile and Peru, has resulted in twenty vegetable seed varieties adapted to Arctic conditions. These vegetables are now grown on taiga farms throughout the Soviet northlands.

Leningrad has numerous consumer goods industries: cotton, linen, and wool textiles, footwear manufacture, knitting mills, and fine chemicals.

At Cherepovets, east of Leningrad, a full-cycle integrated iron and steel plant began operation in 1955. It has a current production of steel of 1·2 million tons annually, destined mainly for Leningrad user-industries. Cherepovets' blast-furnaces use prepared flux-sinter (60 per cent iron) derived from the ores of Olenogorsk and Yensko-Kovdor, from the Kola Peninsula. Coking coal arrives by train from Vorkuta, 1600 kilometres northeast of Cherepovets.

Over the past two decades or so, many new industrial centres have grown up in the Northwest, and historic centres have added new and sophisticated manufactures. Examples are: Vologda (machine tools) Petrozavodsk (lumber and fishing industry equipment, and tractors), Pskov (flax scutchers, electrical machinery, telephone equipment and kapron and rayon staple fibres), and Velikiy Ustyug (river vessels). Karelia is the Soviet Union's chief source of mica, and this has given rise to many mica-using industries, particularly electrical and electronic engineering.

At many locations in the Northwest non-ferrous metal smelting and refining have become major economic activities. Leningrad refines copper and nickel (Krasnyy Vyborzhets and Sovkabel plants). Aluminium refining, originally based on one of the Soviet Union's first hydroelectric plants (Volkhov, 1932), is now carried on at Volkhov, Kandalakhsha and Nadvoitsy. Aluminous ores for these plants are received from the Khibiny mountains, Kola Peninsula (nephelites), and the Tikhvin (and newly developed associated areas) deposits of bauxite. Electrical energy for the reduction plants comes from stations on the Volkhov, Sina, Niva, Vyga, and other rivers.

The Northwest has substantial development in the food processing industries. The Atlantic fishing fleet based in Murmansk ranks first after overtaking the Far East and the Caspian as the Soviet Union's chief producer of fish (Table 22.1). The waters of the Barents Sea, North Atlantic, Iceland, Greenland, and Newfoundland, fished regularly by the Murmansk fleet, yield cod, haddock, sea perch, and herring. Other fisheries of the White Sea and Baltic land herring, navaga, and smelt; and halibut, eels, sprats, and herring respectively. Many fresh-water fish are also taken in the rivers and lakes of the Northwest. Fish canneries and freezing plants are located in Murmansk, Arkhangel'sk, and Leningrad.

TABLE 22.1

Soviet Fish Catch by Principal Regions, 1950–1970 (in million centners)

	1950	1960	1970 (e)
North Atlantic	2·90	12·80	30·15
South Atlantic	—	0·44	9·60
Baltic Sea	1·13	1·55	3·77
Azov and Black Seas	2·34	1·80	1·92
Caspian Sea	3·19	3·85	3·75
Aral Sea	0·35	0·44	0·76
Far East	4·84	8·61	25·33
Other Inland Waters	2·21	1·37	3·72
Total	16·96	30·86	79·00

Source: L. G. Vinogradov *et. al.*, 'Fisheries Resources,' in I. P. Gerasimov *et al.*, *op. cit.*, p. 304. 1970 estimated by author from Landings by Republics; *Narodnoe Khozyaistvo, 1970*, Moscow, 1971, p. 257.

Butter and processed milk surplus to the region's own requirements are produced in the Northwest, especially in Vologda and Arkhangel'sk oblasts. Many other types of food industries, including confectionery and preserve manufacturing, are located in Leningrad oblast. Major elements of the tobacco manufacturing industry are also located here.

The Northern Development

The vast areas of the Soviet northlands with their proven resources of timber, non-ferrous metals, gold, diamonds, coal, oil, and natural gas have given an uncompromising challenge to Soviet planners. How could this Pandora's box and Siberian treasure house be opened up? For many years it seemed

that even the resources of modern technology would be inadequate to ensure *economically viable* development of these Soviet northlands. But such an assessment would underestimate the degree of urgency and Soviet zeal to possess and settle this inhospitable frontier land and win its treasures.

Nevertheless there are very severe disabilities in undertaking northern development. Production costs are many times greater than they are in the south and there are physical problems in ensuring the stability of houses and industrial structures built on the permafrost. Oil-wells must be electrically heated if the oil is to flow at all. Again, there are problems of maintaining adequate food supplies.

In the event, nevertheless, the Soviet authorities have developed several well-established mining complexes of tremendous importance to the national economy. It is true, however, that due to higher costs incurred because of distance and accessibility, only the most valuable materials are being worked at the moment. Known mineral resources in small ore-bodies are being left untapped for the time being.

Nickel (and its co-products cobalt and copper) are currently mined at two locations north of the Arctic Circle: Pechenga and its neighbouring prospects in northern Karelia, and Noril'sk near the Lower Yenisey. The latter stands as a monument to man's determination – a town of 135,000 persons set in an icy wilderness on the margin of the tundra, and 700 kilometres from the nearest rail link to 'civilization' although Noril'sk has a short isolated rail link to the port of Dudinka on the Lower Yenisey, through which blister copper and smelted nickel and cobalt are shipped (Fig. 22.2).

The Yenisey valley is an historic gold-mining area, but its placer mines have now given out and have been overtaken by other gold-working areas in the Far East. The gold lode at Bilibino, near Pevek in the Chukotska Peninsula, has the distinction of being the first mining centre north of the Arctic Circle to install a small atomic power station.

Tin-mining is also a feature of northern development. Deposits are worked in Iul'tin (Chukotska) and between the Indigirka and Yana rivers at Deputatskiy and Ege-Khaya.

Diamonds (both gem-stones and industrial diamonds) are won from the alluvial gravels and

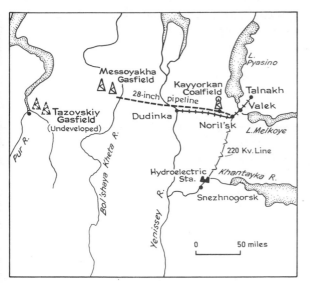

FIG. 22.2   The Noril'sk Complex and Associated Fuel and Power Developments.

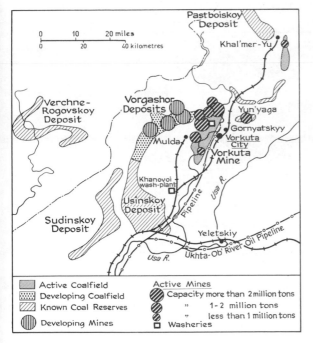

FIG. 22.3   The Vorkuta Coalfield – Recent Developments.

kimberlite pipes in the Vilyuy basin, a tributary of the Lena. There are a number of workings but the chief centre of the industry is Mirnyy (population about 20,000).

One of the earliest northern developments was the Vorkuta bituminous coal-mining township in the Pechora Basin (Fig. 22.3). This expanded greatly during World War II. There are now several new townships working these coals: Severnyy, Promyshlennyy, Komsomol'skiy, Gornyatskiy, and Inta. These fields now produce 20 million tons of coal annually and supply coking coal to the Cherepovets blast furnaces. As a consequence, the Vorkuta conurbation has a population of 200,000 persons, more than double the population of the city itself.

While the early oil-field centre of Ukhta has contributed to Leningrad's fuel supplies in ample measure, this role is soon to be taken over by new oil and natural gas-fields on the other side (eastern flank) of the northern Urals. Pre-eminently, the gasfields located between the Lower Ob' and the settlement of Nadym (Medvezh'ye, Zapolyarnoy, Urengoy, and others) will provide gas flows through large diameter pipelines now under construction to feed Northwestern industrial centres, including Leningrad. A pipeline from the Messoyakha gasfield to Noril'sk has been built already to serve that city's smelters and power-station.

Finally, the mountains of the Kola Peninsula, 160 kilometres south of Murmansk, supply large quantities of phosphatic ores required by the Northwest's fertilizer industry.

One of the very vital ways in which Soviet development of its northlands was achieved in recent years, is by a system of wage incentives and regional allowances for workers in these inhospitable zones. Before the war, attempts were made to use political and civil prisoners under M.V.D. surveillance to open up the northlands. This system broke down not so much because of its inhumanity and penal excesses, but simply because it proved an inefficient and time-consuming way in which projects reached fruition.

With the development of the labour incentive scheme, workers attracted into the northlands from the south receive higher wages. These are calculated to more than cover the additional cost of living. They also receive an additional payment called 'regional coefficients' depending on the remoteness and isolation of their work-place. These 'regional coefficients' amount to from 30–100 per cent margins over and above basic wages. Despite such high incentive payments workers rarely settle permanently in the northlands. They prefer to return south after four or five years taking accumulated savings with them. Since 1960 'regional coefficients' have been given to indigenous national groups and not just workers attracted from the south. This has given more stability to the northlands' labour-force and, through job competition, has somewhat

reduced the turn-over of labour from the south. To a large extent this accounts for the greater growth in permanent settlement since the 1960s.

Nevertheless, the authorities are taking a much more pragmatic view of northern development. Apart from essential resource-winning operations, the planners are content to allow settlements to grow at their own pace. Gone are the days when starry-eyed visions of great cities springing up in the tundra in a grandiose science-fiction transformation of Nature style were entertained as serious possibilities.

113. A community in the Vuktyl' gas-fields, near Ukhta, Komi A.S.S.R., far into the northern taiga.

CHAPTER TWENTY-THREE

THE URALS REGION

Reference	Appendix 6 for details by administrative region of population, area, density, and urbanization
Area	753·0 thousand square kilometres
Population	about 17·9 million
Average Density	23·8 persons per square kilometre
Urbanization (Per cent)	58
Largest Cities	1970 Population (in thousands)

The Urals
(*including Bashkir A.S.S.R.*)

Sverdlovsk	1025	Orsk	225
Chelyabinsk	875	Zlatoust	180
Perm'	850	Kamensk-Ural'skiy	169
Ufa	771	Kopeysk	156
Izhevsk	422	Berezniki	146
Nizhniy Tagil	378	Miass	131
Magnitogorsk	364	Pervoural'sk	117
Orenburg	344	Serov	101
Kurgan	244	Solikamsk	89
		Novo-Troitsk	83

The Urals Region comprises four oblasts of the Russian Federation (Chelyabinsk, Orenburg, Perm', and Sverdlovsk); the Komi-Permyak National Okrug, and the Udmurt A.S.S.R. The Bashkir A.S.S.R., lying between the Tatar A.S.S.R. and the southern Urals, is also a part of the Urals Region for the purposes of this study (Fig. 23.1).

The Ural Mountains, from which the region takes its name, are wild and rugged expanses of range country, much broken up by the dissection of numerous valleys. The highest peaks in the Urals only reach elevations of 5000–6000 feet; Narodnaya Gora, the highest point, is 6183 (2377 metres). On the western flanks the rivers – Pechora, Kama, Chusovaya, Ufa, and Belaya – are deeply entrenched in low-lying forelands. The Chusovaya, in particular, has cut a swathe through the Central Urals giving easy gradients for the Trans-Siberian to Sverdlovsk and various branch lines across the Urals Divide. Again, to the extreme south the Ural River runs through a gorge separating the Southern Urals from the Mugodzhar Mountains of Kazakhstan.

The Northern Urals are little developed except for the heavily glaciated country now covered with coniferous forest which sustains a vigorous timber industry. The Pechora and Kama rivers give access to these forests.

The Central Urals have been long settled and achieved the greatest economic growth. In this area both the western and eastern forelands are quite densely settled (for this particular region) reaching 80 persons per square kilometre. Four of the major cities of the region, two on each flank of the mountains, now dominate the industrial life of the area. These are Sverdlovsk, Chelyabinsk, Perm', and Ufa which throughout their history have controlled the trans-Urals trade.

The Central Urals have somewhat more fertile soils than the north, developed under a cover of wooded steppe. Although originally clothed with mixed coniferous–deciduous forest, great changes have taken place in the ecological structure due to forestry. Second-growth aspen and birch copses are now frequently all that remain, dotted over a landscape cleared for agriculture.

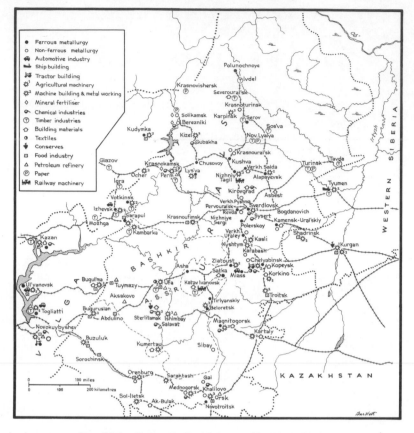

FIG. 23.1   Economic Development: The Urals Region.

Agriculture in the Urals Region

Although agricultural potentials in the Urals Region are somewhat limited, every effort has been made over the last three decades to stimulate progress and improve its condition. There is an urgent need to feed the region's increasing population, now more than ever concentrated in cities and towns.

Every area with favourable topography and a suitable micro-climate is pressed into service. The wooded steppe and steppe chernozem soils are most suitable, but climate, with harsh winter régimes and with a serious drought hazard in summer, especially in the south, leads to low yields and frequent crop failures.

Nevertheless, the Urals possesses some notable grain-growing areas. Orenburg and Chelyabinsk oblasts, and the neighbouring Kurgan oblast outside the region, are well-suited to spring grains. Spring wheat and barley are the most prevalent crops. Rye and oats are planted in late summer and are harvested in the following early summer, thus ensuring heavier yields than is possible from spring-sown crops. Rye dominates the wooded steppe of Perm' oblast and the Udmurt A.S.S.R. Maize is another crop found wherever sufficiently humid conditions prevail, principally therefore along the warm windward margins of Obshchiy Syrt and the Orenburg piedmont.

Spring wheat is far and away the dominant grain crop in the Urals and, indeed, the region ranks only after Western Siberia and Kazakhstan in the quantity of spring wheat grown. The region also has some plantings of winter wheat in Orenburg oblast, but this represents only a small proportion of the total wheat area of the region.

One of the major innovations of the past decade or so has been the upgrading of lands, formerly suitable only for hardy grains, particularly oats, or grasslands. These have been deep-ploughed, treated with trace elements, and given heavy applications of mineral fertilizers so that they can now be used for wheat culture. At the same time, pasture improvement in areas not suitable for arable cultivation has more than made up for the loss of former grasslands now used for wheat. Such a systems approach to planned farm regeneration is typical of Soviet agricultural methods in the post-1960 period.

The Urals are distinctly marginal for industrial crops – unless, indeed, second-growth timber is considered an industrial crop, an appropriate concept for there is much collective farm production of timber in the Urals.

Nevertheless, the Urals Region does grow some flax and sugar-beet in small, well-favoured locations. Flax is grown for fibre in the Udmurt A.S.S.R. and Perm' oblast, but further south, in areas subjected to the hazard of summer drought, the crop is grown for linseed. Sugar-beet is grown in relatively minor quantities under more humid conditions on the chernozem soils of the Bashkir A.S.S.R.

Around all major cities of the Urals regions market-intensive crops are grown – potatoes, vegetables, and salad crops such as cucumbers and radishes – and dairying is also a prime activity. Some beef cattle and pigs are raised particularly on the western and southwestern flanks of the mountains. In pig-raising there is some association with maize-growing and market-gardening.

In the drier areas of the feather-grass steppe, sheep flocks become a dominant form of land-use. Cross-bred sheep suitable for both wool and meat production are favoured.

Despite the considerable animal populations in the Central and Southern Urals, however, local meat supplies are inadequate and consequently additional quantities have to be brought in from the Volga and Kazakhstan regions.

Transport in the Urals Region

Throughout history the Urals Mountains have been a barrier to movement, far greater in fact than one would expect from the physical constraint presented by their rather low and eroded profiles. Partly, the barrier-effect was psychological; the inhibition that after all this mountain range was the boundary between two worlds: the European and the Asiatic. Nevertheless natural passes through the Urals have from time immemorial permitted trappers and prospectors to explore the Asiatic frontier. Another reason for the Urals' constraining influence, up to the coming of the Trans-Siberian Railway at least, was political in overtone. Soviet governments, as imperialist governments before them, had considered the lands beyond the Urals, lands of exploitation rather than lands of settlement. Relative growth rates in regional populations over time prove that it is only comparatively recently that the settlement and economic generation thesis has had real meaning in the trans-Urals frontier lands.

Yet other evidence is available on the constraining effect of the Urals on eastward migration: the piling-up of population along the western flanks of the Urals accounting for the higher densities of these areas. Again, the drift of major population migrations was around the Southern Urals rather than through the mountains. The attenuation of density east of Orsk and north of Sverdlovsk illustrates this point.

With the development of the railways and more recent changes in incentives to settlement, there have been great changes in population patterns. Not only are settlements along the west–east railway lines growing apace, but the same development is taking place along the north–south lines running down each flank of the Urals.

The Trans-Siberian line runs through Kuybyshev–Ufa–Chelyabinsk–Kurgan and on to the east. Other trans-Ural lines run through Kirov–Sverdlovsk–Tyumen' and beyond; another line from Kazan' to Sverdlovsk; and the Ufa–Magnitogorsk line. Lateral lines run from Zlatoust to Polunochnaya and from Orsk to Nadezhdinsk along the flanks of the Urals.

Major elements in railway freights are Kuznetsk and Karaganda coal bound for Urals' steelworks as well as oil, Siberian timber, grains, and non-ferrous metals or concentrates, flowing from eastern areas to and beyond the Urals. Freights originating in the Urals are dominantly iron-ore (Magnitogorsk, Kachkanar), iron and steel, non-ferrous metals, timber, pyrites, building materials, and machinery.

The importance of waterways does not compare with the Volga, but the Kama tributary of the Volga carries bulk freights of timber, building materials,

oil, and some grain. On the eastern flank, the Ob'
tributaries, the Tavda and Tobol, carry much the
same river cargoes.

The barrier effect of the Urals is especially
noticeable in the oil and gas pipeline network.
Pipelines link together the North Urals gas-fields as
well as the Tyumen' oil-fields with their counterparts in the European part of the Soviet Union via
routes which skirt the northern or southern extremities of the mountain chain.

The building of the new 40-inch diameter gas
pipeline from Nadym through heavy permafrost
terrain to the north is considered by some Soviet
authorities to be costly and unwise. An additional
argument, other than the question of higher cost, is
that, had the southern route been chosen, natural
gas could serve southern Urals industries as well as
fulfilling its long-term function of boosting the
Centre and Northwest power supplies.

Industry in the Urals Region

Power resources in the Urals Region itself are generally poor, although the historic Urals iron
industry used wood (charcoal) for smelting. Only
the low-quality Kizel bituminous coals, some
brown coal, and the western oil-fields from Perm' to
Ufa, pre-date the current expansion of power from
outside the Urals Region. Because of its industrial
growth the region has always needed large trans-
fusion of energy sources.

In 1932 Urals–Kuznetsk iron and steel
Kombinat was set up on the basis of an exchange of
Kuznetsk coking coal for Magnitogorsk iron-ore,
with steel plants 1200 miles (1931 kilometres)
apart at both terminals. Since that time, the Urals
receives coal over a 600-mile (935 kilometres) haul
from the Karaganda and Ekibastuz coalfields. Small
quantities of Kuznetsk coal are still needed for
admixture to make good-quality metallurgical coke
in the Urals.

The Urals also receive West Siberian oil and
natural gas by pipeline, principally from the
Tyumen' oil-fields and the Berezovo and Tazovskiy
gas-fields. Coal, oil, and gas are used in large thermal power stations located at Nizhniy Tagil,
Troitsk, and Yuzhnoural'sk. These are linked
together and to major industrial centres through a
powerful regional grid system.

Further energy sources are the hydroelectric

power stations (Votkinsk, Perm', and Naberezhnyye Chelny) on the Kama and a major atomic
power station at Beloyarsk, southeast of
Sverdlovsk. These plants are also locked into the
Urals' regional grid. Some Urals industrial centres
now form intermediary switching points for the new
1500-kilovolt D.C. transmission line which brings
power from the Angara and Yenisey hydroelectric
power stations via Itat to the Chelyabinsk terminal.
Another 500-kilovolt line connects the Urals' grid
system to the Volga hydroelectric system at
Kuybyshev and thence another link provides transmission to Moscow. Thus the Urals Region is now
virtually the centre of a unified electricity grid
system that extends from the COMECON countries to Lake Baikal.

If the power resources of the Urals Region have
been weak until recently, its timber and metallic
mineral resources have always been superlatively
strong. A steady development during the Soviet
period of non-ferrous metal mining, smelting, refining, and fabrication have given the Urals international renown. Similarly the Urals–Kuznetsk
iron and steel *kombinat* built during the Second
Five-Year Plan (1933–37) captured the world's
imagination for its seeming audacity. Here was a
double-ended iron and steel enterprise exchanging
coking coal for iron-ore over a rail distance of 1200
miles when it was customary in other countries to
insist upon cheap waterborne transport before such
projects could be economically viable. Examples
are the U.S. Great Lakes and the Japanese coastal
steel plants. It should be borne in mind, however,
that the Soviet Union has power to determine
freight rates and steel prices so that the success of
the Urals–Kuznetsk *kombinat* owes much to
political considerations.

That the Urals end of the Urals–Kuznetsk
scheme was a dramatic success is testified by the
fact that the Magnitogorsk iron and steel complex is
one of the most prosperous steel centres in the
world. The Urals Region is now the second most
important steel-making area in the Soviet Union –
after the Donbas – accounting for an output of 36
million tons in 1970. Of this amount, the
Magnitogorsk mills alone contributed about 12 million tons.

The Urals–Kuznetsk concept was considered to
be so successful by the Soviet authorities, that other

114. Construction of the pipeline from the Samotlor oil-fields, Tyumen' oblast, to Al'metyevsk on the Volga.

Urals steel plants were set up on the same bases. These were also based on Kuznetsk coking coal or Kuznetsk plus Karaganda–Ekibastuz coals blended to a suitable blast furnace fuel – a task made easier by the use of natural gas enrichment. New mills sprang up at Chelyabinsk, Novo-Tagil, Chusovoy, and Orsk-Khalilovo.

The original Magnitogorsk iron-ore bodies – at Magnitnaya, Vysokaya and Blagodat – no longer produce enough ore to sustain all mills. But fortunately new iron-ore deposits have been opened up in recent years in Kustanay oblast in northern Kazakhstan (and these are very rich), and also the very large – much nearer low grade but easily dressed – iron-ores of the Kachkanar deposit, near Nizhniy Tagil on the Urals' eastern flank. The Peschanka mine in the northern Urals is worked to a depth of 800 metres and yields 45 per cent magnetite. All of these iron-ore sources have been progressively substituted for the now-depleted Magnitogorsk ores.

Fortuitously, the Kuznetsk end of the *kombinat* has also found alternative sources of iron-ore for its blast-furnaces, so that only minimal flows of ore now move eastwards from the Urals. Since, also the Karaganda–Ekibastuz coals have reduced the requirements for Kuznetsk coal, rail freights have retained a fair measure of balance in both directions.

Another indicator of the success of the Urals steel mills is their low production costs, due largely to economies of scale and high technological performance. It is reported that Urals steel is only half the cost of that from the Donets-Dnieper mills. This must have a tremendous influence on the engineering and other steel-user industries established in the Urals, especially for those products to be sold in the eastern and southern parts of the Soviet Union.

Ferro-alloys, particularly ferro-chrome, ferro-vanadium and ferro-nickel, are made in electric furnaces attached to the Chelyabinsk and Chusovoy steel-works. In many areas of the Urals sheet steel- and tube-mills exist, including those at Sverdlovsk and Chelyabinsk. Large diameter pipes for pipelines are made in Chelyabinsk, Sinarsk, and Pervoural'sk.

Many non-ferrous metal industries have emerged in the Urals Region. Excellent resources of copper, nickel, zinc, aluminium, and magnesium exist. For this reason many specialized plants for non-ferrous metallurgy have been set up in the Urals, and their importance has hardly declined with the opening up of new deposits in other parts of the country.

The Urals ranks first in the Soviet Union for its production of blister and refined copper. There are copper smelters at Krasnoural'sk, Kirovograd, and Mednogorsk and refineries at Sredneural'sk (Revda), Karabash, and Kyshtym. Zinc concentrates are sent to the Chelyabinsk smelter from concentration plants in Kazakhstan; additional materials are the by-product zinc sulphides derived from Urals' copper concentration plants. One new series of copper deposits which are of considerable significance to the Urals' economy, are those located at Gay, north of Orsk. These are extremely rich ores containing 8 per cent copper and since their development in the early 1960s they now produce well over half of the copper from the Urals Region.

115. The control desk of the Beloyarsk atomic power station, Sverdlovsk oblast. The gauges in the centre reflect operating conditions of each fuel rod in the reactor core.

116. Vast new discoveries of oil and natural gas in the Soviet Union have called for more and more large-diameter pipelines. This Chelyabinsk, Urals, pipe-rolling mill produces 122 cm (48 inch) and is soon to make 254 cm (100 inch) pipes. Such huge capacity pipelines save large quantities of steel since the weight of pipe required to ship each thousand tons of oil is sharply reduced.

Bauxite deposits of the northern (Krasnaya Shapochka) and central (Kamensk-Ural'skiy) Urals account for a considerable proportion of Soviet alumina production. Alumina is sent to reduction plants at hydroelectric power sites at Shelekhov, near Irkutsk, Anzeb near Bratsk, and Krasnoyarsk, and also the Novokuznetsk aluminium plant on the Kuznetsk coal field. Aluminium reduction plants in the Urals are located at Kamensk-Ural'skiy and Krasnoturinsk.

Other metals and minerals of importance occurring in the Urals include lead, silver, gold (east of Chelyabinsk, near Sverdlovsk, and with platinum at Serov), nickel, cobalt, and chrome (Svetlyy and Orsk-Khalilovo), asbestos (east of Sverdlovsk), mineral salts (Solikamsk and Berezniki) as well as gem-stones such as emeralds and malachite.

Engineering industries in the Urals are principally concerned with the manufacture of mining, metallurgical, power engineering, and transport equipment. There are about sixty large-scale engineering enterprises in the Urals Region and many smaller plants and industrial works. The Urals Machine Factory (Uralmashzavod) at Sverdlovsk and the massive tractor works (converted during the last war to tank-building) at Chelyabinsk are the most outstanding. These two enterprises are among the largest in the Soviet Union and compare in sophisticated manufacturing techniques with those in the United States.

About half of the remaining engineering plants in the Urals specialize on heavy engineering products – mining, metallurgical and power engineering and equipment especially. They manufacture turbines, generators, electrical apparatus and heavy industrial equipment and plant. Some enterprises are multi-product factories, particularly in the larger, diversified industrial cities, but others concentrate on a single product line; often these plants are situated in the smaller industrial nodes of the Urals.

Automotive and transport industries are well represented in the Urals. Chelyabinsk builds tractors, mobile cranes, and self-propelled farm machinery; Miass, Izhevsk, and Naberezhnyye Chelny have modern motor vehicle manufacturing or assembly plants, Izhevsk builds railway locomotives, Nizhniy Tagil has a railway carriage works, and Irbit a motorcycle factory. Other industrial centres manufacture a wide range of products: machine tools, cranes, construction machinery, and many other classes of steel-using products.

The chemical industries of the Urals are based on the potassium and magnesium salts found at Solikamsk and Berezniki, the iron pyrites of the central Urals, limestone, rock salt, and similar basic raw materials. Also the oil refineries at Orsk and Ufa and 'imported' natural gas have given rise to organic petrochemical industries of some significance. Again, smelting and refining operations in the region provide ample by-products – sulphur dioxide, flue dusts containing arsenic, selenium, chromium, cadmium, etc. – to sustain branches of the chemical industries such as the manufacture of pesticides, paints, and varnishes.

The Urals now accounts for approximately 40 per cent of Soviet production of calcined soda and 20 per cent of its mineral fertilizers. Berezniki and Solikamsk (Perm' oblast) account for a high proportion of the potash fertilizers, while Berezniki, Perm', and Krasnoural'sk make nitrogenous, phosphatic, and complex fertilizers such as 'nitrophos' and 'ammophos'.

Pyrites obtained from mining operations in the central Urals, or as by-products from metal concentrators, are the Soviet Union's chief source of sulphur. The Urals manufacture considerable quantities of sulphuric and other industrial acids.

Other Urals industries worthy of mention are the timber-based industries, and a miscellany of consumer goods and products such as hand tools, electrical appliances, various household equipment, and the leather and clothing industries.

In the timber industries, saw-milling is important in Perm' and Sverdlovsk oblasts and the Bashkir A.S.S.R.; pulp mills abound in Urals Mountains and three integrated pulp and paper mills are located in Perm' oblast and the Bashkir A.S.S.R. These now produce about one-fifth of the Soviet Union's paper requirements. Furniture factories also exist in the Udmurt A.S.S.R.

From many points of view the Urals Region is now moving towards a much better balanced economy. Its main problems are in ensuring adequate food supplies for its growing conurbations, such as those of Sverdlovsk and Chelyabinsk, and their respective satellite urban centres, and reducing in some measure the region's over-dependence on mining and heavy engineering enterprises for its regional income.

CHAPTER TWENTY-FOUR

KAZAKHSTAN

Reference	Appendix 7 for details by administrative region of population, area, density, and urbanization
Area	2715·1 thousand square kilometres
Population	about 13·1 million
Average Density	4·8 persons per square kilometre
Urbanization (Per cent)	51
Largest Cities	1970 Population (in thousands)

Kazakhstan

Alma-Ata	730	Petropavlovsk	173
Karaganda	523	Temirtau	166
Chimkent	247	Aktyubinsk	150
Semipalatinsk	236	Ural'sk	134
Ust'-Kamenogorsk	230	Kustanay	124
Dzhambul	187	Gur'yev	114
Pavlodar	187	Rudnyy	96
Tselinograd	180	Balkhash	76

The Kazakhstan Region is one of the fastest growing economic regions in the Soviet Union. Its northern and southern oblasts, the most densely settled parts of Kazakhstan, are separated by a broad expanse of desert that runs from the Caspian Sea to the border mountains with China (Fig. 24.1).

Since World War II, and particularly with the emergence of the Virgin Lands scheme, huge population migrations have swept into Kazakhstan. With government encouragement Komsomol youth, farm families, and even whole village communities have opened up the frontier lands as a patriotic duty.

The northern most populated oblasts include Kustanay, North Kazakhstan, Kokchetav, Tselinograd, Pavlodar, and East Kazakhstan oblasts. Here population densities range from 5·6 to 12·5 persons per square kilometre. South of these areas lie the desert oblasts of Semipalatinsk, Karaganda, Aktyubinsk, Ural'sk, and Gur'yev; population densities here are much lower. Only Karaganda oblast, having substantial industrial development within its ambit, has managed to sustain a larger population.

The southern oblasts include Alma-Ata, Dzhambul, and Chimkent and also have somewhat higher population densities, ranging from 5·6 to 14·1 persons per square kilometre. Although Kazakhstan's population is very small for its vast area, and is very unevenly distributed, its urban centres have shown remarkable growth in the Soviet period. There are now 13 cities with populations in excess of 100,000 persons and another 7 with between 50,000 and 100,000. Very substantial in-migration of Slavs, especially Great Russians and Ukrainians, has occurred from the late 1930s and especially since the 1959 census. Many large cities now have minority populations of the indigenous Kazakhs. Some indication of these changes is given in Table 24.1 for northern Kazakhstan (the Virgin Lands).

With the increasing russification of Kazakhstan, similar to changes in Central Asia, Islamic culture and old folk-ways, such as nomadic herding, have retreated. Although native language schools, mosques, and traditional craft industries still persist, they are now less important than they were. Institutions of higher education, research, and tech-

FIG. 24.1   Economic Development: Kazakhstan and Central Asia Region.

nological advance project a Russian image, and a knowledge of Russian language and literature are prerequisites for university entry.

Nevertheless, much of this modernization is a rather thin veneer, and lack of ordinary amenities causes a high turnover of the in-migrant workers. Very few of the 'Westerners', particularly families, who come to Kazakhstan's Virgin Lands or industrial projects find it possible to establish roots. Higher wages and regional coefficients have not adequately compensated for the lack of domestic and social amenities.

Agriculture in the Kazakhstan Region

Kazakhstan has many more state farms than collectives (1609 against 449 in 1970) and this reflects the Soviet government's determination to convert the republic into the nation's reserve granary.

Despite its general characteristic of aridity, Kazakhstan plays a substantial role in supplying pastoral and agricultural commodities to the Soviet economy. The main products are spring wheat, cattle (for beef), cotton, and linseed. It currently embraces 30·9 million hectares, 14 per cent of the Soviet Union's agricultural area, following the great

TABLE 24.1

Ethnic Groups in Northern Kazakhstan (Virgin Lands) (in Per cent of Total Population)

Ethnic Group	1897	1926	1959	1970
Kazakhs	79·2	40·1	19·0	20·6
Russians	10·3	26·5	46·2	51·0
Ukrainians	3·5	27·0	14·0	10·8
Germans	—	—	12·1	9·0
Others	7·0	6·4	8·7	8·6
	100·0	100·0	100·0	100·0

Sources: *S.G.*, April, 1962, p. 37. 1970 percentages calculated by author from *S.G.*, **7** (7) 1971: 447–48.

land reclamations of the 1954–62 period. Then over 23 million hectares of Virgin and Long-Fallow land was brought under the plough and cultivated in spring wheat. A total of 544 newly created state grain farms were then set up. Since then more steppe and semi-arid pasture land has been ploughed. Between 1954 and 1970 a four-fold increase in grain output occurred.

Kazakhstan is now the second ranking grain-farming republic in terms of gross production, following the Ukraine. About 80 per cent of sown land is in grain-growing. The lands reclaimed under the Virgin Lands Scheme (40 million hectares) produced 22·2 million tons of grain in 1970, about 11·8 per cent of the Soviet's total output. Spring wheat is by far the most important grain in these northern areas. The winter wheat variety 'Ukrainka' is used for spring wheat cultivation. Winter wheat is also grown in the southern oblasts of Kazakhstan, mainly under irrigation because of summer drought. Total irrigated area in Kazakhstan now amounts to 1,338,000 hectares.

A new 500-kilometre Irtysh–Karaganda Canal threads its way along the deepened courses of the Shiderta, Tuzda and Nura rivers. This canal irrigated 60,000 hectares in northern Kazakhstan and provides domestic water for Karaganda and other industrial centres.

Unfortunately, Kazakhstan's wheat and other grain output fluctuates wildly from year to year depending on the amount and incidence of precipitation and also the occurrence of frequent droughts. In consequence, there are sympathetic fluctuations in government grain procurements according to Kazakhstan's harvest conditions (Table 24.2). Fortunately, the Western winter wheat-growing areas (Ukraine, North Caucasus) seldom experience drought conditions in the same year as Kazakhstan, and there is in consequence, a countervailing grain production in one or the other.

There is some suggestion that agricultural mismanagement is a factor in fluctuating grain output from the Virgin Lands. On the evidence of mean yields compared to specific climatic indices in given years, there is substantiation of this claim. Undoubtedly, many lands have been over-used,

117. Northern Kazakhstan's former Virgin Lands are one of the Soviet Union's chief granaries. Test sampling of grain arriving at the Atbassor elevators, Tselinograd oblast.

inadequately fertilized and/or fallowed, and pushed beyond their natural capacities.

Wheat monoculture in Tselinograd oblast, the centre of the Virgin Lands Scheme, has begun to convert the area into a 'dust-bowl' as dramatic as any experienced in the United States in the 1930s. During the wheat-growing season, strong and desiccating westerly and southwesterly winds flow into Tselinograd oblast, and Tselinograd city experiences dust-storms on 53 days per year on average.

Exploitation of Kazakhstan's manifest potential for further dry-lands grain farming will largely depend on the efficiency with which current problems are solved. At this stage, dry-farming techniques and machinery better adapted to Kazakhstan's soil and climatic conditions are helping. Agricultural aviation is also becoming important, not only in spreading fertilizers on the wheat fields, but also in the application of pesticides. In other areas, particularly the more humid areas of the southeast, aircraft are used to spread fertilizers, pesticides, and pollinating agents for orchards.

TABLE 24.2

State Grain Procurements from Kazakhstan's Harvests (in millions of tons)

1960	10·5	1965	2·4	1968	11·7
1963	4·8	1966	17·0	1969	11·0
1964	15·4	1967	8·2	1970	13·4

Source: *Statesman's Yearbook, 1972–73*, p. 1446.

The southern areas of Kazakhstan fall naturally into two divisions as far as agriculture is concerned. First, the arid desert margins which grow drought-resistant crops – cotton, kok-sagyz, mustard, and linseed – and, secondly, the more favoured loess-covered uplands and mountains of the Taldy-Kurgan, Alma-Ata and Dzhambul oblasts. The cool slopes of the Talasskiy and Dzungarskiy Ala-Tau and other piedmont areas grow many orchard and vegetable crops to perfection. These include apples, grapes, melons, potatoes, market garden salads, and high-class tobacco. Orchards and vineyards amounted to 109,000 and 18,000 hectares respectively in 1970. Small areas of sugar-beet are cultivated: a new crop for Kazakhstan. Fodder crops, e.g. lucerne, are also grown to serve southern Kazakhstan's thriving animal industries.

Kazakhstan was once the heritage of steppe horsemen, cattle-raisers, and nomadic sheep-and goat-herders. During the early years of Soviet power, it suffered grievous losses in animal numbers as the authorities tried to wrest control over

118. The semi-arid floodplains on Aktyubinsk sovkhoz, Kazakhstan, are ideal for fully mechanized vegetable farming once adequate spray irrigation (background) is installed to supply moisture.

lands and animals alike. Now however, the cattle, sheep, goat, and pig populations have been regenerated to unprecedented levels. Kazakhstan is again one of the nation's foremost meat-producing republics.

Grazing is commonplace on the drier lands of the desert margins and also in the mountains of Kazakhstan. Much of the arid-land grazing for sheep and camels, between the Caspian to Lake Balkhash, is confined to spring and early summer months, taking advantage of the flush of vegetation which follows the melting of the snows.

In the mountainous areas, where warm 'ebe' (föhn) winds may melt snow on the piedmont slopes even in winter months, grazing is feasible for all or many months of the year. In the severest winter months cattle, sheep and goats, however, may be brought down to the desert herbage, but return the following spring and summer in massive trans humance drives. Many areas can support year-round grazing without over-wintering cattle in stalls.

Great efforts are being made to reduce the animal industry's dependence on natural vegetation. Fodder crops and meadow hay are being increasingly grown in rotation with grains and cotton. Lucerne hay is havested four or five times each year, and provides excellent feed in the winter months when natural herbage is scarce.

Another tremendous innovation are the plans to construct ground-water bores in the deserts of Kazakhstan. According to research carried out by Kazakh Academy of Sciences (Institute of Hydrogeology and Hydrophysics) huge artesian basins of freshwater underlie the desert sands of Kyzyl Kum, Betpak-Dala and Ust'-Yurt at depths of less than 80 metres. The source of these supplies, accumulated over many centuries, are the mountain regions to the south. These release snow- and ice-melt amounting to 5000 million cubic metres annually, and this water percolates underground to join the artesian reservoirs. Therefore, scientists believe, this is the quantity of bore-water that could be withdrawn safely each year without affecting the base reservoirs, estimated to aggregate 4000 billion cubic metres.[1]

[1] I. Ivanov, *Soviet News Bulletin*, No. 10/283, 14/5/1973, Canberra, Australia, 1973.

119. Planting out tomato seedlings with simultaneous watering-in on Aktyubinsk sovkhoz, Kazakhstan. Note the excellent tilth of the soil.

Kazakhstan's sheep are noted for their fine fleeces and good fleece weights. The republic ranks second after the Russian Federation in sheep numbers (31·2 million in 1970). One of the most suitable breeds for the sparse desert vegetation is the 'Akharomerino' which is a new cross-breed derived from the Australian merino ewe and the native Akhar mountain ram. The latter is a semi-wild variety well adapted to Kazakhstan's environment. Currently Kazakhstan accounts for over one-quarter of the Soviet Union's wool production, and also about one-third of the Karakul sheepskins. Karakul skins are taken from new-born lambs and are popular in the world's fur markets, where they are known as Astrakhan or Persian lamb.

In 1970 Kazakhstan had 7·2 million head of cattle, 2·2 million pigs, and 521,000 goats as well as the 31·2 million sheep already mentioned. Quite significant amounts of meat are processed in refrigeration and freezing works and shipped to other parts of the Soviet Union. Most of the beef, mutton, and goat-meat is transported in carcass form, but Semipalatinsk has a large meat cannery, which is perhaps the first example of a 'Chicago-type' integrated meat packing plant in Kazakhstan.

Transport in Kazakhstan

Economic growth in Kazakhstan has been greatly stimulated by the development of new railways. Even sparsely settled areas that are crossed by railways to tap remote resources, have felt the impact of the new communications. Settlements have grown substantially as a consequence. For instance, the small settlement of Syrdar'inskiy in the Kyzyl Kum desert was raised to town status and renamed Chardara in August, 1968.

The trend of the earliest railway lines in Kazakhstan is dominantly north–south, but recently there has been an in-filling of the network in the north as east–west lines parallel to the Trans-Siberian Railway were built. The north–south lines were necessary due to the absence of navigable rivers in Kazakhstan. Economic penetration could only be secured by railways and roads. Kazakhstan is thus quite unlike other areas of the country where river navigation has traditionally sustained the thrust of early economic penetration. It is not too much to claim that the comparative lateness of Kazakhstan's economic development was due to this cause rather than the machinations of Moscow-dominated bureaucracies.

At present four major railways link the Kazakhstan–Central Asian republics with the northern east–west trunk lines. These are: the Turk–Sib (Novosibirsk–Alma-Ata); the Trans-Kazakh line (Petropavlovsk–Karaganda–Chimkent) – also called the Mointi–Chu line from the first 430-kilometre link built in 1953; the Orenburg–Aktyubinsk–Tashkent, and the newly extended Astrakhan–Gur'yev–Chardzhou–Dushanbe line. These railways haul Karaganda coal, non-ferrous metals and concentrates, cotton, wool, grains, and timber.

In 1970 total railway length in Kazakhstan was 13,700 kilometres, giving it a very low network density compared to the railways of European Russia. Between 1951–57 about 600 kilometres of narrow gauge railway were built as a stop-gap measure in the Virgin Lands, but most of these routeways have now been incorporated in the new conventional broad-gauge lines of the Central Siberian Railway (Kustanay–Kokchetav–Barnaul) which despite its name runs through the northern oblasts of Kazakhstan for most of its length – as does, of course, its counterpart, the South Siberian Railway.

120. The Trans-Ilian Ala-Tau alpine pastures provide first-rate grazing for sheep. Supplies and veterinary services are flown in by helicopter.

121. Harvesting sunflowers for oil-seed and silage in southern Kazakhstan.

122. The 475-kilometre Irtysh–Karaganda Canal, Kazakhstan, seen here under construction, now brings water from the Ob' basin to the industrial centres of Ekibastuz, Karaganda, and Temir-Tau and also irrigates several thousand hectares of arid steppe.

Industry in Kazakhstan

The mineral resources of Kazakhstan are very considerable, but widely scattered (Fig. 24.1). Since 1945 a vigorous programme of prospecting has opened up useful new deposits of coal, iron-ore, non-ferrous metals, oil, and natural gas, and such useful minerals as asbestos (at Dzhetygara) and borax (at Inderborskiy). A major iron and steel complex has been built at Karaganda. These activities have projected Kazakhstan forward at a great pace; it has virtually entered the technological age over the last two decades only.

The Karaganda coal basin covers a small area, but has reserves estimated at no less than 51 thousand million tons. Another deposit at Ekibastuz, 385 kilometres north of Karaganda, was opened up after World War II and, since it is worked by open-cut methods, produces the cheapest coal in the Soviet Union. Coal seams are as thick as 100 metres at Ekibastuz, which has reserves estimated at 12 thousand million tons.

In 1970 Kazakhstan produced 61·6 million tons of coal altogether, of which Karaganda and Ekibastuz produced about 30 million and 14 million tons of bituminous coal respectively.

Kazakhstan also has useful brown coal at Lengren in the south and at Kumertau, near Aktyubinsk. The open-cut here produces 6–7 million tons annually for a power station in Kumertau. Other major thermal power stations are located at Karaganda (Temirtau and Topar), Petropavlovsk, and, in the south, at Chimkent, Dzhambul, and Alma-Ata. Hydroelectric power stations are located at Bukhtarma and Ust'-Kamenogorsk on the Irtysh river and in the south at Kapchagay on the Ili river.

Oil and natural gas production in Kazakhstan is growing year by year. In 1970 oil production had reached 13·2 million tons and natural gas 2092 billion cubic metres. Kazakhstan yields a high-grade oil suitable for aviation fuel when refined.

Major oil-fields lie along a course north of the Emba River on the flanks of the Mugozhary Hills and their extension towards the Caspian. Another oil-field opened up in the late 1950s lies on the Mangyshlak Peninsula inland from the Caspian. The principal centres of oil production are Martyshi, Dossor and Maket, near the Gur'yev refinery, and at Saghiz, Kenkiyak, and Kulsary in Aktyubinsk oblast. The Mangyshlak oil-fields are at Uzen' and Zhetybay; both sites have just begun volume production and have now probably reached the scheduled output of 20 million tons annually.

Natural gas is also produced at the Mangyshlak locations, and at Bazay, Aktyubinsk oblast, on the northwestern shores of the Aral Sea. Both gas-fields are linked into pipelines running from the Gazli gas-fields of Uzbekistan. The Mangyshlak gas feeds the Donbas and Centre, and the Bazay gas joins the Gazli–Chelyabinsk line via the southern Urals.

Undoubtedly, Kazakhstan's excellent resources of coal, oil, and natural gas stand it in good stead for further industrial development. In the recent past, non-ferrous metal mining has grown substantially, making Kazakhstan one of the Soviet Union's foremost mining and metal-winning republics.

Copper ores are found in the Dzhezkazgan area of eastern Karaganda oblast (Baykonur, Karsakpay and Nikol'skiy deposits); Lake Balkhash

(Kounradskiy, Vostochno-Kounradskiy, and Sayak deposits), and in East Kazakhstan oblast (Orlovka and Glubokoye). The latter area also has several copper–zinc ore deposits at Nikolayevka, Verkhneberezovskiy, and Belousovka. Copper smelters in Kazakhstan exist at Karsakpay, Dzhezazgan, Balkhash, and Glubokoye. The Balkhash plant also has a copper refinery.

Polymetallic ores, particularly the lead–zinc group, are found in considerable abundance in Kazakhstan. The main mines are located in East Kazakhstan oblast (Leninogorsk, Zyryanovsk, and Ust'-Kamenogorsk); in the Taldy-Kurgan area north of the Kapchagay reservoir (Tekeli deposit), and in the Karatau Mountains (Kentau and Baydzhansay). There is a lead smelter and refinery at Leninogorsk and Ust'-Kamenogorsk and a smelter at Chimkent.

Kazakhstan's aluminium industry resources are located in Kustanay oblast at Arkalyk. This is an excellent source of bauxite which is sent by rail to Pavlodar and Ust'-Kamenogorsk where it is converted to alumina and aluminium metal. Expanding production at these centres required additional raw materials and a second bauxite mine was opened up at Krasnooktayabr'skiy. Alumina surplus to Pavlodar's own reduction mill requirements is sent to the hydroelectric power site refineries at Krasnoyarsk, Shelekhov (Irkutsk oblast), and Bratsk. Some alumina also goes to the Novokuznetsk reduction plant in the Kuzbas.

The Kalba Mountains in particular also have many deposits of other non-ferrous metals, including titanium, magnesium, lithium, columbium, and tantalum. Ferro-alloys are mined at Akchatau (tungsten–molybdenum) and Dzhezdy (manganese) in Karaganda oblast, and also at Batamshinskiy (nickel) and Khromtau (chromium) in Aktyubinsk oblast.

At the moment most non-ferrous metal concentrates or smelter production move out of Kazakhstan, particularly to the Urals and Centre for further processing. The example of ferro-alloys that are currently used in the Karaganda iron and steel (Fourth Metallurgical Complex) works, however, indicates the prospective future trend of using more of Kazakhstan's resources in the republic itself.

The Karaganda integrated iron and steel plant

123. The automatic control panel for the Bogatyr open-cut coal mine in the Ekibastuz basin, Kazakhstan.

opened in 1960 and quickly supplanted the small steel works built at Temirtau and Aktyubinsk during the last war. The Karaganda Metallurgical Plant situated at Temirtau where the Samarkand reservoir provides process water now has four blast-furnaces and both open-hearth and oxygen converter steel-making furnaces. It also has hot-strip, cold-sheet, and pipe-mills. These last can manufacture the large diameter pipes required for oil- and gas-transmission lines, now in great demand in the south.

Currently the Karaganda complex makes slightly more than two million tons of rolled steel products annually. Another 400,000 tons of steel comes

124. The desert oil-field at Shevchenko, Mangyshlak peninsula, Kazakhstan. Shown here is the desalination plant operated by atomic energy which provides drinking water from a Caspian Sea intake.

from the old Temirtau steel-mill, giving Kazakhstan a total of about 2·4 million tons in 1970.

The Karaganda blast-furnaces are charged with iron-ore from West Karazhal (Atasu deposit) and Bol'shoy Ktay, 241 kilometres southwest of the plant. These open-cut mines supply about 2·2 million tons of lump ore (55 per cent iron content) and the underground mine a further 2·3 million tons. The West Karazhal iron-ores serve the Kuzbas as well as the Karaganda plant, and consequently other ores are railed in from the Kustanay iron-ore fields to supplement Karaganda's needs.

The Kustanay iron-ores are located at Rudnyy (Sokolovka and Sarbay deposits) with total reserves of 1·4 million tons of magnetite (45 per cent iron content) and also at Lisakovsk and Kachar. Open-cut mines in Kustanay currently have a production capacity of about 30 million tons of crude ore annually. In 1970, the pellet plant had an output of about 8 million tons. Much of the output from the Kustanay deposits goes to Magnitogorsk (354 kilometres) and other Urals blast furnaces; some to

Kuzbas mills (1,465 kilometres), and finally some to the Karaganda plant (644 kilometres). Production of iron-ore in Kazakhstan was 18·2 million tons in 1970.

Coking coal for the Karaganda iron and steel mills is obtained from local sources: Karaganda itself and its suburban coal-mining centres at Saran, Abay (Churubay–Nura deposits), and Shakhtinsk (Tentek–Shakhan deposits) all to the southwest. Since the 1930s the Karaganda Basin coal has been increasingly exploited by underground mining, but the most vigorous phase dates from wartime expansion when the Urals steel plants needed more coking coal due to the loss of the Donbas. At the present time, the Karaganda district produces about 30 million tons of coal annually; more than one-third of it high-quality coking coal.

On the margins of the Karaganda Basin some brown coal and sub-bituminous coal of low quality and high ash content are worked by open-cut methods.

The Ekibastuz coals have a high ash content and

are not suitable for coking. The coal is obtained from four large open-cut mines; the largest of these will eventually sustain an output of 45 million tons annually. Production of the whole Ekibastuz coalfield in 1970 amounted to about 25 million tons. The planned use for Ekibastuz coal is in coalfield power stations – four are to be built in future. Meanwhile, coal is sent by rail to thermal power stations elsewhere, particularly in the Southern Urals (Sredneural'sk and Troitsk).

Engineering industries in Kazakhstan are still comparatively lightly developed: the economy at this stage is much more oriented towards raw materials and semi-manufactures in the metal fields. Several locations however, are showing incipient signs of engineering development. Currently some 35–40 industrial plants are in operation. Pavlodar, Karaganda, and Chimkent have engineering works specializing in the manufacture of coal-mining machinery, metallurgical plant and equipment, and forges and presses. Gur'yev makes oil industry equipment; Pavlodar has a large tractor works, and both Tselinograd and Alma-Ata manufacture agricultural implements. The centre for steel supplies for all of these works is the two steel mills at Temirtau (the Fourth Metallurgical Complex or Karaganda mill) and the small Temirtau mill.

The most important branch of the chemical industries is the manufacture of phosphatic fertilizers. There is a superphosphate plant at Dzhambul in the south that uses local phosphate rock mined at Karatau (the deep Molodezhnyy mine at Chulak-Tau – renamed Karatau after the mountain range in 1963). An open-cut mine on the Aksay phosphate deposit has been set up at Koktal. Both of these mines send crude phosphate rock to the concentrator at Karatau which removes gangue (15–25 per cent). Annual output is about 1·4 million tons of concentrate which goes to the Chimkent electric furnaces to yield phosphorus or to the Dzhambul superphosphate fertilizer works.

Total production of mineral fertilizers in Kazakhstan was over 1·9 million tons in 1970. Part of this production comes from Aktyubinsk superphosphate plant. Borax mined at Inderborskiy is processed at the Alga plant south of Aktyubinsk.

The only food processing and manufacturing plants that are noteworthy are the fish canneries of Gur'yev and the meat processing and canning plant at Semipalatinsk. Elsewhere in Kazakhstan food processing is at an elementary stage.

CHAPTER TWENTY-FIVE

CENTRAL ASIAN REGION

Reference   Appendix 8 for details by administrative region of population, area, density, and
                     urbanization
Area   1,279·3 thousand square kilometres
Population   about 20·5 million
Average Density 16·0 persons per square kilometre
Urbanization (Per cent) 40
Largest Cities   1970 Population (in thousands)

Central Asia

Tashkent	1385	Osh	126
Frunze	431	Bukhara	112
Dushanbe	374	Chirchik	111
Samarkand	267	Fergana	111
Ashkhabad	253	Leninabad	103
Andizhan	188	Almalyk	81
Namangan	181	Nebit Dag	56
Kokand	136	Krasnovodsk	n.a.

Soviet Central Asia embraces four separate Soviet Socialist Republics each of which enjoys a specific ethnic identity, although they share affinities in common culture, history, and present-day economies. These republics are: Uzbekistan which runs from the Aral Sea to the Fergana Basin, and includes the large Kara-Kalpak A.S.S.R.; Turkmenistan, between the Caspian Sea and the Amu-Darya River; Tadzhikistan, which embraces the high plains and mountain ranges of the Pamirs, and finally Kirghizia, with its high mountain ranges, the Talasskiy Ala Tau and western Tien Shan (Fig. 24.1 above).

Agriculture in Soviet Central Asia

Soviet Central Asia has vast areas of desert, and in consequence, has developed highly specialized forms of land-use and adapted agriculture (Table 25.1). Apart from those oasis-crops well-suited to desert conditions – dates, figs, pomegranates, and vegetable pulses – most crops are grown under irrigation.

Cotton is by far the pre-eminent crop in all Central Asian republics, but especially in Uzbekistan. Here two-thirds of all Soviet cotton are grown, and in Central Asia, Turkmenistan, Tadzhikistan, and Kirghizia follow in this order. Over the past two decades Central Asia has been directed by Soviet policy towards more and more cotton production, as former cotton lands in the North Caucasus and Trans-Caucasus have been progressively diverted to other irrigated crops. Total regional output of the four republics is now 5·6 million tons annually: 80 per cent of the Soviet production of 7·0 million tons in 1971. Turkmenistan grows much Egyptian-strain cotton from which all long-staple cottons grown in the Soviet Union are derived.

The Central Asian republics supply their own cotton-textile industries, but more importantly, also the enormous requirements of the Centre's textile plants. Moreover, since the Soviet Union now ranks first in world cotton production – ahead of the U.S.A., India, and Mainland China – it now produces somewhat more than its own needs. Some Central Asian cotton is therefore exported.

Central Asia's agriculture has indeed been transformed by irrigation. Many very large, and sometimes expensive schemes – the Kara Kum and Amu-Darya–Karshi canals, for instance – have been pressed into service, far outweighing the

TABLE 25.1
Agriculture in Central Asia: A Comparison, 1970

	Uzbekistan	Turkmenistan	Tadzhikistan	Kirghizia
Area under Sown Crops (thousand hectares)	3589	636	765	1264
Irrigated Area (thousand hectares)	2809	543	518	883
Proportion of Crops Irrigated (Per cent)	78·4	85·3	67·4	69·6
Number of State Farms	377	49	89	103
Number of Collectives	1056	331	282	243
Production of:				
(thousand tons)				
Cotton	4666	869	727	187
Wheat	409	28	127	595
Maize	70	1	5	103
Potatoes	184	—	67	278
Fruit	410	21	143	85
Grapes	310	36	95	21
Meat	214	51	64	134
Milk	1374	192	285	548
Wool	22·1	14·0	4·9	27·1

Source: *Narodnoe Khozyaistvo, 1970*, Moscow, 1971, *passim*.
    N.B. The figure for Turkmenistan's irrigated area is incorrectly stated in this source (p. 348). The correct figure is given above.

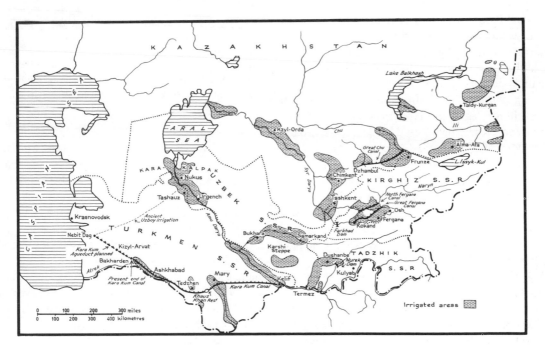

FIG. 25.1   Soviet Central Asia – Irrigation Agriculture.

elemental irrigation that has existed around oases since time immemorial (Fig. 25.1).

Since Central Asia's precipitation is so scanty, and moreover arrives as convectional showers, the only water provenance on which irrigation can be based is the high snow accumulation and orographic rainfall of the mountain girdles to the south-east. These feed waters into perennial streams such as the Amu-Darya and Syr-Darya, along which are strung oasis cities and towns of great antiquity. Other rivers, the Murgab, Zeravshan, Chirchik, and Chu also provide irrigation schemes. Over half a million hectares of the Hungry Steppe (Golodnaya Steppe) are irrigated and planted in cotton.

Central Asia's irrigation developments emphasize the building of modern irrigation projects by constructing dams with reservoirs whose main, if not only, purpose is to provide storage of water for release to agriculture. A few dams have hydroelectric facilities, but in the major agricultural areas these are always subordinate to the irrigation requirements. Only in the mountains of the south are pure hydroelectric power sites found. The Soviet authorities have also built modern canals with concrete revetments to prevent percolation losses. In all projects, great efforts have been made to regulate and conserve the region's water resources. And with the recent discovery of huge ground-water resources, prior-streaming through subsurface sands and gravels, sometimes in artesian basins, the exploitation of these in conjunction with perennial streams is now feasible, ensuring maximum agricultural use. In 1963 about 40,000 square kilometres of the Hungry Steppe was transferred from Kazakhstan to Uzbekistan to ensure unified control of irrigation developments.

Major irrigation projects include the Farkhad dam, the North Fergana Canal, and the new Great Fergana and South Fergana Canals, all of which draw their water resources from the upper headwaters of the Syr-Darya. New canals are located at Amu-Darya–Bukhara and the Karshi steppe. Another major dam is the Nurek structure on the Vakhsh river, a tributary of the frontier river, the Pyandzh.

But perhaps the most audacious project of all is the Kara-Kum Canal, which crosses the desert for over 600-kilometres between the upper Amu-Darya at Kelif to Ashkhabad. This first section, completed

125. Tashkent, capital of Uzbekistan, has recently completed this 504-suite air conditioned 'Uzbekistan' hotel. Rapid construction has been perfected in the Soviet Union by the use of pre-cast modular units, high-speed tower cranes and other building machinery.

in 1962, carries Amu-Darya water westwards linking up with ancient irrigation systems on the Murgab and Tedzhen rivers, and the oases of Ashkhabad and Kizel-Arvat.

Currently the final section of the Kara-Kum Canal is being extended from Ashkhabad along a route afforded by a post-glacial spillway from the Aral Sea. This embraces the western end of the ancient Uzboy irrigation system, long since defunct, and will eventually terminate at Krasnovodsk on the Caspian. When completed the Kara-Kum Canal will irrigate one million hectares of land. Quite apart from the dubious economic viability of irrigation provided by such a costly scheme as the

Kara-Kum Canal, there are also questions of silting and sand-blow to be faced. About 8 million cubic metres of sediments enter the canal from the Amu-Darya each year and, despite settlement reservoirs near Kelif and the regulating reservoir at Khauz Khan, the Canal is silting up at many points. Sand blown from the scantily vegetated Kara-Kum desert dunes is another problem as well as the endemic dust storms. Some other schemes (Bukhara–Karakul) have large tree plantings to protect them from drifting sands.

The irrigation agriculture of the Fergana Basin and the Zeravshan Valley may be taken as typical examples of developments throughout Central Asia.

The Fergana Basin is pre-eminently a cotton-growing district. Many collective farms are approaching mono-culture of cotton with a consequent neglect of subsistence crops. This does not matter so much when ample grain supplies are available by long rail hauls from the Virgin Lands of Kazakhstan and Western Siberia, but in years of stringency, Fergana often lacks adequate food supplies.

The Soviet government is anxious to develop greater self-sufficiency in the Fergana Basin. Much of the new or improved land for irrigation farms – 30,000 and 20,000 hectares respectively – in the Namangan scheme is given over to diversified crop production. Rice is very important, and other grains – irrigated winter wheat, barley, and maize – are also grown.

Other crops which are prominent in the farming pattern of the Fergana Basin are irrigated vegetable crops and potatoes; sugar-beet, groundnuts, and essential oil crops. Kenaf, a fibre, and hemp are also grown. Fruit trees in small clumps and also vine-yards cover the unirrigated slopes above the valley farms.

The Zeravshan valley trends away from the Tien Shans across the southern margins of the Kyzyl Kum desert. Additional irrigation water is now brought in via the new Amu-Darya–Bukhara and Amu-Darya–Karakul canals and also the Kashka Darya link canal. Zeravshan is the site of very ancient oasis settlements which are now linked by a modern irrigation reticulation system, 300 kilometres long by 15–40 kilometres wide. The Zeravshan valley has a high intensity agriculture, typical really of the classical oasis, but spread over a much broader area. The central area from the settlement of Karakul to Bukhara grows mainly cotton, but wheat, rice, tobacco, kenaf, fruit and vegetables, mulberry, and silkworms are important subsidiary crops. Lucerne is grown in rotation with cotton as a means of restoring fertility and tilth to the loess and alluvial soils.

In addition to the intensive irrigation agriculture of the Zeravshan valley, the higher terraces are

126. Tashkent. The Uzbekistan branch of the Lenin Central Museum (foreground) and government offices (background).

planted in unirrigated crops, particularly wheat and barley, and orchards and vineyards. The Viticulture Research Institute has bred a frost-resistant variety of grape suitable for planting in areas where the risk of temperature inversion is high. This is a cross between the Amur Valley grape of the Far East and selected western European varieties. The piedmont of the mountains on either side of the valley have long been famed for their flocks of karakul sheep. The valley has the greatest concentration of these sheep, bred for their wool or the fine lambskins taken prematurely from the ewes, of any region of Central Asia or Kazakhstan. Another area of lesser concentration is in the Kara-Kalpak A.S.S.R., south of the Aral Sea.

Animal husbandry plays a considerable role in the Central Asian economy (Table 25.2).

Turkmenistan and Uzbekistan have vast areas of desert and semi-arid plains. Sheep thrive in both republics, but Turkmenistan is somewhat too dry for cattle to do well. Their place in animal industries land-use is taken by goats, camels, and the famous Turkoman horses.

The place of pig-raising in the Central Asian economy is somewhat confined due to Moslem religion, or at least antecedents, of their populations. The Kazakhs on the other hand are not Moslems and pork figures prominently in their diet.

In Uzbekistan, karakul sheep grazing on the dry western pastures of the collectives receive breeding stock from the Karakul Research Institute in Samarkand. Camel breeding is still practised in the desert areas, although the long caravans of transport animals of the past are now a rare sight.

The mountainous areas of the south graze large flocks of karakul sheep for their wool, while the sturdy Gissar sheep provide meat and fat; important elements in the Central Asian diet.

Kirghizia has heavy concentration of domestic cattle and sheep grazing in its wild mountainous terrain. The high altitude pastures, however, are unsuited to these animals and their place is taken by the semi-domesticated yaks. These are reared to yield milk and meat. One innovation of interest is the crossing of yaks and cattle, particularly the native Kirghiz cattle, to breed an animal that yields more milk and meat than either. There are now serious possibilities that such a strain might become widely distributed in the Soviet Union's wilder and harsher climatic zones.

Similarly, the small-statured Kirghiz horse, well-known for its stamina and quarter-horse performance, has been successfully cross-bred with Don, Arabian, Turkoman, and other horse strains.

Transport in Soviet Central Asia

As for Kazakhstan, the building of railways (6083 kilometres) and oil and gas pipelines have been vital means of ensuring the economic development of Central Asia. Construction of all-weather roads, however, has not kept pace with the required rate of development, and many localities such as the

TABLE 25.2
Central Asia: Animal Husbandry, 1971

	Cattle (millions)	Sheep (millions)	Goats (thousands)	Pigs (thousands)
Uzbekistan	2·95	7·6	438	335
Turkmenistan	0·44	4·3	198	69
Tadzhikistan	1·01	2·2	452	78
Kirghizia	0·91	9·2	255	244
Total Central Asia	5·31	23·3	1343	726
For comparison: Kazakhstan	7·20	31·2	521	2227

Source: *Narodnoe Khozyaistvo, 1970*, Moscow, 1971, pp. 354–56.

127. The new KhV-5·4 cotton-picker shown working in Uzbekistan's cotton fields, has a capacity of 30 tons per 8-hour shift.

128. Uzbekistan is the Soviet Union's chief cotton growing Republic. Here cotton stockpiles are awaiting ginning at Ak-Kurgan, near Tashkent.

Gorno-Badakhshan autonomous oblast, and the fastnesses of Tadzhikistan and Kirghizia lack modern transport facilities.

As can be expected from the regional climate, rivers — fed from mountain waters far away — provide little opportunity for transport, especially in summer when they are frequently reduced to chains of pools by high evaporation rates. At present, the rivers provide about 3000 kilometres of navigation for small boats in the high-water season, but the facility is not of great economic benefit. Of much greater use are the Caspian and Aral Seas which are used to transport cotton and oil from their railway ports at Krasnovodsk, Gur'yev, Muynak (the port for Kungrad) and Aral'sk.

The major railways of Central Asia are the east–west Andizhan–Samarkand–Krasnovodsk line; the Tashkent–Orenburg line which follows the route of the Syr-Darya between the Kyzyl-Kum and Golodnaya Steppe; the Chardzhou–Kungrad line which has now been extended to Gur'yev, thus providing a parallel alternative route to the Centre in European Russia.

Tadzhikistan is linked into the Central Asian railway system via the Bukhara–Termez–Dushanbe line, and also the new broad-gauge railway from Termez to Yavan west of the Karatau mountains. Another narrow gauge railway runs from Dushanbe to Kulyab, intersecting the broad-gauge line previously mentioned at Kurgan-Tyube.

Industry in Soviet Central Asia

Over the past two decades, the Soviet government has made vigorous attempts to provide more industrial development in Central Asia. The aim has been to encourage the more balanced growth of the agrarian–industrial economies of the four republics.

Fortunately, Central Asia possesses minor quantities of fuel at various bituminous coal deposits at Takchiyan (Uzbekistan) and at Tash-Kumyr and Kok-Yangok (Kirghizia). Brown coal is mined at several locations including Angren in Tashkent oblast (Uzbekistan); the mines at Min-Kush, Dzhergalan, Almalyk (coal-mine), Kyzyl-Kiya, Dzhin-Dzhigan, and Salyukta (Kirghizia), and the mine at Shurab (Tadzhikistan). Total coal output (all grades) in Central Asia in 1970 was about 8·5 million tons.

Coal is used dominantly in thermal power stations and steam raising for factory processes. The chief fuel resources, however, of the Central Asia republics are the large volumes of oil and natural gas that they possess.

Oil and natural gas are exploited on the eastern buried flank of the Kopet Dag mountain (Turkestan) that runs under the below-sea-level plains of the southeastern Caspian. The principal wells are at Okarem, Nebit Dag, Cheleken, and the Zhdanov Bank in the Caspian Sea. Oil pipelines run from Nebit Dag and Koturdepe to Krasnovodsk,

129. Placing the concrete revetment along the Karshi Canal. The Karshi steppes cover wide expanses of Kashka-Darya oblast, Uzbekistan. The additional irrigation will supply new cotton-farming sovkhozes along each bank of the new canal.

and a new gas pipeline has been constructed linking the Okarem and other *en route* gas-fields with Krasnovodsk and western Kazakhstan. Cheleken is also a source of natural paraffin wax (ozocerite).

Uzbekistan produces oil and natural gas from the Fergana Basin and Surkhan-Darya. The Fergana Basin deposits are along the northern flanks of the Alayskiy Khrebet from Nefteabad (Tadzhikistan) through Ravat, Shorsu, Chimion to the principal fields of Andizhan oblast extending across the Kirghizia border at Changyr-Tash. Other nearby fields in Kirghizia include the Kok-Tash and Kochkor-Ata wells.

Elsewhere in Central Asia it is the natural gas-fields which are of pre-eminent importance, serving the Soviet Union through a large-capacity pipeline system. Astride the Uzbekistan–Turkmenistan border are the Gazli gas-fields situated on the central Amu-Darya; the Bukhara gas-field, and the recently developed gas-fields of the Kashka steppe (Urta-Bulak and Saman-Tepe) are the most prominent. Gas is also brought into the Soviet Union from the Shibarghan gas-field, Afghanistan. Unlike these foregoing gas-fields that are linked into the national pipeline system, the Mayskoye gas-field on the Kara-Kum Canal at Mary serves as a domestic and industrial gas supply for Ashkhabad and Bezmein. Tadzhikistan has a small oil-field at Kichik-Bel' and a gas-field at Kyzyl-Tumshuk. The latter is linked to the Dushanbe area's gas-fields by pipeline for local use.

The industrialization programme for Central Asia has required increasing quantities of steel. The small steel mill at Begovat (Bekabad) in Uzbekistan is quite inadequate to supply the amounts now needed and large 'imports' are obtained from the Urals iron and steel plants and Karaganda.

Non-ferrous metal mining is considerably developed in Central Asia. A copper–molybdenum complex ore is worked south of Tashkent at the Kalmakyr mine, near Almalyk. The plant at Almalyk has a copper concentrator, smelter, electrolytic refinery, and also a rolling mill producing sheet copper.

Lead–zinc ores are mined at several centres in Tadzhikistan (Altyn-Topkan, Kurusay, and Kansay). Lead is obtained in Kirghizia (Sovetskiy – lead–antimony ore – and at Bordunskiy and Ak-Tyuz – lead–gold ores), and also in Turkmenistan

130. The Tashkent area, despite its general aridity, has developed into a first-rate citrus-growing district. Over the years new varieties of lemons, developed from Caucasian strains, have been acclimatized. In the photograph the horticulturist-selector Z. Fakhrutdinov is shown holding the *Tashkentskiy* (right) and *Yubileinyy* (left) lemons.

131. Harvesting winter barley on the Turkmenistany kolkhoz, Turkmenistan.

132. Syr-Darya oblast, Uzbekistan, is famed for its irrigation agriculture and horticulture. Musk melons are produced in great abundance.

133. Cotton-picking on the '40 years of Komsomol' sovkhoz, Turkmenistan. This farm harvests 4500–5500 tons of cotton annually.

(Kugitang). There is a zinc smelter and refinery at
Almalyk (Uzbekistan) and an antimony refinery at
Kadamdzhay (Kirghizia). Mercury is mined at
Chauvay and also at Khaydarken where there is a
refining plant.

Ferro-alloys include not only the antimony mentioned, but also tungsten and molybdenum. Tungsten ores are mined at Igichka near Samarkand
(Uzbekistan), and at a mine in the Mogoltau and
concentrated at Chorukh-Dayron (Tadzhikistan).
Complex ores of tungsten–molybdenum occur at
Koytash, Lyangar, and Chirchik (Uzbekistan). All
of these mine concentrates as well as the other

134. Picking table grapes in Turkmenistan. The Central Asian
Republics have surged ahead in economic development with
the twin blessings of irrigation water and petroleum deposits.

135. A herd of Akhal–Tekin horses graze on the alpine
pastures of the Kopet Dag mountains, Turkmenistan.

136. The Syr-Darya power station on the Hungry Steppe, Uzbekistan, operates on natural gas. In 1973 one of its 300,000 kilowatt generators was working – it is to have three more of equal capacity – and this serves the new town of Shirin (population, 13,000).

137. The Vakhsh River Project, Tadzhikistan. The township of Nurek is now a major electro-chemical centre based on the Vakhsh hydroelectric station.

molybdenum concentrates from the Kalmakyr working are sent to the Chirchik alloys plant. Here they are made into welding rods or ferro-alloys.

Uranium ores occur at several places in Central Asia. The main mining areas are at Yangiabad and Charkesan (Uzbekistan); Taboshar (Tadzhikistan), and at Min-Kush and Kyzyl Dzhar (Kirghizia). These ores are processed at either the Kosh-Tegirmen or Tynya-Muyan uranium refineries.

Alumina is manufactured at Akhangaran, north of Almalyk (Uzbekistan). This plant uses a process that converts kaolin into alumina for a high grade cement plant, but there are longer term prospects that the alumina may be suitable for the aluminium reduction plant situated at Regar, near the Nurek hydroelectric power station.

Central Asia has an important segment of Soviet cement industry (1970 production 4·4 million tons) using local supplies of clay, limestone, and natural gas for firing the kilns. This cement is used in many of the hydroelectric power and other structures during the current building boom in Central Asia.

Soviet Central Asia's chemical industries are mainly concerned with fertilizer manufacture since the cotton-fields provide an exceptionally heavy demand. With the building of many large-scale hydroelectric power stations on the rushing torrents of the southern mountains, however, there is an incipient development of many branches of the electro-chemical industries.

Fertilizer plants manufacturing superphosphates are located at Almalyk, Kokand, Samarkand, and across the Kazakhstan border, at Dzhambul. The latter obtains its phosphate rock from the Karatau and Zhanatas deposits, northwest of Dzhambul. Another superphosphate plant is located at Komsomol'sk south of Chardzhou. Nitrogenous fertilizers are made at Fergana, Navoy, and Chirchik. Throughout Central Asia fertilizer plants receive local natural gas via pipelines for processing.

Other chemical industries are based on a variety of raw materials: sulphur (Gaudak), fluorspar (Lyangar), potash (Karlyuk), sodium chloride (Krasnovodsk), bentonite (Oglanly), and sodium sulphate (Kara-Bogaz-Gol). Examples are the iodine–bromine plant and carbon-black works at Cheleken (Turkmenistan); the anhydrous sodium sulphate and hydrous magnesium chloride plant at Bekdash on the Kara-Bogaz-Gol of the Caspian, and the Yavan valley electro-chemical complex which is due to begin production in 1973 and will make sodium chloride, magnesium chloride, chlorine, soda ash, and magnesium metal. The Yavan project is the largest single electro-chemical complex in the Soviet Union. These chemicals and metals will be made from local dolomite by electrolytic processes. Water for the Yavan project is brought in from the Vakhsh river via an 8-kilometre long tunnel through the Karatau mountains.

A giant hydroelectric power station — the Golovnaya (3·2 million kilowatts capacity) has been built on the Vakhsh river to service the Yavan valley complex. Other hydroelectric power stations of importance are at Nurek (2·7 million kilowatt), Toktogul' dam (1·2 million kilowatts), and two dams now being built at Ragun (3·2 million kilowatts) on the Vakhsh and at Dashtidzhum on the Pyandzh, the border river with Afghanistan (4·3 million kilowatts).

Central Asia has petroleum refineries at Fergana, Krasnovodsk, and Khanza-Khazimzade and these each have petro-chemical units incorporated.

Another recent petro-chemical complex is located at Shagal, 55 kilometres northwest of Chardzhou. This plant, brought on stream in 1970, manufactures synthetic rubber, synthetic fibres, and plastic intermediates.

Over recent years, Central Asia has developed into an important source of cotton and natural silk fabrics. In 1970 the region produced over 330 million metres of cotton textiles, dominantly from large *kombinats* in Uzbekistan and Tadzhikistan. Tashkent, the capital of Uzbekistan, was the largest single cotton manufacturing centre producing nearly half of the region's output. Production of natural silk fabric amounted to over 102 million metres in 1970. Again output came principally from Uzbekistan and Tadzhikistan, although the Kirghiz Republic has retained a small craft industry in silk weaving that goes back to ancient times. This

138. Despite modern developments, Tadzhik girls still learn traditional crafts like carpet weaving and the art of gold-thread embroidery in Leninabad, Tadzhikistan.

marks these republics' location on the historic Great Silk Road that ran from China to Europe. Dushanbe is the chief centre of the modern silk industry in the Soviet Union.

In keeping with Central Asia's influence in textile manufacturing, it also has many engineering plants making textile machinery. Large cities make cotton and silk roving, spinning and weaving machines, and associated with the region's large wool sheep industry there are plants manufacturing modern carpet-looms. These are installed in up-to-date factories that nevertheless make carpets to the traditional designs of the various areas within the republics. This machine–carpet industry exists side-by-side with the historic hand-weaving of carpets which is traditionally women's work in the mountain villages of Central Asia.

With the further development of small manufacturing industries in Central Asia, there has been a substantial rise in the proportion of the work-force engaged in secondary and tertiary activities. By 1970 over 4·4 million persons were classified as industrial or office workers; or about 21·4 per cent of the Central Asian population.

CHAPTER TWENTY-SIX

WESTERN SIBERIAN REGION

Reference	Appendix 9 for details by administrative region of population, area, density, and urbanization
Area	2498·2 thousand square kilometres
Population	about 13·2 million
Average Density	5·3 persons per square kilometre
Urbanization (Per cent)	54
Largest Cities	1970 Population (in thousands)

Western Siberia

Novosibirsk	1161	Kurgan	244
Omsk	821	Biysk	186
Novokuznetsk	499	Rubtsovsk	145
Barnaul	439	Leninsk-Kuznetskiy	128
Kemerovo	385	Kiselevsk	127
Tomsk	338	Belovo	108
Prokop'yevsk	272	Anzhero-Sudzhensk	106
Tyumen'	269	Gorno-Altaisk	34

The region comprises a huge area of nearly 2·5 million square kilometres, embracing six oblasts (Tyumen', Kurgan, Omsk, Novosibirsk, Tomsk and Kemerovo) each served by the Trans-Siberian Railway or one of the alternative west–east railway routes. In addition to these, the most densely settled areas of Western Siberia, there are two very sparsely settled areas to the north (the Khanty–Mansi N.O. and the Yamal–Nenets N.O.) and, to the south of the Trans-Siberian, the relatively well settled Altay Kray. Because of its severe climate and intense winter cold, only the southern margins of Western Siberia have been developed economically to any great extent. This zone lies between Ural Mountains and the Kuznetsk Ala-Tau.

In its western part, the region is a windswept, low-lying, and featureless plain drained by major tributaries of the mighty Ob' river and the Tobol, Ishim, and Irtysh rivers. This includes the Ishim and Baraba steppes which have rich chernozem soils, but are afflicted with the twin constraints of a short growing season and frequent summer drought.

In its eastern part, Western Siberia's southern margin is a complex of mountains, rising to 14,600 feet (4393 metres) in the Rudnyy Altay, near the Kazakhstan–Chinese border. These mountains are drained by headwaters of the Tom and Ob' rivers. From the Altay Mountains substantial ranges thrust northwestward – the Salair and Kuznetsk Ala-Tau – virtually enclosing the Kuznetsk Basin and diverting the Trans-Siberian Railway northwards so that it skirts the mountains until it reaches the Yenisey river. To the southwest of the Salair Range is the dry Kulunda steppe.

The Western Siberian Region has had considerable difficulty in maintaining its rate of economic growth despite the government's very progressive re-structuring of its developmental activities. It has vast raw material and industrial potentials and many new agricultural developments. These include the ploughing of Virgin Lands and provision of about 2 million hectares of irrigation in the Kulunda steppe and neighbouring areas of northern Kazakhstan.

Nevertheless, climate with sub-zero temperatures

for all but a few months in the year, has greatly inhibited permanent settlement. The region has difficulty in attracting and settling labour, particularly semi-skilled and skilled labour, despite higher money wages and substantial regional coefficients. According to a survey conducted by the Novosibirsk Institute of Economics in 1967 oilfield labour turn-over was some 76 and 87 per cent in Nefteyugansk and Surgut respectively, while other surveys by the same Institute showed that between 1959–65, Siberia lost about 350,000 persons, and that more than one-third of these went to warmer parts of the Soviet Union (European western parts, the Caucasus and Central Asia). Moreover, these areas receiving migrants from Western Siberia already have a surplus of labour.[1]

In consequence, the vast Siberian migrations of the recent past have done very little to boost the region's labour pool to a status needed for current and planned development projects. Few cities have managed to retain more than 40–50 per cent of their migrant intake (many of them are workers already acclimatized from the surrounding countryside). Between 1959 and 67 the Western Siberian able-bodied rural population declined by 550,000 persons (19 per cent of the initial population), partly as a result of the drift to cities and towns. This decline caused an acute labour shortage in agriculture. Some farms were only at 70–80 per cent of their establishment strength. This shortage was only made good by appealing to Soviet youth – especially Komsomol members – to work in these inhospitable lands as a patriotic duty. Similar problems of industrial and agricultural labour shortages are experienced in Eastern Siberia and the Far East.

Agriculture in the Western Siberian Region
Western Siberia's troubles in agricultural development stem principally from the Soviet authorities' zealous intent to turn the region into a huge 'machine' to produce grain, meat, eggs, and honey to serve its European area markets. Physical problems loom large, however.

The taiga abuts on the narrow grassland chernozem zone with great abruptness, marking a change from a severe to a slightly less severe climate – comparable to that of the Clay Belt of Canada. This is Western Siberia's most favoured agricultural area and has been a substantial source of spring wheat for many decades. The southern fringe of this ribbon – incidentally followed by the Trans-Siberian – is, however, increasingly subject to drought and seasonal dust storms of great severity. Sandwiched between winter cold and accompanying late spring frosts as the main 'northern' characteristics and the summer drought and early onset of cold *purga* winds as the chief 'southern' characteristics, the spring-sown wheatlands face critical agricultural management problems. The farm soils cannot be prepared early enough to achieve good germination levels and establish vegetative growth before drought strikes on the one hand, and on the other hand, the harvest all too frequently cannot be fully garnered before the onset of cold weather. Naturally, under these circumstances wheat production and yields fluctuate from year to year, to the detriment of regional shipments.

Although wheat is the main grain crop, oats and rye, which can tolerate cold conditions better, are planted in less favoured areas to the north of the spring wheat belt. These areas are the small fingers of wooded steppe which penetrate the taiga along river valleys. The natural cover of these areas is aspen and birch, but these forests have been largely cleared for the cultivation of hardy grains, flax, and dairy pastures. Southward wheat farming and some dairying become prominent.

The drier parts of the Ishim and Baraba steppes, and especially the Kulunda steppe, are unsuited to wheat cultivation except under irrigation, and consequently barley, millet, and buckwheat are the favoured dry-land crops. Small amounts of oil-seed, especially sunflower and linseed, are grown.

In the Baraba and Kulunda steppes there are numerous ephemeral streams. These rise swiftly following the cyclonic storms of summer, but their waters soon become lost in the many terminal playas and lakes which dot the areas east of the Salair Range and Altay Mountains. These steppes are far from featureless. They are rolling plains and hillocks, whose deflation hollows fill with dry snow during the 150–80 snow-days that mark the region's winter.

Supplementing the spring moisture availability

by the construction of irrigation works on the region's main rivers has given the steppe-lands a vigorous irrigation agriculture. Spring wheat is irrigated with very beneficial results in output and yields. Other crops which are favoured as elements in irrigation agriculture of the Altay Kray, and the Gorno-Altay autonomous okrug to the south, are maize, sugar-beet, and sown pasture, especially lucerne, for dairy herds. On the piedmont slopes of the Salair Range and Kuznetsk Ala-Tau, makhorka, hemp, fruit, and berry crops have expanded considerably due to the growing urban markets of the last decade or so.

As in the Kulunda steppe, and areas served by the Irtysh–Karaganda Canal in Kazakhstan, sugar-beet cultivation has been largely introduced by Ukrainian in-migrants, who now make up a substantial proportion of Western Siberia's farming community.

While grain-growing, dairy and poultry-farming have been the traditional farm enterprises of Western Siberia and these, despite all problems, are continuing an upward swing in production, new avenues of expansion are being sought by Soviet authorities.

Almost as a counter-measure, beef cattle raising has grown in Western Siberia, expanding northwards from Kazakhstan. At the same time, spring-wheat farming has spread southwards away from the 250–350-kilometre-wide wheat belt of Siberia into the Virgin and Long-Fallow lands of the five northern oblasts of Kazakhstan. This, of course, is not just an economic *quid pro quo*, but a real attempt to diversify and balance agricultural enterprises in climatically sensitive regions; a process that is evident in many other regions of the Soviet Union also.

Moreover, there is sound economic sense in breeding beef cattle in the warmer pasture lands of Kazakhstan and then moving store-cattle to the cooler, richer pastures of Western Siberia's mountain pastures for fattening and finishing. Because of the severity of winter conditions cattle have to be stall-fed and consequently harvesting of summer hay and the feeding of oil-seed cake concentrates are inherent elements in the system.

As a conservation measure, some wheat land in Western Siberia is rested by fallowing, or alternatively, the planting of rotation leys for several years to restore fertility. This is the *perelog* system, now common practice in many of the over-extended wheat areas of the Virgin Lands.

In addition to the upgrading of cattle pastures, much more fencing off of grazing areas has been introduced, and many new bore-watering points assist in the management of herds. Another growing innovation is the seasonal transhumance of cattle herds. The cattle are moved from the holding areas near farming communities in spring to graze on distant mountain pastures, particularly those with good ephemeral streams resulting from the snow-melt.

Sheep grazing for wool production is a feature of land-use in the drier steppe and also in the remoter and sparser mountain pastures not suited to cattle. Very large flocks are involved, usually under the care of Kazakh shepherds. Western Siberia has a considerable production surplus of wool and meat – both beef and mutton – which are sent to markets in European Russia.

Another expanding animal industry is pig-raising. Nearly all valley communities, especially those in the wooded steppe 'fingers', throughout Western Siberia keep pigs. They are fed on urban swill and off-farm vegetable waste. Poultry-keeping – egg-producing hens, geese and ducks – is also prevalent in these same rural communities.

The wild mountain ranges have a profusion of wild flowers from early spring to autumn and, in consequence, Western Siberia has been one of the traditional and justly famed areas for honey production. The hives containing the bee-swarms are scattered far and wide over the mountains and ranges early in spring.

Transport in Western Siberia
Compared with the Urals and Central Asian regions, and even more so compared with the European parts of the Soviet Union, the Western Siberia Region has a very tenuous and incomplete railway network.

The main, and virtually the only east–west railway route, is the Trans-Siberian Railway. This branches at Omsk; the northern route leading to Tyumen' and Sverdlovsk and beyond to Leningrad or Moscow, and the southern route leading to Kurgan and Chelyabinsk and thence to Kuybyshev and Moscow.

139. The Belovo thermal power station in the Kuznetsk Basin, Western Siberia. The turbo-alternator room has six units with an aggregate capacity of 1·2 million kilowatts.

140. The Ust'-Khantayskaya hydroelectric power scheme on a tributary of the Yenisey in the Taymyr tundra. The 440,000-kilowatt scheme, farthest north in the whole of the Soviet Union, serves the nickel-copper mining settlement at Noril'sk and dozens of reindeer and hunting townships of the tundra.

The Middle Siberian Railway runs from Kiselevsk in the Kuznetsk Basin to Barnaul and, thence branches three ways, the Middle Siberian running on to Kamen' and Omsk across the Kulunda steppe; the South Siberian running to Pavlodar to join the Trans-Kazakhstan line at Tselinograd, and the Turk–Sib Railway heading south to Semipalatinsk and beyond. All of these lines are vital communication links serving the industrial cities of the Kuzbas, the ore-mining and pastoral areas of the Altay Mountains, and the wheatlands of the southeastern parts of Western Siberia.

The Trans-Siberian Railway carries the heaviest traffic of any Soviet railway, especially over the Omsk-Novosibirsk section. The line is now electrified from Moscow all the way to Irkutsk in Eastern Siberia. The Novosibirsk line to Barnaul is also electrified.

A complex subsidiary rail network with many industrial spur-lines and marshalling yards connects the numerous industrial cities of the Kuzbas – Anzhero-Sudzhensk, Kemerovo, Leninsk-Kuznetskiy, Belovo, Kiselevsk, and Novokuznetsk – into a unified system. The main line continues south from Novokuznetsk to the iron-ore mines of the Gornaya Shoriya and then eastwards to Abakan.

The waterways of Western Siberia, especially the Tom', Ob', and Irtysh rivers, carry heavy industrial freight (coal and oil) and the immense timber production of the region. North of the steppe lands, where the rivers enter the unending taiga on their journey to Arctic seas, an immense expanse of ill-drained lowland occurs. When the rivers thaw in their upper reaches each spring they are still blocked downstream by huge ice-jams causing rivers to over-spill their banks. At the height of the flood waters the Lower Ob' reaches a channel-width of some 20 miles (32·2 kilometres) and the northern parts of Western Siberia become virtually a vast inland sea. Permafrost inhibits any groundwater drainage and consequently in summer the river channels, now shrunken in size, are flanked by vast expanses of swampland infested with mosquitoes and other insect plagues. It is little wonder that the foresters, hunters, and oil-men who carry forward the economy of northern Western Siberia need special incentives to remain for long at their posts.

With the rise of oil and natural gas production in Western Siberia, pipeline networks have been built. The Tyumen' and other oil-fields are connected southwards to Omsk where pipelines join the main east–west trunk line that links the Volga with Angarsk, Eastern Siberia.

In northern Siberia the Lower Ob' gas-fields serve pipelines from Urengoy and Gubkin eastward to Noril'sk and westward to Ukhta. Another West Siberia pipeline runs from the Myl'dzhino gas-field to Novokuznetsk.

Industry in Western Siberia

During World War II, Western Siberia with the Urals became the major arsenals of the Soviet war effort. The coal and steel producing Kuznetsk Basin at that time gained second rank as the country's chief heavy industrial district and has continued in that role ever since.

As a result of government investment decisions, the expansion of industry has continued at a high rate, not only in the Kuzbas, but also in Novosibirsk, Tomsk, Omsk, and other major cities of Western Siberia. The region ranks second in coal production – 199 million tons annually, only slightly less than the Donbas; it ranks high in iron and steel production; in ferro-alloys; in oil and natural gas production and in zinc, aluminium, and other non-ferrous metal production.

The major power resources of Western Siberia are located in Kuznetsk coal basin along the course of the Tom' River. In the northern part of the basin (Anzhero-Sudzhensk and Kemerovo districts) coal seams up to 50 metres thick are worked by shallow shaft mines or open-cut workings. Further south (Leninsk-Kuznetskiy, Kiselevsk, and Novokuznetsk districts), the coal seams are thinner and much more difficult to mine because of their steep pitch. They are generally mined by deep shafts, but at Yerunka, northeast of Novokuznetsk, there are shallow shaft mines and two very large open cuts.

In 1969 the coal output of the Kuznetsk Basin was 107 million tons and slightly more than half of this was metallurgical coking coal. Much of the coking coal, and some of the steam coal, from the Kuzbas serves far distant industrial areas – the Urals, Kazakhstan, and the Centre – as well as its own steel mills, smelters, and power stations. Another coal basin occurs at Kansk-Achinsk and overlaps the eastern area of Kemerovo oblast.

With the weakening of the Urals–Kuznetsk *kombinat*, the two Kuznetsk iron and steel mills located at Novokuznetsk and Antonovskaya (the new West Siberian Iron and Steel Works) on the right bank of the Tom' and 30 kilometres northeast of the other mills, have become almost completely independent of Magnitogorsk iron-ore.

The Kuzbas plants now use iron-ore from the Gornaya Shoriya-Temir Tau (not to be confused with Temir Tau northeast of Karaganda) south of the Kuzbas; the Minusinsk Basin (Abakan-Teisk) to the east, and more recently, iron-ore pellets (65 per cent iron plus the needed ratios of manganese and limestone flux) are obtained from the Sokolov-Sarabay and Lisakovsk ore-fields in Kustanay oblast, Kazakhstan. Pellets are also derived from the Korshunovo concentrator (Irkutsk oblast) or the Kachkanar iron-ores in the Urals. During the late 1960s a large, but low-grade iron-ore body was prospected in Bakchar, northeast of Tomsk. This is very near the Kuzbas and planned mining has now begun. Like the Kustanay and Kachkanar deposits, the Bakchar iron-ore can be mined by open-cut methods and easily dressed to pellet form as an efficient blast furnace charge.

Recent innovations in the steel industry require fuel oil derived from the Volga–Urals and Western Siberian (Tyumen') oil-fields and also natural gas from Myl'dzhino. These high calorific value fuels enrich the fuel charge of blast furnaces and steelmaking open-hearths.

Western Siberia has not only the two large integrated steel mills mentioned, but also small steelmaking or re-melting plants in Novosibirsk, Gur'yev (Kuzbas), and Omsk. Novokuznetsk has an important ferro-alloys plant.

In Western Siberia thermal power stations contribute 95 per cent of the electricity generated. There are major stations at Yuzhno-Kuzbasskaya (near Novokuznetsk), Tom'-Usinskaya (Mezhdurechensk), Novosibirsk, and Omsk. There are small hydroelectric plants at Novosibirsk (400-megawatts) on the Ob' river; at Kamen' (630 megawatts) which generates power and serves the Kulunda steppe with irrigation water, and two other plants now under construction on the Upper Ob' and its Katun tributary.

The most promising discoveries of oil and natural gas in the Soviet Union have been made in Western Siberia. The region has been dubbed 'the Third Baku' so rich and plentiful are the known reserves. Major oil-field locations are at Nizhnevartovskiy, Nefteyugansk, Megion and Surgut (Tyumen' oblast), and Strezhevoy and

141. The Ust'-Khantayskaya hydroelectric power scheme. Power supplies and graded all-weather roads have done much to open up the Soviet northlands.

Aleksandrovskoye (Tomsk oblast). The principal gas-fields are located at Berezovo and Igrim (Tyumen' oblast); the rich Vasyugan river gas-field (Tomsk oblast) near the Ob', and in the extreme north, the many gas-fields centred on the Taz valley adjacent to the Lower Ob', of which the Urengoy, Medvezh'ye, and Novyy Port gas-fields are representative.

Oil pipelines carry Tyumen' crudes south to the refinery at Omsk, including the large 40-inch, 965-kilometre line from Nefteyugansk. Western Siberian crude oil production rose to 6 million in 1967, but is estimated to be at least 20 million tons in 1970, so fast has production been augmented.

Natural gas reserves are phenomenal in Western Siberia; greater than those in any other region. Production has been somewhat hampered by difficulties with pipeline construction, principally shortages of large diameter pipe and compressor equipment needed to boost transmission pressures.

Nevertheless, a 40-inch pipeline from the Berezovo–Igrim gas-fields to Serov in the Urals was completed in 1966. This line joins the pipeline from Central Asia and will later continue westward to bring gas to the Centre and Northwest. The large diameter west-bound pipeline to be built from the Lower Ob' gas-fields north of the Urals has been mentioned in an earlier chapter.

Non-ferrous metallurgy in Western Siberia developed from the polymetallic ores of the Salair Range but these are now exhausted, and metal concentrates are now received from the Altay Mountains of East Kazakhstan. The main zinc smelter is at Belovo in the Kuzbas. In future, the Bozshakul copper deposit will be opened up, and the concentrates shipped via the Irtysk–Karaganda Canal to the smelter at Semipalatinsk. A major aluminium refinery using Urals and Arkalyk alumina is located in Novokuznetsk and depends on cheap thermal electricity for its operation.

Apart from the non-ferrous metal sources mentioned, the southeastern mountain complex yields gold, mercury, and other useful metals. The Gorno-Altay autonomous oblast is particularly rich in these ores.

After the wartime frenetic expansion, engineering industries in Western Siberia have developed rather slowly. Consequently, a high proportion of the region's iron and steel, non-ferrous metals, and bituminous coal, is shipped out of Western Siberia in a raw or semi-finished state.

Nevertheless, some cities are accomplishing steady if slow industrial growth and among these Novosibirsk, Omsk, Tomsk, and Barnaul are the most outstanding. These industrial centres manufacture steam and hydraulic turbines, machine tools, electric tramway equipment, and instruments of various sorts. Agricultural machinery manufacture, geared to wheat land farming, is made in Novosibirsk, Omsk, Rubtsovsk, and Kemerovo.

The coal, oil, and natural gas resources of Western Siberia give it thriving chemical industries. These include explosives, aniline dyestuffs, nitrogenous fertilizers, and synthetic polymers and resins. The Vasyugan natural gas fortuitously contains large amounts of liquid hydrocarbons (casing-head oil) ideally suited for a petrochemical industry. There is an established petrochemical industry based on the Omsk refinery and another based on Vasyugan hydrocarbons is planned for a site near Tomsk. Barnaul manufactures viscose and kapron tyre cord which supplies a tyre factory using synthetic rubber in that city and another at Omsk (which produces the rubber also). Barnaul also has a well developed cotton textile industry due largely to its situation on the Turk–Sib Railway, the route along which cotton from Central Asia reaches Western Siberia.

Timber working industries are among the oldest established enterprises in the region. The taiga and its southern margins yield pine, fir, larch, and aspen. While most timber is shipped westward as semi-finished products there are growing attempts to add more value by manufacturing in Western Siberia itself. Biysk, Barnaul, and Tomsk make matches and match boxes. Tomsk makes pencils from Siberian cedar, and both Novosibirsk and Barnaul make a wide range of wood chemicals, including turpentine and resin.

If there is one particular industrial group that is especially weak in its development in Western Siberia it is the food industries. Despite its vast array of food production – wheat, meat, milk, etc. – very little is processed beyond an elemental stage in the region. There is, however, an incipient development of flour-milling and dairy-product manufacture that augurs well for this branch in the years to come.

CHAPTER TWENTY-SEVEN

EASTERN SIBERIAN REGION

Reference   Appendix 10 for details by administrative region of population, area, density, and urbanization
Area   7226·0 thousand square kilometres
Population   about 8·2 million
Average Density 1·1 persons per square kilometre
Urbanization (Per cent) 48
Largest Cities   1970 Population (in thousands)

	Eastern Siberia		Bratsk	155
Krasnoyarsk	648		Noril'sk	135
Irkutsk	451		Yakutsk	108
Ulan-Ude	254		Cheremkhovo	99*
Chita	241		Achinsk	97
Angarsk	203		Kansk	95

* Cheremkhovo declined from 122,000 (1959) to 99,000 (1970). It was a major coal mining centre.

The Eastern Siberian Region clearly indicates a general characteristic of the Soviet Union: the declining intensity of economic activities as the eastern regions are approached. Eastern Siberia is considerably less developed than its neighbour Western Siberia, but nevertheless great efforts are currently being made to develop the region's not inconsiderable resource potential more fully.

Eastern Siberia comprises two oblasts of the Russian Federation, Chita and Irkutsk. Within these are two ethnically separated groups; the Aga Buryat national okrug in Chita oblast and the Ust'-Orda Buryat national okrug in Irkutsk oblast. Next, the extremely extensive Krasnoyarsk Kray which stretches from Tannu Ola (mountains on the Mongolian border) to the Laptev Sea in the far north. Embraced within Krasnoyarsk Kray are the Khakass autonomous oblast, and in the north, the Evenki and Taymyr national okrugs. In addition, Eastern Siberia enfolds three Autonomous Soviet Socialist Republics: Tuva and Buryat, both flanking the Mongolian People's Republic, and Yakut which covers an immense area – even larger than Kazakhstan – drained by the north-flowing Lena and Kolyma rivers in the northeastern segment of the Soviet Union.[1]

Agriculture in Eastern Siberia

Compared with its two neighbouring regions, the Far East and Western Siberia, the vast expanse of Eastern Siberia is even less suited by climate, soils, and topography to intensive agricultural development.

If Yakutia is excluded because of its slight agricultural potential, the area of Eastern Siberia is only a little smaller than the whole of the European part of the Soviet Union, and yet this vast expanse has only about the same population as Greater Moscow. Dominantly this population is concentrated along the region's southern fringe, along the routeway of Trans-Siberian Railway, the only line crossing the region on its way to the Soviet Far East. More than half of Eastern Siberia's cities and

[1] Although the Yakut A.S.S.R. has been joined administratively with the Far East since 1962, it will be treated here with Eastern Siberia because of their considerable community of economic interest.

towns have been established during the Soviet period. This is a mark of slow, but on-going, economic expansion.

The total agricultural–pastoral area of Eastern Siberia is 22 million hectares, and of this about 36 per cent is suitable for sown crops. The region has a very short growing season due to intensely cold conditions in late spring, and the early onset of winter. Frosts can occur even in the summer months. Heavy falls of dry snow give little moisture provenance during the spring melt, and summer precipitation, most beneficial for agriculture, is light and of uncertain incidence.

Agriculture is for the most part organized on a state farm basis. Good management and a high level of farm mechanization have succeeded in compressing the farming year into the few short months available.

Under this system, large areas of spring wheat are planted, and the cold-tolerant grains, rye, oats, and barley, play a special role in allowing late summer harvesting under conditions that would devastate standing wheat crops. Potatoes are also grown on the more marginal lands where soils generated under taiga cover are acidic podzols.

The hardy grains and potatoes are displaying an important function in extending agriculture northwards: they are the pioneer crops. Gradually, farming is moving into new frontier lands along the Angara and Yenisey valleys; into the Trans-Baykal lands of the Buryat A.S.S.R., and the Vitim–Patom plateau. Another avenue of farming development is the new railway line that leaves the Trans-Siberian at Tayshet and now terminates at Ust'-Kut. In future it is possible that this line will be extended eastwards to open up new mineral and agricultural resources along the middle Lena Valley.

Grain production in Eastern Siberia has now reached the point where it has a surplus available for shipment to other parts of the Soviet Union. Even the Yakut A.S.S.R. planted 71,000 hectares in grain in 1970 on its 49 state and 24 collective farms. Before World War II Eastern Siberia was a deficit area for grains, despite its very small population. This creation of a surplus is a tremendous agronomic achievement and transport saving considering the inhibiting factors faced by the region's farms. Most surplus grain now flows to the Far East via the Trans-Siberian, or by lorry convoys to the northeast. Some also moves north along the Angara–Yenisey waterway and east via the Lena. River vessels carrying grain return with cargoes of Eastern Siberian timber.

Aside from its surplus of grain crops, the region has an inadequate production of other agricultural commodities. Potatoes, vegetables, and fruit have to be brought in from neighbouring regions in substantial quantities.

Eastern Siberia has very good pasture lands, however, and cattle grazing is an important enterprise, despite the inclement winter climate. Meadows along the stream courses are prepared for hay each summer and cattle are over-wintered in substantial barns. So significant is the beef cattle industry in Eastern Siberia, that it now ranks as the largest single meat-shipping region in the Soviet Union. Beef cattle herds are located mainly in the southern parts of Krasnoyarsk Kray as well as in the well-watered areas of the Khakass autonomous oblast and Tuva A.S.S.R. Irkutsk oblast, and especially the Ust'-Orda Buryat national okrug, also have very large numbers of cattle. In many respects, Eastern Siberia's cattle industry is similar to the grasslands cattle industry of the northern United States–Canadian Great Plains.

The Tannu Ola, Eastern Sayan Mountains, Yablonovyy Khrebet, and other mountainous areas of Eastern Siberia afford excellent short-grass pasturage for sheep flocks. Khakassia, the Tuva and Buryat A.S.S.R.s, and Chita oblast have many areas grazing fine-wool and medium-wool sheep. In particular, the Trans-Baykal areas are expanding this line of enterprise. In some areas however, precipitation is so low that it is necessary to irrigate holding pastures to preserve the flocks over the low natural feed period.

There have been marked changes in animal husbandry. Indigenous shepherds and cattle herders were until recently completely nomadic in their lifestyle. Now, however, great encouragement is given to sedentary cattle ranching, and sheep flocks are held within confined areas for long periods. Nevertheless, transhumance of both sheep and cattle to upland pastures in summer remains an accepted practice, and indeed, shows an excellent adaptation of land-use to historic folk-customs.

The Tuva A.S.S.R. is concerned with the grazing of yaks, needed for milk and meat supplies. The republic ships out yak and cattle hides, hair, and large amounts of wool.

The Yakut A.S.S.R. is famed for its hunting and trapping of fur-bearing animals. Each year it sends great numbers of pelts of sable, squirrel, silver fox, and other fur species to European markets. A recent innovation has been the breeding of fur-bearing animals in captivity, especially mink and foxes.

Transport in Eastern Siberia

Apart from the Trans-Siberian Railway, Eastern Siberia is ill-served with railway lines. One other line runs from the Kuzbas to Abakan and then north to join the Trans-Siberian at Achinsk. This line transports Khakassian iron-ore and Krasnoyarsk timber to Western Siberian industrial areas, particularly the Kuzbas. Yet another line, recently built, is the Abakan–Tayshet–Ust'-Kut line. This joins the Lena River navigation system at Ust'-Kut, and is ostensibly the first section of the long-mooted northern railway to the Far East. This is projected to run 400–500 kilometres to the north of the present Trans-Siberian Railway, and thus well away from the sensitive border area with China.

The main purpose served by the Tayshet–Ust'-Kut line at the moment is to tap the important Angara-Ilim iron-ores and timber resources and carry these to industrial centres in the west. Previously the line had been used to freight construction materials for the building of the Bratsk dam on the Angara River.

Over the last decade new railway lines have been constructed between Reshety and Boguchany, and also from Achinsk to Abalakovo. These lines tap new mineral workings and the forests of Krasnoyarsk Kray, and are part of the progressive in-filling of the railway network of Eastern Siberia.

Three main events have led to an improvement on the heavily burdened Trans-Siberian railway system. First, the construction of the Ust'-Kut–Tayshet and Achinsk–Abakan links has diverted much heavy industrial freight bound for the Kuzbas away from the main trunk route. Secondly, the building of the Tuimazy–Irkutsk main trunk oil pipeline has virtually eliminated oil tank-car trains running on the Eastern Siberian section of the Trans-Siberian, and thirdly, the electrification and adoption of centralized traffic control over the main line has greatly increased its freight capacity.

While railways carry most east–west freight and passengers in Eastern Siberia, the rivers, particularly the Yenisey and Lena, carry much river freight and many passengers. Roads also reach far to the north from stations along the Trans-Siberian. The rivers forge an essential link between the many riverside settlements scattered along their length and both the Trans-Siberian in the south and the Northern Sea Route along the Arctic coast.

On the Yenisey, ocean-going vessels can reach the interior Eastern Siberian timber port of Igarka, 400 kilometres upstream from the broad Yeniseyskiy Zaliv (inlet). During the short open season river vessels can continue on for a further 2700 kilometres as far as the Minusinsk rapids, near Abakan. The Yenisey's major tributaries, the Nizhnyaya Tunguska, Podkamennaya Tunguska, and Angara, are also navigable for much of their length.

The Lena–Vitim system of waterways is also navigable for some 4000 kilometres, and serves the important Vilyuy and Aldan basins carrying freight to the Northern Sea Route and upstream to the Irkutsk region.

While railways and waterways handle a considerable proportion of Eastern Siberia's external freight traffic, all-weather roads and airlines are the only means of reaching the remoter areas of the taiga and tundra. More than half of the region's internal freight (i.e. not inter-regional) is carried by motor lorries in terms of ton-kilometres hauled. This is a measure of Eastern Siberia's dire need for the strengthening of its railway network.

Air freight traffic is centred on the region's main airport at Irkutsk. This airport also handles much local air passenger traffic to all points north, north-west, and northeast, but regular air services direct from Moscow and Leningrad also reach centres like Noril'sk, Tiksi, and Yakutsk.

Industry in Eastern Siberia

Eastern Siberia has a rich endowment: iron-ore, ferro-alloy metals, non-ferrous and valuable metals, various qualities of coal, mica, asbestos, graphite, and fluorspar. Gold, diamonds, and other gemstones complete the impressive list of mineral resources. In addition, the region possesses vast resources of timber and hydroelectric energy on massive rivers that are well-suited to harnessing. Many developments in all fields have already occurred and the immediate future holds further prospects for resource exploitation and industrial growth.

In 1970, Eastern Siberia ranked first in the Soviet Union in the development of electrical power installations. This was almost wholly due to continuing expansion of the region's hydroelectric power resources.

So many large hydroelectric power stations have been built that Eastern Siberia now has a substantial surplus of electrical energy to 'export' to the European parts of the Soviet Union. This will become feasible with the completion of the 1500-kilovolt D.C. transmission line from Irkutsk and Bratsk to the Urals via the transformer station at Itat, east of Krasnoyarsk.

Hydroelectric power stations have been built at Krasnoyarsk (5000 megawatts) on the Yenisey, and the Sayan dam (6500 megawatts) on the same river is under construction. Other major hydroelectric power plants are at Bratsk (4500 megawatts) and Ust'-Ilimsk (4500 megawatts) on the Angara. There are also a number of smaller plants at Irkutsk (660 megawatts) and another on the Vilyuy tributary of the Lena at Chernyshevskiy (312 megawatts).

Many other large hydroelectric plants are projected or already building to complete the outstanding Yenisey power scheme. These plants are the Yeniseyskaya, Osinovskaya, and Nizhne-Tungusskaya on the Yenisey, and the Boguchanskaya on the Angara. Each plant is projected to have a capacity in excess of 4000 megawatts. Another smaller plant at Snezhnogorsk (441 megawatts) is situated just south of Noril'sk on the Khantayka tributary of the Yenisey.

It is the Yenisey–Angara power schemes that have captured the popular imagination as they rank as the largest hydroelectric power plants in the world. Both the Bratsk and Krasnoyarsk stations have capacities considerably more than double that of the Coulee Dam in the Pacific Northwest of the United States, previously the world's largest.

The immense availability of electrical energy in Eastern Siberia has given rise to many power-consuming industries. Aluminium reduction plants have been set up in Krasnoyarsk, Irkutsk, and at Anzeb, near Bratsk. Alumina is made at Achinsk and railed to these three reduction plants; other supplies come from Pavlodar in Kazakhstan. These plants probably produce the cheapest aluminium in the Soviet Union, since it is reported that, due to the favourable hydrological and geological conditions found at power sites of Eastern Siberia, the cost of

142. A sheep-farming kolkhoz in the Tuva A.S.S.R.

143. The Vilyuy hydroelectric power station, Yakut A.S.S.R., serves the diamond mining centres of Mirnyy, Aikhal, and Udachnyy. Yakutia has vast resources of timber, coal, natural gas, gold, tin, and antimony as well as its time-honoured fur trade. Road connections to the Northern Sea Route and the Trans-Siberian Railway are gradually opening up this vast and forbidding northland. A new seaport has been set up on the Kolyma estuary at Zelyonyy Mys, Arctic coast.

generating electrical energy is only 30–50 per cent of that in western parts of the Soviet Union.

Other power-consuming industries are the wood-pulp mills. In 1967, a very large mill opened at Bratsk. The output of this mill supplies a 200,000-ton capacity cellulose plant which manufactures rayon tyre cord.

Apart from the on-going development of hydroelectric power resources in Eastern Siberia, there have been many changes in the coal-mining industry of the region. Output of all coal is about 50 million tons annually. The main mining areas are the Kansk-Achinsk brown coal basin. Irsha-Borodino, and Berezovskoye, Nazarovo open-cuts); the Minusinsk bituminous coal basin (Chernogorsk); the Cheremkhovo steam coal basin; and the brown coal of Chita oblast: the Chernovskoye mines in a suburb of Chita, and at Tarbagatay, Morday, and Kharanor in the south. Bituminous coal is mined at Bukachacha.

Open cut coal-mining accounts for all of the brown coal mined, and about 70 per cent of the bituminous coal is obtained in this way. Some shaft mines have been closed because their resources have been depleted and they are no longer economic to operate.

With the adoption of electric or diesel locomotives there has been a sharp falling off in steam coal requirements. Cheremkhovo, which has mined steam coal for Trans-Siberian Railway locomotives since the 1890s is one of the few examples in the Soviet Union of a declining urban settlement. Population rose from 56,000 to 122,000 persons between 1939 and 1959, the heyday of steam locomotives, but has since fallen back to 99,000 persons in 1970, while in 1971 the population was continuing an even faster decline to reach 96,000.

Most coal is now used in coalfield power stations – the Irsha-Borodinskaya, Azeyskaya, Nazarovskaya, and several others – or for industrial purposes in Krasnoyarsk and other major industrial nodes.

Non-ferrous metals are obtained in abundance in Eastern Siberia. Moreover, absence of good transport facilities is inhibiting the development of known deposits of commercial significance, for example, the Udokan copper prospect in northern Chita oblast, and the Gorev lead deposit, Angara River.

Metals currently mined in Eastern Siberia include cobalt (Khovo-Aksy, Tuva A.S.S.R.), antimony (Rozdolinsk), molybdenum–tungsten complex (Zakamensk), molybdenum (Tüim-Sorsk on the Achinsk–Abakan railway and also at Davenda and Vershakhtaminskiy, Chita oblast). The space-age metals – tantalum, columbium, beryllium, and lithium – are mined in numerous parts of the southeastern mountains of Chita oblast.

Mica is mined at a new working on the Mama–Chuya rivers (Irkutsk oblast). This is muscovite mica but the more useful phlogopite mica comes from Kankunskiy and Emel'dzhak (Yakut A.S.S.R.).

Gold has always been one of the most sought-after metals in Eastern Siberia. At the moment gold is mined in the Yeniseyskiy Hills (Severo-Yeniseysk gold lode and Yuzhno-Yeniseyskiy placers), the Lena goldfields (Bodaybo on Vitim River), the Nerchinsk district (Taseyevo and Baley lodes), northeastern Chita oblast (Vershino-Durasunskiy

and Klyuchevskiy lodes), and in the Vitim headwaters of the Buryat A.S.S.R. (Bagdarin and Karaftit).

The Yakut A.S.S.R. is also known for its gold deposits; its diamond workings, its non-ferrous metals, and its natural gas-fields. It also has many scattered reserves of bituminous and brown coal not widely used at present because of inadequate lines of communication in this vast and physically uninviting republic.

Gold is found in several locations east of the upper Aldan valley (Aldan, Orochen, Leninskiy placers, and Kuranakh lode). The area is connected to the Trans-Siberian Railway at Never by an all-weather road which then runs northwards to the Tas-Tumus natural gas-field at the Vilyuy–Lena confluence. Power for the Aldan goldfields comes from the Chul'man thermal station.

The Yakut A.S.S.R. is one of the few areas in the Soviet Union where private prospecting parties are encouraged, although all finds must be reported to the controlling authority, Soyuz Zoloto Trest (Union Gold Trust).

The Soviet Union has become one of the world's major producers of industrial and gem-stone diamonds and also gold over the past 15 years. The principal workings are all kimberlite pipes, situated along the upper headwaters of the Vilyuy and its tributary the Markha in the western area of the Yakut A.S.S.R. The chief centre for the industry is Mirnyy, but Aykhal and Udachnyy have grown in importance. Another diamond location is Ebelyakh on an Arctic coast river, the Anabar.

Eastern Siberia has developed a small steel plant at Petrovsk-Zabaikal'skiy. This mill obtains coal from the Tarbagatay shaft at Novopavlovka near the steel mill. Pig-iron is railed in from the Kuzbas to make steel and rolled products.

With the opening up of many iron-ore resources in Eastern Siberia, there are strong possibilities that a fully integrated, modern iron and steel mill will be built in future, especially after the plans to build such a mill at Tayshet, Western Siberia, fell through.

Iron-ore is mined in the southern Khakass autonomous oblast (Teya and Abaza), the Angara-Pitt deposits, and also at Zhelezhnogorsk-Ilimskiy, Rudnogorsk, and Korshunovo, all near the Ust'-Kut–Tayshet railway. Concentrators attached to the Angara-Pitt open-cut workings convert ore to 62 per cent iron content fines (magnetite) which are shipped to the Kuzbas. Small shipments of iron-ore to Petrov-Zabaykal'skiy have partially revived the old iron smelting industry, but it seems likely that a new modern plant would only be set up with assured supplies of coking coal. A two-way shuttle of ore and Kuzbas coking coal with steel mills at each end (on the Urals–Kuznetsk model) is a strong possibility. This would make Bratsk or a centre in the Minusinsk Basin likely contenders for such a new steel mill.

Many branches of manufacturing industries are developed to only a minor degree in Eastern Siberia at the moment. Nevertheless, its very strong industrial resource base, particularly its excellent energy potential, gives the region good prospects for future development of secondary industries.

Heavy engineering at this stage is confined to Krasnoyarsk, Irkutsk, Chita and Ulan-Ude, all historic centres connected with the needs of the Trans-Siberian Railway. These industrial centres now emphasize the manufacture of machinery and equipment for road and railway transport, mining, iron and steel, cranes, and river vessel building. They also supply equipment to the timber-working industries as well as agricultural implements and dairy factory needs.

Eastern Siberia's timber industries produce over 50 million cubic metres of sawn timber annually. Most of this is transported to Central Asia, Kazakhstan, and the Volga region. Timber exports bound for overseas markets are shipped through the Yenisey port of Igarka.

Chemical industries have grown quite vigorously over the past few years. They are premised on the availability of smelter by-products, brown coal, fluorspar (Solonechnyy, Kalanguy and Usugli, Chita oblast), salt (Usol'ye-Sibirskoye and Tyret'), wood derivatives, and oil and natural gas. The region manufactures dyestuffs, chlorine, caustic soda, hydrochloric acid, industrial (wood) alcohol, turpentine, and many petrochemical derivatives, including synthetic rubber and synthetic fibres (Krasnoyarsk and Angarsk).

The food-processing industries are on the threshold of more substantial growth and are at present based on abattoirs, dairy factories – especially butter and cheese – distilleries for alcoholic beverages, and a few fish canneries based on Lake Baykal and river fisheries (Buryat A.S.S.R.).

CHAPTER TWENTY-EIGHT

FAR EASTERN REGION

Reference   Appendix 11 for details by administrative region of population, area, density, and urbanization
Area   3112·7 thousand square kilometres
Population   about 5·2 million
Average Density   1·7 persons per square kilometre
Urbanization (Per cent) 74
Largest Cities   1970 Population (in thousands)

Vladivostok	441	Yuzhno-Sakhalinsk	106
Khabarovsk	436	Nakhodka	104
Komsomol'sk-on-Amur	218	Magadan	92
Petropavlovsk-Kamchatskiy	154	Birobidzhan	56
Blagoveshchensk	128	Nikolayevsk	n.a.
Ussuriysk	128		

The Soviet Far East comprises an enormous area more than 50 per cent greater than the size of European Russia. And yet within this vast and resource-rich area there live fewer people than in the Leningrad conurbation. However, average density belies the actual situation for the majority of population is found in the settlements strung along the Trans-Siberian Railway on its journey east to Khabarovsk and then south to Vladivostok. Also small concentrations of population exist at points along the sea-coast – at Okhotsk, Magadan, Palana, and Petropavlovsk-Kamchatskiy, and also far to the north along the Bering Sea at Beringovskiy and Anadyr (Fig. 28.1).

The principal administrative regions of the Soviet Far East are Amur, Magadan, Kamchatka, and Sakhalin oblasts, and also the very important Khabarovsk and Maritime krays. Since the end of World War II the whole of the Kuril Islands archipelago has belonged to the Soviet Union. These areas include the Far East's greatest cities, Khabarovsk and Vladivostok respectively.

Agriculture in the Soviet Far East

Agricultural possibilities are distinctly limited in the Soviet Far East. Even in the most favoured agricultural areas – the Zeya–Bureya valleys, the Birobidzhan (Jewish) autonomous oblast, the Lower Amur valley and the Ussuri-Khanka lowland – there are serious problems with climatic and soil conditions.

In general, the region is excessively cold, conforming more with the Labrador area of eastern Canada rather than with its homologous zone of the Canadian maritime provinces. In consequence, growing seasons are short, with a late onset of the warmer conditions of spring. Moreover, much of the precipitation falls in the form of dry snow or as sharp monsoonal showers of late summer. Even falls of dry snow accumulating to depths of 15 centimetres are equivalent to little more than 50 millimetres (2 inches) of rainfall and are quite inadequate to start germination processes. Although precipitation on the Sikhote-Alin mountain's Pacific slopes may amount to 1,000 millimetres annually (40 inches) much of this is not available to plants when it is needed for the germination and growth periods of spring and early summer.

Fortunately, however, the seasonal inflow of maritime air masses drawn into a summer low-pressure centre over Lake Baykal renders the

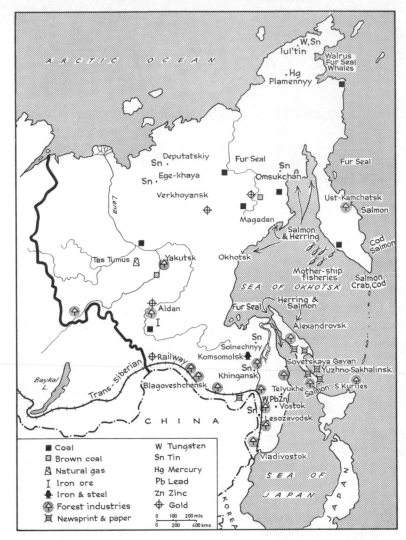

FIG. 28.1   Economic Development: Soviet Far East Region.

southern margins of the region relatively humid. The higher rainfall is sufficient to grow excellent forests, although it is marginal for crop agriculture. From northern Kamchatka to Vladivostok the region is afflicted each summer by dense fogs in coastal areas as the relatively warm air masses flow over the cold Japan current and colder coastlands of the Soviet Far East.

In the northern part of the region the permafrost trends sharply southwards giving rise to shallow-rooted trees such as the larch rather than pines and firs. In these areas, tundra soils and podzols domin-ate, so that, coupled with poor drainage, any hope

of agriculture is severely constrained, quite apart from the climatic aspect. Along the Trans-Siberian Railroad, however, small patches of steppe soils occur – no longer in an attenuated but continuous belt as in the Siberias – and these are given over to a persistent, if somewhat hazardous, cultivation.

South again, in the Maritime Kray the humid, short-summer continental climate is associated with broad-leaf deciduous forests. Soils here, although still podzolic, are richer in humus and better adapted to tillage.

For agricultural prosperity, it is the Zeya-Bureya lowlands and the Suifun-Khankaiskaya districts

(Ussuri-Khanka lowlands) that are most favoured. These lands grow a wide variety of crops suited to the short, humid summers. Spring wheat, rice and maize are among the usual grains, and sugar-beets are grown on the better friable soils. Soya bean is another crop of great significance.

In these lowland areas from the Zeya river to Lake Khanka, about 3 million hectares are under cultivation, and while about half is under spring wheat, other grain crops are also grown. In addition to rice and maize, the next ranking grains, winter rye, barley, and buckwheat, are also grown.

The Far East is the Soviet Union's chief area for the cultivation of soya beans. Of the country's total area under soya bean, about 850,000 hectares (over 98 per cent) are in the Far East, mainly in the warmer humid southwestern areas. Soya bean is an extremely useful crop yielding protein (50 per cent by weight) and oil (20 per cent). In the Soviet Union, soya bean is used both for human food and animal feedstuffs.

In the Amur Valley between Birobidzhan and Nikolayevsk (Khabarovsk Kray) potatoes are grown in huge quantities, along with cold-tolerant vegetables, and a hay and dairy-cattle livestock industry exists. Very little grain is grown in this area as it is too cold.

Another area with a similar agricultural system is a narrow strip of the Sea of Japan coast from Vladivostok to Soviet Harbour (Sovetskaya Gavan). Beef cattle graze also on the seaward slopes of the Sikhote-Alin mountains.

Animal husbandry, although more important than crop cultivation, is not too well developed in the Far East. On the margins of arable farming, large areas of pasture exist, often the result of past clearing of the forest, but so far there is scant use of these. These pasture lands are capable of supporting beef cattle and sheep industries, but at the moment these share the valley meadowlands with dairy cattle and pigs. Only in the interior Zeya valley is there a distinctive fine-wool sheep industry; elsewhere the grazing of sheep is hardly developed.

The Aldan valley, far in the interior, manages to produce excellent market-garden crops, grows some hardy grains, and raises fine beef cattle, all activities

144. The floating factory ship '50-Years Revolution', seen anchored at Petropavlovsk-Kamchatskiy, is flagship of the Kamchatka fishing fleet. At sea, it has a daily production of 150 tons of 'barrel' herring, 90 tons of fresh frozen herring, 50 tons of crated salt herring, 30 tons of canned herring, and 100 tons of herring meal.

driven no doubt by the sheer necessity for a small group of isolated mining settlements to feed themselves as much as possible.

The Far East is perhaps the last frontier for the fur hunter in the Soviet Union. Khabarovsk Kray and the Sikhote-Alin mountains as well as Sakhalin island and the Kamchatka peninsula abound in fur-bearing animals – sable, squirrel, ermine, racoon, marten, fox, and bear. The offshore islands, and especially the Kuril archipelago, have large colonies of sea otter and fur-seal. These animals are currently undergoing great depredation and there seem to be no sufficient control measures to ensure the maintainance or, in some cases, regeneration of wild animal populations. Nevertheless, the recent moves to rear sable, arctic fox, silver fox, and the musk-deer on fur-farms in the Far East may show a innate response to the hunting pressures that evidently exist. The musk-deer supplies an important ingredient for expensive perfumes.

145. The Primoriye king crab fishing fleet serving their 'mother-ship' 'Mikhail Tukhachevsky' in the Sea of Okhotsk off the Kamchatka coast.

Transport in the Soviet Far East

The Skovorodino–Khabarovsk–Vladivostok section of the Trans-Siberian Railway is the only line of any note in the Far East. During World War II a new 200-kilometre branch line was built from Izvestkovaya on the Trans-Siberian railway to coal-mines at Urgal and the Chegdomyn railhead. Another important line runs northward from Khabarovsk to Komsomol'sk and Nikolayevsk, and another, built more recently, from Komsomol'sk to Sovetskaya Gavan on the Gulf of Tartary, opposite Sakhalin. This harbour is now one of the Soviet Union's major naval dockyards, and it enjoys a much more strategic location than Vladivostok on Peter the Great Bay (Japan Sea) which is only 60 kilometres from the Chinese border. While Vladivostok remains the pre-eminent commercial and naval port in the Far East, much foreign freight is moved through Nakhodka, somewhat to the east, where an excellent deep-water harbour has been developed, and also through Posvet, another deep-water harbour near the Korean–Chinese–Soviet common border. These last two ports are not so much affected by winter ice as Vladivostok which occupies a shallow embayment.

The three ports mentioned handle a thriving export trade based on timber, metal concentrates, fish products, and other commodities for the overseas trade. Much of the Far East's trade is with Japan, Australia, and other Pacific Basin countries.

Since the early 1960s the existing railway line on Sakhalin island from Korsakov to Poronaysk has been progressively extended to Nysh on the Tym' river. Currently a short cross link is under construction to Katangli to connect with the existing line to Okha.

Before the last war the Soviet Union had a joint financial interest in the Chinese Eastern Railway with the Japanese who, at that time, administered Manchuria. Subsequently, the Russians handed over their operational control and rolling stock on the Chinese Eastern Railway to the Chinese Communist authorities. Since that time, the short route from the Trans-Siberian Railway at Chita via Manchouli (Chinese border) and Harbin to Vladivostok, has been denied to the Russians.

The Soviet Union acquired the southern part of Sakhalin island (Karafuto) and Kuril Islands from the Japanese as a result of World War II, and consequently the Sea of Okhotsk – which has very significant fisheries – has gravitated towards Soviet control and become a Russian sphere of influence. The salmon, Pacific crab, herring, cod and other fisheries to the north of Japanese Hokkaido, long the preserve of Japanese mother-ship fisheries, have now come quite substantially under Russian dominance.

Industry in the Soviet Far East

Over the last twenty years, the Soviet Far East has expanded industries quite rapidly, although the region still remains one of the least developed parts of the Soviet Union. In particular, the region's timber, non-ferrous metals, and fisheries resources have given a first-rate economic basis for the growth of industry, but major problems that have had to be faced are the region's inhospitable physical environment, its poor communications, and the latent threat of Chinese claims to Soviet territory (Fig. 28.1).

The Chinese claim that the Treaty of Peking (1860) was an 'unequal' treaty imposed on them by the then Tsarist government and that they have a natural right to some 200,000 square kilometres of Soviet territory formerly colonized by them, stretching from the Pamirs to the Far East. The Soviet government denies the claim, and this has been the principal ground for friction between the two powers since 1963.

Easily accessible fuel resources of the Far East are not really adequate for the region's needs and consequently any expansion of industry will make augmented coal, oil, and natural gas production, or 'importation' of electricity or fuel from neighbouring regions, absolutely essential.

Resources of bituminous coal at present developed in the Soviet Far East occur at Suchan and Lipovtsy within the Vladivostok area of Primorskiy Kray; at Urgal on the upper Bureya river (Khabarovsk Kray); at Kadykchan on the Kolyma river in the far north, at the widely separated Galimyy and Beringovskiy mines in Magadan oblast, and at a number of underground mines near Uglegorsk and Aleksandrovsk on the east coast of Sakhalin and at Dolinsk on the west coast.

Brown coal is worked at Artem and Tavrichanka, near Vladivostok and the new open-cuts at Novoshakhtinskiy and Rettikhovka northeast of Ussuriysk. The Bikin river open-cut brown coal at Nadarovka near Luchegorsk serves the Primorskiy power station opened in 1970. Final capacity of these open-cuts is planned to reach 12 million tons annually, making it one of the largest power resource developments in the Far East. Another significant brown coal-field is at Raychikhinsk on the lower Bureya river, Amur oblast. This currently produces 12 million tons annually from four open-cut mines and supplies the local Progress power station. On Sakhalin island, brown coal is worked at two open-cuts; one at Vakhrushev on the east coast, and the other at Gornozavodsk in the southwest.

Currently both bituminous and brown coals are used for thermal power stations – Vladivostok, Ussuriysk, Artem, the new Primorskiy station (1·2 million kilowatts capacity), and many smaller plants. Some coal goes to domestic and industrial consumers, but since the electrification of the Trans-Siberian between Vladivostok and Khabarovsk and the use of diesel locomotives on other sections, direct railway consumption of coal has fallen drastically.

Oil and natural gas from Sakhalin island and the Tas-Tumus gas-field on the Lena are the Soviet Far East's only petroleum sources at present. There are oil-fields at Kolendo, Tungor, Okha, Ekhabi and Katangli, all in the northern part of Sakhalin island. Current production is about 2·4 million tons annually. A double pipeline has been built under the Strait of Tartary to the Komsomol'sk refinery. Another refinery is located at Khabarovsk. There are advanced plans for the construction of a natural gas pipeline from Sakhalin's gas-fields to a new chemical complex which will make fertilizers and other chemicals at Komsomol'sk. This pipeline will also convey casing-head gas from the Sakhalin oil-fields.

Apart from the Zeya hydroelectric power station (scheduled capacity 1·47 million kilowatts) now in operation (1970), the vast hydroelectric potential in the Far East is virtually untapped. Rivers like the Amur and its tributaries, the Zeya and Selemdzha have high potential, but as feed sources for the border river Amur, their future development is likely to be fraught with political problems as long as the Chinese maintain their critical stance.

Kamchatka, which is very isolated from the main stream of Far Eastern developments, has special power problems and its mineral resources lie idle for the most part. As it is a centre of volcanic activity, however, there are hopes that the development of geothermal steam power may be feasible. Currently a small geothermal station (5000 kilowatts) operates at the Pauzhetka hot-spring in southern Kamchatka, but this is largely experimental. It serves only the fish cannery at Ozernovskiy. Petropavlovsk, the capital of Kamchatka, uses 'imported' fuel oil for its 70,000 kilowatt steam-powered station.

The Soviet Far East has a wealth of non-ferrous metal resources, although mining operations are still on a limited scale, even where the workings themselves have been known for many years.

In the northeast part of Magadan oblast (Chukotsk N.O.) there are deposits of tungsten–tin ore (Iul'tin), tin (Val'kumey and Krasnoarmeyskiy), and mercury (Plamennyy). Gold placer deposits near the Arctic port of Pevek occur at Komsomol'skiy, Bilibino on the Malyy Anyuy river, at Aliskerovo, and further east at Polyarnyy.

The upper Kolyma valley's rich surface gold placers have been exploited for many years, and are now nearly exhausted. However, with the introduction of drag-lines and power-shovels in the early 1960s, it is now possible to remove overburden to great depths, thus exposing the buried placer deposits. Currently gold-mining is taking place at Susuman, Yagodnoe, and Ust'-Omchug (Magadan oblast).

In Kamchatka gold placers were discovered in the Sredinnyy Khrebet near Mil'kovo in 1965, and there are possibilities that further gold or non-ferrous metals may be discovered in these little explored mountains. Currently much geological prospecting is under way not only in Kamchatka, but throughout the Far East.

Amur oblast has an old-established gold-mining area near Ekimchan in the headwaters of the Selemdzha river. The mines at Ogodzha and elsewhere have been worked since the nineteenth century, but the lode at Tokur still produces payable quantities of gold.

Southern Khabarovsk Kray and also the Primorskiy Kray have many useful non-ferrous

146. The floating cannery ship 'Kronid Korenov' operates in the Sea of Okhotsk off Sakhalin Island. It packs 200,000 cans of fish, principally salmon, in each 8-hour shift. It has a crew including factory workers of some 500. The vessel is served by several swarms of catching boats such as those shown alongside.

metal deposits. Tin occurs at Gornyy and Solnechnyy, west of Komsomol'sk; at Sinacha, Lifudzin, and Khrustal'nyy on the eastern piedmont of the Sikhote-Alin; at Yaroslavskiy near Ussuriisk (with co-products, lead, zinc, silver, and fluorspar); and at Khingansk, west of Birobidzhan, which however has now reached a waning phase. The Khrustal'nyy district tin ores are concentrated at Kavalerovo, before being sent to Novosibirsk for smelting.

In addition to the lead–zinc by-products of the Yaroslavskiy tin deposits, rich polymetallic ores occur at Tetyukhe. Lead concentrates from the Tetyukhe mill are smelted locally, but the zinc concentrates have to be sent westward over the Trans-Siberian to areas with greater resources of electrical energy; principally to Belovo (Kuzbas), Ordzhonikidze (North Caucasus) and Konstantinovka (Ukraine) before smelting and refining can take place.

Other non-ferrous metals occur at Vostok (tungsten) on the western side of the Sikhote-Alin, and at Umal'tinskiy (molybdenum) which mine, however, is now approaching the end of its useful life.

Chemical industries are very little developed in the Soviet Far East at the moment. Native sulphur is found in northern Kamchatka, fluorspar at Voznesenka in the Primorskiy Kray and natural gas and liquid hydro-carbons in Sakhalin. An incipient development of fertilizer and basic chemical plants is taking place at Komsomol'sk, particularly associated with the refinery complex. Nevertheless, it will be many years before the Far East can become self-sufficient in its chemical needs.

At the moment even oil has to be brought in from the west to supplement Sakhalin's production. One longer-term possibility is the extension of the existing trunk oil pipeline from its present terminal at Angarsk (Lake Baykal) to Khabarovsk, a distance of 2500 kilometres. Another possibility is the further development of the Tas-Tumus natural gasfield (northwest of Yakutsk), and a pipeline from there to the southern part of the Far East. This would involve a pipeline of about 1600 kilometres. Either project would present such formidable construction costs that the Soviet authorities may well opt for a large atomic power station – perhaps of 2000 megawatt capacity – as perhaps the best solution to the region's energy scarcity.

Engineering works in the Far East are frequently merely extensions of necessary repair and maintenance services required by transport, mining, and agriculture. The small 'Amurstal' steel-works at Komsomol'sk makes rolled steel products and tin-plate, but does not have integrated facilities to supply all the needs of the Far East. Substantial 'imports' of steel are brought in from the Urals and Kuzbas to serve engineering industries.

The Far East has major shipyards and repair slipways in Vladivostok, Nakhodka, and Sovetskaya Gavan and for river vessels at Blagoveshchensk and Khabarovsk. In Khabarovsk there is also an engineering plant making agricultural machinery, particularly ploughs and harvesters. Other cities of the Far East, not mentioned so far, have a number of machine-building plants, but the main emphasis is on jobbing engineering to keep machinery brought in from other parts of the Soviet Union in good condition and repair.

There are, however, two industries in the Soviet Far East that are of more than regional significance. These are the timber industries, and the fisheries and fish-processing industries.

The location of saw-mills in the Far East region is dominantly along the Trans-Siberian Railway, although some major rivers in the taiga far from the railways have major mills. This is due to the ease with which log-rafts can be assembled upstream and floated to the mill-site, the sawn timber then continuing downstream by river vessel to meet railways or market centres.

Timber industries of the Far East are mainly concentrated along the middle Amur and Ussuri rivers; in the Zeya and Bureya lowlands; in the Sikhote-Alin mountains, and in the central valleys of Sakhalin island. The main species include cedar, fir, spruce, and larch. Major saw-milling centres are located at Birobidzhan, Khabarovsk, Lesozavodsk, Ussuriysk, Vladivostok, and Tymovskoye and Pobedino in Sakhalin. Many other smaller mills occur wherever railways or roads cross major streams. Vladivostok and Nakhodka export Russian timber.

Pulp- and paper-mills are located mainly in central and southern Sakhalin, although there is one major centre at Izvestkovaya (Khabarovsk Kray) at the junction of the Trans-Siberian and Urgal railways.

The marine fisheries of the Far East represent one of the best developed industries in the world, similar to the American and Japanese North Pacific fisheries. It was, of course, the wealth of furs and marine life which carried Russian venturers into Alaska before its sale to the United States in 1867.

By far the greatest asset in the Far East's fisheries is the salmon. Altogether Kamchatka's numerous fishing collectives and the Russian mother-ship fishing vessels account for about two-thirds of the Soviet salmon catch; mostly the species, quinnat, humpback, chinook, and silver salmon. There are major salmon canneries in Kamchatka at Petropavlovsk-Kamchatskiy and Ozernovskiy; along the Sea of Okhotsk coast at Magadan and Okhotsk; at Nikolayevsk at the mouth of the Amur; and at Okha and Yuzhno-Sakhalinsk in Sakhalin.

The annual spawning migrations of salmon are particularly heavy around the Amur estuary and in the Gulf of Penzhina, north of the Kamchatka Peninsula, but with the development of off-shore fisheries, in which gill-net boats deliver their salmon catch to mother-ships that then process and can the fish, fewer salmon now have the opportunity to get near to their natal streams. Problems have ensued since insufficient salmon now spawn to regenerate the stock on which the long-term viability of the fishery depends. In consequence, the Russians have now established salmon hatcheries to breed finger-lings for release in the rivers.

Another fisheries product of great importance is the Pacific or Kamchatka crab, which grows to half a metre measured across the extremities. Both coasts of Kamchatka have very significant crab fisheries, and shore-based canneries prepare crab-meat which is sold on world markets. The Soviet Union is also renowned as an exporter of salmon, especially the red variety which brings the highest price.

Other fisheries include herring and cod in nor-thern waters of the cold Japan current, and sole,

147. Tyuleniy Island (Seal Island) in the Sea of Okhotsk is visited annually by huge colonies of seals. The Soviet sealing industry produces seal furs, blubber oil, and preserved meat (pemican). Seen here are the blubber oil storage tanks. Soviet authorities have introduced vigorous conservation measures to protect the long-term viability of the sealing and whaling industries.

smelt, mackerel, and shark in the south, off the Kuril Islands and Vladivostok coast. Seals, walrus, and sea otter are taken for their furs in the Kuril Islands, off the rocky Shantarskiy Island in the Sea of Okhotsk and around the Komandorskiy group of islands east of Kamchatka.

The large mother-ships and many types of catcher boat over-winter in the safe anchorages of Vladivostok and Nakhodka. These ports are also the home bases for the Pacific whaling fleets, consisting of factory ships, harpoon-chaser vessels and towing vessels. These fleets make annual visits to Antarctic waters during the Southern Hemisphere's summer, when the whales are heading north towards the Equator on their seasonal breeding migrations.

Thus it appears quite evident that the Far East Region has very handsome resources: some exploited as a long-standing tradition — forests, fur-animals, and fisheries — but others hardly touched in the vast Pandora's Box that is the Soviet Far East.

CHAPTER TWENTY-NINE

SOVIET PERSPECTIVES AND THE FUTURE

The Soviet Union currently has some 32,000 collective farms, 15,500 state farms (including other state agricultural enterprises such as animal husbandry units, research stations, etc.), and about 50,000 major industrial enterprises. These are the working units that are co-ordinated in the unified, planned system of economic management undertaken by the Soviet authorities. It is believed that only public ownership of the means of production, state control of the exploitation of natural resources, and the harmonious organization of Soviet manpower can lead ultimately to a Communist society where the principle: 'From each according to his ability, to each according to his needs', is supreme.

As can be imagined the planning and control of such a vast state undertaking is no mean task. Under a system of Five-Year Plans (and sometimes longer, Seven-Year or Twenty-Year Plans), however, the main guidelines for the country's future development are laid down. This centralized planning allows for the full participation on the part of individual enterprises, their associations, and the working people in the affairs of economic management.

The Communist Party of the Soviet Union, following the principles of Marxist–Leninist theory, and acting in accordance with the wishes and experience of the people, works out a socio-economic policy for future implementation. The aim is to create an abundance of material and cultural wealth for all citizens.

The Directives of the current ninth Five-Year Economic Development Plan of the U.S.S.R. for 1971–75, endorsed by the 24th Congress of the Soviet Communist Party, emphasize that 'The main task of the Five-Year Plan is to ensure a considerable rise of the people's material and cultural level on the basis of a high rate of development of socialist production, enhancement of its efficiency, scientific and technical progress and acceleration of the growth of labour productivity.'

During the 1971–75 Plan the national income is to rise by 38·6 per cent – in 1971 it was more than 304,000 million roubles – and output of the means of production is to increase by 46·3 per cent and that of consumer goods by 48·6 per cent.

Future Soviet Industrial and Mining Developments
The immense expansion to be undertaken during the ninth Five-Year Plan (1971–75) rests quite fundamentally on the rate of future developments in production of energy and heavy industries and mining. Consequently, this concluding chapter reviews some of the major projects scheduled in these fields for the 1971–75 period (Table 29.1).

Power Engineering Industries
Major developments are scheduled for the power engineering industries during the ninth Five-Year Plan. Although hydroelectric power stations are much more expensive to build (per kilowatt of installed capacity) than large thermal power stations, and moreover, they take much longer to build, they have certain advantages: the flow of water is a renewable resource and therefore, unlike mineral fuels, has an indefinite life span; the electric power produced is comparatively cheap; and large hydroelectric power stations are frequently built in areas remote from other sources of energy.

Although there are many new power stations to be built – coal-fired, oil or natural gas-fired, hydroelectric and nuclear-powered – the lion's share of development will go to the Russian Federation with major projects in thermal and nuclear power stations (Table 29.2). Belorussia, Kazakhstan, and Uzbekistan will also expand their electrical energy output. There will, however, be some slight readjustments in the percentage share of power output by 1975 largely at the expense of the Russian Federation, which is notably the dominant republic with over 60 per cent of all power production. All other republics, except Latvia and

TABLE 29.1
Major Projects Scheduled for Ninth Five-Year Plan, 1971–75

Planned Expansion of the Means of Production	1970 Output	1975 Plan
Electrical energy output (thousand million kWh)	740	1030–1070
Petroleum (million tons)	353	480–500
Natural Gas (thousand million cubic metres)	200	300–320
Percentage of all Energy from oil and gas	56·4	67
Coal (million tons)	624	685–695
Iron and Steel: Crude Steel (million tons)	116	142–150
Rolled Steel (million tons)	80·6	101–105
Non-Ferrous Metals (Primary Production)		
Aluminium production (thousand tons)	2000	3000–3200
Copper production (thousand tons)	900	1215–1260
Chemical Industries		
Plastics and Resins (million tons)	1·67	3·34
Synthetic Rubber (thousand tons)	500 (e)	plus 70%
Mineral Fertilizers (million tons)		
conventional units	55·4	90·0
100%-nutrients basis	13·1	c25·0
Man-made Fibres (million tons)	0·623	1·05–1·10

Source: *USSR, 1972, Novosti Press Agency Year Book*, Moscow, 1972, *passim*, especially pp. 182–96; *S.G.*, **12** (9), 1971: 615–35.
(e) estimated by the author from value output of synthetic rubber divided by price per ton.

TABLE 29.2
Planned Expansion of Electrical Energy in The Soviet Republics, 1970–75 (in thousand million kilowatt-hours of output)

Republic	1970 Output	1975 Plan	1970 %	1975 %	Republic	1970 Output	1975 Plan	1970 %	1975 %
Soviet Union	741·0	1067·6	100·0	100·0	Georgia	9·0	15·5	1·2	1·5
R.S.F.S.R.	470·0	660·0	63·5	61·8	Armenia	6·1	10·5	0·8	1·0
Ukraine	138·0	200·0	18·6	18·7	Azerbaydzhan	12·0	15·0	1·6	1·4
Belorussia	15·1	26·0	2·0	2·4	Kazakhstan	34·7	52·0	4·7	4·9
Moldavia	7·6	10·0	1·0	1·0	Uzbekistan	18·3	30·0	2·5	2·8
Estonia	11·6	16·7	1·6	1·6	Turkmenistan	1·8	3·5	0·2	0·3
Latvia	2·7	3·6	0·4	0·3	Tadzhikistan	3·2	6·8	0·4	0·6
Lithuania	7·4	11·0	1·0	1·0	Kirghizia	3·5	7·0	0·5	0·7

Source: 1970, *Narodno Khozyaistvo, 1970*, Moscow, 1971, p. 180, 1975 Plan, *S.G.*, **12** (9), 1971: 615–35. Percentages calculated by the author.

TABLE 29.3

Soviet Power Station Projects, 1971–75 (in thousands kilowatt designed capacity)

Location	Type	Capacity	Status	Location	Type	Capacity	Status
Kola	N	880	U/C	Novovoronezh	N	820	U/C
Leningrad	N	2000	P	Yerevan	N	815	U/C
Kirishi	T	2000	U/C	Surgut	G	1200	U/C
Kashira	T	2000	P	Iriklinskiy	O/G	2400	U/C
Ryazan'	T	1800	U/C	Beloyarskiy	N	600	U/C
Smolensk	N	1000	P	Ust'-Ilimsk	H	5000	P
Kursk	N	2000	P	Sayan	H	6500	U/C
Ladyzhin	T	1800	P	Zeya	H	1470	U/C
Tripol'ye	T	1200	P	Luchegorsk	T	1200	U/C
Kurakhovo	T	1600	P	Toktogul	H	1200	P
Krivoi Rog (2nd)	T	3000	P	Kurpsay	H	800	P
Uglegorsk	T/O/G	3600	U/C	Syr-Dar'ya	G	4000	U/C
Zaporozh'ye	T/O/G	3600	U/C	Mary	G	1400	P
Chernobyl'	N	1000	P	Nurek	H	2700	U/C
Novolukoml'	T	2400	P	Ekibastuz	T	4000	P
Kishinev	T	2000	U/C				

Source: *S.G.*, **12** (9) 1971: 615–35. Updated by author.

Notes: *Types*: T = Thermal, coal-fired, G = Natural gas-fired, O/G = Fuel oil- and natural gas-fired, T/O/G = coal-, oil-, and natural gas-fired, N = Nuclear-powered, H = Hydroelectric station.
Status: P = Planned for completion in 1971–75 Plan.
     U/C = Under Construction in June, 1973.

Azerbaydzhan, will either hold or increase their percentage share of power output.

Major power station developments envisaged for completion by the end of the 1971–75 Plan are shown above (Table 29.3).

Some of the other industries due for expansion during the ninth Five-Year Plan are discussed below.

Coal Industry Developments. The Soviet authorities do not intend that the Soviet coal industry should undertake great expansion during the current Five-Year Plan (about 61 million tons: 9·8 per cent) although there are several developments mooted that call for comment.

The greatest growth in coal output is planned for Kazakhstan, the Kuznetsk Basin (R.S.F.S.R), and the Donets Basin (Ukraine) (Table 29.4). Open-cut mining is to be emphasized wherever possible because of its economy.

Production from the Karaganda and Ekibastuz coal-mines is to rise by 32·4 million tons over the 1971–75 Plan period to reach a total of 94 million tons. Out of this increment Karaganda will supply an additional six million tons of coking coal to serve the Fourth Metallurgical Plant making a total output of coking coal of 23 million tons by 1975. Ekibastuz coal, mined by open-cut methods, will more than double its output. Because of its good steam-raising quality it will continue to serve power stations and industries in the Urals and elsewhere.

It is planned to increase coal production from the Kuznetsk Basin by about 23 million tons over the five-year period. Total output will then reach 135 million tons annually, an important proportion, coking coal, to serve the new iron and steel mill at Antonovskaya. New shaft mines are to be built at Berezovskiy and Mezhdurechensk and there will be additional workings at the Yerunak open-cut coal mine. In 1970 the Yerunak open-cut had an output of 30 million tons, but this will now increase quite substantially.

The Russian Federation will also increase production from the Kansk-Achinsk coal basin. These lower-grade steam coals will be used for the thermal power stations of Eastern Siberia.

The 1971–75 Plan will bring about ration-

TABLE 29.4
Recent Coal Output in Major Growth Localities (1950–1975 Plan) (in million tons)

	Kazakhstan		R.S.F.S.R.	Ukraine-R.S.F.S.R.	Total all Localities
	Karaganda	Ekibastuz	Kuznetsk	Donets Basin	
1950	17·4	—	46·6	78·0	142·0
1960	25·8	6·6	84·0	172·1	288·5
1965	31·5	14·3	103·2	194·3	343·3
1970	40·0	21·6	112·0	207·1	380·7
1975P	44·0	50·0	135·0	215·0*	444·0

Sources: Kazakhstan, *S.G.*, **12** (9) 1971, p. 627, *Narodnoe Khozyaistvo, 1970*, Moscow, 1971, p. 188.
  * This figure already reached by 1971 with 7 new mines in operation. See *S.G.*, **14** (3) 1973, p. 208.

alization of the coal industry in the Donbas. Many of the older, partially worked out, and inefficient mines will be closed, but the output will in fact increase due to the construction of fourteen new mines equipped with modern technological facilities. Emphasis is to be given to the production of coking coal.

The small coal-mine at Tkibuli in Georgia is now somewhat depleted. The construction of two new shafts at a different locality, however, will maintain the republic's production at its existing level (2·3 million tons annually) for some years ahead.

Belorussia, which is a fuel-deficit area, will nearly double its production of peat-briquettes for use in minor power stations and domestic heating. Planned output in 1975 is 3·5 million tons.

Oil and Natural Gas Industries. Whereas the planned increase in bituminous coal production is to be quite modest between 1971 and 1975, the Soviet Union is anticipating an enormous expansion of the oil and natural gas industries. By 1975 oil production is expected to reach 480 million tons and natural gas at least 300 thousand million cubic metres. These figures represent a growth in the five-year period of 36·0 per cent and 50·0 per cent respectively. The oil-fields that will contribute most to the expansion are those of Western Siberia, Western Kazakhstan, Western Turkmenistan, and the new Rechitsa oil-field in Belorussia (Table 29.5).

The prolific Western Siberian oil-fields will contribute most – about 74·4 per cent – of the planned increase in oil production and in the longer term

even greater output is expected from these oil-fields. But significant increases from the other oil-fields mentioned are also scheduled, and a continuing vigorous oil-search programme may well open-up new prospects.

Consonant with expanding oil output, the pipeline network is to be improved and several new refineries are to be built during the 1971–75 Plan (Table 29.6).

The Western Siberian oil-fields are to be linked via the Omsk–Chimkent pipeline to the new refineries at Chimkent, Pavlodar, and Achinsk. Another major pipeline to the west will reach Al'metyevsk (Volga–Urals) and from there link into the 'Friendship' pipeline to Eastern Europe. As a result of the better availability of Western Siberian oil, new petrochemical plants are to be built at Tomsk and Tobol'sk during the Plan period.

TABLE 29.5
Planned Oil-Field Expansion, 1971–75 (in million tons)

Oil-fields	1970	1975 Plan	Approximate Increase
Western Siberia (Tyumen', Middle Ob')	31·4	120–25	90
Western Kazakhstan (Mangyshlak)	13·2	30	17
Western Turkmenistan (Nebit Dag, Cheleken)	14·5	22	8
Belorussia (Rechitsa)	4·2	10	6

Source: *S.G.*, **12** (9) 1971: 615–35; *passim.*

TABLE 29.6
Oil Refineries Planned, 1971–1975

Name	Location	Source of Oil
Chimkent	Kazakhstan (south)	Western Siberia
Pavlodar	Kazakhstan (north)	Western Siberia
Achinsk	Eastern Siberia	Western Siberia
Arkhangel'sk	Northwest	Pechora
Lisichansk	Donbas	Chernigov–Poltava
Mozyr'	Belorussia	Volga–Urals; Rechitsa
Mažeikiai	Lithuania	Volga–Urals
Shagal	Turkmenistan	Nebit Dag–Cheleken

Source: *USSR, 1972*, Novosti Press Agency Year Book, Moscow, 1972, *passim.*

The Azerbaydzhan oil industry centred around Baku will be maintained at its present level of production, 19–20 million tons annually. The off-shore wells in the Caspian Sea, especially those at Neftyanyye Kamni, now account for about two-thirds of the oil output. Much casing-head gas and natural gas comes from these sources too.

Expansion of production from the Western Siberian oil-fields will be particularly vigorous during the ninth Five-Year Plan. Augmented output will serve Eastern Siberia, Kazakhstan, and the European parts of the Soviet Union via long-distance, large diameter pipelines.

In Western Kazakhstan, the Uzen' and Zhetybay oil-fields on the Mangyshlak Peninsula, which first yielded oil in 1965, will be expanded further. Oil will be piped to the Gur'yev refinery which is to be re-equipped to handle the larger throughput.

The Krasnovodsk refinery currently handles all oil produced in the Western Turkmenistan oil-fields, but a new refinery and synthetic rubber plant is to be built under the Five-Year Plan at Shagal, west of Chardzhou. This is expected to handle much of the republic's additional oil production.

In the Ukraine, the Chernigov–Poltava oil-fields are linked to the existing refinery at Kremenchug, but a new 28-inch diameter pipeline is to be built under the plan to link up with the two Black Sea refineries at Kherson and Odessa. These refineries are to be extended and, together with the new Donbas refinery to be built at Lisichansk, will serve the important markets of the southern Ukraine.

Belorussia and the Baltic Republics are oil-deficit areas, and most oil therefore has to be brought in by pipeline. The small Rechitsa oil-field in Belorussia will, however, more than double its current output to 4·2 million tons during the period 1971–75. This will provide additional crude for the existing refinery at Novopolotsk, completed in 1963, and also serve the planned new refinery at Mozyr'. Both of these refineries, however, must rely on Volga–Urals crude oil received by pipeline for most of their throughput. The same pipeline system will extend to a new refinery to be built at Mažeikiai, Lithuania, 100 kilometres east of the Baltic port of Liepaja.

As in the case of oil, the contribution of natural gas output to the Soviet fuel-balance will be increased considerably during the ninth Five-Year Plan (1971–75). The principal new gas-field developments are shown below (Table 29.7).

The Medvezh'ye natural gas areas of northern Tyumen' oblast in Western Siberia, were discovered in 1964–66. Work was in progress in 1970 on the construction of a 48-inch, 300-mile pipeline from Nadym, the collecting point, to the Urals via the existing terminal at Igrim and another 56-inch pipeline is to be built to the existing terminal at Ukhta. However, even these very rich natural gas resources have been overtaken in terms of reserves by the Krasnyy Kholm deposit, southwest of Orenburg. By 1975 pipelines will connect Krasnyy Kholm with the Zainsk power station and the Salavat petrochemical plant. Orenburg oblast gas has a high hydrogen sulphide content and may well serve a sulphuric acid plant in future.

Development of the Okarem and associated gas-fields of western Turkmenistan is now in progress. A 48-inch pipeline is to be built northward from Okarem to link into the system now under construction from the Mangyshlak gas-fields (Zhetybay–Uzen') to the Centre. Two other gas-fields are currently under development in Turkmenistan. The Achak gas-field, now linked into the Bukhara pipeline system, and the new Shatlyk gas-field west of Mary from which a new 56-inch, 1700 mile pipeline will be built to a junction with the Caucasus–Moscow line at Ostrogozhsk. With the immediate future expansion of the Turkmenistan gas-fields, Uzbekistan will no longer be Soviet Central Asia's chief source.

Iron and Steel Industries. The continued expansion of the iron and steel industries during the

TABLE 29.7
Planned Natural Gas-field Expansion, 1971–75 (in thousand million cubic metres)

Gas-field Location	1970	1975 Plan	Approximate Increase
Medvezh'ye (Lower Ob', W. Siberia)	Small output	40*	40
Krasnyy Kholm (Orenburg oblast)	1·0	25–30	24
Myl'dzhino (Tomsk oblast)	Small output	8–10	8
Zhetybay (W. Kazakhstan)	2·2	6–7	4
Bukhara district (Uzbekistan)	32·1	35–36	3
Achak (N.E. Turkmenistan)	12·7	16–17	3
Okarem (W. Turkmenistan)	17·0	28–30	11

Source: *S.G.,* **12** (9) 1971: 615–35 (updated and tabulated by the author).

* The Medvezh'ye gas-fields embrace six separate major gas-fields now under active development. By 1980 the collecting centre at Nadym will handle 270 thousand million cubic metres of natural gas and two 100-inch diameter pipelines are to be built to convey it to European Russia (81·5 per cent) and the Urals (18·5 per cent).

ninth Five-Year Plan (1971–75) – raising crude steel production from 116 million tons to 142–50 million tons (22·4 per cent) and rolled steel products from 80·6 million to 101–5 million tons (25·3 per cent) – will call for greatly increased supplies of iron-ore. Major ore developments planned are located at the Kursk Magnetic Anomaly (R.S.F.S.R.), at Rudnyy and Lisakovsk (Kazakhstan), and Zhelezhnogorsk (Eastern Siberia) (Table 29.8).

These projects will provide sufficient ore to support the planned expansion of the iron and steel industries. During the ninth Five-Year Plan many new facilities are to be built in various Soviet iron and steel works. Some of the most important construction projects to be undertaken are the following:

(1) Construction of a 3000-cubic metre blast furnace (No. 9) at Krivoy Rog that is scheduled for completion by 1973. This will raise the works' iron

TABLE 29.8
Planned Iron-Ore Expansion, 1971–75 (in million tons)

Iron-Ore Workings	1970	1975 Plan	Approximate Increase
Kursk Magnetic Anomaly	18	40	22
Krivoy Rog district (Ukraine)	103	107*	4
Rudnyy district (Sokolovka–Sarbay)	30	53*	23
Lisakovsk (Kazakhstan)	—	36*	36
Kachkanar (Urals)	25	33*	8
Belozerka (Ukraine)	Small output	7	7
Abaza-Teya (Krasnoyarsk Kray)	Small output	8–10	8
Zhelezhnogorsk–Rudnogorsk	12	18*	6
Karazhal (Kazakhstan)	5·7	11–12	5

Source: *S.G.,* **12** (9) 1971: 615–35 for 1975 Plan figures. 1970 production and calculation by author.

* These mines now express their output in terms of iron-ore concentrates (sinter fines or pellets) and consequently the author has converted back to a crude ore basis to preserve comparability.

output to 10 million tons annually. Another oxygen steel converter (No. 6) is also to be added to the Krivoy Rog plant, completing a programme begun in the 1960s. This converter will raise crude steel production by 1·4 million tons to a total of about 8·5 million tons annually.

Other planned developments in the Ukraine include a large-diameter pipe-forming mill at Khartsyzsk; a railway-wheel plant at Dnepropetrovsk, and two 350-ton oxygen converters and a large plate-mill in Zhdanov (Azovstal Works). The latter improvements will add 5 million tons to crude steel-making and 1·7 million tons to plate-rolling output. In Dneprodzerzhinsk modern BOS converters are to replace the inefficient open-hearth and Bessemer furnaces now in use.

Development of the Kursk Magnetic Anomaly iron-ores will contribute substantially to the expansion of the Novo-Lipetsk iron and steel works, raising its steel output to 6 million tons by 1975. During the Plan, the works is to add a new 3,200-cubic metre blast furnace (No. 5), having an annual capacity of 2 million tons of iron, and a second oxygen steel converter.

Other iron and steel works in the Russian Federation are to undertake expansion during the 1971–75 period. These include improvements at Cherepovets (Northwest), at Nizhniy Tagil and Chelyabinsk (Urals), and at Novokuznetsk (Western Siberia). The Cherepovets plant will receive augmented ore supplies from Olenegorsk, Kola Peninsula; the Urals plants (including not only those under extension, but also the Magnitogorsk and Novo-Troitsk plants) will use more Rudnyy and Lisakovsk ores, and the two Kuzbas plants (Novokuznetsk and Antonovskaya) will receive additional ore supplies from the Abaza-Teya mines and also Zhelezhnogorsk.

During the 1971–75 Plan, the Karaganda iron and steel works (Kazakhstan) will expand by the construction of a fourth blast furnace. With the steel-making facilities currently operating – two open-hearth furnaces and three 250-ton converters – the works' output is to reach 5 million tons of pig-iron and 6 million tons of crude steel by 1975. This more than doubles its 1970 steel output (2·25 million tons).

The small steel-making plant at Begovat, Uzbekistan, is to have its capacity increased by 50 per cent to reach 600,000 tons by 1975. This will be achieved by the addition of a 200,000 ton scrap steel recovery mill.

To support this widespread expansion of steel-making facilities in the Soviet Union, the Yermak (Kazakhstan) ferro-alloys plant, opened in 1968, is to undertake considerable growth during the ninth Five-Year Plan. It will supply ferro-manganese, ferro-chrome, and ferro-silicon. The other ferro-chrome plant at Aktyubinsk is also to expand its output, and to this end the Khromtau chromite mine is to raise its ore output to 4 million tons during the 1971–75 period. At Zhireken in Chita oblast (Eastern Siberia) a new molybdenum mine is to be opened during the 1971–75 period. Under the Plan, the ferro-nickel works at Pobugskoye, Ukraine, is to be completed also.

Despite the lower-grade carbonate manganese ores now being worked at Chiatura, Georgia, ferro-manganese production at Zestafoni is to be greatly expanded. Between 1960 and 1970 manganese ore output dropped from 3 million to 1·57 million tons at Chiatura, consequent upon the working out of the former richer ores. During the Plan period carbonate ore open-cuts will swing from 20 to 100 per cent of the ore production to serve a new concentrator. This will expand Zestafoni ferro-maganese output sufficiently to permit some export of the product.

The Non-Ferrous Metal Industries
The Aluminium Industry. Aluminium reduction plants now building at Bratsk and Krasnoyarsk will be completed during the 1971–75 Plan. Another plant is envisaged in connection with the giant Sayan hydro-electric station now under construction on the Yenisey river. In Tadzhikistan, the Regar aluminium reduction plant in the Gissar valley, west of Dushanbe, is to be built.

To serve these aluminium industries, new alumina facilities will be built at Pavlodar, Kazakhstan (its second alumina plant). This will obtain additional bauxite from the existing Arkalyk mine and a new working at Krasnooktyabr'skiy.

In the northwest the existing alumina plants at Volkhov, Boksitogorsk and Pikalevo are to be expanded as additional supplies of nephelite and bauxite become available from the newly opened Onega river deposits.

The Kirovabad alumina plant will also be expanded using additional alunite from Alunitedag. Alumina from this plant will raise aluminium production from the Sumgait reduction works to serve a new strip-rolling mill to be built there during the ninth Five-Year Plan. Sumgait is also to build a secondary aluminium recovery plant.

In Armenia, the Razdan alumina plant will process local supplies of nephelite–syenite so that the Kanaker aluminium reduction plant at Yerevan can expand its output further.

Copper and Associated Metal Industries. Kazakhstan is to undertake a major expansion of its copper industries during the ninth Five-Year Plan. The Sayak mine and concentrator will supply copper concentrates to the Balkhash refinery, replacing material formerly received from the Kounradskiy mine that is now approaching exhaustion.

The Orlovka and Nikolayevka copper deposits and the old Glubokoye centre, all in East Kazakhstan, are to provide increased output, and a concentrator is to be built at the Nikolayevka mine. A new copper mine is to be set up in the south at the Chatyrkul deposit (Dzhambul oblast).

The copper smelter and refinery at the Dzhezkazgan copper mines are to be modernized during the 1971–75 period. Completion of these projects by 1975 is planned to raise Kazakhstan's copper output by 70 per cent above 1970 output.

During the ninth Plan the Noril'sk district nickel–copper mines will expand their output by opening up new deposits near Talnakh and at Oktyabr'skoye (formerly Khara-Yelakh).

In Georgia, a complex ore-body at Madneuli, southwest of Tbilisi, containing copper–lead–zinc–barite, is to be further expanded during the 1971–75 period.

In the Tien Shan mountains of Kirghizia a tin deposit at Sarydzhaz is to be mined during the ninth Plan.

Lead–Zinc and Associated Metal Industries. The Soviet economy now needs considerably more non-ferrous and other special metals. In consequence, considerable expansion is envisaged for the lead–zinc group of industries during the ninth Five-Year Plan.

In Kazakhstan, the Chimkent lead smelter, the Leninogorsk zinc refinery, and the Ust'-Kamenogorsk lead–zinc refinery are all to increase their capacities. This will increase Kazakhstan's output of zinc metal by 19 per cent and lead by 10 per cent in 1975.

New ore supplies for these operations are to come from the Tishinka mine, near Leninogorsk, and recently developed deposits at Zhayrem (Karaganda oblast) and Karagayly, east of Karaganda. The latter prospect is a lead–zinc–barite deposit.

In Tadzhikistan a new lead–zinc mine is to be opened during the ninth Plan at the East Karamazar deposit. Raw ore from this source will supplement ores now received from local mines by the Adrasman concentrator, near Leninabad.

Also in Tadzhikistan, the Zarashan concentrator will double its 1970 output of antimony and mercury concentrates when the new mine at Anzob comes into production before 1975. Another antimony–mercury operation will be the expansion of production at the Kadamdzhay and Khaydarken smelters in Kirghizia during the ninth Plan.

The foregoing sections reveal that in the immediate future the Soviet Union is undertaking a quite formidable expansion programme in creating new means of production. Often this will be in resource-rich, but manpower- and communications-poor regions. Clearly this mammoth task will require a high order of economic management and great investments in the latest technology. Past experience would suggest that the Soviet people will accomplish the tasks they have set for themselves, but at what costs and at what level of social deprivation only time will tell. If happily the increase in the gross national product mooted for 1975 filters down in new consumer goods, new social and cultural amenities, then surely the arduous labours of the Soviet working people will not be in vain.

APPENDICES

Source for all Appendices, 1–11, *Narodnoe Khozyaistvo, 1970,* Moscow, 1971: 27–32.

CHAPTER 18: THE WESTERN REGION

	Population (Thousands) 1971	Area (Thousands Sq. km)	Density (Persons/Sq. km)	Per cent Urban Population 1971
ESTONIAN S.S.R.	1374	45·1	30·5	66
LATVIAN S.S.R.	2386	63·7	37·5	63
LITHUANIAN S.S.R.	3166	65·2	48·6	51
BELORUSSIAN S.S.R.	9074	207·6	43·7	45
Brest Oblast	1302	32·3	40·3	36
Gomel' Oblast	1545	40·4	38·2	41
Grodno Oblast	1123	25·0	44·9	34
Minsk City Soviet	955	} 40·8	} 61·1	100
Minsk Oblast	1539			27
Mogilev Oblast	1231	29·0	42·4	44
Vitebsk Oblast	1379	40·1	34·4	47
UKRAINE S.S.R. (WESTERN PART)	20997	277·4	75·7	33
Chernigov Oblast	1546	31·9	48·5	36
Chernovtsy Oblast	855	8·1	105·5	35
Ivano-Frankovsk Oblast	1264	13·9	90·9	31
Khmel'nitskiy Oblast	1617	20·6	78·5	28
Kiev City	1693	} 29·0	} 121·7	100
Kiev Oblast	1837			37
L'vov Oblast	2454	21·8	112·5	48
Poltava Oblast	1720	28·8	59·7	41
Rovno Oblast	1060	20·1	52·7	28
Ternopol Oblast	1164	13·8	84·4	24
Transcarpathian Oblast	1071	12·8	83·6	30
Vinnitsa Oblast	2125	26·5	80·2	27
Volyn Oblast	983	20·2	48·7	33
Zhitomir Oblast	1608	29·9	58·3	36
MOLDAVIAN S.S.R.	3619	33·7	107·4	32
Kaliningrad Oblast (R.S.F.S.R.)	741	15·1	49·1	74
Western Region	41357	707·8	58·4	52

CHAPTER 19: SOUTH UKRAINE–DONETS-DNIEPER REGION

	Population (Thousands) 1971	Area (Thousands Sq. km)	Density (Persons/Sq. km)	Per cent Urban Population 1971
Cherkassy Oblast	1539	20·9	73·7	38
Crimea Oblast	1851	27·0	68·6	64
Dnepropetrovsk Oblast	3382	31·9	106·0	77
Donetsk Oblast	4943	26·5	186·2	88
Khar'kov Oblast	2852	31·4	90·9	70
Kherson Oblast	1045	28·3	36·9	55
Kirovograd Oblast	1264	24·6	51·4	45
Nikolayev Oblast	1156	24·7	46·8	55
Odessa Oblast	2417	33·3	72·6	57
Sumy Oblast	1498	23·8	62·9	44
Voroshilovgrad Oblast (Lugansk)	2759	26·7	103·3	83
Zaporozh'ye Oblast	1801	27·2	66·2	66
South Ukraine–Donets-Dnieper Region	26507	326·3	81·2	62

CHAPTER 20: NORTH CAUCASUS–TRANS-CAUCASUS REGION

	Population (Thousands) 1971	Area (Thousands Sq. km)	Density (Persons/Sq. km)	Per cent Urban Population 1971
NORTH CAUCASUS (R.S.F.S.R.)	14707	430·6	35·0	46
Krasnodar Kray	4542	83·6	54·3	48
Adygey A.O.	(389)	(7·6)	51·2	41
Stavropol' Kray	2323	80·6	28·8	43
Karachay–Cherkess A.O.	(347)	(14·1)	24·6	33
Rostov Oblast	3874	100·4	38·4	64
Chechen–Ingush A.S.S.R.	1084	19·3	56·2	42
Dagestan A.S.S.R.	1457	50·3	29·0	36
Kabardino–Balkar A.S.S.R.	600	12·5	48·0	53
Kalmyk A.S.S.R.	267	75·9	3·5	36
North Ossetian A.S.S.R.	560	8·0	70·0	65
GEORGIAN S.S.R.	4734	69·7	67·9	48
Abkhaz A.S.S.R.	489	8·6	56·9	44
Adzhar A.S.S.R.	316	3·0	105·2	44
South Ossetian A.O.	(100)	(3·9)	25·7	37
AZERBAYDZHAN S.S.R.	5219	86·6	60·3	50
Nagorno-Karabakh A.O.	(152)	(4·4)	34·6	38
Nakhichevan A.S.S.R.	206	5·5	37·4	25
ARMENIAN S.S.R.	2545	29·8	85·4	60
North Caucasus–Trans-Caucasus Region	27205	616·7	44·1	50

N.B. Figures in brackets are included in S.S.R. or A.S.S.R. or Kray totals.

All figures for Autonomous Oblasts (A.O.s) (which are here bracketed), although given, are already included in the next higher order administrative region. It is therefore necessary to exclude these in summation to avoid double counting. The same applies to National okrugs.

APPENDIX 4

CHAPTER 21: THE CENTRAL AND VOLGA REGION

	Population (Thousands) 1971	Area (Thousands sq. km)	Density (Persons/sq. km)	Per cent Urban Population 1971
Astrakhan' Oblast	874	44·1	19·8	61
Belgorod Oblast	1259	27·1	46·5	36
Bryansk Oblast	1579	34·9	45·2	49
Gor'kiy Oblast	3674	74·8	49·1	66
Ivanovo Oblast	1332	23·9	55·7	76
Kalinin Oblast	1710	84·1	20·3	58
Kaluga Oblast	993	29·9	33·2	53
Kirov Oblast	1708	120·5	14·1	56
Kostroma Oblast	851	60·1	14·1	56
Kursk Oblast	1469	29·8	49·3	34
Kuybyshev Oblast	2809	53·6	52·4	73
Lipetsk Oblast	1226	⌐24·1	50·9⌐	45
Moscow City Soviet	7172	{ 47·0	276·7 }	100
Moscow Oblast	5830			70
Orel Oblast	926	⌊24·7	37·5⌋	40
Penza Oblast	1530	43·2	35·4	45
Ryazan' Oblast	1409	39·6	35·6	48
Saratov Oblast	2466	100·2	24·6	66
Smolensk Oblast	1098	49·8	22·0	49
Tambov Oblast	1499	34·3	43·7	40
Tula Oblast	1949	25·7	75·9	73
Ul'yanovsk Oblast	1234	37·3	33·1	54
Vladimir Oblast	1519	29·0	52·4	68
Volgograd Oblast	2345	114·1	20·5	66
Voronezh Oblast	2523	52·4	48·2	46
Yaroslavl' Oblast	1397	36·4	38·4	71
Chuvash A.S.S.R.	1237	18·3	67·6	36
Mari A.S.S.R.	687	23·2	29·6	42
Mordovian A.S.S.R.	1029	26·2	39·3	37
Tatar A.S.S.R.	3165	68·0	45·5	53
Central and Volga (R.S.F.S.R.) Region *	58499	1376·3	42·5	54

* See note to Appendix 3.

APPENDIX 5

CHAPTER 22: THE NORTHWESTERN REGION AND NORTHLANDS*

	Population (Thousands) 1971	Area (Thousands sq. km)	Density (Persons/sq. km)	Per cent Urban Population 1971
Arkhangel'sk Oblast	1404	587·4	2·4	67
Nenets N.O.	(39)	(176·7	0·2	56
Leningrad City Soviet	4002	85·9	63·5	100
Leningrad Oblast	1451			62
Murmansk Oblast	815	144·9	5·6	89
Novgorod Oblast	719	55·3	13·0	55
Pskov Oblast	870	55·3	15·7	44
Vologda Oblast	1288	145·7	8·8	49
Karelian A.S.S.R.	711	172·4	4·1	70
Komi A.S.S.R.	974	415·9	2·3	63
Northwestern and Northern (R.S.F.S.R.) Region	12234	1662·8	7·3	62

N.B. Figures in brackets are included in Oblast total.

* Details for Northlands administrative regions are given in appropriate Appendices: viz. Urals, Western Siberia Eastern Siberia and Far Eastern of which the Northlands are administratively a part.

APPENDIX 6

CHAPTER 23: THE URALS REGION

	Population (Thousands) 1971)	Area (Thousands sq. km)	Density (Persons/sq. km)	Per cent Urban Population 1971
Chelyabinsk Oblast	3296	87·9	37·5	78
Orenburg Oblast	2057	124·0	16·6	54
Perm' Oblast	3003	160·6	18·7	68
Komi-Permyak N.O.	(206)	(32·9)	6·3	19
Sverdlovsk Oblast	4137	194·8	22·2	81
Bashkir A.S.S.R.	3838	143·6	26·7	49
Udmurt A.S.S.R.	1422	42·1	33·8	58
Urals (R.S.F.S.R.) Region	17933	753·0	23·8	58

N.B. Figures in brackets are included in the Oblast or Kray totals.

APPENDIX 7
CHAPTER 24: KAZAKHSTAN

	Population (Thousands) 1971)	Area (Thousands sq. km)	Density (Persons/sq. km)	Per cent Urban Population 1971
Aktyubinsk Oblast	562	299·8	1·9	45
Alma-Ata City	753	104·7	14·1	100
Alma-Ata Oblast	724			19
Chimkent Oblast	1152	114·1	10·1	41
Dzhambul Oblast	806	144·6	5·6	41
East Kazakhstan Oblast	854	97·3	8·8	57
Gur'yev Oblast	515	278·6	1·8	67
Karaganda Oblast	1590	398·8	4·0	81
Kokchetav Oblast	590	78·1	7·6	31
Kustanay Oblast	901	114·6	7·9	42
Kzyl-Orda Oblast	504	227·0	2·2	54
North Kazakhstan Oblast	555	44·3	12·5	39
Pavlodar Oblast	714	127·5	5·6	50
Semipalatinsk Oblast	721	179·6	4·0	45
Taldy-Kurgan Oblast	617	118·5	5·2	40
Tselinograd Oblast	763	124·6	6·1	54
Turgay Oblast	224	111·8	2·0	26
Ural'sk Oblast	523	151·2	3·5	31
Kazakh S.S.R. Region	13068	2715·1	4·8	51

APPENDIX 8
CHAPTER 25: CENTRAL ASIAN REGION

	Population (Thousands) 1971	Area (Thousands sq. km)	Density (Persons/sq. km)	Per cent Urban Population 1971
UZBEK S.S.R.	12305	449·6	27·4	36
Andizhan Oblast	1089	4·3	253·3	24
Bukhara Oblast	963	143·2	6·7	31
Fergana Oblast	1370	7·1	192·9	33
Kashkadarya Oblast	828	28·4	29·1	17
Khorezm Oblast	570	4·5	126·6	19
Namangan Oblast	875	7·8	112·2	29
Samarkand Oblast	1511	29·2	51·8	26
Surkhand-Darya Oblast	683	20·8	32·8	16
Syr-Darya Oblast	757	23·1	32·8	24
Tashkent City	1424	} 15·6	} 188·2	100
Tashkent Oblast	1512			40
Kara-Kalpak A.S.S.R.	723	165·6	4·4	36
TURKMEN S.S.R.	2223	488·1	4·6	48
Chardzhou Oblast	474	93·6	5·1	44
Mary Oblast	642	133·0	4·8	33
Tashauz Oblast	421	75·4	5·6	29
KIRGHIZ S.S.R.	3003	198·5	15·1	38
Issik-Kul' Oblast	318	43·2	7·4	29
Naryn Oblast	192	50·6	3·8	15
Osh Oblast	1266	73·9	17·1	31
TADZHIK S.S.R.	2987	143·1	20·9	37
Gorno-Badakhshan A.O.	(101)	(63·7)	1·6	13
Leninabad Oblast	964	26·1	36·9	38
Central Asian Region	20518	1279·3	16·0	40

N.B. Figures in brackets are included in S.S.R. total.

APPENDIX 9
CHAPTER 26: WESTERN SIBERIAN REGION

	Population (Thousands) 1971	Area (Thousands sq. km)	Density (Persons/sq. km)	Per cent Urban Population 1971
Kemerovo Oblast	2909	95·5	30·5	83
Kurgan Oblast	1085	71·0	15·3	44
Novosibirsk Oblast	2507	178·2	14·1	66
Omsk Oblast	1826	139·7	13·1	57
Tomsk Oblast	795	316·9	2·5	60
Tyumen' Oblast	1421	1435·2	1·0	51
Khanty–Mansi N.O.	(286)	(523·1)	0·5	65
Yamal–Nenets N.O.	(85)	(750·3)	0·1	43
Altay Kray	2647	261·7	10·1	47
Gorno-Altay A.O.	(167)	(92·6)	1·8	26
Western Siberian Region	13190	2498·2	5·3	54

N.B. Figures in brackets are included in the Oblast or Kray totals.

APPENDIX 10
CHAPTER 27: EASTERN SIBERIAN REGION

	Population (Thousands) 1971	Area (Thousands sq. km)	Density (Persons/sq. km)	Per cent Urban Population 1971
Chita Oblast	1152	431·5	2·7	58
Aga Buryat N.O.	(66)	(19·0)	3·5	25
Irkutsk Oblast	2300	767·9	3·0	73
Ust'-Orda Buryat N.O.	(145)	(22·0)	6·6	18
Krasnoyarsk Kray	2970	2401·6	1·2	63
Evenki N.O.	(13)	(767·6)	0·02	28
Khakass A.O.	(447)	(61·9)	7·2	61
Taymyr N.O.	(39)	(862·1)	0·05	63
Tuva A.S.S.R.	235	170·5	1·4	39
Buryat A.S.S.R.	817	351·3	2·3	45
Yakut A.S.S.R.	676	3103·2	0·2	57
Eastern Siberian Region	8180	7226·0	1·1	48

N.B. Figures in brackets are included in Oblast or Kray totals.

APPENDIX 11
CHAPTER 28: FAR EASTERN REGION

	Population (Thousands) 1971	Area (Thousands sq. km)	Density (Persons/sq. km)	Per cent Urban Population 1971
Amur Oblast	808	363·7	2·2	62
Kamchatka Oblast	297	472·3	0·6	77
Koryak N.O.	(31)	(301·5)	0·1	35
Khabarovsk Kray	1369	824·6	1·7	78
Jewish A.O.	(176)	(36·0)	4·9	68
Magadan Oblast	364	1199·1	0·3	75
Chukchi N.O.	(106)	(737·7)	0·1	70
Maritime Kray	1753	165·9	10·6	74
Sakhalin Oblast	622	87·1	7·1	80
Far Eastern Region	5213	3112·7	1·7	74

N.B. Figures in brackets are included in Oblast or Kray Totals.

APPENDIX 12

LIST OF SOVIET CITIES THAT HAVE CHANGED THEIR NAMES SINCE WORLD WAR II

Present Name (1974)	Former Name	Year of Change
Donetsk	Stalino	1961
Dushanbe	Stalinabad	1961
Kaliningrad	Königsberg (Germany)	1945
Klaypeda	Memel (Lithuania)	1945
Kommunarsk	Voroshilovsk	1959
⎧Lugansk	Voroshilovgrad ⎫	1958
⎩Voroshilovgrad	Lugansk ⎭	1970
Novokuznetsk	Stalinsk	1961
Novomoskovsk	Stalinogorsk	1961
Orenburg	Chkalov	1957
Ordzhonikidze	Dzaudzhikau	1954
Pechenga	Petsamo (Finland)	1945
Perm'	Molotov	1957
Severodvinsk	Molotovsk	1957
Tallin	Revel (Estonia)	1945
Tol'yatti	Stavropol' (Kuybyshev Ob.)	1964
Tselinograd	Akmolinsk	1961
Ussuriysk	Voroshilov	1957
Volgograd	Stalingrad	1961
Zhdanov	Mariupol'	1948

BIBLIOGRAPHY

Chapter 1

A. D. Breyterman, *Ekonomicheskaya Geografiya SSSR, Chast 1, Geografiya Tyazheloy Promyshlennosti* (Economic Geography of the USSR, Part 1, Geography of Heavy Industry), Moscow, 1965 (in Russian).

C. D. Harris (ed.), *Soviet Geography: Accomplishments and Tasks*, Amer. Geogr. Soc., New York, 1962.

R. Hutchings, *Soviet Economic Development*, Bannes and Noble, New York, 1971.

G. Kish (with I. M. Matley and B. Bellaire), *Economic Atlas of the Soviet Union*, Univ. of Michigan Press, Ann Arbor, 1960.

A. N. Lavrishchev, *Ekonomicheskaya Geografiya SSSR* (Economic Geography of the USSR), 3rd ed., English trans., Moscow, 1967.

R. S. Mathieson, 'The Soviet Contribution to Regional Science: A Review Article', *Journal of Regional Science*, 9 (1), 1969: 125–40.

I. M. Matley, 'The Marxist Approach to the Geographical Environment', *A. A. A. G.*, 56, 1966: 97–111.

N. P. Nikitin, Ye. D. Prozorova and B. A. Tutykhin (eds.). *Ekonomicheskaya Geografiya SSSR* (Economic Geography of the USSR), Moscow, 1966 (in Russian).

V. V. Pokshishevskiy (ed.), *Geograficheskiye Problemy Razvitiya Krupnykh Ekonomicheskikh Raionov SSSR* (Geographical Problems of the Development of Macro-Economic Regions of the USSR), Moscow, 1964.

Y. G. Saushkin, 'A History of Soviet Economic Geography', *S.G.*, 7 (8) 1966: 31–104.

E. L. Shubalov, *Ekonomicheskaya Geografiya SSSR*, Progress Publishers, Moscow, 1965.

Chapter 2

D. L. Armand, 'Das Studium der Erosion in der Waldsteppen- und Steppengebieten der UdSSR', *Petermanns Mitteilungen*, 98, 1954, 233–39.

L. S. Berg, *Natural Regions of the U.S.S.R.*, Macmillan, New York, 1950.

J. K. Charlesworth, *The Quaternary Era, With Special Reference to its Glaciation*, 2 vols., Arnold, London, 1957 (for discussion of continental glaciation, origin of loessal soils, etc.).

I. P. Gerasimov, D. L. Armand, and K. M. Yefron, *Natural Resources of the Soviet Union: Their Use and Renewal*, English ed. (Trans J. I. Romanovski), ed. W. A. D. Jackson, W. H. Freeman, San Francisco, 1971.

D. V. Nalivkin, *The Geology of the U.S.S.R.* (Trans. J. E. Richey), Pergamon Press, New York, 1960.

Yu. G. Saushkin, 'Comparison of the Main Economic and Tectonic Regions of the U.S.S.R.', *Voprosy Geografii*, 47, 1959, Moscow [in Russian].

G. Seger, *Physische Geographie der Sowjetunion*, Lehrberichte für das Fernstudium der Lehrer, Geographie, 16, Berlin, 1960.

S. P. Suslov, *Physical Geography of Asiatic Russia* (Trans. N. D. Gershevsky, ed. J. E. Williams), W. H. Freeman, San Francisco, 1961.

G. A. Taskin, 'The Falling Level of the Caspian Sea', *G.R.*, 44, 1954: 508–27.

Chapter 3

B. P. Alisov, *Climates of the USSR* [in Russian], Moscow State University, Moscow, 1956.

L. S. Berg, *The Natural Regions of the USSR* (Trans.), Macmillan, New York, 1950.

A. A. Borisov, *Climates of the USSR* (Trans. R. A. Ledward), Oliver and Boyd, London, 1965.

V. F. Burkhanov, 'Criteria for Determining an Engineering–Geographic Boundary of the North of the USSR'. *S.G.*, January, 1970: 24–32.

F. F. Davitaya and S. A. Sapozhnikova, 'Agro-climatic Resources', Chapter 4 *in* Gerasimov *et. al.*, *Natural Resources of the Soviet Union: Their Use and Renewal*, Freeman, San Francisco, 1971.

F. F. Davitaya, O. A. Drozdov, and Ye. S. Rubinshteyn, 'Study of the Climatic Resources of the USSR and their Economic Utilization', *S.G.*, 1 (6), June, 1960: 11–35.

B. L. Dzerdzeevskii, 'On Some Climatological Problems and Micro-climatological Studies of Arid and Semi-Arid Regions in USSR', Proc. Arid Zone Research Symposium, UNESCO, Canberra, 1958.

Ya. I. Feldman, 'Effects of Ground Cover and Surface on Climatic Conditions', Chapter 5 *in* Gerasimov *et. al.*, *op. cit.*

N. C. Field, 'Environmental Quality and Land Productivity: 'A comparison of the Agricultural Land Base of the USSR and North America', *Canadian Geographer*, January, 1968: 1–14.

I. P. Gerasimov, 'Reducing the Dependence of Soviet Agriculture on Natural Elements to the Minimum', *S.G.*, 4 (2), February, 1963: 3–11.

A. A. Grigor'yev and M. I. Budyko, 'Classification of the Climates of the USSR', *S.G.*, 1 (5), 1960: 3–24.

V. N. Kunin, 'The Study of Local Waters in the Deserts of the USSR', *S.G.*, 9 (6), 1968: 469–84.

P. E. Lydolph, The Russian Sukhovey, *AAAG*, 54, 1964: 291–309.

——, 'Schemes for use Amelioration of Soils and Climate in the USSR', *in* R. D. Laird, *Soviet Agriculture and Peasant Affairs*, Univ. of Kansas Press, Lawrence, 1963: 204–12.

S. A. Sapozhnikova and D. I. Shashko, Agro-climatic Conditions of the Distribution and Specialization of Agriculture', *S.G.*, **1** (9), 1960: 20–43.

D. I. Shashko, 'Climate Resources of Soviet Agriculture', *in Soil-Geographical Zoning of the USSR*, Academy of Sciences, Moscow, 1962, trans. A. Gourevitch, Israel Program for Scientific Translation, Jerusalem, 1963.

Chapter 4

A. V. Al'benskiy and P. D. Nikitin (eds.), *Handbook of Afforestation and Soil Melioration*, trans. A. Gourevitch, Israel Program for Scientific Translations, Jerusalem, 1967.

S. F. Averyanov *et al.*, 'Increasing Agricultural Productivity Through Irrigation and Drainage', Chapter 9 *in* Gerasimov *et. al.*, *op. cit.*, 1971.

B. M. Barr, 'The Importance of Regions in Analysis of the Soviet Forest Resource: A Reply', *Canadian Geographer*, **20** (4), 1966: 234–37.

R. M. Bone, 'The Soviet Forest Resources', *Canadian Geographer*, **10** (2), 1966: 94–116.

D. Fogel and B. Shiglovskiy, *Perebros stoka severnykh rek* (Transfer of Run-off of the Northern Rivers), Lesnaya promyshlennost, No. 5, 1961.

I. P. Gerasimov, 'Basic Problems of the Transformation of Nature in Central Asia', *S.G.*, **9** (6), 1968: 444–58.

E. M. Ivanova *et al.*, *Soil-Geographical Zoning of the USSR*, trans. A. Gourevitch, Israel Program for Scientific Translations, Jerusalem, 1963 [published in Russian by Academy of Science of the U.S.S.R., Moscow, 1962].

P. E. Lydolph, in R. D. Laird, *op. cit.*

W. Pfeifer, 'Soviet Timber Shipping', *Bulletin of the Institute for the Study of the U.S.S.R.*, March, 1967: 14–21.

N. N. Rozov, 'Pedological Description of Land Resources', Chapter 8 in Gerasimov *et al.*, *op. cit.*, 1971.

——, *Pochvennaya Karta SSSR* (Soil Map of the U.S.S.R.), Dokl. VI Mezhdunarodnomu Kongressu Pochvovedov (Report to Sixth International Congress of Soil Scientists), Fifth Commission, 1956.

S. P. Suslov, *The Physical Geography of Asiatic Russia*, trans. N. D. Gershevsky, ed. J. E. Williams, W. H. Freeman, San Francisco, 1961.

V. P. Tseplyaev, *The Forests of the USSR*, trans. A. Gourevitch, Daniel Davey and Co., New York, 1966.

P. V. Vasilyev, 'Forest Resources and Forest Economy', Chapter 11 *in* Gerasimov *et al.*, *op. cit.*, 1971.

D. G. Vilenski, *Soil Science*, trans. A. Birron and Z. S. Cole, Israel Program for Scientific Translation, 1960 (3rd ed., Moscow, 1957).

G. S. Vyzgo, 'O generalnom plane ispolzovaniya vodnykh zemelnykh i energeticheskikh resursov' (Concerning a General Plan of Utilization of Water, Land and Energy Resources), *Geografiya i Khozyaystvo No. 6*, Moscow, 1960.

K. V. Zvorykin and P. N. Lebedev, 'The Task of Rational Utilization of Land Resources', *S.G.*, **9** (3), March, 1968: 154–61.

Chapter 5

V. V. Aspaturian, 'The Non-Russian Nationalities', *in* A. Kassof (ed.), *Prospects for Soviet Society*, Praeger, New York, 1968: 143–202.

R. Conquest, *Soviet Nationalities Policy in Practice*, Praeger, New York, 1967.

W. W. Eason, 'Population Changes', *in* A. Kassof, *op. cit.*

N. C. Field, 'Land Hunger and the Rural Depopulation Problem in the U.S.S.R.', *AAAG*, 1963: 465–78.

R. A. French, 'Recent Population Trends in the U.S.S.R.' *in* M. Kaser (ed.), *Soviet Affairs No. 4*, St. Antony's Papers, No. 19, O.U.P., 1966: 68–95.

B. Z. Goldberg, *The Jewish Problem in the Soviet Union, An Analysis and Solution*, Crown, New York, 1961.

E. Goldhagen (ed.), *Ethnic Minorities in the Soviet Union*, Praeger, New York, 1968.

D. G. Khodzhayev, 'The Planning of the Distribution of Production in Population Centres and Some Problems in Population Geography', *S.G.*, **8** (8), 1967: 618–29.

S. A. Kovalev, 'Die Entwicklung des Netzes der stadtischen Siedlungen in Sowjetunion ind den ersten drei Jahren des fünften Fünfjahrplans', *Petermanns Geographische Mitteilungen*, **99**, 1955: 159–63.

F. M. Listengurt, 'Problems in the Formation of the Population of Cities in the RSFSR', *S.G.*, **7** (2), 1971: 116–23.

A. Melezin, 'Trends and Issues in the Soviet Geography of Population', *AAAG*, **53**, 1963: 144–60.

J. A. Newth, 'Some Trends in the Soviet Population, 1939 to 1956', *Soviet Studies*, January, 1959: 252–78.

V. I. Perevedentsev, 'The Influence of Ethnic Factors on the Territorial Redistribution of Population', *S.G.*, **6** (8), 1965: 40–50.

V. V. Pokshishevskiy, 'On the Geography of Population Employed in the U.S.S.R. in the Sphere of Services and Non-Material Production' [in Russian], *Geografiya Naseleniya i Naselennykh Punktov SSSR*, L. Nauka, 1967: 103–28. English abstract: 127–28. An earlier version in English translation, 'Soviet Geography, Accomplishments and Tasks', *Amer. Geog. Soc.*, 1962.

——, 'Prospects of Population Migration in the USSR', *S.G.*, **4** (1), 1963: 13–25.

——, *et al.*, 'On Basic Migration Patterns', *S.G.*, **5** (10), December, 1964: 3–18.

S. G. Prociuk, 'The Manpower Problem in Siberia', *Soviet Studies*, October, 1967: 190–210.

M. K. Roof and F. A. Leedy, 'Population Redistribution in the Soviet Union, 1939–1956', *G.R.*, **49** (2), 1959: 208–21.

D. Shimkin, 'Demographic Changes and Socio-Economic Forces within the Soviet Union, 1939–1959', *in Population Trends in Eastern Europe, the USSR and Mainland China*, Milbank Memorial Fund, 1960: 224–62.

C. Thomas, 'Population trends in the Soviet Union, 1959–1964', *Geog.*, **52**, 1967: 193–97.

Karl-Eugen Wädekin, 'Internal Migration and the Flight from the Land in the U.S.S.R. 1939–1959', *Soviet Studies*, October, 1966: 131–52.

D. M. Zakharina, 'Manpower Resources as a Key Element in the Economic Geography of an Area', *S.G.*, **3** (4), 1962: 38–44.

Chapter 6

N. I. Blazkho, 'A System of Urban Places of the Donets Territorial-Production Complex', *S.G.*, **5** (2), 1964: 11–16.

V. G. Davidovich, 'Satellite Cities and Towns of the USSR', *S.G.*, **3** (3), 1962: 3–34.

——, 'On the Patterns and Tendencies of Urban Settlement in the USSR', *S.G.*, **7** (1), 1966: 3–31.

——, 'Quantitative Regularities in the Urbanization of the USSR', *S.G.*, **13** (2), 1972: 79–98.

P. George, 'Population Urbaine et Population Rurale en USSR', *Annales de Géographie*, **70**, 1961: 206–10.

C. D. Harris, 'Cities of the Soviet Union: Studies in their Functions, Size, Density, and Growth', *Assoc. Amer. Geogr.* Monograph Series, No. 5, Rand McNally, 1970.

——, 'City and Region in the Soviet Union', in R. P. Beckinsale and J. M. Houston, *Urbanization and its Problems*, B. Blackwell, Oxford, 1968: 277–96.

B. S. Khorev, 'A Study of the Functional Structure of Urban Places of the USSR', *S.G.*, **7** (1), 1966: 31–51.

H. Knübel, Verstädterung und Gross-stadtentwicklung in der Sowjet-Union, *Geographische Rundschau*, **16**, 1964: 244–46.

O. A. Konstantinov, 'Some Conclusions About the Geography of Cities and Urban Population of the USSR, Based on the Results of the 1959 Census', *S.G.*, **1** (9), 1960: 59–74.

O. Langbein, 'Les Grandes Villes de l'USSR', *Annales de Géographie*, **67**, 1958: 286–88.

O. V. Larmin, V. M. Moiseyenko, and B. S. Khorev, 'Social-Demographic Aspects of Urbanization in the USSR', *S.G.*, **13** (2), 1972: 99–113.

F. M. Listengurt, 'Prospects of Economic and Territorial Growth of Small and Medium Cities in the Central Economic Region', *S.G.*, **6** (8), 1965: 51–60.

——, 'Problems in the Formation of the Population of Cities of the RSFSR', *S.G.*, **12** (2), 1971: 117–23.

D. N. Lukhmanov, 'Changes in the Distribution of Rural Settlements in Northern Kazakhstan from 1959 to 1964', *S.G.*, **9** (8), 1968: 699–710.

W. Meckelein, 'Gruppengross-stadt und Gross-stadtballungen in der Sowjet-Union', *Tagessbericht und Wissenschaftliche Abhandlungen*, Vol. 32, 1960, Steiner Verlag, Wiesbaden.

Yu. G. Saushkin, 'The Study of a System of Cities in the Soviet Union', *S.G.*, **1**, 1960: 44–51.

R. V. Tatevosyan, 'Methods of Analysis of Inter-regional Migration in the USSR in Relation to the Process of Urbanization', *S.G.*, **13** (2), 1972: 126–131.

V. V. Vladimirov, F. M. Listengurt, and N. I. Naymark, 'Some Aspects of the Formation of Urban Settlement Patterns' (Illustrated by the Tatar A.S.S.R., Bashkir A.S.S.R., and Kuybyshev Oblast)', *S.G.*, **8** (2), 1967: 58–69.

Chapter 7

P. Alampiev, *Economic Areas in the USSR*, Gosplanizdat, Moscow, 1965.

I. I. Belousov, 'Transportation and the Formation of Economic Regions', *S.G.*, **5** (9), 1964: 19–23.

P. J. Bernard, *Planning in the Soviet Union*, Pergamon, 1966.

R. M. Bone, 'Regional Planning and Economic Regionalization in the Soviet Union', *Land Economics*, August, 1967: 347–54.

J. C. Dewdney, 'Patterns and Problems of Regionalization in the USSR', Univ. of Durham. Dept. of Geography, Research Paper No. 8, 1967.

O. Hoeffding, 'The Soviet Industrial Reorganization of 1957', *Amer. Econ. Review*, May, 1959: 65–77.

V. V. Kistanov, 'On Indicators of Regional Specialization and Integration', *S.G.*, **6** (8), 1965: 16–26.

R. E. Lonsdale, 'The Soviet Concept of the Territorial-Production Complex', *Slavic Review*, **24**, 1965: 466–78.

A. Melezin, 'Soviet Regionalization: An Attempt at the Delineation of Socio-Economic Integrated Regions', *G.R.*, **58**, 1968: 593–621.

Z. Mieczkowski, 'The 1962–63 Reforms in Soviet Economic Regionalization', *Slavic Review*, **24**, 1965: 479–96.

——, 'The Major Economic Regions of the USSR, in the Krushchev Era', *Canadian Geographer*, September, 1965: 19–30.

——, 'The Economic Administrative Regions in the USSR', *Tijdschrift voor Econ. en Soc. Geografie*, July–August, 1967: 209–19.

N. N. Nekrasov, 'Scientific Principles for a General Long-Range Scheme of Location of the Productive Forces of the USSR', *S.G.*, **5** (9), 1964: 13–18.

A. Ye. Probst, 'Calculation of the Economic Effect of Regional Productive Specialization', *S.G.*, **5** (2), 1964: 32–41.

T. Shabad, 'The Soviet Concept of Economic Regionalization', *G.R.*, **43**, April, 1953: 214–22.

——, 'Soviet Economic Regions', *S.G.*, 1963: 58–61.

Chapter 8

M. Bornstein, 'The Soviet Debate on Agricultural Price and Procurement Reforms', *Soviet Studies*, **21**, 1969: 1–20.

R. A. Clarke, 'Soviet Agricultural Reforms Since Khrushchev', *Soviet Studies*, **20**, 1969: 159–78 (October, 1968, *according to Shabad, p. 458*).

N. C. Field, 'Land Hunger and the Rural Depopulation Problem in the USSR', *AAAG*, **53**, 1963: 465–78.

W. A. D. Jackson, 'The Problem of Soviet Agricultural Regionalization', *Slavic Review*, **20**, 1961: 656–78.

R. G. Jensen, 'Land Evaluation and Regional Pricing in the Soviet Union', *S.G.*, **9** (3), 1968: 145–49.

A. Kahan, Agriculture, *in* A. Kassof (ed.), *Prospects for Soviet Society*, Praeger, New York, 1968: 263–90.

G. A. Knox-Lovell, 'The Role of Private Subsidiary Farming during the Soviet Seven-Year Plan', 1959–65, *Soviet Studies*, July, 1968: 46–66.

C. Krylov, 'The Sovkhoz Dilemma', *Bulletin of the Institute for the Study of the USSR*, June, 1967: 15–18.

R. D. Laird (ed.), *Soviet Agriculture and Peasant Affairs*, Univ. of Kansas Press, Lawrence, 1963.

V. Matskevich, *Agriculture*, Novosti Press Agency, Moscow, 1971.

M. P. Mensheha, 'Soviet Agricultural Potentialities and Reality', *AAAG* (Abstract), **57**, 1967: 184.

J. A. Newth, 'Soviet Agriculture: The Private Sector 1950–1959', *Soviet Studies*, October, 1961: 160–71; April, 1962, 414–32.

J. W. de Pauw, 'The Private Sector in Soviet Agriculture', *Slavic Review*, March, 1969: 63–71.

S. I. Ploss, *Conflict and Decision-Making in Soviet Russia: A Case Study of Agricultural Policy 1953–1963*, Princeton U.P., 1965.

A. N. Rakitnikov, 'Agricultural Regionalization', *S.G.*, **5** (9), 1964: 24–33.

A. N. Rakitnikov and V. G. Kryuchkov, 'Agricultural Regionalization', *S.G.*, **7** (5), 1966: 48–58.

H. Swearer, 'Agricultural Administration under Khrushchev' *in* R. D. Laird (ed.) *Soviet Agriculture and Peasant Affairs*, Univ. of Kansas Press, Lawrence, 1963.

P. F. Vedenichev and P. P. Marakulin, 'Basic Principles of Economic Evaluation of Agricultural Lands', *S.G.*, **9** (3), 1968: 172–80.

C. K. Wilber, 'The Role of Agriculture in Soviet Economic Development', *Land Economics*, **45**, 1969: 87–96.

Chapter 9

K. Braekhus, 'Some Geographical Aspects of Soviet Agriculture', *Norsk Geografisk Tidsskrift*, **22**, 1968: 39–55.

F. F. Davitaya, 'A Natural Transmission Belt for the Year-Round Supply of Fresh Farm Products', *S.G.*, **4** (2), February, 1963: 25–31.

F. Dovring, 'Soviet Farm Mechanization in Perspective', *Slavic Review*, **25** (2), 1966: 287–302.

R. A. French, 'Contemporary Landscape Change in the USSR', *in* R. W. Steel and R. Lawton (eds.), *Liverpool Essays in Geography*, Longmans, London, 1967: 547–63.

R. G. Jensen, 'Regionalization and Price Zonation in Soviet Agricultural Planning', *AAAG.*, June, 1969: 324–47.

V. S. Mikheyeva, 'Application of Mathematical Methods and Computer Techniques in Economic–Geographic Research', *S.G.*, **6** (9), 1965: 39–45.

J. A. Newth, 'Soviet Agriculture: The Private Sector 1950–1959: Animal Husbandry', *Soviet Studies*, April, 1962: 430–31.

R. Schlesinger, 'The New Structure of Soviet Agriculture', *Soviet Studies*, January, 1959: 228–251.

E. Smith, 'Soviet Agriculture: The Khrushchev Era and Afterwards', *Journ. Agric. Economics*, **8**, 1967: 387–402.

E. Strauss, *Soviet Agriculture in Perspective*, Allen and Unwin, London, 1969.

K. E. Wädekin, 'Manpower in Soviet Agriculture: Some Post-Khrushchev Developments', *Soviet Studies*, **20**, 1969: 281–305.

K. V. Zvorykin, 'Study and Classification of Agricultural Lands', *S.G.*, **5** (8), 1964: 15–23.

Chapter 10

J. Anderson, 'Fodder and Livestock Production in the Ukraine: A Case Study of Soviet Agricultural Policy', *The East Lakes Geographer*, October, 1967: 29–46.

R. M. Bone, 'Soviet Tea Cultivation', *AAAG*, **53**, 1963: 161–173.

Commonwealth of Australia, *The Economics of the Soviet Wheat Industry*, B. A. E. Commodity Research Report No. 1, Canberra, December, 1966.

I. P. Gerasimov, 'Lands of the USSR Used for Agriculture', *G. J.*, December, 1958: 452–63.

A. Ye. Granovskaya, 'Specialization of Agriculture in Relatively Similar Natural Environments of the USSR and the United States', *S.G.*, **9** (10), 1968: 830–37.

W. A. D. Jackson, 'The Russian Non-Chernozem Wheat Base', *AAAG*, June, 1959: 97–109.

R. G. Jensen, 'Soviet Sub-tropical Agriculture: A Microcosm', *G.R.*, **54**, 1964: 185–202.

F. Karcz (ed.), *Soviet and East European Agriculture*, Univ. of California Press, Berkeley, 1967.

P. Krug, 'Theecultuur in de Sowjet-Unie en Turkije', *Tijdschift voor Econ. en Soc. Geografie*, **54**, 1963: 278–79.

E. Strauss, 'The Soviet Dairy Economy', *Soviet studies*, **21**, 1970: 269–96.

C. Zoerb, 'The Virgin Land Territory: Plans, Performance, Prospects', *Studies on the Soviet Union*, **3** (4), 1964: 29–44.

Chapter 11

J. S. Berliner, *Factory and Manager in the USSR*, Harvard U.P., Cambridge, Mass., 1957.

——, 'The Informal Organization of the Soviet Firm', *in* F. D. Holzman, *op. cit.*, pp. 408–31.

D. Granick, 'An Organizational Model of Soviet Industrial Planning', J.P.E., **67** (2), April, 1959: 109–30.

D. Granick, *Management of Industrial Firms in the USSR*, Columbia U.P., New York, 1953.

D. R. Hodgman, *Soviet Industrial Production, 1928–1951*, Harvard U.P., Cambridge, Mass., 1954.

F. D. Holzman, *Readings in the Soviet Economy*, Rand McNally, Chicago, 1962.

R. Krengel, 'Soviet, American, and West German Basic Industries: A Comparison', *Soviet Studies*, October, 1960: 113–25.

H. S. Levine, 'Industry', *in* A. Kassof, *Prospects for Soviet Society*, Praeger, New York, 1968: 291–317.

R. E. Lonsdale and J. H. Thompson, 'A Map of the USSR's Manufacturing', *E.G.*, January, 1960: 36–52.

A. Nove, 'The Industrial Planning System Reforms in Prospect', *Soviet Studies*, July, 1962: 1–15.

G. W. Nutter, *The Growth of Industrial Production in the Soviet Union*, Princeton U.P., 1962.

——, 'Industrial Growth in the Soviet Union', *American Econ. Review*, Proc., May, 1958: 398–411.

V. P. Petrov, *Geography of the Soviet Union*, Part IV, Soviet Industry, V. P. Kamkin Inc., Washington. 1960.

S. G. Prociuk, 'The Territorial Pattern of Industrialization in the USSR', *Soviet Studies*, July, 1961: 69–95.

T. Shabad, *Basic Industrial Resources of the USSR*, Columbia U.P., New York, 1969.

——, 'Changing Resource Policies of the Soviet Union', *AAAG* (Abstract), **59**, 1969: 202.

D. B. Shimkin and F. A. Leedy, 'Soviet Industrial Growth – Its Cost, Extent and Prospects', *Automotive Industries*, 1/1/1958, 118: 4–35.

U.S. Congress (Foreign Economic Policy Joint Economic Committee), *Soviet Economic Performance: 1966–1967*, Washington, D.C., May, 1968: 1–29.

Chapter 12

R. Belousov, *USSR Heavy Industry*, Novosti Press Agency Publishing, Moscow, 1972.

M. S. Buyanovskiy, 'On the Questions of the Prospects of Development of the Pechora Coal Basin', *S.G.*, **1** (3), March, 1960: 9–20.

R. W. Campbell, *The Economics of Soviet Oil and Gas*, Johns Hopkins Press, Baltimore, 1968.

B. Ross Guest, 'The Soviet Seven-Year Plan for Gas Pipelines', *AAAG* (Abstract), **57**, 1967: 176.

——, 'Soviet Gas Pipeline Development during the Seven-Year Plan', *The Professional Geographer*, July, 1967: 189–192.

H. Hassmann, *Oil in the Soviet Union* (trans. A. M. Leeston), Princeton U.P., 1953.

J. A. Hodgkin, *Soviet Power, Energy Resources, Production and Potentials*, Prentice-Hall, Englewood Cliffs, 1961.

P. E. Lydolph and T. Shabad, 'The Oil and Gas Industries in the USSR', *AAAG*, December, 1960: 461–68.

A. A. Michel and S. A. Klain, 'Current Problems of the Soviet Electric Power Industry', *E.G.*, July, 1964: 206–20.

V. P. Petrov, *Geography of the Soviet Union*, Part IV–B, Electric Power, V. P. Kamkin Inc., Washington, 1959.

A. Rodgers, 'Coking Coal Supply: Its Role in the Expansion of the Soviet Steel Industry', *E.G.*, April, 1964: 113–50.

T. Shabad, *Basic Industrial Resources of the USSR*, Columbia U.P., New York, 1969.

A. Sudoplatov, *Coal Industry of the USSR,* Foreign Language Publishing House, Moscow, 1959.

G. A. Vvedensky, 'The Soviet Fuel and Power Industry', *Bulletin of the Institute for the Study of the USSR*, January, 1968: 18–25.

M. K. Zaytsev, 'The Development of Oil and Gas Industry of Turkmenia', *S.G.*, **9** (6), 1968: 503–510.

Chapter 13

American Iron and Steel Institute, *Steel in the Soviet Union*, New York, 1959.

M. Gardner Clark, *The Economics of Soviet Steel*, Harvard U.P., Cambridge, Mass., 1956.

——, 'Economics and Technology: The Case of Soviet Steel', *in* N. Spulber (ed.), *Study of the Soviet Economy: Direction and Impact of Soviet Growth, Teaching, and Research in Soviet Economics*, Russian and East European Series, Indiana Univ. Publication, Vol. 25, Bloomington, 1964: 17–31.

——, 'Magnitogorsk: A Soviet Iron and Steel Plant in the Southern Urals', *in* Thoman and Patton (eds.), *Focus on Geographic Activity*, McGraw-Hill, New York, 1964: 128–34.

D. Granick, *Soviet Metal-Fabricating and Economic Development: Practice Versus Policy*, Univ. of Wisconsin Press, Madison, 1967.

——, 'Organization and Technology in Soviet Metalworking: Some Conditioning Factors', *Amer. Econ. Review*, Papers and Proc. **47** (2), May, 1957: 633–40.

V. P. Gukov, 'The Location of the Cement Industry of Eastern Siberia within the Long-Term Future', *S.G.*, **5** (5) 1964: 64–72.

F. D. Holzman, 'Soviet Ural–Kuznetsk Combine: A Study in Investment Criteria and Industrialization Policies', *Q.J.E.*, 1957: 368–405.

N. Jasny, 'Prospects of the Soviet Iron and Steel Industry', *Soviet Studies*, January, 1963: 275–94.

T. Shabad, 'The Soviet Aluminium Industry', *Amer. Metal Market*, New York, 1958.

D. B. Shimkin, *Minerals: A Key to Soviet Power*, Harvard U.P., Cambridge, Mass., 1953.

G. A. Vvedensky, 'The Soviet Copper Industry', *Bulletin of the Institute for the Study of the USSR*; August, 1967: 22–27.

Alfred Zimm, *Industriegeographie der Sowjetunion*, Deutscher Verlag der Wissenschaft, Berlin, 1963.

Chapter 14

H. G. Cordero (ed.), 'Iron and Steel Works of the World', 4th ed., Metal Bulletin Books Ltd., London, 1965.

L. Dienes, *Locational Factors and Locational Developments in the Soviet Chemical Industry*, Univ. Chicago, Dept. of Geography, Research Paper No. 119, 1969.

N. D. Matrusov, 'Geographical Problems in the Development of Machine-Building in the Ob'–Irtysh Complex', *S.G.*, **11** (6), June, 1970: 464–71.

Y. L. Meltzer, *Soviet Chemical Industry*, Noyes Development Corp., Park Ridge, N.J., 1967.

M. N. Meshcheryakova, 'The Integrated Development and Location of the Petro-chemical Industry in the Industrial Nodes of the Middle Volga Region', *S.G.*, **8** (2), 1967: 81–87.

A. G. Omarovskiy, 'Changes in the Geography of Machine Building in the USSR', *S.G.*, **1** (3), March, 1960: 42–56.

A. Rodgers, 'Changing Locational Patterns in the Soviet Pulp and Paper Industry', *AAAG*, March, 1955: 85–104.

T. Shabad and P. E. Lydolph, 'The Chemical Industries in the USSR', *Tijdschrift voor Econ. en Soc. Geografie*, August–September, 1962: 169–79.

A. S. Shaposhnikov, 'The Middle Volga Economic Region – Outpost of the Chemical Industry', *S.G.*, **8** (2), 1967: 87–93.

Chapter 15

P. Hanson, 'Marketing and the Consumer in Communist Society' *in* G. Schöpflin (ed.), *The Soviet Union and Eastern Europe*, Blond, London, 1970.

P. R. Pryde, 'The Areal Deconcentration of the Soviet Cotton Textile Industry', *G.R.*, October, 1968: 575–92.

Chapter 16

T. Armstrong, 'The Soviet Northern Sea Route', *G.J.*, **120**, 1955: 136–48.

Chief administration Geodesy and Cartography of the M.V.D., SSSR, *Atlass skhem zheleznykh dorog SSSR*, (Atlas of Railway Networks of the U.S.S.R.), Moscow, 1960.

A.J. Grajdanzev, 'The Trans-Siberian Railway and the Problem of Soviet Supply', *Pacific Affairs*, **14** (4), 1941: 389–415.

B. R. Guest, 'The Growth of Soviet Air Cargo', *Journal of Geography*, October, 1966: 323–27.

H. Hunter, *Soviet Transportation Policy*, Harvard, 1957.

——, *Soviet Transport Experience: Its Lessons for other Countries*, The Brooking Institution, Washington, 1968.

G. Kish, 'Soviet Air Transport', *G.R.*, **48**, July, 1958: 309–20.

——, 'Railway Passenger Transport in the Soviet Union', *G.R.*, July, 1963: 363–76.

C. Krypton, *The Northern Sea Route*, Research Program on the USSR, New York, 1953.

C. Krypton, *The Northern Sea Route and the Economy of the Soviet North*, Praeger, New York, 1956.

M. B. Mazanova, 'Marine Transport as a National Specialized Activity of a Major Economic Region', *S.G.*, May, 1963: 3–9.

R. E. H. Mellor, 'Through-Railway Links Between USSR and its Neighbours', *Geography*, **49**, 1964: 416–17.

——, 'Narrow-gauge Railways in Russia's Virgin Lands', *Geography*, **41**, 1956: 191–92.

K. W. Muckleston and F. E. Dohrs, 'The Relative Importance of Transport on the Volga before and after the Communist Revolution', *The Professional Geographer*, March, 1965: 22–25.

I. V. Nikolskiy, *Geography of Soviet Transport* (in Russian) 1960, [Excerpts. trans. *S.G.*, June, 1961: 39–92].

I. V. Nikolskiy, 'Railroad Freight Traffic of the USSR', *S.G.*, **2** (6), 1961: 39–92.

Yu. N. Paleyev, 'Transport Problems of the Volga Region in Connection with Development of its Productive Forces', *S.G.*, **8** (2), 1967: 117–25.

Yury Pavlov and Yefim Khokovsky, 'The Trans-Siberian Railway of the USSR', *Railway Gazette*, **116** (14), 6/4/1962.

V. P. Petrov, *Geography of the Soviet Union*, Vol. V: Transportation, V. Kamkin, Washington, 1967.

N. Spulber, 'The Danube–Black Sea Canal and the Russian Control over the Danube', *E.G.*, 1954: 236–45.

R. Taaffe, *Rail Transportation and the Economic Development of Soviet Central Asia*, Univ. of Chicago, Dept. of Geography Research Paper No. 64, 1960.

——, 'Inter-regional Passenger Movement in the Soviet Union', *The East Lakes Geographer*, October, 1967: 47–79.

D. Turnock, 'Transportation in the Soviet Union and Eastern Europe', *in* G. Schöpflin, *The Soviet Union and Eastern Europe*, Anthony Blond, London, 1970.

A. A. Vorob'yev, 'Problems in the Location of Transportation in the Southern Part of Eastern Siberia', *S.G.*, **5** (5), 1964: 3–13.

J. N. Westwood, *Soviet Railways Today*, Ian Allan Ltd., Hampton Court, 1963 (also the Citadel Press, New York, 1964).

——, *A History of the Russian Railways*, Allen and Unwin, London, 1964.

Ernest W. Williams, *Freight Transportation in the Soviet Union, Including Comparisons with the United States*, National Bureau of Economic Research, General Series, No. 76, Princeton, U.P., 1962.

V. V. Yegorova, 'The Economic Effectiveness of the Construction of Pioneering Railroads in Newly Developed Areas', *S.G.*, **5** (4), 1964: 46–55.

V. V. Zvonkov, *Principles of Intergrated Transport Development in the USSR*, Univ. of Chicago, 1957.

Chapter 17

R. B. Adam, 'Soviet Foreign Trade', *Focus*, Amer. Geog. Soc., New York, June, 1968: 8–11.

A. Bromke and P. E. Uren (eds.), *The Communist States and the West*, Praeger, New York, 1967.

J. C. Campbell, 'The Soviet Union in the International Environment', *in* A. Kassof, *Prospects for Soviet Society*, Praeger, New York, 1968: 473–96.

J. Gittings, *Survey of the Sino-Soviet Dispute*, O.U.P., London, 1968.

M. I. Goldman, *Soviet Foreign Aid*, Praeger, New York, 1967.

M. C. Kaser, *COMECON: Integration Problems of the Planned Economies*, 2nd ed., O.U.P., London, 1967.

J. S. Prybyla, 'Recent Trends in Sino-Soviet Economic Relations', *Bulletin of the Institute for the Study of the USSR*, May, 1967: 11–21.

F. L. Pryor, 'Foreign Trade Theory in the Communist Bloc', *Soviet Studies*, July, 1962: 41–61.

——, *The Communist Foreign Trade System*, M.I.T. Press/Allen and Unwin, London, 1963.

C. A. Sawyer, *Communist Trade with Developing Countries: 1955–1965*, Praeger, New York, 1966.

S. C. Stolte, 'Features of Soviet Bloc Economic Development', *Bulletin of the Institute for the Study of the USSR*, May, 1968: 3–13.

S. Tekiner, 'Sinkiang and the Sino-Soviet Conflict', *Bulletin of the Institute for the Study of the USSR*, August, 1967: 9–16.

A. Todd, 'Soviet and East European Aid to Developing Countries', *in* G. Schöpflin, *The Soviet Union and Eastern Europe*, Blond, London, 1970, pp. 307–14.

S. Wellisz, *The Economics of the Soviet Bloc*, McGraw-Hill, New York, 1964.

P. J. D. Wiles, *Communist International Economics*, Blackwell, Oxford, 1968.

G. J. Zablocki (ed.), *Sino-Soviet Rivalry: Implications for U.S. Policy*, Praeger, New York, 1966.

Chapter 18

J. A. Armstrong, *Ukrainian Nationalism*, Columbia U.P., New York, 1963.

V. Druzhinin, *Soviet Estonia*, Foreign Languages Publishing House, Moscow (English edition), 1953.

D. J. Fox, 'Odessa', *S.G.M.*, **79** (1), 1963: 5–22.

R. A. French, 'Drainage and Economic Development of the Poles'ye, USSR', *E.G.*, **35**, April, 1959: 172–80.

G. Metelsky, *Lithuania, Land of the Niemen*, Foreign Languages Publishing House, Moscow, 1959.

T. B. Rea, 'On the Ways of Development and Genetic Classification of Estonian Urban Settlements', Uchenye zapiski Tartuskogo gos. universiteta, Trudy po geografii, No. 156, 1964 (with Russian summary); presented before 20th International Geographical Congress, London, 1964 (Nelsons, London, 1965).

V. Swoboda, 'The Ukraine', pp. 209–16, *in* G. Schöpflin, *The Soviet Union and Eastern Europe*, Blond, 1970.

S. Tarvydas, 'A Short Review of Lithuanian Urban Geography', Papers, 19th International Geographical Congress, Vilnius, 1960: 431–36.

N. P. Vakar, *Belorussia*, Harvard U.P., Cambridge, Mass., 1956.

V. S. Vardys, *Lithuania Under the Soviets*, Praeger, N.Y., 1965.

——, 'How the Baltic Republics Fare in the Soviet Union', *Foreign Affairs*, **44** (3), 1966: 512–17.

Y. Zlatova and V. Kotelnikov, *Across Moldavia*, Foreign Languages Publishing House, Moscow (English edition), 1959.

Chapter 19

J. Anderson, 'Fodder and Livestock Production in the Ukraine: A Case Study of Soviet Agricultural Policy', *East Lakes Geographer*, 3 October, 1967: 29–46.

N. I. Blazhko, 'On Methods of Studying the Place of a City in The System of Cities of the USSR (as Illustrated by Odessa)', *S.G.*, **3** (3), 1963: 69–74.

——, 'The System of Urban Places of the Donets Territorial-Production Complex', *S.G.*, February, 1964: 11–16.

B. G. Bondarchuk *et al.*, 'The Natural Resources of the Ukrainian S.S.R. and Ways of Using Them Rationally', *S.G.* **2** (1), January 1961: 12–34.

N. L. Chirovsky, *The Ukrainian Economy*, Shevenko Scientific Society of the Ukraine, Vol. 16 (English Edition), New York/Paris, 1965.

L. V. Gnatyuk, 'Some Aspects of the Economic–Geographic Situation of Odessa', *S.G.*, **4** (9), 1963: 43–52.

V. Holubnychy, *The Industrial Output of the Ukraine: 1913–1956*, Institute for the Study of the USSR, Munich, 1957.

I. A. Kugukalo *et al.*, 'Economic Regionalization of the Ukrainian SSR', *S.G.*, October, 1960: 23–32.

A. I. Lanko *et al.*, 'The Physical–Geographic Regionalization of the Ukrainian SSR for Agricultural Purposes', *S.G.*, December, 1960: 33–50.

M. Y. Nuttonson, 'Agroclimatology and Crop Ecology of the Ukraine and Climatic Analogues in North America', *G.R.*, April, 1947: 213–31.

V. P. Popov *et al.*, 'The Study of the Heat and Moisture Balance of the Ukraine as a Basis for Measures to Raise the Productivity of Agriculture', *S.G.*, September, 1960: 16–27.

N. B. Vernander *et al.*, 'The Land Resources of the Ukraine: Their Evaluation and Inventory Methods', *S.G.* **2** (1), January, 1961: 35–43.

Chapter 20

R. M. Bone, 'Soviet Tea Cultivation', *A. A. A. G.*, June, 1963: 161–73.

N. H. Greenwood, 'Developments in the Irrigation Resources of the Sevan–Razdan Cascade of Soviet Armenia', *A. A. A. G.*, June, 1965: 291–307.

L. N. Gumilev, 'Khazaria and the Caspian (Landscape and Ethnos)', Part I, *S.G.*, **5**, June, 1964: 54–68.

R. G. Jensen, 'Soviet Sub-tropical Agriculture: A. Microcosm', *G.R.*, **54**, April, 1964: 185–202.

P. Krug, 'Theecultuur in de Sowjet-Unie en Turkije' (in Dutch), *Tijdschrift Voor Econ. en Soc. Geografie*, **54**, 1963: 278–79.

D. M. Lang, *A Modern History of Soviet Georgia*, Grove Press, New York, 1962.

G. L. Magakyan, 'The Mingechaur Multi-Purpose Water Management Project', *S.G.*, December, 1964: 43–50.

M. Matossian, *The Impact of Soviet Policies in Armenia*, Brill, Leiden, 1962.

M. Shaginyan, *A Journey Through Soviet Armenia*, Foreign Languages Publishing House, Moscow (English edition), 1954.

G. A. Taskin, 'Falling Level of the Caspian Sea in Relation to Soviet Economic Development', *G.R.*, **44**, 1954: 508–27.

D. Tutaeff, *The Soviet Caucasus*, Harrap, London, 1942.

Chapter 21

R. J. Fuchs, 'Moscow', *Focus*, Amer. Geog. Soc., N.Y., January, 1966.

P. Hall, *The World Cities*, World Univ. Press, London, 1966, pp. 158–181 (Chapter on Moscow).

D. J. M. Hooson, *A New Soviet Heartland*, Van Nostrand Searchlight Books, Princeton, 1964.

——, 'A New Soviet Heartland', *G.J.*, **128** (1), 1962: 19–29.

——, 'The Middle Volga: An Emerging Focal Region in the Soviet Union', *G.J.*, **126** (2), 1960: 182–90.

Ye. I. Kapitonov, 'The Kursk Magnetic Anomaly and its Development', *S.G.*, May, 1963: 10–15.

B. S. Khorev, 'Prospects of Development of the Industrial Complex of the Volga–Vyatka Major Economic Region', *S.G.*, **3** (9), 1962: 39–49.

——, 'Satellite Cities and Towns of Gor'kiy', *S.G.*, **3** (3), 1962: 51–64.

F. S. Kurnikov, 'The Basic Tendencies of Development of the Industrial Complex of the Volga Region', *S.G.*, **8** (2), 1967: 107–17.

F. M. Listengurt, 'Prospects of Economic and Territorial Growth of Small and Medium Cities of the Central Economic Region', *S.G.*, **6** (8), 1965: 51–59.

M. N. Meshcheryakova, 'The Integrated Development and Location of the Petrochemical Industry in Industrial Nodes of the Middle Volga Region', *S.G.*, **8** (2), 1967: 81–87.

R. Milner-Gulland, 'Moscow's Countryside', *Geog. Magazine*, **35** (4), 1962: 19–30.

G. Ye. Mishchenko, 'Satellite Cities and Towns of Moscow', *S.G.*, March, 1962: 35–42.

K. W. Muckleston, 'Volga Transport System', *Yearbook Assoc. Pac. Coast Geog.*, **27**, 1965: 67–76.

K. W. Muckleston and F. E. Dohrs, 'The Relative Importance of Transport on the Volga before and after the Communist Revolution', *Professional Geog.*, **17** (2), 1965: 22–25.

C. Padick, 'Reorientation in Power Generation in the Volga Basin, USSR', *Yearbook Assoc. Pac. Coast Geog.*, **27**, 1965: 27–37.

P. R. Pryde, 'The Area Deconcentration of the Soviet Cotton-Textile Industry', *G.R.*, **58** (4), 1968: 575–92.

S. G. Prociuk, 'The Territorial Pattern of Industrialization in the USSR: A Case Study in Location of Industry', *Soviet Studies*, July, 1961: 69–95.

Yu. G. Saushkin, *Moscow*, Progress Publishers, Moscow, 1966.

Yu. G. Saushkin and A. S. Shcherbakov, 'The Industrial Nodes of the Middle Volga', *S.G.*, **8** (2), 1967: 70–80.

Yu. N. Savenko, 'The Fuel Balance of Kuybyshev Oblast', *S.G.*, **2**, 1961: 8–13.

A. S. Shaposhnikov, 'The Middle Volga Economic Region – Outpost of the Chemical Industry', *S.G.*, **8** (2), 1967: 87–93.

R. N. Taaffe, 'Volga River Transportation: Problems and Prospects', *in* R. S. Thoman and D. J. Patton, *Focus on Geographic Activity*, McGraw-Hill, New York, 1964, pp. 185–93.

S. L. Vendrov et al., 'The Problem of Transformation and Utilization of the Water Resources of the Volga River and Caspian Sea', *S.G.*, September, 1964: 23–34.

V. V. Vladimirov, F. M. Listengurt, and N. I. Naimark, 'Some Aspects of the Formation of Urban Settlement Patterns (Illustrated by the Tatar ASSR, Bashkir ASSR and Kuybyshev Oblast)', *S.G.*, **8** (2), 1967: 58–70.

D. S. Wood, 'The New Volga: A Soviet Transformation of Nature', *J. of Geography*, **57** (2), 1963: 49–56.

Chapter 22

L. P. Altman and M. L. Dolkart, 'Problems of Economic Development in the Northwest Economic Region during the New Five-Year Plan (1966–70), *S.G.*, **9** (1), January, 1968: 11–23.

T. E. Armstrong, *Russian Settlement in the North*, Cambridge U.P., 1965.

——, 'The Soviet North', pp. 384–90, *in* G. Schöpflin, *The Soviet Union and Eastern Europe*, Anthony Blond, London, 1970.

——, 'The Soviet Northern Sea Route', *G.J.*, 120, 1955: 136–48.

——, 'The Population of the North of the USSR', *Polar Record*, **11**, No. 71, 1962: 172–78.

——, 'Soviet Sea Fisheries Since the Second World War', *Polar Record*, **13**, No. 83, May, 1966: 155–86.

——, 'Labour in Northern U.S.S.R.', *Polar Record*, **13**, No. 87, 1967: 769–74.

V. F. Burkhanov, 'Criteria for Determining an Engineering–Geographic Boundary of the North of the USSR', *S.G.*, January, 1970: 24–32.

V. Connolly, *Beyond the Urals*, O.U.P., 1967.

F. A. D'yakanov, 'Productive Forces and Productive Territorial Complexes in the Northeast of the USSR', *S.G.*, **5** (1), 1964: 40–52.

V. K. Fry, 'Reindeer Herding in Northern Russia', *Professional Geographer*, **23** (2), 1971: 146–51.

V. L. Gorovoy, 'The Timber Industry of Northern European Russia', *S.G.*, **2**, April, 1961: 53–59.

R. A. Helin, 'Soviet Fishing in the Barents Sea and North Atlantic, *G.R.*, **54** (3), 1964: 386–408.

C. Krypton, *The Northern Sea Route and the Economy of the Soviet North*, Methuen, London, 1956.

T. Lloyd, 'The Soviet–Norwegian Frontier', *Norsk Geografisk Tidsskift*, 1955–56: 187–242.

Ye. B. Lopatina, 'The Formation of Leningrad's Satellite Places', *S.G.*, **3** (3), 1962: 43–51.

A. Rodgers, 'Changing Locational Patterns in Soviet Pulp and Paper Industry', *AAAG*, March, 1955: 85–104.

N. I. Shishkin, 'On the Diversion of the Vychegda and Pechora Rivers to the Basin of the Volga', *S.G.*, May, 1962: 46–56.

O. N. Shubnikova, 'Resources of Fur-Bearing and Game Animals in Yakutia and their Utilization', *S.G.*, **8** (10), 1967: 792–799.

G. A. Taskin, 'The Soviet Northwest: Economic Regionalization', *G.R.*, **51** (2), 1961: 213–35.

S. L. Vendrov, 'Geographical Aspects of the Problems of Diverting Part of the Flow of the Pechora and Vychegda Rivers to the Volga Basin', *S.G.*, June, 1963: 29–41.

S. L. Vendrov, 'A Forecast of Changes in Natural Conditions in the Northern Ob' Basin in the case of Construction of the Lower Ob' Hydro Project', *S.G.*, December, 1965, 3–18.

V. V. Vladimirov, 'Settlement in Lumber-Industry Regions of the USSR', *S.G.*, **9** (8), 1968: 710–25.

Chapter 23

M. G. Clark, 'Magnitogorsk: A Soviet Iron and Steel Plant in the Southern Urals', *in* R. S. Thoman and D. J. Patton, *Focus on Geographic Activity*, McGraw-Hill, New York, 1964, pp. 128–34.

V. Connolly, *Beyond the Urals: Economic Development in Soviet Asia*, Oxford U.P., London, 1967.

I. P. Gerasimov *et al.*, *Ural i Priural'ye* [in Russian], Nauka, Moscow, 1968.

M. N. Stepanov, 'Development of the Satellite Places of Perm', *S.G.*, **3** (3), 1962: 65–69.

V. S. Varlamov, 'The Economic–Geographic Situation of Orenburg', *S.G.*, **2** (6), 1961: 14–21.

——, 'On the Economic Links of the Industry of Orenburg', *S.G.*, March, 1961: 54–60.

Chapter 24

V. A. Adamchuk, 'The Problem of Creating a Kazakhstan Metallurgical Base', *S.G.*, **5** (6), 1964: 20–35.

P. Alampiev, *Soviet Kazakhstan*, Foreign Languages Publishing House, Moscow, 1958.

A. G. Babayev *et al.*, 'Basic Problems in the Study and Development of Desert Territories of the USSR', *S.G.*, **9** (6), 1968: 430–43.

S. N. Bobrov, 'The Transformation of the Caspian Sea', *S.G.*, September, 1961: 47–59.

M. I. Buyanovskiy, 'On the Question of Iron and Steel Plant Location in Kazakhstan', *S.G.*, **2**, 1961: 44–59.

——, 'Balkhash-Ili, A Potential Major Industrial Complex', *S.G.*, October, 1965: 3–15.

V. Conolly, *Beyond the Urals; Economic Development in Soviet Asia*, Oxford U.P., London, 1967.

F. A. Durgin, 'The Virgin Lands Programme, 1954–1960', *Soviet Studies*, 1962: 255–80.

S. Yu. Geller, 'On the Question of Regulating the Level of the Caspian Sea', *S.G.*, January, 1962: 59–66.

——, 'The Transformation of Nature and the Development of Natural Resources of Arid Areas', *S.G.*, **5**(6), September 1964: 34–42.

D. J. M. Hooson, *A New Soviet Heartland*, Van Nostrand, Princeton, 1964.

W. A. D. Jackson, 'The Virgin and Idle Lands Program Re-appraised', *A. A. A. G.*, March, 1962: 69–79.

A. A. Karsten, 'The Virgin Lands Kray and Its Prospects of Development', *S.G.*, **4**, 1963: 37–46.

I. V. Nikol'skiy, 'The Geography of Transportation of Kazakhstan', *S.G.*, **2** (3), 1961: 44–54.

A. Nove and J. A. Newth, *The Soviet Middle East: A Model for Development*, F. A. Praeger, New York, 1967.

G. A. Taskin, 'The Falling Level of the Caspian Sea in Relation to Soviet Economy', *G.R.*, October, 1954: 508–27.

Chapter 25

E. Allworth (ed.), *Central Asia: A Century of Russian Rule*, Columbia U.P., New York, 1967.

E. E. Bacon, *Central Asia under Russian Rule: A Study in Cultural Change*, Cornell U.P., Ithaca, 1966.

N. A. Belyayev, 'Industrial Development of the Desert of West Turkmenia', *S.G.*, **9** (6), 1968: 511–37.

V. Conolly, 'Soviet Central Asia', pp. 377–83, *in* G. Schöpflin (ed.), *The Soviet Union and Eastern Europe: A Handbook*, Anthony Blond, London, 1970.

L. Ya Feygin, 'Problems of Improving Inter-Regional Productive Relationships of the Central Asian Economic Region', *S.G.*, **5** (6), June, 1964: 3–10.

N. C. Field, 'The Amu Darya: A Study in Resource Geography', *G.R.*, **44** (4), 1954: 528–42.

J. F. Gellert and G. Engelmann, 'Entwicklung und Struktur einiger sowjetischer Grossstädte in Mittelasien', *Geographische Berichte*, **12** (No. 44), 1967, No. 3: 175–203.

R. A. Lewis, 'The Irrigation Potential of Soviet Central Asia', *A.A.A.G.*, **52** (1), 1962: 99–114.

——, 'Early Irrigation in West Turkestan', *A.A.A.G.*, September, 1966: 467–91.

P. Luknitsky, *Soviet Tadzhikistan*, Foreign Languages Publishing House, Moscow (English Edition), 1954.

I. M. Matley, 'The Golodnaya Steppe: A Russian Irrigation Venture in Central Asia', *G.R.*, **60** (3), 1970: 328–46.

V. F. Pavlenko, 'The Transport–Geography Situation and the Inter-regional Links of Central Asia', *S.G.*, **4**, November, 1963: 27–33.

A. Ye. Probst, 'Further Productive Specialization of the Central Asian Region', *S.G.*, **5** (6), 1964: 11–20.

T. Rakowska-Harmstone, *Russia and Nationalism in Central Asia: The Case of Tadzhikistan*, Johns Hopkins Press, Baltimore, 1969.

S. N. Ryazantsev, *Kirghizia*, Foreign Languages Publishing House, Moscow, 1951.

E. Schuyler, *Turkistan*, G. Wheeler (ed.), Routledge and Kegan Paul, London, 1966.

R. Taaffe, *Rail Transportation and Economic Development of Soviet Central Asia*, University of Chicago Research Paper, No. 64, 1960.

——, 'Transportation and Regional Specialization: The Example of Soviet Central Asia', *A.A.A.G.*, **52** (1), March, 1962: 80–98.

M. Tikhomirov, *Cities of Central Asia*, Central Asia Research Centre, London, 1961.

G. Wheeler, *The Modern History of Soviet Central Asia*, Weidenfeld, London, 1965.

——, *The Peoples of Soviet Central Asia: A Background Book*, Bodley Head, London, 1966.

D. S. M. Williams, 'The City of Tashkent, Past and Present', *Royal Central Asian Journal*, **54** (1), 1967: 33–43.

M. K. Zaytsev, 'The Development of the Oil and Gas Industries of Turkmenia', *S.G.*, **9** (6), 1968: 503–10.

Chapter 26

F. A. Durgin, 'The Virgin Lands Programme, 1954–1960', *Soviet Studies*, 1962: 255–80.

F. V. D'yakonov, 'The Development of New Areas and Economic Complexes in the West Siberian Plain', *S.G.*, June, 1969: 327–38.

S. Le Fleming, 'Novosibirsk: The City', *Geog. Magazine*, **39** (7), November, 1966: 495–503.

F. D. Holzman, 'The Soviet Ural–Kuznetsk Combine: A Study in Investment Criteria and Industrialization Policies', *QJE*, August, 1958: 368–405.

W. A. D. Jackson, 'Durum Wheat and the Expansion of Dry Farming in the Soviet Union', *AAAG*, 1956: 405–10.

V. A. Krotov, 'The Economic Geography of Siberia and the Far East in its Present Stage', *S.G.*, **5** (5), 1964: 56–64.

——, 'Geographical Aspects and Problems of the Industrialization of Siberia', *S.G.*, **5** (9), 1964: 50–57.

M. G. Levin and L. P. Potapov (ed.), *The Peoples of Siberia*, Univ. of Chicago Press, 1964.

N. D. Matrusov, 'Geographical Problems in the Development of Machine–Building Complexes in the Ob'-Irtysh Complex', *S.G.*, June, 1970: 464–71.

N. Nekrasov, 'The Industrial Development of Siberia and the Far East', *Sovetskiy Voyn*, No. 14, July, 1966: 38–40, Trans. in U.S. Joint Publications Research Service, **37** (382), September 1, 1966: 9–12.

B. P. Orlov, 'Tendencies of Economic Development in Siberia', *S.G.*, January, 1970: 1–13.

V. V. Pokshishevskiy, V. V. Vorob'yev, Ye. N. Gladysheva, and V. I. Perevedentsev, 'On Basic Migration Patterns', *S.G.*, **5** (10), 1964: 3–18.

Y. Semyonov, *Siberia: Its Conquest and Development* (trans. J. R. Foster), Hollis and Carter, London, 1963.

D. W. Treadgold, *The Great Siberian Migration*, Princeton U.P., 1957.

V. S. Varlamov, 'Problems of Transport Development in the West Siberian Plain in conjunction with the Formation of a New Economic Complex in its Territory', *S.G.*, June, 1969: 312–26.

S. L. Vendrov, 'A Forecast of Changes in Natural Conditions in the North Ob' Basin in Case of Construction of the Lower Ob' Hydro Project', *S.G.*, December, 1965: 3–18.

Chapter 27

B. M. Barr, 'The Krasnoyarsk Region: An Emerging Industrial Centre', *Occasional Papers*, British Columbia Division, Canadian Assoc. of Geog., No. 4, June, 1963: 26–38 (reprinted 1965).

G. G. Burmantov, 'The Formation of Functional Types of Settlements in the Southern Tayga (With Particular Reference to the Angara River District of Krasnoyarsk Kray)', *S.G.*, **9** (2), 1968: 112–19.

V. P. Gukov, 'The Location of the Cement Industry of Eastern Siberia within the Long-Term Future', *S.G.*, **5** (5), 1964: 64–72.

W. A. D. Jackson, *The Russo-Chinese Border-lands: Zone of Peaceful Contact or Potential Conflict?* 2nd edn., Van Nostrand, Princeton, 1968.

V. A. Krotov, 'The Economic Geography of Siberia and of the Far East in Its Present Stage', *S.G.*, **5** (5), 1964: 56–64.

——, 'Geographical Aspects and Problems of the Industrialization of Siberia', *S.G.*, **5** (9), 1964: 50–57.

—— *et al.*, 'The Role of Eastern Siberia in Solving Some of the Economic Problems of the Pacific Basin', *S.G.*, **9** (2), 1968: 142–44.

I. Naymushin and A. Gindin, 'Problems of the Angara Series of Hydroelectric Stations', *S.G.*, **1**, June 1960: 61–67.

B. P. Orlov, 'Tendencies of Economic Development in Siberia', *S.G.*, January, 1970: 1–13.

S. G. Prociuk, 'The Manpower Problem in Siberia', *Soviet Studies,* **19** (2), 1967: 190–210.

D. L. Treadgold, *The Great Siberian Migration*, Princeton U.P., 1957.

A. A. Vorob'yev, 'Problems in the Location of Transportation in the Southern Part of Eastern Siberia', *S.G.*, **5**, May, 1964: 3–12.

V. V. Yegorova, 'The Economic Effectiveness of the Construction of Pioneering Railroads in Newly Developed Areas (As illustrated by the Lena Railway)', *S.G.*, April, 1964: 46–55.

Chapter 28

M. Beloff, *Soviet Policy in the Far East, 1944–1951*, Oxford, 1953.

F. V. D'yakonov, 'Productive Forces and Productive Territorial Complexes in the Northeast of the U.S.S.R.', *S.G.*, January, 1964: 40–52.

C. P. Fitzgerald, 'Tensions on the Sino-Soviet Border', *Foreign Affairs*, **45** (4), 1967: 683–93.

J. R. Gibson, 'Russia on the Pacific: The Role of the Amur', *Canadian Geog.*, **12** (1), 1968: 15–27.

E. S. Kirby, *The Soviet Far East*, Macmillan, London, 1971.

M. A. Kravanja, 'Soviet Far Eastern Fisheries Expansion', *Commercial Fisheries Review*, November, 1964.

Z. Mieczkowski, 'The Soviet Far East; Problem Region of the USSR', *Pacific Affairs*, **41** (2), 1968: 214–29.

H. L. Moore, *Soviet Far Eastern Policy, 1931–1945*, Princeton/O.U.P., 1946.

W. Pfeifer, 'The Development of the Soviet Fishing Fleet', *Bulletin of the Institute for the Study of the USSR*, Vol. **14** (5), 1967: 22–30.

V. V. Pokshishevskii, 'On the Geography of Pre-Revolutionary Colonization and Migration Processes in the Southern Part of the Soviet Far East', *S.G.*, **4** (4), 1963: 17–31.

E. Thiel, *The Soviet Far East: A Survey of Its Physical and Economic Geography*, Praeger, 1957.

V. V. Vorob'yev, 'The Principal Changes in the Geography of Urban Population and Urban Settlements of the Soviet Far East', Eleventh Pacific Science Congress, Tokyo, 1966, Proc. Vol. 10.

Chapter 29

A. Bromke and P. E. Uren (eds.), *The Communist States and the West*, Praeger, New York, 1967.

24th Congress of the Communist Party of the Soviet Union, March 30–April 9, 1971; Documents, pp. 239–324, Directives of the 24th Congress of the C.P.S.U. for the Five-Year Development Plan of the USSR for 1971–75 (English edition), Novosti Press Agency Publishing House, Moscow, 1971.

J. Gittings, *Survey of the Sino-Soviet Dispute*, O.U.P., London, 1968.

A. L. Horelick and M. Rush, *Strategic Power and Soviet Foreign Policy*, Praeger, New York, 1966.

M. Kaser, *Comecon: Integration Problems of the Planned Economies*, O.U.P., London, 1967.

A. Kassof (ed.), *Prospects for Soviet Society*, Praeger, New York, 1968.

J. S. Prybyla, 'Recent Trends in Sino-Soviet Economic Relations', *Bull. Inst. Study of the USSR*, May, 1967: 11–21.

C. A. Sawyer, *Communist Trade with Developing Countries 1955–1965*, Praeger, New York, 1966.

S. Tekiner, 'Sinkiang and the Sino-Soviet Conflict', *Bull. Inst. Study of the USSR*, August, 1967: 9–16.

A. B. Ulam, *Expansion and Coexistence: The History of Soviet Foreign Policy, 1917–1967*, Praeger, New York, 1968.

C. J. Zablocki (ed.) *Sino-Soviet Rivalry: Implications for U.S. Policy*, Praeger, New York, 1966.

AUTHOR INDEX

GENERAL INDEX